The 70-296 Cram Sheet

This Cram Sheet contains the distilled, key facts about Exam 70-296, "Planning, Implementing, and Maintaining a Microsoft Windows Server 2003 Environment." Review this information as the last thing you do before you enter the testing center, paying special attention to those areas where you feel that you need the most review. You can transfer any of these facts from your head onto a blank sheet of paper immediately before you begin the exam. Terms that appear in the glossary are not defined again here and instead are listed only as appropriate.

WINDOWS SERVER 2003 BUILT-IN SECURITY TEMPLATES

1. Know the uses for the built-in security templates: Default Security (Setup security.inf), Default DC Security (DC security.inf), Compatible (compatws.inf), Secure (securews.inf and securedc.inf), and Highly Secure (hisecws.inf and hisecdc.inf).

SECURITY CONFIGURATION MANAGER TOOLS

2. *The Security Configuration and Analysis snap-in*—A GUI tool that enables you to create, configure, test, and implement security template settings for a local computer.
3. *The Security Templates snap-in*—An MMC snap-in that enables you to create new or modify existing security templates to be imported using Security Configuration and Analysis, `secedit.exe`, or Group Policy.
4. *The `secedit.exe` command*—A command-line tool that enables you to create, configure, test, and implement security template settings for any computer on the network.
5. *Group Policy security extensions*—A feature that enables you to quickly and uniformly apply security and configuration settings over an OU, domain, or site.

DNS NAMESPACE PLANNING

6. *Existing DNS namespace*—Uses the same namespace for both the internal (corporate network) and external (Internet) portions of your network. This is the easiest method to implement and provides simple access to both internal and external resources.
7. *Delegated DNS namespace*—Uses a delegated domain of the public namespace. If your domain name is `bigcorp.com`, you might consider using `corp.bigcorp.com` for the internal namespace. This provides a namespace that is easy to understand and remember, and that fits nicely with the existing registered domain name.
8. *Unique DNS namespace*—Uses a completely separate but related domain name for your internal namespace. As an example, if you are using `bigcorp.com` for your external namespace, you might use `bigcorp.net` for your internal namespace.

DNS ZONE TYPES

9. *Standard primary*—Holds a master copy of a zone and can replicate it to all configured secondary zones in standard text format.
10. *Standard secondary*—Holds a read-only copy of the zone information in standard text format. Secondary zones are created to increase performance and resilience of the DNS configuration.
11. *Active Directory–integrated*—Available only on Windows 2000 Server and Windows Server 2003 DNS servers in an Active Directory domain. The zone information is contained within the Active Directory database and is replicated using Active Directory replication.
12. *Stub*—Contains only those resource records that are necessary to identify the authoritative DNS servers for that zone. Those resource records include Name Server (NS), Start of Authority (SOA), and possibly glue host (A) records.

STANDARD ZONE FEATURES

13. A single DNS server is the master, holding the only writable copy of the DNS zone file.
14. Zone transfers can be conducted using either incremental or full zone transfer.

15. Fully compatible with Berkeley Internet Name Domain (BIND) DNS servers by using the standard DNS methods in place.

ACTIVE DIRECTORY–INTEGRATED ZONE FEATURES

16. A multimaster arrangement enables any DNS server to make updates to the zone file.
17. Zone data is replicated with Active Directory data.
18. Increased security is provided on the zone file.
19. Redundancy is provided for DNS dynamic update.
20. Replication scope is adjustable by the administrator. Additionally, the zone file can be replicated to a standard secondary DNS server, a common practice for DNS servers placed on screened subnets.
21. A zone appears to be a standard primary zone to a BIND DNS server, thus allowing the usage of BIND DNS as a standard secondary zone server.

DNS FORWARDING AND NAME RESOLUTION

22. Refer to the Glossary and familiarize yourself with the following: recursive query, iterative query, DNS forwarder, DNS slave server, and conditional forwarding.

BIND DNS FEATURES BY VERSION

23. 4.9.4—Support for fast zone transfers
24. 4.9.6—Support for SRV resource records
25. 8.1.2—Support for dynamic DNS (DDNS)
26. 8.2.1—Support for incremental zone transfer (IXFR) between DNS servers
27. 8.2.2—Full support for all Active Directory features

WINDOWS SERVER 2003 DNS OPERABILITY WITH OTHER DNS SYSTEMS

28. You can use any DNS system that meets the following specifications: support for SRV (Service) resource records, and dynamic updates per RFC 2136.
29. If you have Unix BIND servers in your DNS infrastructure, you should consider placing them as secondaries instead of primaries.
30. If you are using an earlier version of BIND or another third-party DNS system that does not support fast zone transfers, you must disable fast zone transfers by selecting the BIND Secondaries option.

HIGHLY AVAILABLE SOLUTIONS

31. Clustering is accomplished by grouping independent servers into one large collective entity that is accessed as if it were a single system.
32. Server clustering uses a group of between two and eight servers that all share a common storage device.
33. Network load balancing (NLB) uses a mathematical algorithm to distribute all incoming connection requests to members of NLB cluster.
34. NLB clusters are composed of between 2 and 32 nodes, each of which must contain the same applications and content.
35. Port rules are used to determine what types of traffic are to be load-balanced across the NLB nodes.

BACKUP TYPES

36. Refer to the Glossary and familiarize yourself with the characteristics of the following backup types: normal (full), incremental, copy, daily, and differential.

SYSTEM STATE FILES

37. The following files make up the System State: Registry, COM+ class-registration database, critical boot and system files, system files that are protected by Windows File Protection, the Certificate Services database (if the server is a Certificate Authority), Active Directory directory service (if the server is a domain controller), SYSVOL directory (if the server is a domain controller), Cluster Service information (if the server is a member of a cluster), and IIS metadirectory (if IIS is installed on the server).

AUTOMATED SYSTEM RECOVERY (ASR)

38. ASR can be used to restore the operating system to a previous state, which enables you to start Window Server 2003 if other methods do not work.
39. You should always consider ASR as your last resort for recovery, after Safe Mode, the Recovery Console, and Last Known Good Configuration (LKGC).
40. ASR sets are created by the Automated System Recovery Preparation Wizard from the Backup utility.
41. ASR restorations are started during server startup by pressing F2 when prompted.

REMOTE ASSISTANCE

42. Remote Assistance enables the Expert to create a connection to the Novice's computer, view the desktop, communicate with the Novice, and even take remote control of the Novice's computer if allowed by the Novice. The Expert can be located on the same internal network or even somewhere else on the Internet.
43. Remote Assistance can be performed only on computers running Windows XP or Windows Server 2003.

Join the CRAMMERS CLUB

Are you interested in an exclusive discount on books, special offers on third-party products and additional certification resources? Join our online certification community and become a member of The Crammers Club today!

Visit our site at **www.examcram2.com** and sign up to become a Crammers Club Member. By answering a few questions you will be eligible for some exciting benefits, including

- **Free practice exams**
- Special third-party offers and discounts
- Additional discounts on all book purchases
- The latest certification news
- Exclusive content
- Newsletters and daily exam questions
- Author articles and sample chapters
- Contests and prizes

Win a library of five Exam Cram 2 books of your choice!

Join The Crammers Club today and you will automatically be entered in our monthly drawing for a free five-book library.

Exam Cram 2 or Training Guide books only. Random monthly drawing of all Crammers Club Members, limitations may apply.

EXAM CRAM™ 2

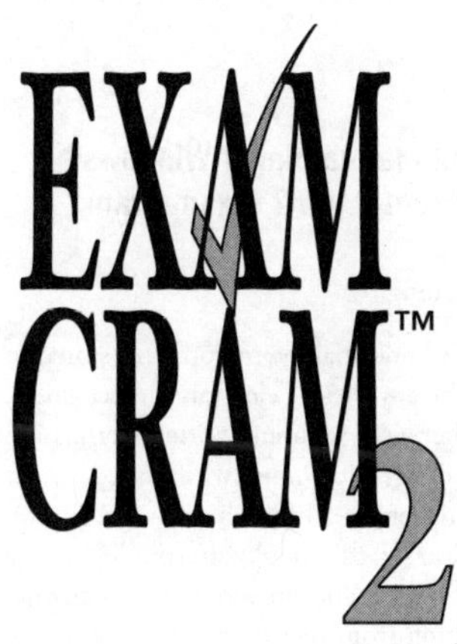

Planning, Implementing, and Maintaining a Windows® Server™ 2003 Environment

Will Schmied

Planning, Implementing, and Maintaining a Windows® Server™ 2003 Environment Exam Cram 2 (Exam Cram 70-296)

International Standard Book Number: 0-7897-3014-6

Library of Congress Catalog Card Number: 2003103930

Printed in the United States of America

First Printing: December 2003

06 05 04 4 3 2

Trademarks

Warning and Disclaimer

Bulk Sales

Que Publishing offers excellent discounts on this book when ordered in quantity for bulk purchases or special sales. For more information, please contact:

U.S. Corporate and Government Sales
1-800-382-3419
corpsales@pearsontechgroup.com

For sales outside of the U.S., please contact:

International Sales
1-317-428-3341
international@pearsontechgroup.com

Publisher
Paul Boger

Executive Editor
Jeff Riley

Acquisitions Editor
Jeff Riley

Development Editor
Ginny Bess Munroe

Managing Editor
Charlotte Clapp

Project Editor
Tricia Liebig

Copy Editor
Krista Hansing

Indexer
Mandie Frank

Proofreader
Juli Cook

Technical Editors
Ken Peterson
Ed Tetz

Team Coordinator
Pamalee Nelson

Multimedia Developer
Dan Scherf

Interior Designer
Gary Adair

Cover Designer
Anne Jones

Page Layout
Michelle Mitchell
Ron Wise

Que Certification • 800 East 96th Street • Indianapolis, Indiana 46240

A Note from Series Editor Ed Tittel

You know better than to trust your certification preparation to just anybody. That's why you, and more than two million others, have purchased an Exam Cram book. As Series Editor for the new and improved Exam Cram 2 series, I have worked with the staff at Que Certification to ensure you won't be disappointed. That's why we've taken the world's best-selling certification product—a finalist for "Best Study Guide" in a CertCities reader poll in 2002—and made it even better.

As a "Favorite Study Guide Author" finalist in a 2002 poll of CertCities readers, I know the value of good books. You'll be impressed with Que Certification's stringent review process, which ensures the books are high-quality, relevant, and technically accurate. Rest assured that at least a dozen industry experts have reviewed this material, helping us deliver an excellent solution to your exam preparation needs.

We've also added a preview edition of PrepLogic's powerful, full-featured test engine, which is trusted by certification students throughout the world.

As a 20-year-plus veteran of the computing industry and the original creator and editor of the Exam Cram series, I've brought my IT experience to bear on these books. During my tenure at Novell from 1989 to 1994, I worked with and around its excellent education and certification department. This experience helped push my writing and teaching activities heavily in the certification direction. Since then, I've worked on more than 70 certification-related books, and I write about certification topics for numerous Web sites and for *Certification* magazine.

In 1996, while studying for various MCP exams, I became frustrated with the huge, unwieldy study guides that were the only preparation tools available. As an experienced IT professional and former instructor, I wanted "nothing but the facts" necessary to prepare for the exams. From this impetus, Exam Cram emerged in 1997. It quickly became the best-selling computer book series since "*…For Dummies*," and the best-selling certification book series ever. By maintaining an intense focus on subject matter, tracking errata and updates quickly, and following the certification market closely, Exam Cram was able to establish the dominant position in cert prep books.

You will not be disappointed in your decision to purchase this book. If you are, please contact me at etittel@jump.net. All suggestions, ideas, input, or constructive criticism are welcome!

Ed Tittel

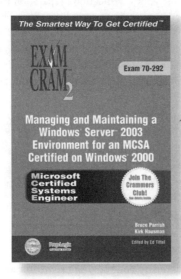

For my family—thank you for your love and support.

– Will Schmied

About the Author

Will Schmied, BSET, MCSE, CWNA, TICSA, MCSA, Security+, Network+, A+, is the president of Area 51 Partners, Inc., a provider of wired and wireless networking implementation, security, and training services to businesses in the Hampton Roads, Virginia, area. Will holds a Bachelor's degree in mechanical engineering technology from Old Dominion University along with his various IT industry certifications. In addition to his activities with Area 51 Partners, Inc., Will operates the MCSE certification portal MCSE World located at `www.mcseworld.com`.

Will has previously authored and contributed to several other publications from Que Publishing, including *MCSE 70-293 Training Guide: Planning and Maintaining a Windows Server 2003 Network Infrastructure* (2003), *MCSA/MCSE 70-291 Training Guide: Implementing, Managing, and Maintaining a Windows Server 2003 Network Infrastructure* (2003), *MCSA Training Guide (70-218): Managing a Windows 2000 Network Environment* (2002), *MCSE Windows 2000 Server Exam Cram 2 (Exam 70-215)* (2003), *Special Edition Using Windows XP Professional, Bestseller Edition* (2003), and *Platinum Edition Using Windows XP* (2003). Will has also worked with Microsoft in the MCSE exam-development process.

Will currently resides in Newport News, Virginia, with his wife, Chris; their children, Christopher, Austin, Andrea, and Hannah; their dogs, Peanut and Jay; and their cat, Smokey. When he's not busy working, you can find Will enjoying time with his family or reading a Douglas Adams book. You can visit Area 51 Partners at `www.area51partners.com`.

About the Technical Reviewers

Ken Peterson (MCSA, MCSE + I, MCT) is an independent technical consultant and technical editor. A resident of Las Vegas, NV for the past 20 years with his wife, Carol, and daughter, Emily, Ken has been an active member of the IT community since 1987, as a technical consultant for IT companies specializing in enterprise network design and support. As an MCSE and MCT through all versions of Microsoft Windows, his professional time is spent tech editing books, planning and implementing Active Directory and Exchange 2000, and teaching Microsoft Certified classes throughout North America. His off-time is spent perfecting his golf game.

Edward Tetz graduated in 1990 from Saint Lawrence College in Cornwall, Ontario with a diploma in business administration. He spent a short time in computer sales, which turned into a computer support position. Since then he has been performing system administration and LAN support for small and large organizations. In 1994, he added training to his repertoire. He currently holds the following certifications: MCT, MCSE, MCDBA, CTT+, A+, CIW MA, CIW SA, and CIW CI. He has experience with Linux, Apple Macintosh, IBM OS/2, Novell NetWare, and all Microsoft operating systems. Over the years he has delivered training on many Microsoft products through Microsoft's CTEC channel. He currently works as a consultant for IMP Solutions in Halifax.

Over the years, he has worked on many titles with New Riders and Que Publications. He enjoys working with Jeff Riley, Ginny Bess, and the rest of the crew at Que.

When he isn't working, Ed spends time with his wife, Sharon, and their two daughters. He can be reached at `ed_tetz@hotmail.com`.

Acknowledgments

I would like to say thanks to the entire team of professionals at Que Publishing: You are the best when it comes to taking tech-speak and making it reader-friendly.

I would also like to give thanks to the entire team at LANWrights, Inc., for their help during this project.

—Will Schmied

Contents at a Glance

Table of Contents

We Want to Hear from You!

As the reader of this book, *you* are our most important critic and commentator. We value your opinion and want to know what we're doing right, what we could do better, what areas you'd like to see us publish in, and any other words of wisdom you're willing to pass our way.

As executive editor for Que, I welcome your comments. You can email or write me directly to let me know what you did or didn't like about this book—as well as what we can do to make our books better.

Please note that I cannot help you with technical problems related to the topic of this book. We do have a User Services group, however, where I will forward specific technical questions related to the book.

When you write, please be sure to include this book's title and author as well as your name, email address, and phone number. I will carefully review your comments and share them with the author and editors who worked on the book.

Email: `feedback@quepublishing.com`

Mail: Jeff Riley
Executive Editor
Que
800 East 96th Street
Indianapolis, IN 46240 USA

For more information about this book or another Que title, visit our Web site at `www.examcram2.com`. Type the ISBN (excluding hyphens) or the title of a book in the Search field to find the page you're looking for.

Introduction

Welcome to the *70-296 Exam Cram 2!* Whether this is your first or your fifteenth *Exam Cram 2* series book, you'll find information here that will help ensure your success as you pursue knowledge, experience, and certification. This introduction explains Microsoft's certification programs in general and talks about how the *Exam Cram 2* series can help you prepare for the Microsoft Certified Systems Engineer and Microsoft Certified Systems Administrator exams. Chapter 1, "Microsoft Certification Exams," discusses the basics of Microsoft certification exams, including a description of the testing environment and test-taking strategies. Chapters 2–10 are designed to remind you of everything you'll need to know to take—and pass—the 70-296 exam. The two practice exams at the end of the book should give you a reasonably accurate assessment of your knowledge—and, yes, we've provided the answers and their explanations to the tests. Read the book and understand the material, and you'll stand a very good chance of passing the test.

Exam Cram 2 books help you understand and appreciate the subjects and materials you need to pass Microsoft certification exams. *Exam Cram 2* books are aimed strictly at test preparation and review. They do not teach you everything you need to know about a topic. Instead, we present and dissect the questions and problems we've found that you're likely to encounter on a test. We've worked to bring together as much information as possible about Microsoft certification exams.

Nevertheless, to completely prepare yourself for any Microsoft test, we recommend that you begin by taking the self-assessment that is included in this book, immediately following this introduction. The self-assessment tool will help you evaluate your knowledge base against the requirements for a Microsoft Certified Systems Engineer (MCSE) under both ideal and real circumstances.

Based on what you learn from the self-assessment, you might decide to begin your studies with some classroom training, some practice with Windows Server 2003, or some background reading. On the other hand, you might decide to pick up and read one of the many study guides available from Microsoft or third-party vendors on certain topics, including the award-winning *MCSE Training Guide* series from Que Publishing. We also recommend that you supplement your study program with visits to `www.examcram2.com` to receive additional practice questions, get advice, and track the MCSE program.

We also strongly recommend that you install, configure, and work with Windows Server 2003 because nothing beats hands-on experience and familiarity when it comes to understanding the questions you're likely to encounter on a certification test. Book learning is essential, but without a doubt, hands-on experience is the best teacher of all!

The accompanying CD contains the PrepLogic Practice Tests, Preview Edition exam-simulation software. The Preview Edition exhibits most of the full functionality of the Premium Edition but offers questions sufficient for only one practice exam. To get the complete set of practice questions and exam functionality, visit `www.preplogic.com`.

Taking a Certification Exam

After you've prepared for your exam, you need to register with a testing center. Each computer-based Microsoft Certified Professional (MCP) exam costs $125, and if you don't pass, you can retest for an additional $125 for each additional try. In the United States and Canada, tests are administered by Prometric and by VUE. Here's how you can contact them:

- *Prometric*—You can sign up for a test through the company's Web site, at `www.prometric.com`. Within the United States and Canada, you can register by phone at 1-800-755-3926. If you live outside this region, you should check the Prometric Web site for the appropriate phone number.
- *VUE*—You can sign up for a test or get the phone numbers for local testing centers through the Web at `www.vue.com/ms`.

To sign up for a test, you must possess a valid credit card or contact either Prometric or VUE for mailing instructions to send a check (in the United States). Only when payment has been verified or your check has cleared can you actually register for the test.

To schedule an exam, you need to call the number or visit either of the Web pages at least one day in advance. To cancel or reschedule an exam, you must call before 7 p.m. Pacific standard time the day before the scheduled test time (or you might be charged, even if you don't show up to take the test).

When you want to schedule a test, you should have the following information ready:

- Your name, organization, and mailing address.
- Your Microsoft test ID. (Inside the United States, this usually means your Social Security number; citizens of other nations should call ahead to find out what type of identification number is required to register for a test.)
- The name and number of the exam you want to take.
- A method of payment. (As mentioned previously, a credit card is the most convenient method, but alternate means can be arranged in advance, if necessary.)

After you sign up for a test, you are told when and where the test is scheduled. You should try to arrive at least 15 minutes early. You must supply two forms of identification—one of which must be a photo ID—and sign a nondisclosure agreement to be admitted into the testing room.

All Microsoft exams are completely closed-book. In fact, you are not permitted to take anything with you into the testing area, but you are given a blank sheet of paper and a pen (or, in some cases, an erasable plastic sheet and an erasable pen). We suggest that you immediately write down on that sheet of paper all the information you've memorized for the test. In *Exam Cram 2* books, this information appears on a tearout sheet inside the front cover of each book. You are given some time to compose yourself, record this information, and take a sample orientation exam before you begin the real thing. We suggest that you take the orientation test before taking your first exam, but because all the certification exams are more or less identical in layout, behavior, and controls, you probably don't need to do this more than once.

When you complete a Microsoft certification exam, the software tells you immediately whether you've passed or failed. If you need to retake an exam, you have to schedule a new test with Prometric or VUE and pay another $125.

The first time you fail a test, you can retake the test as soon as the next day. However, if you fail a second time, you must wait 14 days before retaking that test. The 14-day waiting period remains in effect for all retakes after the second failure.

Tracking MCP Status

As soon as you pass any Microsoft exam, you attain MCP status. Microsoft generates transcripts that indicate which exams you have passed. You can view a copy of your transcript at any time by going to the MCP secure site and selecting Transcript Tool. This tool enables you to print a copy of your current transcript and confirm your certification status.

After you pass the necessary set of exams, you are certified. Official certification is normally granted after three to six weeks, so you shouldn't expect to get your credentials overnight. The package for official certification that arrives includes a welcome kit that contains a number of elements (see Microsoft's Web site for other benefits of specific certifications):

- A certificate that is suitable for framing, along with a wallet card and a lapel pin.
- A license to use the applicable logo, which means you can use the logo in advertisements, promotions, and documents, and on letterhead, business cards, and so on. Along with the license comes a logo sheet, which includes camera-ready artwork. (Note that before you use any of the artwork, you must sign and return a licensing agreement that indicates you'll abide by its terms and conditions.)
- A free subscription to *Microsoft Certified Professional Magazine*, which provides ongoing information about testing and certification activities, requirements, and changes to the MCP program.

Many people believe that the benefits of MCP certification go well beyond the perks that Microsoft provides to newly anointed members of this elite group. We're starting to see more job listings that request or require applicants to have MCP, MCSE, and other certifications, and many individuals who complete Microsoft certification programs can qualify for increases in pay or responsibility. As an official recognition of hard work and broad knowledge, one of the MCP credentials is a badge of honor in many IT organizations.

How to Prepare for an Exam

Preparing for any MCSE-related test (including Exam 70-296) requires that you obtain and study materials designed to provide comprehensive information about the product and its capabilities that will appear on the specific exam for which you are preparing. The following list of materials can help you study and prepare:

- *The Microsoft Windows Server 2003 Resource Kit*, (Microsoft Press, 2003). The Resource Kit can also be accessed online at `www.microsoft.com/windowsserver2003/techinfo/reskit/resourcekit.mspx`.
- *Microsoft Windows Server 2003 Deployment Kit*, (Microsoft Press, 2003). The Deployment Kit can also be accessed online at `www.microsoft.com/windowsserver2003/techinfo/reskit/deploykit.mspx`.
- The exam preparation materials, practice tests, and self-assessment exams on the Microsoft Training and Services page, at `www.microsoft.com/traincert`. The Exam Resources link offers examples of the new question types found on the MCSE exams. You should find the materials, download them, and use them!
- The exam preparation advice, practice tests, questions of the day, and discussion groups on the `www.examcram2.com` e-learning and certification destination Web site.
- Study guides. Several publishers, including Que Publishing, offer certification titles. Que Publishing offers the following:
    - The *Exam Cram 2* series—These books give you information about the material you need to know to pass the tests.
    - The *MCSE Training Guide* series—These books provide a greater level of detail than the *Exam Cram 2* books and are designed to teach you everything you need to know about the subject covered by an exam. Each book comes with a CD-ROM that contains interactive practice exams in a variety of testing formats.

  Together, these two series make a perfect pair.
- Classroom training. CTECs, online partners, and third-party training companies (such as New Horizons, ECPI, and Entré) all offer classroom training on Windows Server 2003. These companies aim to help you prepare to pass Exam 70-296 (or other exams). Although such training runs upward of $350 per day in class, most of the individuals lucky enough to partake usually find this training to be worthwhile.
- Other publications. There's no shortage of materials available about Windows Server 2003. The "Need to Know More?" resource sections at the end of each chapter in this book give you an idea of where we think you should look for further discussion.

This set of required and recommended materials represents a wide variety of sources and resources for Windows Server 2003 and related topics. We hope you'll find that this book belongs in this company.

What This Book Will Not Do

This book will *not* teach you everything you need to know about computers or even about a given topic. Nor is this book an introduction to computer technology. If you're new to Windows administration and looking for an initial preparation guide, check out `www.quepublishing.com`, where you will find a whole section dedicated to the MCSE certifications. This book reviews what you need to know before you take the test, with the fundamental purpose dedicated to reviewing the information needed on the Microsoft 70-296 certification exam.

This book uses a variety of teaching and memorization techniques to analyze the exam-related topics and to provide you with ways to input, index, and retrieve everything you'll need to know to pass the test. Once again, it is *not* an introduction to Windows administration.

What This Book Is Designed to Do

This book is designed to be read as a pointer to the areas of knowledge you will be tested on. In other words, you might want to read the book one time, just to get an insight into how comprehensive your knowledge of computers is. The book is also designed to be read shortly before you go for the actual test and to give you a useful review in as few pages as possible. We think you can use this book to get a sense of the underlying context of any topic in the chapters—or to skim-read for Exam Alerts, bulleted points, summaries, and topic headings.

We've drawn on material from Microsoft's own listing of knowledge requirements, from other preparation guides, and from the exams themselves. We've also drawn from a battery of third-party test-preparation tools and technical Web sites, as well as from my own experience with Windows administration and the exam. Our aim is to walk you through the knowledge you will need—looking over your shoulder, so to speak—and point out those things that are important for the exam (Exam Alerts, practice questions, and so on).

Exam 70-296 makes a basic assumption that you already have a strong background of experience with the Windows 2000 Server and Windows Server 2003 products and their applicable terminology. On the other hand, because

Windows Server 2003 is so new, no one can be a complete expert. We've tried to demystify the jargon, acronyms, terms, and concepts. Also, wherever we think you're likely to blur past an important concept, we've defined the assumptions and premises behind that concept.

About This Book

If you're preparing for the 70-296 certification exam for the first time, we've structured the topics in this book to build upon one another. Therefore, the topics covered in later chapters might refer to previous discussions in earlier chapters.

We suggest that you read this book from front to back. You won't be wasting your time because nothing we've written is a guess about an unknown exam. We've had to explain certain underlying information on such a regular basis that we've included those explanations here.

After you've read the book, you can brush up on a certain area by using the index or the table of contents to go straight to the topics and questions you want to reexamine. We've tried to use the headings and subheadings to provide outline information about each given topic. After you've been certified, we think you'll find this book useful as a tightly focused reference for administering Windows Server 2003.

Chapter Formats

Each *Exam Cram 2* chapter follows a regular structure, along with graphical cues about especially important or useful material. The structure of a typical chapter is as follows:

- *Opening hotlists*—Each chapter begins with lists of the terms you'll need to understand and the concepts you'll need to master before you can be fully conversant with the chapter's subject matter. We follow the hotlists with a few introductory paragraphs, setting the stage for the rest of the chapter.
- *Topical coverage*—After the opening hotlists, each chapter covers the topics related to the chapter's subject.
- *Alerts*—Throughout the topical coverage section, we highlight material most likely to appear on the exam by using a special Exam Alert layout that looks like this:

This is what an Exam Alert looks like. An Exam Alert stresses concepts, terms, software, or activities that will most likely appear in one or more certification exam questions. For that reason, we think any information found offset in Exam Alert format is worthy of unusual attentiveness on your part.

Even if material isn't flagged as an Exam Alert, *all* the content in this book is associated in some way with test-related material. What appears in the chapter content is critical knowledge.

- *Notes*—Where a body of knowledge is deeper than the scope of the book, we use notes to indicate areas of concern or specialty training.

Cramming for an exam will get you through a test, but it won't make you a competent IT professional. Although you can memorize just the facts you need to become certified, your daily work in the field will rapidly put you in water over your head if you don't know the underlying principles of application development.

- *Tips*—We provide tips that will help you to build a better foundation of knowledge or to focus your attention on an important concept that will reappear later in the book. Tips provide a helpful way to remind you of the context surrounding a particular area of a topic under discussion.

You should also read Chapter 1 for helpful strategies used in taking a test. The introduction to Sample Test #1 in Chapter 11 contains additional tips on how to figure out the correct response to a question and what to do if you draw a complete blank.

- *"Exam Prep Questions"*—This section presents a short list of test questions related to the specific chapter topic. Each question has a following explanation of both correct and incorrect answers. The practice questions highlight the areas we've found to be most important on the exam.
- *"Need to Know More?"*—Every chapter ends with a section titled "Need to Know More?" This section provides pointers to resources that we've found to be helpful in offering further details on the chapter's subject matter. If you find a resource that you like in this collection, use it, but don't feel compelled to use all these resources. We use this section to recommend resources that we have used on a regular basis, so none of the recommendations will be a waste of your time or money. These resources might go out of print or be taken down (in the case of Web sites), so we've tried to reference widely accepted resources.

The bulk of the book follows this chapter structure, but there are a few other elements that we want to point out:

- *Practice exams*—The practice exams, which appear in Chapters 11 and 13 (with answer keys in Chapters 12 and 14), are very close approximations of the types of questions you are likely to see on the current Exam 70-296.
- *Answer keys*—These provide the answers to the sample tests, complete with explanations of both the correct and incorrect responses.
- *Glossary*—This is an extensive glossary of important terms used in this book.
- *The Cram Sheet*—This appears as a tear-away sheet inside the front cover of this *Exam Cram 2* book. It is a valuable tool that represents a collection of the most difficult-to-remember facts and numbers we think you should memorize before taking the test. Remember, you can dump this information out of your head onto a piece of paper as soon as you enter the testing room. These are usually facts that we've found require brute-force memorization. You need to remember this information only long enough to write it down when you walk into the test room. Be advised that you will be asked to surrender all personal belongings before you enter the exam room itself.

  You might want to look at the Cram Sheet in your car or in the lobby of the testing center just before you walk into the testing center. The Cram Sheet is divided into headings, so you can review the appropriate parts just before each test.
- *The CD*—The CD contains the *PrepLogic Practice Tests, Preview Edition* exam simulation software. The Preview Edition exhibits most of the full functionality of the Premium Edition but offers only questions sufficient for only one practice exam. To get the complete set of practice questions and exam functionality, visit `www.preplogic.com`.

Contacting the Author

I've tried to create a real-world tool that you can use to prepare for and pass the 70-296 MCSE certification exam. I'm interested in any feedback you care to share about the book, especially if you have ideas about how I can improve it for future test-takers. I'll consider everything you say carefully and will respond to all reasonable suggestions and comments. You can reach me via email at `feedback@area51partners.com`.

Let me know if you found this book to be helpful in your preparation efforts. I'd also like to know how you felt about your chances of passing the exam *before* you read the book and then *after* you read the book. Of course, I'd love to hear that you passed the exam—and even if you just want to share your triumph, I'd be happy to hear from you.

Thanks for choosing me as your personal trainer, and enjoy the book. I would wish you luck on the exam, but I know that if you read through all the chapters and work with the product, you won't need luck—you'll pass the test on the strength of real knowledge!

Self-Assessment

The reason we included a self-assessment in this *Exam Cram 2* book is to help you evaluate your readiness to tackle Microsoft certifications. It should also help you understand what you need to know to master the topic of this book—namely, Exam 70-296: "Planning, Implementing, and Maintaining a Microsoft Windows Server 2003 Environment." But before you tackle this self-assessment, let's talk about concerns you might have when pursuing certification as an MCSE (Microsoft Certified Systems Engineer) on Windows Server 2003 and what an ideal MCSE candidate might look like.

MCSEs in the Real World

In the next section, we describe an ideal MCSE candidate, knowing full well that only a few real candidates will meet this ideal. In fact, our description of that ideal candidate might seem downright scary. But take heart: Although the requirements to obtain an MCSE may seem formidable, they are by no means impossible to meet. However, be keenly aware that it does take time, involves some expense, and requires real effort to get through the process.

Increasing numbers of people are attaining Microsoft certifications, so the goal is within reach. You can get all the real-world motivation you need from knowing that many others have gone before you, so you can follow in their footsteps. If you're willing to tackle the process seriously and do what it takes to obtain the necessary experience and knowledge, you can take—and pass—all the certification tests involved in obtaining an MCSE.

In addition to MCSE, some of the other Microsoft certifications available include the following:

- *MCSA (Microsoft Certified Systems Administrator)*—A newer certification that Microsoft has provided for those Microsoft professionals who are not going to design networks but rather administer them. This certification includes three core exams and a single elective.

- *MCSD (Microsoft Certified Solutions Developer)*—This certification is aimed at software developers and requires one specific exam, two more exams on client and distributed topics, plus a fourth elective exam drawn from a different, but limited, pool of options.
- *MCAD (Microsoft Certified Application Developer)*—This is aimed at software developers functioning at a departmental level with one to two years of application-development experience. The MCAD certification requires two specific exams, plus a third elective exam drawn from a limited pool of options.
- *MCDBA (Microsoft Certified Database Administrator)*—This is aimed at database administrators and developers who work with Microsoft SQL Server. The MCDBA certification requires three core exams and one elective exam.
- *Other Microsoft certifications*—The requirements for these certifications range from one test (MCP) to several tests (MCSE).

The Ideal MCSE Candidate

This MCSE exam is aimed at experienced Windows 2000 MCSEs who need to upgrade their certification status to include Windows Server 2003. The 70-296 exam that this book helps you to prepare for fulfills one of two required exams for the MCSE upgrade. The other exam is 70-292, "Managing and Maintaining a Microsoft Windows Server 2003 Environment for an MCSA Certified on Windows 2000," which is required for both MCSAs and MCSEs on Windows 2000 to upgrade to Windows Server 2003 status.

Microsoft specifies the following audience profile for this exam, which also summarizes the experience level that a typical MCSE candidate should possess:

- The MCSE on Windows Server 2003 credential is intended for IT professionals who work in the typically complex computing environment of medium to large companies.
- Candidates should have experience implementing and administering a network operating system in environments that have the following characteristics:
  - 250 to 5,000 or more users
  - Three or more physical locations

  - Three or more domain controllers
  - Network services and resources such as messaging, database, file and print, proxy server, firewall, Internet, intranet, remote access, and client computer management
  - Connectivity requirements such as connecting branch offices and individual users in remote locations to the corporate network and connecting corporate networks to the Internet
- In addition, candidates should have experience in the following areas:
  - Implementing and administering a desktop operating system
  - Designing a network infrastructure

Fundamentally, this boils down to a bachelor's degree in computer science (or equivalent experience on the job), plus two to three years' experience working in a position involving network design, installation, configuration and maintenance. I believe that well under half of all certification candidates meet these requirements. In fact, most meet less than half of these requirements—at least, when they begin the certification process. But because all the people who already have been certified have survived this ordeal, you can survive it too—especially if you heed what this self-assessment can tell you about what you already know and what you need to learn.

Put Yourself to the Test

The following series of questions and observations is designed to help you figure out how much work you must do to pursue Microsoft certification and what kinds of resources you should consult on your quest. Be absolutely honest in your answers; otherwise, you'll end up wasting money on exams you're not yet ready to take. There are no right or wrong answers—only steps along the path to certification. Only you can decide where you really belong in the broad spectrum of aspiring candidates.

However, two things should be clear from the outset:

- Even a modest background in computer science and programming will be helpful.
- Hands-on experience with Microsoft products and technologies is an essential ingredient to Microsoft certification success.

Educational Background

1. Have you ever taken any computer-related classes? [Yes or No]

   If Yes, proceed to question 2; if No, proceed to question 4.

2. Have you taken any classes on computer operating systems? [Yes or No]

   If Yes, you'll probably be able to handle Microsoft's architecture and system component discussions. If you're rusty, brush up on basic operating system concepts and general computer security topics.

   If No, consider some basic reading in this area. We strongly recommend a good general operating systems book, such as *Operating System Concepts, 6th Edition*, by Abraham Silberschatz and Peter Baer Galvin (John Wiley & Sons, 2001). If that title doesn't appeal to you, check out reviews for other, similar titles at your favorite online bookstore.

3. Have you taken any networking concepts or technologies classes? [Yes or No]

   If Yes, you'll probably be able to handle Microsoft's networking terminology, concepts, and technologies (brace yourself for frequent departures from normal usage). If you're rusty, brush up on basic networking concepts and terminology, especially networking media, transmission types, the OSI Reference Model, and networking technologies such as Ethernet, token ring, and WAN links.

   If No, you might want to read one or two books in this topic area. The two best books that we know of are *Computer Networks, 4th Edition*, by Andrew S. Tanenbaum (Prentice-Hall, 2002, ISBN 0-13-066102-3) and *Computer Networks and Internets with Internet Applications, 3rd Edition*, by Douglas E. Comer (Prentice-Hall, 2001, ISBN 0-130-91449-5).

   Skip to the next section, "Hands-On Experience."

4. Have you done any reading on operating systems or networks? [Yes or No]

   If Yes, review the requirements stated in the first paragraphs after questions 2 and 3. If you meet those requirements, move on to the next section.

   If No, consult the recommended reading for both topics. A strong background will help you prepare for the Microsoft exams better than just about anything else.

Hands-on Experience

The most important key to success on all the Microsoft tests is hands-on experience, especially with Windows Server 2003, Windows 2000 Server, and Windows XP/2000 Professional, plus the many add-on services and BackOffice components around which so many of the Microsoft certification exams revolve. If we leave you with only one realization after taking this self-assessment, it should be that there's no substitute for time spent installing, configuring, and using the various Microsoft products on which you'll be tested repeatedly and in depth.

5. Have you installed, configured, and worked with Windows Server 2003 and Windows 2000 Server? [Yes or No]

   If Yes, make sure you understand the basic concepts covered in the following exams:

   - 70-290, "Managing and Maintaining a Microsoft Windows Server 2003 Environment"
   - 70-291, "Implementing, Managing, and Maintaining a Microsoft Windows Server 2003 Network Infrastructure"
   - 70-293, "Planning and Maintaining a Microsoft Windows Server 2003 Network Infrastructure"
   - 70-294, "Planning, Implementing, and Maintaining a Microsoft Windows Server 2003 Active Directory Infrastructure"

   If you don't have a lot of experience with Windows Server 2003, you should consider obtaining two or three machines and a copy of Windows Server 2003 (you can get a 180-day evaluation copy from Microsoft in most of the MS Press books for Windows Server 2003 as well as from the Microsoft Web site at `www.microsoft.com/windowsserver2003/evaluation/trial/evalkit.mspx`).

6. Have you installed, configured, and worked with Windows XP Professional or Windows 2000 Professional? [Yes or No]

   If Yes, make sure that you understand the concepts covered in Exam 70-210, "Installing, Configuring, and Administering Microsoft Windows 2000 Professional" and 70-270, "Installing, Configuring, and Administering Microsoft Windows XP Professional."

   If No, you'll want to obtain a copy of Windows XP Professional or Windows 2000 Professional and learn how to install, configure, and maintain it. You can use the *70-210* or *70-270 Exam Cram 2* to guide your activities and studies, or work straight from Microsoft's test objectives if you prefer.

You can download objectives, practice exams, and other data about Microsoft exams from the Training and Certification page at **http://www.microsoft.com/traincert/**. Use the Microsoft Certifications link to obtain specific exam information.

Before you even think about taking a Microsoft exam, make sure that you've spent enough time with the related software to understand how it may be installed and configured, how to maintain such an installation, and how to troubleshoot that software when things go wrong. This will help you in the exam and in real life!

If you have the funds, or your employer will pay your way, consider taking a class at a Certified Training and Education Center (CTEC). In addition to classroom exposure to the topic of your choice, you usually get a copy of the software that is the focus of your course, along with a trial version of whatever operating system it needs, with the training materials for that class.

Testing Your Exam-Readiness

Whether you attend a formal class on a specific topic to get ready for an exam or use written materials to study on your own, some preparation for the Microsoft certification exams is essential. At $125 (U.S.) a try, pass or fail, you want to do everything you can to pass on your first try—that's where studying comes in.

We have included two practice exams in this book (Chapters 11–13), so if you don't score well on the first, you can study more and then tackle the second.

For any given subject, consider taking a class if you've tackled self-study materials, taken the test, and failed anyway. The opportunity to interact with an instructor and fellow students can make all the difference in the world, if you can afford that privilege. For information about Microsoft classes, visit the Training and Certification page at `www.microsoft.com/education/partners/ctec.asp` for Microsoft Certified Education Centers.

If you can't afford to take a class, visit the Training page at `www.microsoft.com/traincert/training/find/default.asp` anyway because it also includes pointers to free practice exams and to Microsoft Certified

Professional Approved Study Guides and other self-study tools. Even if you can't afford to spend much at all, you should still invest in some low-cost practice exams from commercial vendors.

7. Have you taken a practice exam on your chosen test subject? [Yes or No]

   If Yes and you scored 70% or better, you're probably ready to tackle the real thing. If your score isn't above that threshold, keep at it until you break that barrier.

   If No, obtain all the free and low-budget practice tests you can find and get to work. Keep at it until you can break the passing threshold comfortably.

When it comes to assessing your test-readiness, there's no better way than to take a good-quality practice exam and pass with a score of 70% or better. When I'm preparing myself, I shoot for 80% or more, just to leave room for the "weirdness factor" that sometimes shows up on Microsoft exams.

What's Next?

After you've assessed your readiness, undertaken the right background studies, obtained the hands-on experience that will help you understand the products and technologies at work, and reviewed the many sources of information to help you prepare for a test, you're ready to take a round of practice tests.

When your scores come back positive enough to get you through the exam, you're ready to go after the real thing. If you follow our assessment regimen, you'll not only know what you need to study but also when you're ready to make a test date at Prometric (`www.prometric.com`) or VUE (`www.vue.com`). Good luck!

Exam-taking is not something that most people anticipate eagerly, no matter how well prepared they are. In most cases, familiarity helps offset test anxiety. In plain English, that means you probably won't be as nervous when you take your fourth or fifth Microsoft certification exam as you'll be when you take your first one.

Whether it's your first exam or your tenth, understanding the details of taking the new exam (the environment you'll be in, how much time to spend on questions, and so on) and the new exam software will help you concentrate on the material rather than on the setting. Likewise, mastering a few basic exam-taking skills should help you recognize (and perhaps even outfox) some of the tricks and snares you're bound to find in some exam questions.

This chapter explains the exam environment and software. It also describes some proven exam-taking strategies that you can use to your advantage.

Assessing Exam-Readiness

We strongly recommend that you read through and take the self-assessment included with this book (it appears just before this chapter). The self-assessment will help you compare your knowledge to the requirements for obtaining an MCSE (Microsoft Certified Systems Engineer). It will also help you identify parts of your background or experience that might need improvement, enhancement, or further learning. If you get the right set of basics under your belt, obtaining Microsoft certification will be that much easier.

After you've gone through the self-assessment, you can remedy those topical areas in which your background or experience is lacking. You can also tackle subject matter for individual tests at the same time so that you can continue making progress while you're catching up in some areas.

After you've worked through an *Exam Cram 2* book, have read the supplementary materials, and have taken the practice test, you'll have a pretty clear idea of when you should be ready to take the real exam. Although we strongly recommend that you keep practicing until your scores top the 75% mark, 80% is a better goal because it gives some margin for error when you're in an actual, stressful exam situation. Keep taking practice tests and studying the materials until you attain that score. You'll find more pointers on how to study and prepare in the self-assessment. But now, on to the exam itself.

What to Expect at the Testing Center

When you arrive at the testing center where you scheduled your exam, you must sign in with an exam coordinator and show two forms of identification—one of which must be a photo ID. After you've signed in and your time slot has arrived, you'll be asked to deposit any books, bags, cell phones, and other items you brought with you. Then you'll be escorted into a closed room.

All exams are completely closed book. Although you aren't permitted to take anything with you into the testing area, you're furnished with a blank sheet of paper and a pencil (in some cases, an erasable plastic sheet and an erasable pen). Immediately before entering the testing center, try to memorize as much of the important material as you can so that you can write that information on the blank sheet as soon as you are seated in front of the computer. You can refer to this piece of paper during the test, but you'll have to surrender the sheet when you leave the room. Because your timer does not start until you begin the testing process, it's best to write down the information first, while it's still fresh in your mind. You'll have some time to compose yourself, write down information on the paper you've been given, and take a sample orientation exam before you begin the real thing. We suggest you take the orientation test before you take your first exam. Because the exams are generally identical in layout, behavior, and controls, you probably won't need to do this more than once.

The room typically has one to six computers, and each workstation is separated from the others by dividers. Most test rooms feature a wall with a large picture window. This permits the exam coordinator to monitor the room, to prevent exam-takers from talking to one another, and to observe anything out of the ordinary. The exam coordinator will have preloaded the appropriate Microsoft certification exam (for this book, Exam 70-296), and you'll be permitted to start as soon as you're seated in front of the computer.

All Microsoft certification exams allow a certain maximum amount of time in which to complete your work. (This time is indicated on the exam by an onscreen counter/clock, so you can check the time remaining whenever you like.) All Microsoft certification exams are computer-generated from a larger pool of exam questions. The questions are constructed to check your mastery of basic facts and figures about Windows Server 2003 network administration and to require you to evaluate one or more sets of circumstances or requirements. You'll often be asked to give more than one answer to a question. You might also be asked to select the best or most effective solution to a problem from a range of choices, all of which are technically correct. Taking the exam is quite an adventure, and it involves real thinking. This book shows you what to expect and how to deal with the potential problems, puzzles, and predicaments.

In the next section, you'll learn more about the format of Microsoft test questions and how to answer them.

Exam Layout and Design

The format of Microsoft exams can vary. In addition to the eight exam question types we'll examine next, Microsoft has publicly announced that it might very well include adaptive testing technology and simulation items in its certification exams. You might not know ahead of time what you're getting into and should prepare the same regardless.

Active Screen Questions

The active screen question is one of several new types introduced with the Windows Server 2003 MCP (Microsoft Certified Professional) exams. This question type requires you to configure a dialog box by changing one or more of the options on the dialog box shown in Figure 1.1.

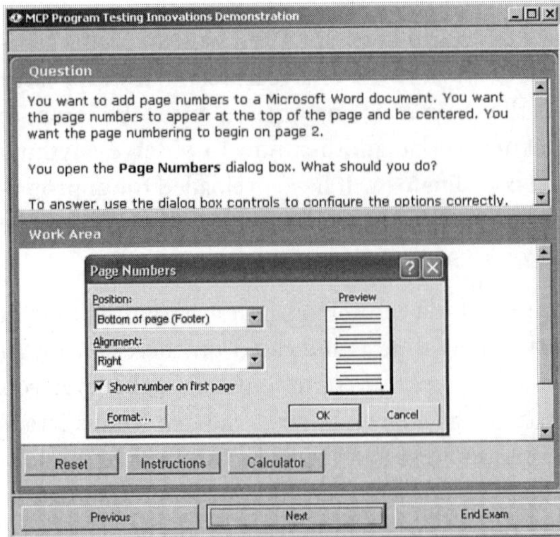

Figure 1.1 The active screen question type requires you to manipulate a dialog box to achieve the desired results.

To answer the active screen question, you might need to change one of several things, including selecting and unselecting options, changing values in drop-down menus, and dragging text elements into text areas within the dialog box. When you're done with your configuration actions, you simply need to click the Next button to progress to the next question. The Reset button can be used to reset the dialog box to its original configuration.

It's important to note that not every element in the dialog box will be active—this can be helpful if you have trouble figuring out where to get started with the question. You can use the scrollbars to view the entire text or dialog box area. In addition, the splitter bar can be used to resize the panes as desired.

Build List and Reorder Questions

The build list and reorder question type is not new to the Windows Server 2003 MCP exams, but has been refined by Microsoft since its initial introduction. In the build list and reorder question shown in Figure 1.2, you're required to build a list in the correct order that represents the steps required in achieving the required result.

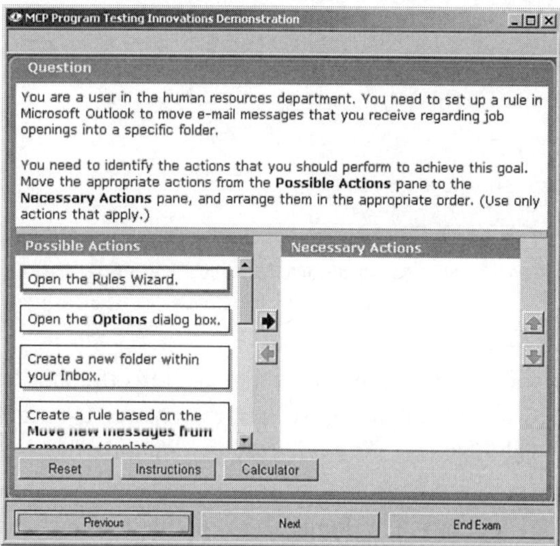

Figure 1.2 The build list and reorder question type requires you to indicate the correct answer by building an answer list.

You can move objects to the workspace by dragging them. You can rearrange objects in the workspace by dragging them up and down within the list. Should you need to remove an object from the workspace, simply drag it out of the workspace. The Reset button can be used to reset the workspace to its original configuration. You can use the scrollbars to view the entire text or dialog box area. The splitter bar also can be used to resize the panes as desired.

Create a Tree Questions

The create a tree question type is also not new to the Windows Server 2003 MCP exams, but has been refined by Microsoft since its initial introduction. In the create a tree question shown in Figure 1.3, you are required to create a tree structure to achieve the required result or answer the question at hand.

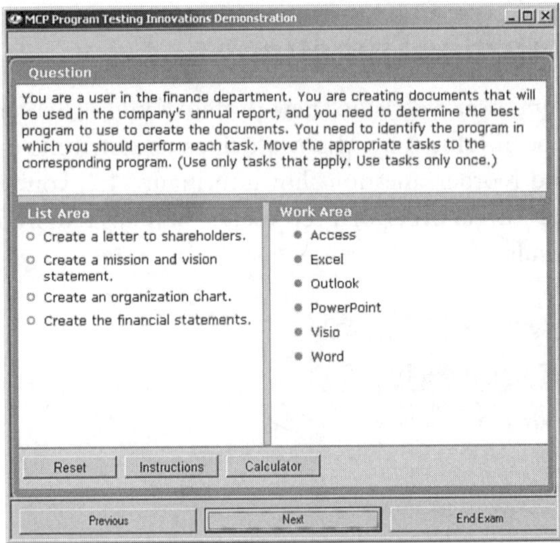

Figure 1.3 The create a tree question type requires you to create a tree structure to answer the question.

You answer this type of question by dragging source nodes into the answer tree in the correct locations. Entries that are present in the answer tree cannot be moved from their initial locations. Answer trees can include five levels of nodes and thus can grow quite complex for some questions. When a source node can no longer be used, it will no longer be available to select and drag. If a source node is still available to select and drag, it can be used again as required. You can remove nodes by dragging them out of the answer tree or by selecting them and pressing the Delete key. The Reset button can be used to reset the answer tree to its original configuration. The + and - icons can be used to expand or hide the child nodes that are under a parent node.

Drag and Drop Questions

The drag and drop question type requires you to drag source objects into their proper places in the work area. In the drag and drop question shown in Figure 1.4, you're required to place the correct text label under the item it's associated with.

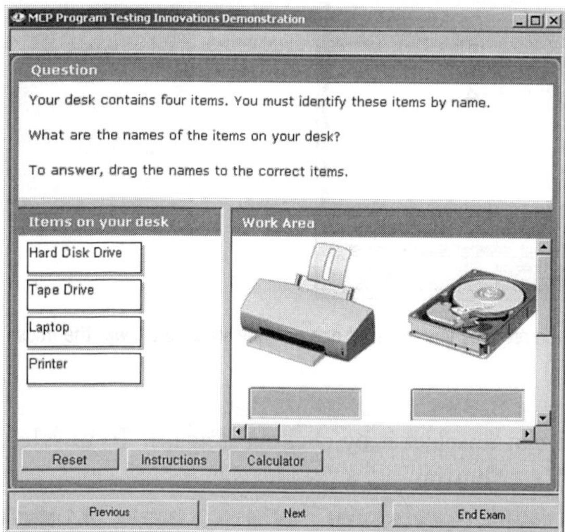

Figure 1.4 The drag and drop question type requires you to create a tree structure to answer the question.

You answer this type of question by dragging source objects into the work area and placing them in the correct locations. Place the source object into the correct target when the target area turns gray. You can delete a source object by dragging it back to its initial location or by clicking on it and pressing Delete. The Reset button can be used to reset the work area to its original configuration.

Hot Area Questions

This type of question asks you to select one or more areas on a graphic to indicate the correct answer to a question as seen in Figure 1.5. A hot spot on the graphic is shaded when you move the mouse over it, and is marked with an obvious border. To select or deselect an element, just click it.

Question-Handling Strategies

For those questions that have only one right answer, usually two or three of the answers will be obviously incorrect, and two of the answers will be plausible. Unless the answer leaps out at you (if it does, reread the question to look for a trick; sometimes those are the questions you're most likely to get wrong), begin the process of answering by eliminating those answers that are most obviously wrong.

At least one answer out of the possible choices for a question can usually be eliminated immediately because it matches one of these conditions:

- The answer does not apply to the situation.
- The answer describes a nonexistent issue, an invalid option, or an imaginary state.

After you eliminate all answers that are obviously wrong, you can apply your retained knowledge to eliminate further answers. Look for items that sound correct but refer to actions, commands, or features that are not present or not available in the situation that the question describes.

If you're still faced with a blind guess among two or more potentially correct answers, reread the question. Try to picture how each of the possible remaining answers would alter the situation. Be especially sensitive to terminology; sometimes the choice of words (*remove* instead of *disable*) can make the difference between a right answer and a wrong one.

You should guess at an answer only after you've exhausted your ability to eliminate answers and are still unclear about which of the remaining possibilities is correct. An unanswered question offers you no points, but guessing gives you at least some chance of getting a question right; just don't be too hasty when making a blind guess.

Numerous questions assume that the default behavior of a particular utility is in effect. If you know the defaults and understand what they mean, this knowledge will help you cut through many Gordian knots. Simple "final" actions might be critical as well. If a utility must be restarted before proposed changes take effect, a correct answer might require this step as well.

Ultimately, how you answer a question might depend on the type of exam being taken: adaptive or nonadaptive. The current standard is for MCP exams to be nonadaptive, although Microsoft has publicly said it might start using adaptive exams at some time in the future. In the standard, nonadaptive exam, you can mark questions that you've skipped or want to look at again for review. You'll get a second chance to look at those questions before you submit your exam for grading. You also can move backward through the exam to get back to a question you want to look at again. When you take an adaptive exam, there is no going back after you've moved on to the next question, nor is there a review screen that gives you the option to look at the question again before the exam is graded.

Mastering the Inner Game

In the final analysis, knowledge gives confidence, and confidence breeds success. If you study the materials in this book carefully and review all the practice questions at the end of each chapter, you should become aware of those areas where additional learning and study are required.

After you've worked your way through the book, take the practice exam in the back of the book. Taking this test provides a reality check and helps you identify areas to study further. Make sure that you follow up and review materials related to the questions that you miss on the practice exam before scheduling a real exam. Don't schedule your exam appointment until after you've thoroughly studied the material and feel comfortable with the whole scope of the practice exam. You should score 80% or better on the practice exam before proceeding to the real thing. Otherwise, obtain some additional practice tests so that you can keep trying until you hit the magic number.

If you take a practice exam and don't get at least 80% to 90% of the questions correct, keep practicing. Microsoft provides links to practice exam providers and also self-assessment exams at **http://www.microsoft.com/traincert/mcpexams/prepare/**.

Armed with the information in this book and the determination to augment your knowledge, you should be able to pass the certification exam. However, you need to work at it, or you'll spend the exam fee more than once before you finally pass. If you prepare seriously, you should do well.

The next section covers other sources you can use to prepare for the Microsoft certification exams.

Additional Resources

A good source of information about Microsoft certification exams comes from Microsoft itself. Because its products and technologies—and the exams that go with them—change frequently, the best place to go for exam-related information is online.

If you haven't already visited the Microsoft Certified Professional site, do so right now. The MCP home page resides at `http://www.microsoft.com/traincert/default.asp`.

Coping with Change on the Web

Sooner or later, all the information we've shared with you about the Microsoft Certified Professional pages and the other Web-based resources mentioned throughout the rest of this book will go stale or be replaced by newer information. In some cases, the URLs you find here will lead you to their replacements; in other cases, the URLs will go nowhere, leaving you with the dreaded **404 File Not Found** error message. When that happens, don't give up.

There's always a way to find what you want on the Web if you're willing to invest some time and energy. Most large or complex Web sites (such as the Microsoft site) offer a search engine. On all of Microsoft's Web pages, a Search button appears along the top edge of the page. As long as you can get to the Microsoft site (it should stay at **www.microsoft.com** for a long time), you can use the Search tool to help you find what you need.

The more focused you make a search request, the more likely it is that the results will include information you can use. For example, you can search for the string

```
"training and certification"
```

to produce a lot of data about the subject in general, but if you're looking for the preparation guide for Exam 70-296, "Planning, Implementing, and Maintaining a Microsoft Windows Server 2003 Environment for an MCSE Certified on Windows 2000," you'll be more likely to get there quickly if you use a search string similar to the following:

```
"Exam 70-296" AND "preparation guide"
```

Likewise, if you want to find the training and certification downloads, try a search string such as this:

```
"training and certification" AND "download page"
```

Finally, feel free to use general search tools—such as **www.google.com**, **www.altavista.com**, and **www.excite.com**—to look for related information. Although Microsoft offers great information about its certification exams online, there are plenty of third-party sources of information and assistance that need not follow Microsoft's party line. Therefore, if you can't find something immediately, intensify your search. You might also want to visit certification-specific Internet portals such as **www.mcseworld.com** and **www.certicities.com** to get a feel for what others are saying about the exam you're preparing for.

Planning and Implementing Server Roles and Server Security

Terms you'll need to understand:

- ✓ Active Directory Users and Computers
- ✓ Group Policy Editor
- ✓ Group Policy Object
- ✓ Principle of least privilege
- ✓ Security Configuration and Analysis
- ✓ **secedit.exe**
- ✓ Security template

Techniques you'll need to master:

- ✓ Analyzing and configuring the server security configuration with the Security Configuration and Analysis Snap-in
- ✓ Using the **secedit.exe** command to analyze and configure server security settings from the command line
- ✓ Importing security templates into Group Policy Objects
- ✓ Modifying Group Policy items to change server security settings
- ✓ Modifying security settings directly in the Domain Controller Security Policy console

Windows Server 2003 is inherently more secure "right out of the box" than any previous version of Windows to come before it. The Trustworthy Computing campaign that Microsoft is leading has shown itself directly in the intrinsic security of Windows Server 2003. Although it is more secure than its predecessors, this does not relieve you of the responsibility to evaluate, implement, and audit security measures for your Windows Server 2003 servers.

The use of security templates, combined with careful planning and attentive administration of the network, will go a long way toward implementing the *principle of least privilege* on the network. Using this principle, users are given only the minimum privileges that are required to perform a specific set of tasks for which they have been assigned.

By using the principle of least privilege, a compromised user account has less of an impact on the overall security of the network than if you had assigned blanket permissions to all users who have no need for them. In addition, by carefully planning the role that each server will fulfill on the network, you can configure it to effectively perform its required duties in a more secure fashion. Windows Server 2003 comes with a complete set of preconfigured security templates that you can use to quickly apply standardized security settings to a single computer, an Organizational Unit, or a domain, if desired.

Configuring Basic Security with Security Templates

As mentioned previously, Windows Server 2003 comes to you out of the box in a more secure form than any other version of Windows before it. In addition, it comes with a full set of preconfigured security templates that you can use to customize the security settings of a server (or other computers in the domain) to your liking. These preconfigured templates can be thought of in one of two ways: either as a starting point from which to make your own customized security template or as a complete solution. Neither thought is more correct than the other.

In simple terms, a *security template* is little more than a specially formatted flat text file that can be read by the Security Configuration Manager tools. These preconfigured templates have an extension of .inf and are located in the %systemroot%\security\templates folder on your Windows Server 2003 computer. You can use the Security Configuration and Analysis console, the `secedit.exe` tool, or the Local Security Policy console to apply these templates to a local computer. Templates that you apply to an Organizational Unit or domain can be applied by importing them into the Security Settings section of the applicable Group Policy, using the Group Policy Editor. In addition, these preconfigured templates can be used to compare the security settings of an unknown system against a known set of configuration settings by using the Security Configuration and Analysis console or the `secedit.exe` tool.

The following sections examine the templates themselves and provide an explanation of how they are configured and when they should be used.

The Windows Server 2003 Security Templates

Table 2.1 details the preconfigured security templates that ship with Windows Server 2003.

Table 2.1 The Preconfigured Security Templates in Windows Server 2003

Template (Filename)	Description
Default Security (Setup security.inf)	This template is created during the installation of Windows Server 2003 on the computer. This template is specific to the computer it was created on and will be different depending on whether the installation was performed as a clean installation or an upgrade. Setup security.inf represents the default security settings that a computer is configured with and thus can be used to reset portions of security as required. This template can be applied to both workstations and member servers, but not to domain controllers; it should never be applied via Group Policy. Because of the large amount of data it contains, its application via a Group Policy can result in performance degradations on your network.
Default DC Security (DC security.inf)	This template is automatically created when a member server is promoted to a domain controller. It represents the file, Registry, and system service default security settings for that domain controller. It can be used later to reset these areas to their default configuration.

(continued)

All of the preconfigured security templates are incremental, meaning that they have been designed to be applied to computers using the default security settings. These templates do not implement the default security settings before applying their security settings.

Security Configuration Manager Tools

Now that you've seen the security templates available for use, let's take a brief look at the tools available for the design, testing, and application of these (and other) security templates. The Security Configuration Manager is not one console or tool, but is actually a collection of tools and utilities that you can use to implement security solutions across your network.

The components of the Security Configuration Manager include these:

- The Security Configuration and Analysis snap-in
- The Security Templates snap-in
- The `secedit.exe` command
- Group Policy security extensions

Each of these tools is examined in the following sections as it relates to implementing security solutions using the preconfigured security templates supplied in Windows Server 2003. Before actually moving forward, however, use the instructions in the following steps to construct a customized Microsoft Management Console (MMC):

1. Open an empty MMC shell by clicking Start, Run, and entering `MMC` in the Open field. Click OK. An empty MMC shell opens.
2. Click File, Add/Remove Snap-In to open the Add/Remove Snap-In dialog box. Click the Add button to open the Add Standalone Snap-In dialog box seen in Figure 2.1.
3. Scroll down the list and select the Security Configuration and Analysis and Security Templates snap-ins by double-clicking on each of them, respectively.
4. Click Close and then click OK to return to the MMC console, as seen in Figure 2.2.

computer. You can use the Security Configuration and Analysis console, the `secedit.exe` tool, or the Local Security Policy console to apply these templates to a local computer. Templates that you apply to an Organizational Unit or domain can be applied by importing them into the Security Settings section of the applicable Group Policy, using the Group Policy Editor. In addition, these preconfigured templates can be used to compare the security settings of an unknown system against a known set of configuration settings by using the Security Configuration and Analysis console or the `secedit.exe` tool.

The following sections examine the templates themselves and provide an explanation of how they are configured and when they should be used.

The Windows Server 2003 Security Templates

Table 2.1 details the preconfigured security templates that ship with Windows Server 2003.

Table 2.1 The Preconfigured Security Templates in Windows Server 2003

Template (Filename)	Description
Default Security (Setup security.inf)	This template is created during the installation of Windows Server 2003 on the computer. This template is specific to the computer it was created on and will be different depending on whether the installation was performed as a clean installation or an upgrade. Setup security.inf represents the default security settings that a computer is configured with and thus can be used to reset portions of security as required. This template can be applied to both workstations and member servers, but not to domain controllers; it should never be applied via Group Policy. Because of the large amount of data it contains, its application via a Group Policy can result in performance degradations on your network.
Default DC Security (DC security.inf)	This template is automatically created when a member server is promoted to a domain controller. It represents the file, Registry, and system service default security settings for that domain controller. It can be used later to reset these areas to their default configuration.

(continued)

Table 2.1 The Preconfigured Security Templates in Windows Server 2003 *(continued)*

Template (Filename)	Description
Compatible (compatws.inf)	The Compatible workstation/member server template provides a means of allowing members of the Users group to run applications that do not conform to the Windows Logo program. In most cases, applications that conform to the Windows Logo program can be successfully run by members of the Users group without any further modifications required. For applications that do not conform, there are two basic choices: Make the users members of the Power Users group or relax the default permissions of the Users group. The Compatible template solves this problem by changing the default file and Registry permissions initially granted to the Users group, to allow those users to run most applications that are not part of the Windows Logo program. As a side effect of applying this template, all users are removed from the Power Users group because the basic assumption is that the template is being applied in an effort to prevent the need for Power Users. This template should not be applied to domain controllers, so be sure not to import it into the Default Domain Policy or the Default Domain Controller Policy.
Secure (securews.inf, securedc.inf)	The Secure templates are used to begin the process of locking down the computer to which they are applied. There are two Secure templates: securews.inf, which is for workstations and member servers, and the securedc.inf template, which is for domain controllers only. The Secure templates prevent the use of the LAN Manager (LM) authentication protocol. Windows 9*x* clients must have the Active Directory Client Extensions installed to enable NT LAN Manager v2 (NTLM v2), which gives them the capability to communicate with Windows 2000 and above clients and servers using these templates. These templates impose additional restrictions on anonymous users, such as preventing them from enumerating account and share information. The Secure templates also enable Server Message Block (SMB) signing on the server side. By default, SMB signing is enabled on client computers. By applying this template, SMB packet signing always is negotiated between clients and servers.

(continued)

Table 2.1 The Preconfigured Security Templates in Windows Server 2003 *(continued)*

Template (Filename)	Description
Highly Secure (hisecws.inf, hisecdc.inf)	The Highly Secure templates impose further restrictions on computers when they are applied. Whereas the Secure templates require *at least* NTLM authentication, the Highly Secure templates *require* NTLM v2 authentication. The Secure templates *enable* SMB packet signing; the Highly Secure templates *require* SMB packet signing. In addition to the various additional security restrictions re-imposed by the Highly Secure templates, these templates make several changes to group membership and the login process. All members of the Power Users group are removed, and only Domain Admins and the local administrative account are allowed to be members of the local Administrators group. When the Highly Secure templates are used, it is assumed that only Windows Logo program–compliant applications are in use. As such, no provision is in place for users to use noncompliant applications because the Compatible template is not needed and the Power Users group has no members. Members of the Users group can use applications that are Windows Logo program–compliant. Additionally, members of the Administrators group can use any application they want.
System Root Security (Rootsec.inf)	The Root Security template defines the permissions for the root of the system volume. If these permissions are changed, they can be reapplied using this template. Additionally, this template can be modified to apply the same permissions to other volumes. Explicitly configured permissions are not overwritten on child objects when using this template.
No Terminal Server Use SID (Notssid.inf)	This template is used to remove the additional permissions granted to users of Terminal Services. By default, additional permissions are used to allow older programs to work properly with Terminal Services. If Terminal Services is not used, this template has no effect.

You can learn more about the Windows logo program by visiting **www.microsoft.com/winlogo/default.mspx**.

All of the preconfigured security templates are incremental, meaning that they have been designed to be applied to computers using the default security settings. These templates do not implement the default security settings before applying their security settings.

Security Configuration Manager Tools

Now that you've seen the security templates available for use, let's take a brief look at the tools available for the design, testing, and application of these (and other) security templates. The Security Configuration Manager is not one console or tool, but is actually a collection of tools and utilities that you can use to implement security solutions across your network.

The components of the Security Configuration Manager include these:

- The Security Configuration and Analysis snap-in
- The Security Templates snap-in
- The `secedit.exe` command
- Group Policy security extensions

Each of these tools is examined in the following sections as it relates to implementing security solutions using the preconfigured security templates supplied in Windows Server 2003. Before actually moving forward, however, use the instructions in the following steps to construct a customized Microsoft Management Console (MMC):

1. Open an empty MMC shell by clicking Start, Run, and entering MMC in the Open field. Click OK. An empty MMC shell opens.
2. Click File, Add/Remove Snap-In to open the Add/Remove Snap-In dialog box. Click the Add button to open the Add Standalone Snap-In dialog box seen in Figure 2.1.
3. Scroll down the list and select the Security Configuration and Analysis and Security Templates snap-ins by double-clicking on each of them, respectively.
4. Click Close and then click OK to return to the MMC console, as seen in Figure 2.2.

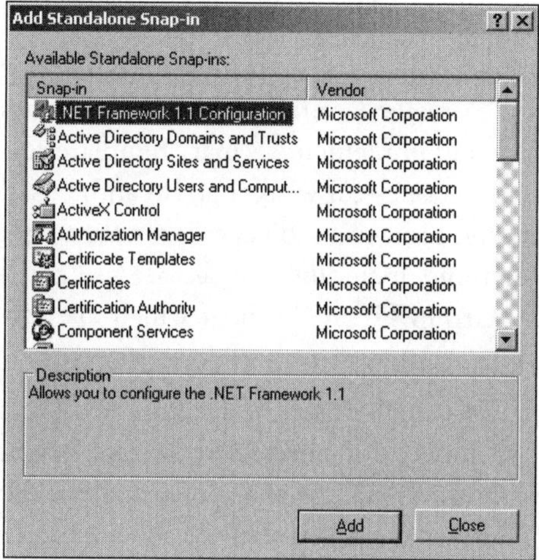

Figure 2.1 You can add any number of snap-ins from the Add/Remove Snap-In dialog box to your custom console.

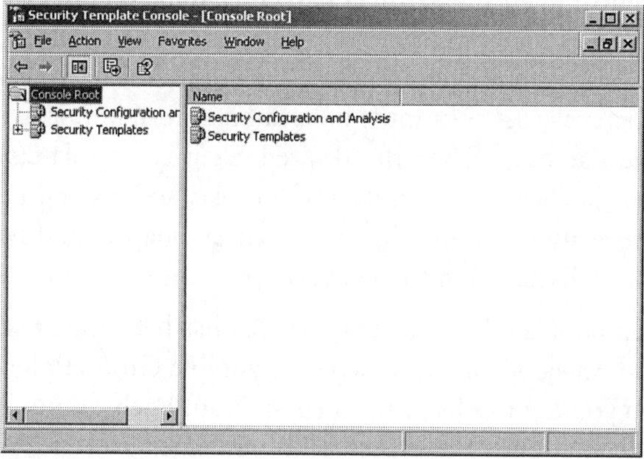

Figure 2.2 A customized MMC console with the Security Configuration and Analysis and Security Templates snap-ins added.

5. Save the console by clicking File, Save. A standard Save dialog box opens; specify the filename and location to save the console to. By default, it is saved in the Administrative Tools folder of the user currently logged in.

Armed with the custom security console, let's move forward and examine how the tools are put to work.

Security Configuration and Analysis

The Security Configuration and Analysis snap-in is the primary tool in your security template toolbox. Using the Security Configuration and Analysis snap-in, you can create, configure, test, and implement security template settings for a local computer. Therein lies its one real weakness: It can be used only with the settings of a local computer. However, you can find ways to get around this limitation by using other tools, including the `secedit.exe` command and the security extensions to Group Policy, both of which are discussed later in this section.

The Security Configuration and Analysis snap-in can be used in two basic modes, configuration and analysis, although not necessarily in that order. When using the Security Configuration and Analysis snap-in to analyze the current system security configuration, no changes are made to the computer being analyzed. The administrator simply selects a security template (either a preconfigured or a custom-created template) to compare the computer's security setting against. The settings from the template are loaded into a database and then are compared to the settings currently implemented on the computer. It is possible to import multiple templates into this database, thus merging their settings into one conglomerate database. You can also specify that any existing database settings must be cleared before importing another template into the database. After the desired security template(s) have been loaded into the database, any number of analysis actions can be performed, both by the Security Configuration and Analysis snap-in and by the `secedit.exe` command, as discussed in the next section.

After the database has been populated and an analysis scan has been initiated, Security Configuration and Analysis examines each configurable Group Policy option and reports back to you the results of the analysis scan. Each setting is marked with an icon that denotes one of several possible outcomes, such as: the settings are the same, the settings are different, or the settings do not apply. Table 2.2 outlines the possible icons that you might see and what they indicate.

Table 2.2 Explanation of Security Analysis Icons

Icon	Description
Red X	The item is defined in the analysis database and on the computer, but it does not match the current configured setting.
Green check mark	The item is defined in the analysis database and on the computer, and it matches the currently configured setting.
Question mark	The item is not defined in the analysis database and was not examined on the computer.
Exclamation point	The item is defined in the analysis database but not on the computer.
Normal	The item is not defined in the analysis database or the computer.

you to enter the path and filename of the security template. Be sure to use a unique name; in other words, do not save over one of the preconfigured security templates because you might need it again in the future.

Security Templates

The Security Templates snap-in (shown in Figure 2.6) displays a list of preconfigured security templates. Using this interface, preconfigured security templates can be modified or new security templates can be created from scratch, without the danger or possibility of accidentally applying the template to the computer or Group Policy Object.

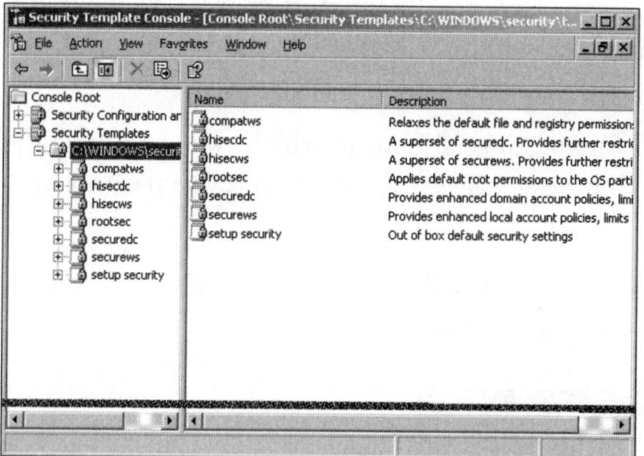

Figure 2.6 The Security Templates snap-in enables you to work with existing or new templates.

To work with an existing template, open the template, expand the subnodes to select the setting to be modified, and simply begin making changes to suit your requirements. When you are done, you should save the template with a new name. This can be done by right-clicking the specific template and selecting Save As from the context menu. This opens the standard Save dialog box that enables you to specify the path and filename of the template.

If you want to start with a completely empty template (no preconfigured settings), you can do so by right-clicking on the template location (for example, C:\WINDOWS\security\templates) and selecting New Template from the context menu.

Group Policy

Up to this point, we have examined how you can apply a security template to a local computer by using the Security Configuration and Analysis snap-in. This is certainly not the only way to apply a security template. Imagine the amount of time and effort involved in applying a security template locally at each computer using Security Configuration and Analysis. As difficult and time-consuming as that project would be, imagine applying different templates to several different types of servers, such as domain controllers, Internet Information Services (IIS) servers, and other member servers. Now you would have the added hassle of trying to remember which template goes with what server.

Fortunately, you can easily and quickly import security templates into your Group Policy Objects using the Group Policy editor, as detailed in the following steps:

1. Open the Active Directory Users and Computers console by clicking Start, Programs, Administrative Tools, Active Directory Users and Computers.
2. Locate the domain or Organizational Unit to which you want to apply the security template. This example applies the securews.inf template to the Sales OU.
3. Right-click the Sales OU and select Properties from the context menu. Switch to the Group Policy page (see Figure 2.7).

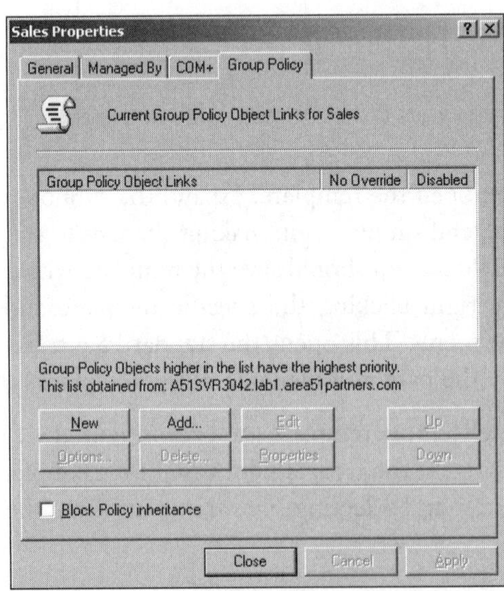

Figure 2.7 Create a new Group Policy Object if none exists already.

4. To create a new Group Policy Object, click the New button. Supply a name for the new GPO and press the Enter key.

5. Click the Edit button to open the Group Policy Editor for the selected GPO.

6. Expand the nodes as follows: Computer Configuration, Windows Settings, Security Settings. Right-click the Security Settings node and select Import Policy from the context menu, as shown in Figure 2.8.

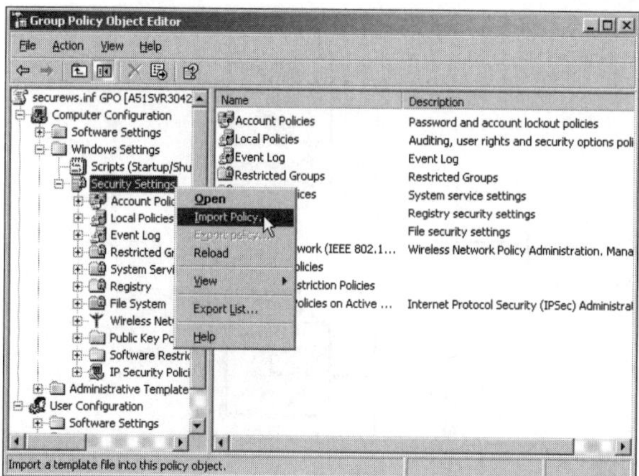

Figure 2.8 Importing a security template into the Group Policy Editor.

7. The Import Policy From dialog box opens, providing you with a list of the preconfigured security templates. You can navigate to another location, if required, to use a custom-created security template. After selecting the desired template and clicking the Open button, the settings configured in the template are now added to the GPO and are applied to all computers that are part of that OU during the next Group Policy refresh cycle.

Note that you can import security settings at the domain level to apply security settings to all computers within the domain. As a general rule, you should apply the most generic settings at the domain level and then apply settings specific to the computers at the OU level. Figure 2.9 provides an example of how this might work for an organization consisting of several OUs.

If you need to apply security templates to the entire domain, right-click on the domain object in Active Directory Users and Computers and select Properties to open its Properties dialog box. The Properties dialog box for your Domain Controllers OU can be accessed by right-clicking on the Domain Controllers OU and selecting Properties.

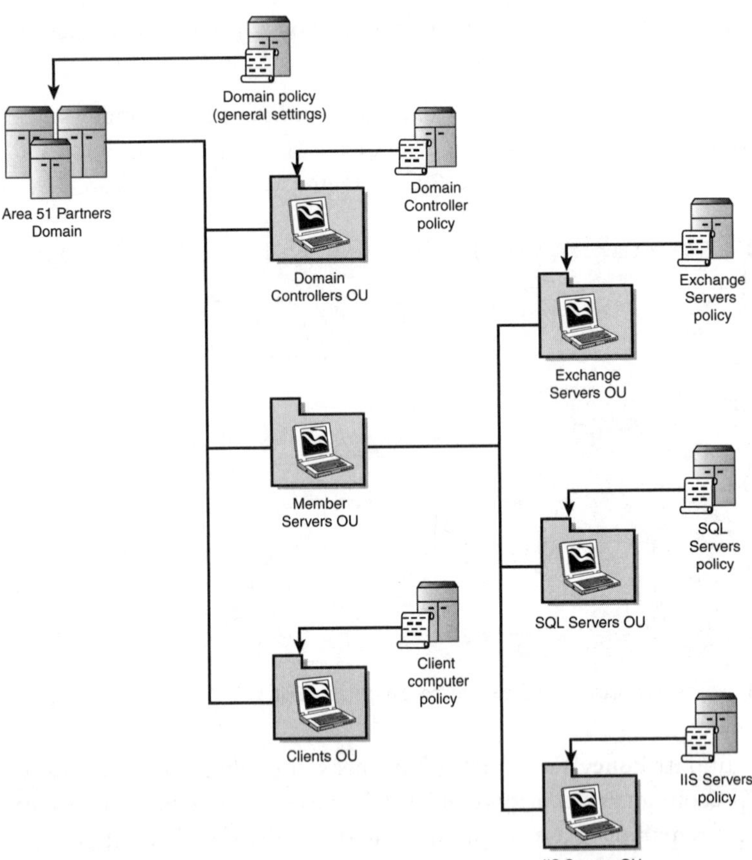

Figure 2.9 You can apply security templates (policies) at several nested levels in Group Policy.

secedit.exe

Up to this point, we have spent a good amount of time examining the ways in which you can work with security templates using the Windows GUI—but what about the command line? As you might have guessed, there is a command-line alternative to the Security Configuration and Analysis snap-in, and it comes in the form of the `secedit.exe` command.

The `secedit.exe` command can be used to perform the same functions as the Security Configuration and Analysis snap-in, with a few additional functions not found in its GUI equivalent. The `secedit.exe` command has the following top-level options available for use:

- `/analyze`—Enables you to analyze the security settings of a computer by comparing them against the baseline settings in a database.

- /configure—Enables you to configure the security settings of the local computer by applying the settings contained in a database.
- /export—Enables you to export the settings configured in a database to a security template (.inf) file.
- /import—Enables you to import the settings configured in a security template (.inf) file into a database. If you are applying multiple security templates to a database, you should perform this option before performing the analysis or configuration.
- /validate—Validates the syntax of a security template to ensure that it is correct before being imported into a database for analysis or configuration.
- /GenerateRollback—Enables you to create a rollback template that can be used to reset the security configuration to the values before the security template was applied.

Of the available options, you will most often make use of the /analyze and /configure switches. To that end, examples and explanations of their usage are provided here.

To analyze the current security configuration of the local computer, you would issue the secedit.exe command with the following syntax:

```
secedit /analyze /db FileName /cfg FileName /overwrite /log FileName /quiet
```

You need to view the results of the analysis in the Security Configuration and Analysis snap-in by opening the database created during the analysis. At first, it might seem like running the analysis from the command line and then viewing the results in the GUI is counterproductive. In reality, the opposite is true. Consider the case in which you run **secedit.exe** from a script on multiple computers. You can then view the databases, one for each computer, in the GUI at your leisure to determine what changes need to be made to the security settings on these computers. The **%computername%** variable can be used when creating the database and log files to create one for each computer being scanned.

The configuration parameters are as follows:

- /db *FileName*—This specifies the path and filename of the database to be used to perform the analysis.
- /cfg *FileName*—This specifies the path and filename of the security template that is to be imported into the database before performing the analysis.
- /overwrite—This specifies that the database is to be cleared before importing the security template.

- `/log` *`FileName`*—This specifies the path and filename of the file that is used to log the status of the analysis process. By default, a log named scesrv.log is created in the %windir%\security\logs directory.

- `/quiet`—This specifies that the analysis process should be completed without more onscreen comments.

As an example, suppose that you wanted to analyze the settings on a computer to compare them to the security settings contained in the securews.inf template. You would issue the following command to perform this function:

```
secedit /analyze /db c:\sectest\1.sdb /cfg
C:\WINDOWS\security\templates\securews.inf /log c:\sectest\1.log
```

If all goes well, you should see something like that shown in Figure 2.10.

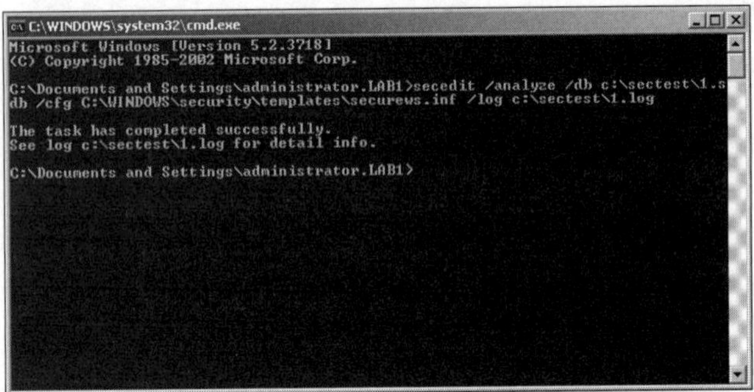

Figure 2.10 A command-line analysis performed using the **secedit.exe** command.

To configure the current security configuration of the local computer, you would issue the `secedit.exe` command with the following syntax:

```
secedit /configure /db FileName /cfg FileName /overwrite /areas Area1 Area2
... /log FileName /quiet
```

The configuration parameters are defined as follows:

- `/db` *`FileName`*—This specifies the path and filename of the database to be used to perform the configuration.

- `/cfg` *`FileName`*—This specifies the path and filename of the security template that is to be imported into the database before performing the configuration.

- `/overwrite`—This specifies that the database is to be cleared before importing the security template.

- /areas—This specifies the security areas that are to be applied to the system. By default, when this parameter is not specified, all security areas are applied to the computer. The available security area options are as follows:
  - SECURITYPOLICY—This area includes Account Policies, Audit Policies, Event Log settings, and Security Options.
  - GROUP_MGMT—This area is the Restricted Group settings.
  - USER_RIGHTS—This area is the User Rights Assignment settings.
  - REGKEYS—This area is the Registry permissions settings.
  - FILESTORE—This area is the File System permissions settings.
  - SERVICES—This area is the System Service settings.
- /log *FileName*—This specifies the path and filename of the file that is used to log the status of the analysis process. By default, a log named scesrv.log is created in the %windir%\security\logs directory.
- /quiet—This specifies that the analysis process should take place without additional onscreen comments.

As an example, suppose that you wanted to configure the settings on a computer with the security settings contained in the securews.inf template. You would issue the following command to perform this function:

```
secedit /configure /db c:\sectest\1.sdb /cfg
C:\WINDOWS\security\templates\securews.inf /log c:\sectest\1.log
```

Configuring Secure Servers

Armed with the knowledge of what security templates are and how you create, modify, and apply them, let's examine how you can use them in your network to secure your servers. In addition, we examine the processes involved in making security configurations directly to your network at several different levels, through direct editing of Group Policy Objects and the use of several management consoles.

Securing Domain Controllers

Your domain controllers are the most important servers on your network, hands down. Not that any server is unimportant; it's just that domain controllers are the most important in terms of security—after all, through authentication mechanisms, they issue the keys to the kingdom.

When it comes time to increase the security level of your domain controllers, you have several options available. Configuring increased security in any of the following ways will have the same net effect:

- Use the securedc.inf or hisecdc.inf security templates (or a custom variation of these security templates). You can apply these templates to your domain controllers by using the Security Configuration and Analysis snap-in, by using the `secedit.exe` command, or by importing them into a Group Policy Object linked to the Domain Controllers Organizational Unit in Active Directory Users and Computers. Of these three options, importing a security template into a GPO is your best choice, in that you will consistently apply the same settings without fail when using a security template.
- Directly edit a Group Policy Object that is linked to the Domain Controllers Group Policy Organizational Unit.
- Configure the settings directly through the use of the Domain Controller Security Policy console.

The general procedure for importing a security template into a Group Policy Object was examined earlier in this chapter. The process of importing a security template is the same as previously outlined, except that, in this case, you import the correct domain controller template to a GPO linked to the Domain Controller OU.

You can also modify the security configuration by directly editing a GPO linked to the Domain Controllers OU. This method is advantageous if you are making a small number of very specific security modifications, but it can quickly become very time-consuming and error-prone if great caution is not exercised. The disadvantage to making changes directly into a GPO is that you lose the capability to analyze the actual results against the intended results. Be sure to always test your modifications in a nonproduction test lab before deploying them to your production network's domain controllers.

The final method available for the configuration of domain controller security is to use the Domain Controller Security Policy console, located in the Administrative Tools folder. Using the Domain Controller Security Policy console enables you to make changes that are directly applied to all domain controllers in the domain, so make the changes with care. Changes made via the Domain Controller Security Policy console are actually implemented into the Default Domain Controller GPO that is linked to the Domain Controllers OU. The Domain Controller Security Policy console is shown in Figure 2.11.

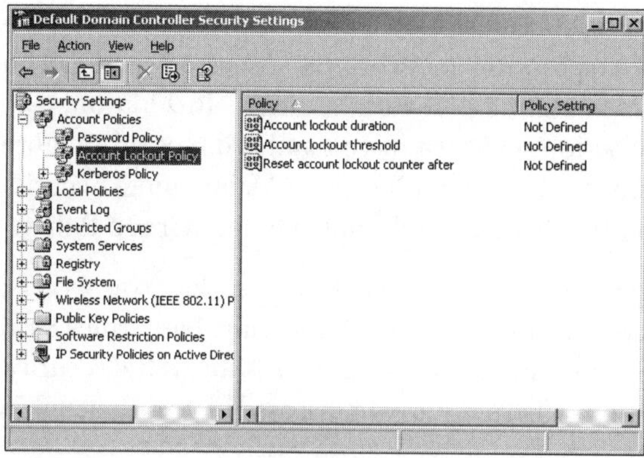

Figure 2.11 Security configuration changes can be made directly to all domain controllers using the Domain Controller Security Policy console.

No matter which way you choose to apply security settings to your domain controllers (with security templates, by direct GPO modification, or with the Domain Controller Security Policy console), the results of the configuration changes are the same. It is absolutely essential that you thoroughly test all configuration changes in a test environment before rolling them out to your production network.

Securing IIS Servers, Exchange Servers, and Other Member Servers

IIS servers (and the Exchange servers that rely on them for secure messaging traffic) have long been the Achilles's heel of Windows security. IIS 5.0 was directly targeted by several dozen exploits and other vulnerabilities that allowed attackers to gain various levels of control over the IIS server and portions of the network behind it.

In Windows Server 2003, the default configuration of IIS 6.0 is inherently more secure than IIS 5.0 was in Windows 2000. IIS 6.0 is no longer installed and enabled on a fresh installation of Windows Server 2003, as it was previously in Windows 2000 Server. The URLScan ISAPI filter and the IIS Lockdown tools (required to secure IIS 5.0) are no longer required in IIS 6.0 because IIS 6.0 is set to a very secure condition by default. You will find yourself needing to enable functionality in IIS 6.0 that will cause it to behave in the same fashion as IIS 5.0 did by default—this is a great benefit to any organization that plans on deploying an IIS server in its Windows Server 2003 network.

With such tools as URLScan and IIS Lockdown no longer necessary, the real work of securing an IIS server is left to the administrator. To properly secure these types of member servers, you must look closely at the process of protecting data while in transit across the network, as discussed in detail in Chapter 5, "Planning and Maintaining Network Security." In addition, user authentication should be of serious concern to you and is discussed in more detail in Chapter 6, "Planning, Implementing, and Maintaining Security Infrastructure," and Chapter 9, "Planning and Implementing Group Policy."

When it comes to securing other member servers, such as database servers, file servers, and print servers (just to name a few), the same basic rules used for IIS servers apply; you must evaluate the requirements for traffic security, user access, and authentication. These topics are discussed in more detail in the chapters previously mentioned.

Every security plan must have a starting point. By making use of the preconfigured security templates supplied with Windows Server 2003, you can quickly and effortlessly implement varying levels of appropriate security within your organization. As discussed in this chapter, you can create customized security templates that specifically meet your needs and security requirements. By configuring and testing security templates in Security Configuration and Analysis, you can avoid mistakenly applying them to a large group of computers via Group Policy until you are ready to do so.

In all but the smallest network, you will most likely have several servers that perform distinctively different functions. No two servers are alike—more specifically, no two types of servers are alike. Because of the nature of each server's unique functionality, you should not just apply a blanket configuration to your network's servers and consider your task as being complete—doing so might not provide your servers or your network with the level of security that you need. By applying different security settings on different groups of servers—domain controllers, IIS servers, file servers, and so on—you can ensure that the correct settings are applied to each type of server. This can be done through the use of the preconfigured default security templates, with additional configuration of security options, network security options, user authentication, and auditing as required by your network implementation.

Exam Prep Questions

Question 1

You are the network administrator for Gus Gus Gas Stations, Inc. You need to implement a more secure network environment across all servers, both domain controllers and member servers. What security templates could you use to provide a higher level of security for these servers and still leave room to increase security again, if desired? (Choose two correct answers.)

- ❑ A. securews.inf
- ❑ B. hisecws.inf
- ❑ C. hisecdc.inf
- ❑ D. securedc.inf

Answers A and D are correct. By using the Secure templates (securews.inf for member servers and workstations and securedc.inf for domain controllers), you can increase the baseline security of your servers and still allow for increasing security later (if desired) through the use of the Highly Secure templates (answers B and C). Answers B and C are incorrect because using the Secure templates prevents the use of the LAN Manager authentication protocol on the network. This results in the need for any Windows 9*x* clients to have the Active Directory Client Extensions installed to enable them to make use of NTLM v2. In addition, SMB signing is configured by default on servers when implementing the secure template. By default, SMB signing is enabled on Windows 2000 and Windows XP client computers.

Question 2

You are the network administrator for Just Right Tops, LLC. Your network consists of three geographically distant sites that function as three different domains. No site has a direct link to any other site. You have recently created two custom security templates that are to be applied to all computers in all three sites of your company network. How can you most easily deploy these security templates at all three sites?

- ❍ A. Create and configure a new domain controller for each remote site. Apply the security templates to the domain controllers. Place a new domain controller in each site, and allow Active Directory to replicate.
- ❍ B. Export the security templates into .inf files using Security Configuration and Analysis. Deliver the security templates to the remote location, and import them into the appropriate Group Policy Objects.

Question 6

You have just completed an analysis of one of your Windows Server 2003 computers using the Security Configuration and Analysis snap-in. Upon opening the Password Policy node, you see the results shown in Figure 2.12. What does the icon on the Enforce Password History policy item denote?

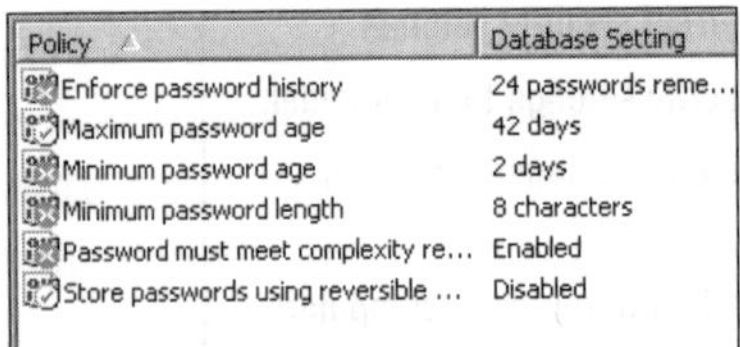

Policy
Database Setting
Enforce password history
24 passwords reme...
Maximum password age
42 days
Minimum password age
2 days
Minimum password length
8 characters
Password must meet complexity re...
Enabled
Store passwords using reversible ...
Disabled

Figure 2.12

- ❍ A. The item is not defined in the analysis database and was not examined on the computer.
- ❍ B. The item is defined in the analysis database and on the computer, and it matches the currently configured setting.
- ❍ C. The item is defined in the analysis database but not on the computer.
- ❍ D. The item is defined in the analysis database and on the computer, but it does not match the current configured setting.

Answer D is correct. A red X icon indicates that the policy item was defined both in the database and on the computer, but the currently configured setting does not match what is held in the database. An item that is not defined in the analysis database and thus not examined on the computer is represented by a question mark icon, so answer A is incorrect. An item that is defined in the database and on the computer and that matches is represented by green check mark, so answer B is incorrect. An item that is defined in the database but not on the computer is represented by an exclamation mark icon, so answer C is incorrect.

Question 7

You have just completed an analysis of one of your Windows Server 2003 computers using the Security Configuration and Analysis snap-in. Upon opening the Password Policy node, you see the results shown in Figure 2.12. What does the icon on the Maximum Password Age policy item denote?

- ❍ A. The item is not defined in the analysis database and was not examined on the computer.
- ❍ B. The item is defined in the analysis database and on the computer, and it matches the currently configured setting.
- ❍ C. The item is defined in the analysis database but not on the computer.
- ❍ D. The item is defined in the analysis database and on the computer, but it does not match the current configured setting.

Answer B is correct. A green check mark icon indicates that the policy item was defined both in the database and on the computer, and that it has the same setting in both locations. An item that is not defined in the analysis database and thus is not examined on the computer is represented by a question mark icon; therefore, answer A is incorrect. An item that is defined in the database but not on the computer is represented by an exclamation mark icon, so answer C is incorrect. An item that is defined in the database and on the computer but that does match is represented by a red X icon, so answer D is incorrect.

Question 8

You've configured settings for an account lockout policy. You check the settings in the Security Configuration and Analysis console and see the icons shown in Figure 2.13. What is the cause for the icons with the question mark?

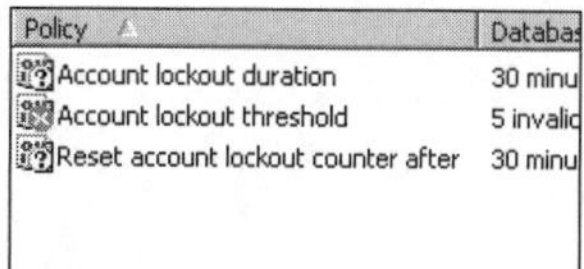

Policy
Databas
Account lockout duration
30 minu
Account lockout threshold
5 invalid
Reset account lockout counter after
30 minu

Figure 2.13

- ❍ A. The item is not defined in the analysis database and was not examined on the computer.
- ❍ B. The item is defined in the analysis database and on the computer, and it matches the currently configured setting.
- ❍ C. The item is defined in the analysis database but not on the computer.
- ❍ D. The item is defined in the analysis database and on the computer, but it does not match the current configured setting.

Answer A is correct. An icon with a question mark indicates that the policy item was not defined in the analysis database and was not examined on the computer during the analysis process. An item that is defined in the database and on the computer and that matches is represented by a green check mark, so answer B is incorrect. An item that is defined in the database but not on the computer is represented by an exclamation mark icon, so answer C is incorrect. An item that is defined in the database and on the computer but that does not match is represented by a red X icon, so answer D is incorrect.

Question 9

You are the network administrator for Gidgets Widgets, LLC. You are trying to explain to one of your assistant administrators, Hannah, how the **secedit.exe** command can be used to apply security templates to computers. Which of the following additional switches will you need to make sure she uses with the **secedit /configure** command? (Select all that apply.)

- ❑ A. **/analyze**
- ❑ B. **/db**
- ❑ C. **/log**
- ❑ D. **/cfg**

Answers B, C, and D are correct. The `/db` switch specifies the path and filename of the database to be used, the `/log` switch specifies the path and filename of the error log to be used during the process, and the `/cfg` switch specifies the path and filename of the security template to be loaded into the database. The `/analyze` switch is used only when performing an analysis operation, so answer A is incorrect.

Question 10

Chris is attempting to configure the Sales OU in her network with the securews.inf template. After she has imported the template and refreshed Group Policy for the domain, she notices that the security settings have not been applied to the computers used by the members of the Sales department. Given Figure 2.14, what is the most likely reason for the problem that Chris is experiencing?

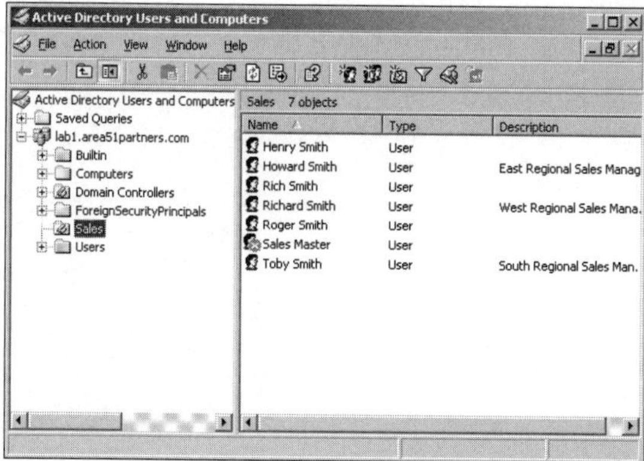

Figure 2.14

❍ A. Chris did not perform the Group Policy modifications locally from a domain controller.

❍ B. There are no computers in the Sales OU to apply the security template settings to.

❍ C. Chris did not restart the Sales department computers after applying the security template.

❍ D. The replication of Group Policy was not successful and needs to be initiated again.

Answer B is correct. The settings in a security template are applied to computers, not users. Because no computer object is found in the OU that Chris applied the security template to, nothing happened after she applied it. If Chris moved computers into this OU, the security settings would be applied to the computers after the next Group Policy refresh. Chris does not need to perform the Group Policy modifications locally on a DC to have them take effect, so answer A is incorrect. There are no computers in the Sales OU, so the Sales department computers will not receive the settings; thus, answers C and D are incorrect.

Need to Know More?

Stanek, William R. *Windows Server 2003 Administrator's Pocket Consultant*, Microsoft Press, Redmond, Washington: 2003.

"Security Configuration Manager Overview," http://www.microsoft.com/technet/prodtechnol/windowsserver2003/proddocs/server/se_scm_overview.asp.

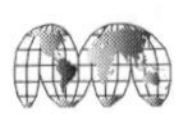

"Security Configuration Manager," http://www.microsoft.com/technet/prodtechnol/windowsserver2003/proddocs/entserver/SEconcepts_SCM.asp.

Planning, Implementing, and Maintaining a Network Infrastructure

Terms you'll need to understand:

- ✓ Active Directory integrated zone
- ✓ Conditional forwarding
- ✓ Domain name service (DNS)
- ✓ DNS forwarder
- ✓ DNS resolver
- ✓ DNS Security (DNSSEC)
- ✓ DNS slave server
- ✓ Fully qualified domain name (FQDN)
- ✓ Iterative query
- ✓ Leaf
- ✓ Recursive query
- ✓ Secure dynamic update
- ✓ Standard primary zone
- ✓ Standard secondary zone
- ✓ Stub zone
- ✓ Top-level domain (TLD)
- ✓ Tree
- ✓ Zone
- ✓ Zone transfer

Techniques you'll need to master:

- ✓ Plan and implement a DNS namespace, the correct DNS zone type, DNS forwarders, and DNS security
- ✓ Integrate with third-party DNS servers

Just a few years ago, TCP/IP was not the king when it came to network communications protocols. Windows NT 4.0 relied on the venerable NetBIOS Extended User Interface (NetBEUI) protocol by default, and NetWare servers could be counted on to understand only IPX/SPX. With the recent widespread adoption of the Internet by the masses, TCP/IP slowly started to creep into private networks of all sizes and purposes. Administrators and network designers began to see the power and flexibility that TCP/IP offered them, and Microsoft and Novell took note of the shift. It wasn't long before all operating systems provided support for TCP/IP, but it still was not the networking protocol of choice. With the introduction of Windows 2000, Microsoft made TCP/IP and the domain name system (DNS) integral parts of Windows Active Directory networks. But how did DNS come into the picture all of a sudden?

If you have ever connected to a Web site by name, you have used DNS. DNS is a service used on the Internet for resolving fully qualified domain names (FQDNs) to their actual Internet Protocol (IP) addresses. For example, suppose you are preparing to take the latest Windows Server 2003 certification exam. You've asked your coworkers what the best study guide available is, and they recommend that you check out Que Publishing's Web site to see what is available. Your obvious question is, "Where can I find Que Publishing's Web site?" Before DNS, the answer would be `165.193.123.44`. If you are like most people, you'll remember that number for less than 30 seconds and will probably never find Que Publishing's site (or get that study guide you were looking for).

DNS puts a user-friendly face on that obscure numeric address. With DNS, your friend can tell you to go to `www.quepublishing.com`, and the DNS infrastructure of the Internet will translate the name to the correct address, `165.193.123.44`. It's like a series of interconnected phone books. You put in a name, and it gives you the correct number. Fortunately for those of us with a limited ability to memorize strings of numbers, the Internet community recognized the benefits of a name-resolution system as a critical part of the infrastructure that would make up the original Internet architecture—and DNS was born.

The DNS Namespace

As we've discussed, you probably have already used DNS, whether you are familiar with the underlying mechanism or not. Domain names are easy to use and remember: The ease at which you can access a Web site using domain names (such as `www.microsoft.com` or `www.quepublishing.com`) is a built-in simplicity that comes at a price; the DNS namespace is complex. DNS names are created as part of a hierarchical database that functions much like the directories in a file system. Hierarchies are powerful database structures because they can store tremendous amounts of data while making it easy to search for specific bits of information. Before examining the specifics of the DNS namespace hierarchy, let's review some rules about hierarchies in general.

Microsoft's Active Directory Service is an excellent example of a hierarchical database. Of course, given that the hierarchy is created on top of the existing rules for a DNS namespace, the information on the DNS hierarchy directly relates to the construction of Active Directory.

Hierarchies

Before getting into the details of a hierarchy, we should introduce some terms:

- *Tree*—This is a type of data structure with each element attached to one or more elements directly beneath it. In the case of DNS, this structure is often called an inverted tree because it is generally drawn with the root at the top of the tree.
- *Top-level domain (TLD)*—TLD refers to the suffix attached to Internet domain names. There are a limited number of predefined suffixes, and each one represents a top-level domain. The more popular TLDs include `.COM`, `.EDU`, `.GOV`, `.MIL`, `.NET`, and `.ORG`.
- *Node*—A node is a point at which two or more lines in the tree intersect. In the case of DNS, a node can represent a TLD, a subdomain, or an actual network node (host).
- *Fully qualified domain name (FQDN)*—A domain name that includes all domains between the host and the root of DNS is an FQDN. For example, `www.microsoft.com` is an FQDN.
- *Leaf*—A leaf is an item at the very bottom of a hierarchical tree structure, and it does not contain any other objects.
- *Zone*—A DNS zone is a logical grouping of hostnames within DNS. For example, `quepublishing.com` is considered the forward lookup zone for Que Publishing. It is where the information about the Que Publishing hosts is contained within DNS.

In DNS, containers called domains hold the information. The hierarchy starts with a root container, called the *root domain*. The root domain doesn't have a name, so it is typically represented by a single period, as shown in

Figure 3.1. The root domain contains pointers to all TLDs, which are directly below the root. These are also sometimes called *first-level domains*. Lower-level domains are second-level, third-level, and so on. Every domain name has a suffix that indicates which TLD domain it belongs to. There are only a limited number of such domains as defined by RFC 1591. Some of the more common TLDs are discussed in the following list:

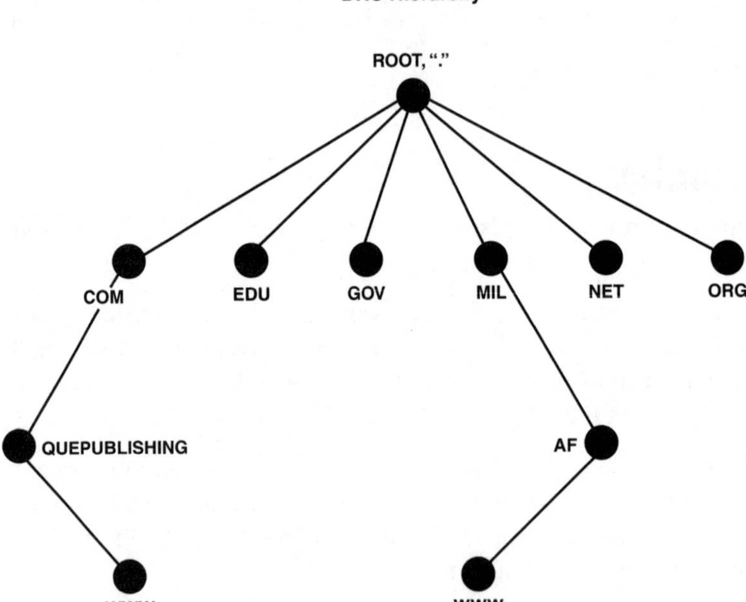

Figure 3.1 This portion of the DNS hierarchy shows the location of two domains in the DNS database in relation to the rest of the DNS database.

- *.COM*—Intended for commercial entities, but it has become the overwhelming favorite top-level domain (example of `.COM`: `area51partners.com`)
- *.EDU*—Intended for higher-education institutions, such as four-year colleges and universities (example of `.EDU`: `berkeley.edu`)
- *.GOV*—Intended for use by agencies of the U.S. Federal Government (example of `.GOV`: `whitehouse.gov`)
- *.MIL*—Intended for use by agencies of the U.S. military (example of `.MIL`: `af.mil`)
- *.NET*—Intended for use by network providers and organizations dedicated to the Internet, such as Internet service providers (example of `.NET`: `ibm.net`)

- .ORG—Intended for nonprofit or noncommercial establishments, such as professional groups, charities, and other such organizations (example of .ORG: npr.org)

Two-letter country code TLDs also exist for nearly all countries on the planet. Examples include **.US** for the United States, **.CA** for Canada, **.JP** for Japan, and **.UK** for the United Kingdom. New TLDs are constantly being added to meet the requirements for new domain names on the Internet. Recent additions include **.BIZ** and **.INFO**, among others.

Fully Qualified Domain Names (FQDNs)

As we have discussed, DNS is used to translate a hostname to an IP address. The FQDN name typically looks something like the following:

```
filesvr042.corporate.area51partners.com
```

This is known as the host's fully qualified domain name (FQDN) because it lists the host's precise location in the DNS hierarchy. The DNS name in the example represents the host FILESVR042 in the subdomain CORPORATE (this is frequently a department or division in a company), which is in the subdomain AREA51PARTNERS (this is frequently the name of the company or organization that has registered the domain), which is in the TLD .COM.

Make sure you have a good understanding of what an FQDN is and how it is represented.

Planning a DNS Namespace Design

Up to this point in our discussion about DNS, we have looked at only the historical and design aspects of DNS—and for good reason. Only by understanding how DNS was created and designed can you effectively plan and implement a DNS design in a Windows Server 2003 Active Directory domain. Because DNS permeates Windows Server 2003, you must deliberately and carefully plan out your DNS namespace *before* you ever perform the first installation of Windows Server 2003 on a computer.

The following list represents some questions you should ask yourself when planning your namespace needs:

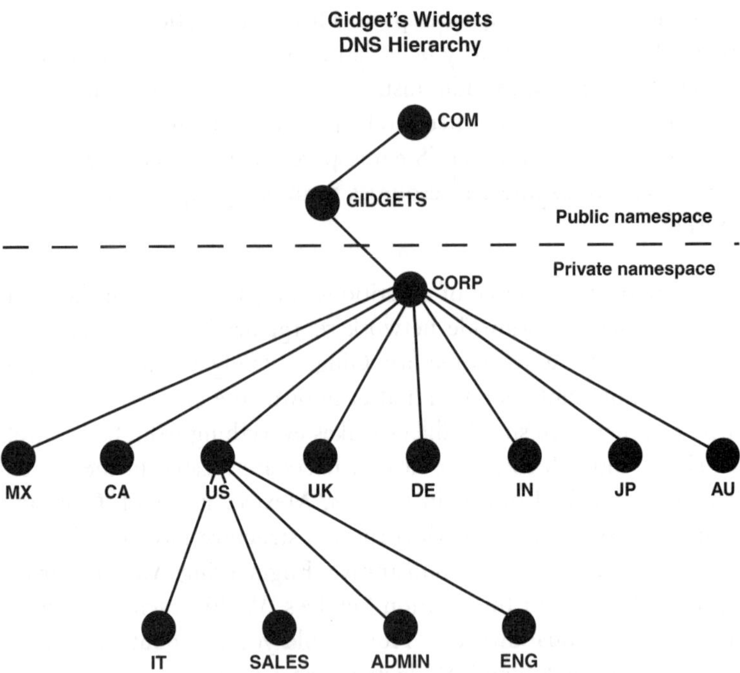

Figure 3.2 Gidget's network has been nicely organized by using countries as third-level domains and major departments as fourth-level domains.

Table 3.1 DNS Name Restrictions

Restriction	Standard DNS	DNS in Windows Server 2003 (and Windows 2000)
Characters	Supports RFC 1123, which permits A to Z, a to z, 0 to 9, and the hyphen (-).	Supports several different configurations: RFC 1123 standard, as well as support for RFCs 2181 and the character set specified in RFC 2044.
FQDN length	Permits 63 bytes per label and 255 bytes for an FQDN.	Permits 63 bytes per label and 255 bytes for an FQDN. Domain controllers are limited to 155 bytes for an FQDN.

After you've planned out your namespace, you're ready to get down to business and start working out the finer points of your DNS implementation. The next thing you need to plan for is the type of zones you will be using. But what exactly is a zone?

- `.ORG`—Intended for nonprofit or noncommercial establishments, such as professional groups, charities, and other such organizations (example of `.ORG`: `npr.org`)

Two-letter country code TLDs also exist for nearly all countries on the planet. Examples include **.US** for the United States, **.CA** for Canada, **.JP** for Japan, and **.UK** for the United Kingdom. New TLDs are constantly being added to meet the requirements for new domain names on the Internet. Recent additions include **.BIZ** and **.INFO**, among others.

Fully Qualified Domain Names (FQDNs)

As we have discussed, DNS is used to translate a hostname to an IP address. The FQDN name typically looks something like the following:

```
filesvr042.corporate.area51partners.com
```

This is known as the host's fully qualified domain name (FQDN) because it lists the host's precise location in the DNS hierarchy. The DNS name in the example represents the host `FILESVR042` in the subdomain `CORPORATE` (this is frequently a department or division in a company), which is in the subdomain `AREA51PARTNERS` (this is frequently the name of the company or organization that has registered the domain), which is in the TLD `.COM`.

Make sure you have a good understanding of what an FQDN is and how it is represented.

Planning a DNS Namespace Design

Up to this point in our discussion about DNS, we have looked at only the historical and design aspects of DNS—and for good reason. Only by understanding how DNS was created and designed can you effectively plan and implement a DNS design in a Windows Server 2003 Active Directory domain. Because DNS permeates Windows Server 2003, you must deliberately and carefully plan out your DNS namespace *before* you ever perform the first installation of Windows Server 2003 on a computer.

The following list represents some questions you should ask yourself when planning your namespace needs:

locations with a high number of clients, you can improve overall network performance.

➤ Standard secondary zone servers reduce the load on the primary servers by distributing name-resolution requests among more DNS servers.

If you are using standard zones, or a secondary zone within an Active Directory–integrated zone implementation, you must ensure that you configure your DNS servers to perform zone transfers only with those servers you trust.

At this point, you have a fair amount of information in hand to start planning your DNS zone requirements. Depending on what type of zones you implement, your zones will use either transfers or replication. Zone transfers occur in standard zones, whereas zone replication occurs in Active Directory–integrated zones.

Unlike WINS, which allows for a push-pull arrangement, zone transfers always originate with the secondary server polling the primary zone at the configured interval. This is accomplished by checking the zone version number on the primary server to see if it has changed in comparison to the version number on the secondary server. If the zone version number on the primary server has been incremented, a zone transfer is required and will be performed. If the secondary zone supports incremental zone transfers (which Windows Server 2003 does), the secondary zone pulls (from the primary zone) only the changes made to resource records for each incremental zone version—meaning that a resource record could potentially be updated one or more times in a single zone transfer. By using incremental zone transfers, network traffic is reduced and zone transfer speed is increased.

Windows Server 2003 supports two zone transfer types for standard zones: full zone transfers and incremental zone transfers. You might also see these abbreviated as AXFR and IXFR, respectively. A full zone transfer causes the entire zone data file to be transferred, which uses a lot of bandwidth and time.

Active Directory–integrated DNS zones replicate data among all domain controllers, allowing any domain controller to modify the zone file and replicate the changes to the rest of the domain controllers. This form of replication is known as multimaster replication because multiple DNS servers are allowed to update the zone data—domain controllers that are running the DNS service, in this case. Replication occurs on a per-property basis, meaning

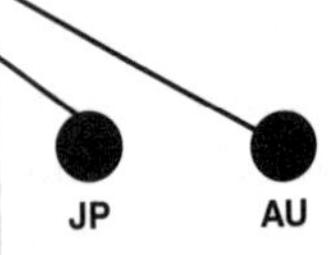

- `.ORG`—Intended for nonprofit or noncommercial establishments, such as professional groups, charities, and other such organizations (example of `.ORG`: `npr.org`)

Two-letter country code TLDs also exist for nearly all countries on the planet. Examples include **.US** for the United States, **.CA** for Canada, **.JP** for Japan, and **.UK** for the United Kingdom. New TLDs are constantly being added to meet the requirements for new domain names on the Internet. Recent additions include **.BIZ** and **.INFO**, among others.

Fully Qualified Domain Names (FQDNs)

As we have discussed, DNS is used to translate a hostname to an IP address. The FQDN name typically looks something like the following:

```
filesvr042.corporate.area51partners.com
```

This is known as the host's fully qualified domain name (FQDN) because it lists the host's precise location in the DNS hierarchy. The DNS name in the example represents the host `FILESVR042` in the subdomain `CORPORATE` (this is frequently a department or division in a company), which is in the subdomain `AREA51PARTNERS` (this is frequently the name of the company or organization that has registered the domain), which is in the TLD `.COM`.

Make sure you have a good understanding of what an FQDN is and how it is represented.

Planning a DNS Namespace Design

Up to this point in our discussion about DNS, we have looked at only the historical and design aspects of DNS—and for good reason. Only by understanding how DNS was created and designed can you effectively plan and implement a DNS design in a Windows Server 2003 Active Directory domain. Because DNS permeates Windows Server 2003, you must deliberately and carefully plan out your DNS namespace *before* you ever perform the first installation of Windows Server 2003 on a computer.

The following list represents some questions you should ask yourself when planning your namespace needs:

- *Is your DNS namespace to be used for internal purposes only?* If so, you can use characters that are not typically used in DNS names, such as those outside of the RFC 1123 standards. An example might be `bigcorp.local`.
- *Is your DNS namespace to be used on the Internet as well?* If you are currently using a corporate DNS namespace on the Internet, or think that you might at any point in the future, you should register your own domain name and conform to Internet naming standards.
- *Will you be implementing Active Directory?* The design and implementation of Active Directory on your network plays a critical role in determining how domains should be created and nested within each other. Chapter 7, "Planning and Implementing an Active Directory Infrastructure," examines the relationship between Active Directory and the domain structure in more detail.

You have the following three basic options to consider when planning the DNS namespace you will be using:

- *Use an Existing DNS Namespace*—This option uses the same namespace for both the internal (corporate network) and external (Internet) portions of your network. If your domain name is `bigcorp.com`, you would use this for both internal and external use. Although this method is the easiest and provides simple access to both internal and external resources, it poses additional administrative requirements because an administrator must ensure that the appropriate records are being stored on the internal and external DNS servers as a security precaution.
- *Use a Delegated DNS Namespace*—This option uses a delegated domain of the public namespace. If your domain name is `bigcorp.com`, you might consider using `corp.bigcorp.com` for the internal namespace. When using this option, the `corp.bigcorp.com` domain becomes the root of the Active Directory forest and domain structure. Internal clients should be allowed to resolve external namespace addresses; however, external clients should not. Using a delegated DNS namespace provides a namespace that is easy to understand and remember, and that fits in nicely with the existing registered domain name. All internal domain data is isolated in the domain or domain tree, thus requiring its own DNS server for the delegated internal domain. The downside to delegated namespaces is that this adds length to the total FQDN.
- *Use a Unique DNS Namespace*—This option uses a completely separate but related domain name for your internal namespace. As an example, if you are using `bigcorp.com` for your external namespace, you might use

bigcorp.net for your internal namespace. This configuration provides the advantage of improving security by isolating the two namespaces from each other. Additionally, the administrative burden is relatively low because zone transfers do not need to be performed between the two namespaces, and the existing DNS namespace remains unchanged. In addition, this prevents internal resources from being exposed directly to the Internet.

Consider the following example of a fictitious company that is in the planning stages of a major worldwide network reorganization and upgrade to Windows Server 2003 Active Directory. Gidget's Widgets, Inc., is a major manufacturer of household goods and already owns the gidgets.com domain name for its Internet Web site. Gidget's makes everything from bath towels to kitchen sinks. Gidget's corporate headquarters are located in the United States, with regional field offices in Canada, Mexico, England, Germany, India, Japan, and Australia. Gidget's corporate structure has the following major departments: Executive, Administrative, Engineering, Manufacturing, Facilities, Sales, Legal, and Information Services. Within each department are one or more individual divisions. How would you go about designing a DNS namespace for the Gidget's Widgets internal network?

You have several options; let's assume for the sake of argument that you are going to first create a delegated domain named corp to serve as the root of the internal network and also as the Active Directory root. Starting with the corp.gidgets.com domain, you could create fourth-level domains by country code. Within these, you could create fifth-level domains, as required, for each of the major departments. You might end up with a configuration that looks something like that shown in Figure 3.2.

If you were a network administrator in the United States working from a computer called GREENGUY42, your FQDN would be greenguy42.it.us.corp.gidgets.com. Of course, you could also design the DNS namespace using continents instead of countries, if desired. When creating DNS namespaces that are several levels deep like the example seen in Figure 3.2, you must keep in mind some general DNS restrictions as outlined in Table 3.1.

No matter what design you settle on, you must (in most cases) get it right the first time. Redesigning a DNS namespace is a difficult and time-consuming task after the fact, at best. In addition, failing to properly design the namespace for Active Directory compatibility can lead to functionality problems in the future.

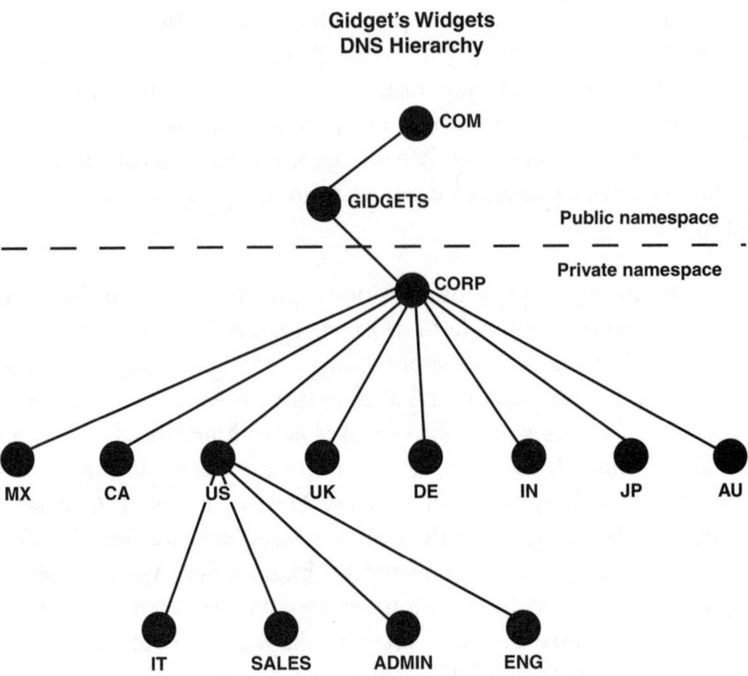

Figure 3.2 Gidget's network has been nicely organized by using countries as third-level domains and major departments as fourth-level domains.

Table 3.1 DNS Name Restrictions

Restriction	Standard DNS	DNS in Windows Server 2003 (and Windows 2000)
Characters	Supports RFC 1123, which permits A to Z, a to z, 0 to 9, and the hyphen (–).	Supports several different configurations: RFC 1123 standard, as well as support for RFCs 2181 and the character set specified in RFC 2044.
FQDN length	Permits 63 bytes per label and 255 bytes for an FQDN.	Permits 63 bytes per label and 255 bytes for an FQDN. Domain controllers are limited to 155 bytes for an FQDN.

After you've planned out your namespace, you're ready to get down to business and start working out the finer points of your DNS implementation. The next thing you need to plan for is the type of zones you will be using. But what exactly is a zone?

Planning DNS Zone Requirements

It is very easy to get lost in the maze of acronyms and buzzwords surrounding DNS, especially if you are having a conversation with someone who has been working with IP networking and DNS for awhile. You have a standard primary server for each zone, which might also be a domain, unless it's a reverse lookup zone; then you have zone transfers happening when you least expect it. To the uninitiated, this can sound alarmingly like some arcane networking ritual, paying homage to the DNS deities.

It's not nearly as bad as it sounds. But before we get any deeper into the Windows Server 2003 DNS infrastructure, we must discuss what exactly is meant when we refer to a DNS zone. First, although it is typically abbreviated in the world of DNS, a zone is actually a *zone of authority*, which means that it contains the complete information on some part of a domain namespace. In other words, it is a subset or root of that portion of a namespace. The nameserver is considered to have authority for that zone, and it can respond to any requests for name resolution from that zone. So, when you look at the DNS name `www.quepublishing.com`, `quepublishing.com` is a DNS zone within the `.com` hierarchy. The `www` denotes the DNS record of a host contained within the `quepublishing.com` zone.

This conceptual representation of a zone also has a physical counterpart—all the information relating to a particular zone is stored in a physical file known as the *zone database file*, or more commonly the *zone file*, that can be found at %systemroot%\system32\dns for zones that are not stored in Active Directory. The types of zones supported by Windows Server 2003 are as follows:

- *Standard primary*—A standard primary zone holds a master copy of a zone and can replicate it to all configured secondary zones in standard text format. Any changes that must be made to the zone are made on the copy stored on the primary.
- *Standard secondary*—A standard secondary zone holds a read-only copy of the zone information in standard text format. Secondary zones are created to increase performance and resilience of the DNS configuration. Information is transferred from the primary zone to the secondary zones.
- *Active Directory*–integrated—Active Directory–integrated zones are available only on Windows 2000 Server and Windows Server 2003 DNS servers in an Active Directory domain. The zone information is contained within the Active Directory database and is replicated using Active Directory replication. Active Directory–integrated zones provide

an increased level of replication flexibility as well as security. Active Directory–integrated zones also operate in a multimaster arrangement because they are hosted within Active Directory itself—this allows any DNS server (domain controller) hosting the Active Directory–integrated zone to update the zone data.

- *Stub*—Microsoft has introduced support for stub zones for the first time in Windows Server 2003. A stub zone contains only those resource records that are necessary to identify the authoritative DNS servers for that zone. Those resource records include Name Server (NS), Start of Authority (SOA), and possibly glue host (A) records. (Glue host records provide A record pointers to ensure that the master zone has the correct nameserver information for the stub zone.)

You might be asking, "What's the difference between a zone and a domain?" Although the two terms can seem as if they are used interchangeably, there is a difference. A DNS domain is a segment of the DNS namespace. A zone, on the other hand, can contain multiple contiguous domains.

For example, **quepublishing.com** is a DNS domain. It contains all the information for that specific portion of the DNS namespace. **Sales.quepublishing.com** is another example of a domain, which is contiguous with the **quepublishing.com** domain—in other words, the two domains "touch." So, if you were to create a DNS forward zone on your DNS server, it could contain records for both domains. Zones allow for the logical grouping and management of domains and resource records on your DNS servers.

Although it might seem that determining the zone type is not an important part of planning your DNS solution, nothing could be further from the truth. The type of DNS zone that you implement ultimately determines the placement of the DNS servers in your network. In addition, the type of DNS zone that you create will, in part, impact the construction of the network and the interoperability with other DNS servers, such as Unix BIND servers.

When using a standard primary/standard secondary DNS zone implementation, the following points are of concern:

- A single DNS server is the master, holding the only writable copy of the DNS zone file.
- Zone transfers can be conducted using either incremental or full zone transfer.
- It is fully compatible with Berkeley Internet Name Domain (BIND) DNS servers by using the standard DNS methods in place.

When using an Active Directory–integrated DNS zone implementation, the following points are of concern:

- A multimaster arrangement allows any DNS server to make updates to the zone file.
- Zone data is replicated with Active Directory data.
- Increased security is provided on the zone file.
- Redundancy is provided for DNS dynamic update.
- Replication scope is adjustable by the administrator. Additionally, the zone file can be replicated to a standard secondary DNS server—a common practice for DNS servers placed on screened subnets.
- It appears to be a standard primary zone to a BIND DNS server, allowing the use of BIND DNS as a standard secondary zone server.

Table 3.2 provides a comparison of Active Directory–integrated zones and standard DNS zones.

Table 3.2 DNS Zone Type Comparison

DNS Feature	Standard DNS Zones	Active Directory–Integrated Zones
Complies with IETF specifications	Yes	Yes
Uses Active Directory for replication	No	Yes
Increases availability by providing a multimaster arrangement	No	Yes
Allows for zone updates after the failure of a single DNS server	No	Yes
Supports incremental zone transfers	Yes	Yes

Regardless of whether you create standard or Active Directory–integrated DNS zones, you should be aware of the benefits of also using standard secondary zones. The following list presents some of the benefits you can realize by placing secondary zones on your network:

- The addition of standard secondary zone servers increases the redundancy of the zone by proving name resolution even if the primary zone server is unresponsive.
- When remote locations are connected to the core network over WAN links, secondary zone servers can greatly reduce costs and network traffic. By placing standard secondary zones in these remote locations or in

locations with a high number of clients, you can improve overall network performance.

- Standard secondary zone servers reduce the load on the primary servers by distributing name-resolution requests among more DNS servers.

If you are using standard zones, or a secondary zone within an Active Directory–integrated zone implementation, you must ensure that you configure your DNS servers to perform zone transfers only with those servers you trust.

At this point, you have a fair amount of information in hand to start planning your DNS zone requirements. Depending on what type of zones you implement, your zones will use either transfers or replication. Zone transfers occur in standard zones, whereas zone replication occurs in Active Directory–integrated zones.

Unlike WINS, which allows for a push-pull arrangement, zone transfers always originate with the secondary server polling the primary zone at the configured interval. This is accomplished by checking the zone version number on the primary server to see if it has changed in comparison to the version number on the secondary server. If the zone version number on the primary server has been incremented, a zone transfer is required and will be performed. If the secondary zone supports incremental zone transfers (which Windows Server 2003 does), the secondary zone pulls (from the primary zone) only the changes made to resource records for each incremental zone version—meaning that a resource record could potentially be updated one or more times in a single zone transfer. By using incremental zone transfers, network traffic is reduced and zone transfer speed is increased.

Windows Server 2003 supports two zone transfer types for standard zones: full zone transfers and incremental zone transfers. You might also see these abbreviated as AXFR and IXFR, respectively. A full zone transfer causes the entire zone data file to be transferred, which uses a lot of bandwidth and time.

Active Directory–integrated DNS zones replicate data among all domain controllers, allowing any domain controller to modify the zone file and replicate the changes to the rest of the domain controllers. This form of replication is known as multimaster replication because multiple DNS servers are allowed to update the zone data—domain controllers that are running the DNS service, in this case. Replication occurs on a per-property basis, meaning that only the relevant changes will be replicated. Active Directory–integrated zones replicate only the final result of multiple changes to a resource record, unlike standard zones, which transfer the changes to a resource record that occurred in each zone version number.

With your namespace and zone type plans complete, you must next evaluate the need for forwarder and slave DNS servers. That is the topic of the next section.

Planning DNS Forwarding Requirements

Before a discussion of forwarding and slave DNS servers can be undertaken, some general knowledge of how DNS clients query a DNS server to resolve IP addresses is of some use.

In a TCP/IP network, a *DNS resolver* is any system that has been configured with one or more DNS server IP addresses and that performs queries against these DNS servers. The DNS resolver is part of the DNS Client service, which is automatically installed when Windows is installed. The resolver can request one of two types of queries from a DNS server: recursive or iterative.

A *recursive query* is a DNS query that is sent to a DNS server from a DNS resolver asking the DNS server to provide a complete answer to the query, or an error stating that it cannot provide the information. If the DNS server is also configured as a forwarder, the query can be forwarded directly to another DNS server. If the query is for a name outside of the local DNS server's zone of authority, it performs an iterative query against a root DNS server, which then responds with the IP address of the DNS server whose zone of authority includes the desired IP top-level domain. Additional iterative queries are then performed until the name is resolved into its IP address or an error is produced.

An *iterative query* is a DNS query that is sent by a DNS server to another DNS server in an effort to perform name resolution. Consider the example of a workstation (DNS resolver) in the `bigcorp.com` domain that wants to communicate with a Web server located in the `smallcorp.com domain`. Figure 3.3 illustrates the process by which the IP address for `www.smallcorp.com` will be resolved to its IP address. Recall that `www` is a typical alias for a Web server or bank of clustered Web servers.

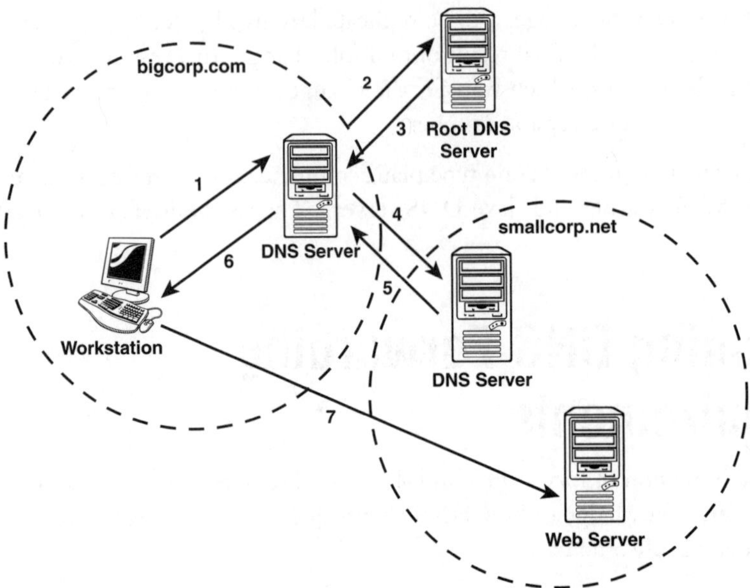

Figure 3.3 The initial recursive query results in several iterative queries in an effort to resolve the name to an IP address.

1. The DNS resolver (the local workstation) sends a recursive query to its local DNS server requesting the IP address of `www.smallcorp.com`.
2. The local DNS server, which is also configured as a forwarder, does not have information about `www.smallcorp.net` in its zone of authority and thus issues an iterative query to a root DNS server for the IP address of `www.smallcorp.com`.
3. The root DNS server does not have the requested information about the IP address of `www.smallcorp.com`, but it does know the IP address of a nameserver for the `smallcorp.com` zone. It provides this information back to the requesting DNS server.
4. The local DNS server next issues an iterative query to the DNS server for the `smallcorp.net` zone asking it for the IP address of `www.smallcorp.com`.
5. The `smallcorp.net` DNS server is authoritative for that zone, so it provides the requested IP address back to the local DNS server for `www.smallcorp.com`.
6. The local DNS server next passes the IP address of `www.smallcorp.com` back to the requesting workstation.
7. The client can now make a connection to `www.smallcorp.com`.

So, with the discussion of how DNS queries are performed and resolved under your belt, you can begin to plan for configuration and usage of DNS forwarders on the network.

A *DNS forwarder* is a DNS server that accepts forwarded recursive lookups from another DNS server and then resolves the request for that DNS server. This can be useful if you do not have local copies of your internal DNS zone and want to have your local DNS server forward DNS queries to a central DNS server that is authoritative for your internal DNS zone. Caching-only servers make good DNS forwarders. If the DNS forwarder does not receive a valid resolution from the server that it forwards the request to, it attempts to resolve the client request itself.

A *DNS slave server* is a DNS forwarder server that will not try to resolve a resolution request if it doesn't receive a valid response to its forwarded DNS request. You will typically see this type of DNS server implemented in conjunction with a secure Internet connection.

A new feature in Windows Server 2003, *conditional forwarding*, enables administrators to direct DNS requests to other DNS servers based on domain. Previous versions of Microsoft DNS supported only one forwarder, so if forwarding were enabled, all requests would be sent to a single server. This is used frequently when you want requests made to the internal network to be forwarded to a master DNS server that stores internal DNS zones, but have resolution requests that are made to Internet domains be sent to the Internet using the standard resolution process.

Because enabling conditional forwarding is a new capability with Windows Server 2003's DNS service, you need to be familiar with how this works and when you might need to use it.

Figure 3.4 shows the Forwarders tab of the DNS server Properties dialog box.

Let's say that you have a single internal domain called `lab1.area51partners.com`. You need to forward any queries to that domain directly to the primary DNS server for the `lab1.area51partners.com` domain. The Windows Server 2003 DNS service enables you to configure forwarding for a single domain, a group of domains, or all domains. Earlier versions of the Windows DNS service supported only forwarding of all domains—it was an all-or-nothing proposition. The functionality of being able to split forwarding among multiple servers while still resolving some domains locally is known as *conditional forwarding*. Figure 3.5 shows the IP address that has been configured for conditional forwarding to the internal domain.

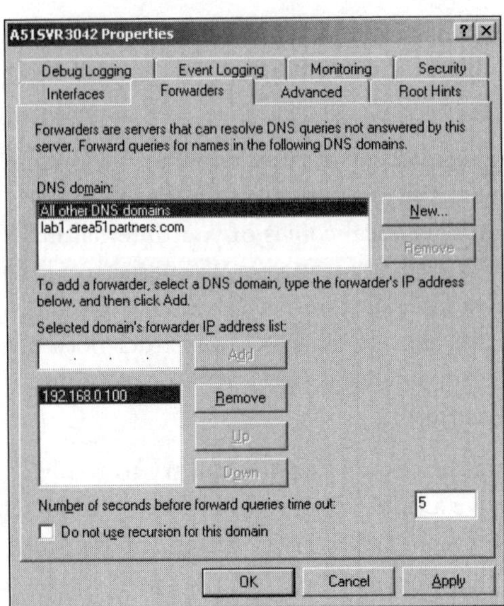

Figure 3.4 The Forwarders tab is used configure where this server will send DNS requests if another DNS server will be supplying some or all of the DNS resolution for that server.

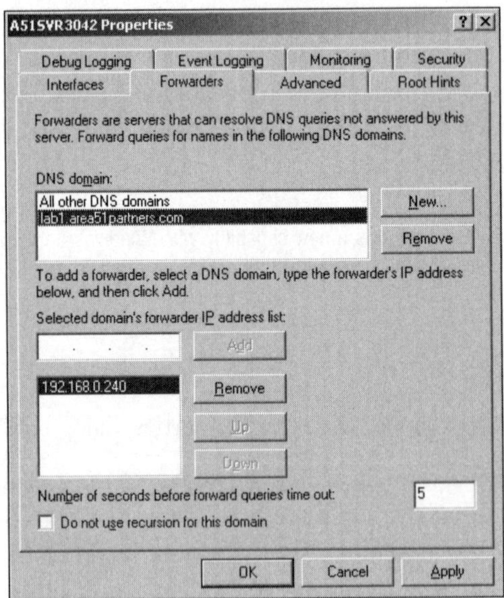

Figure 3.5 Conditional forwarding enables you to configure specific DNS servers by domain.

If you disable recursion in the DNS server properties, you will not be able to use a forwarder. Forwarding DNS requests requires that the DNS server be capable of making recursive queries.

A common implementation of DNS forwarders in a Windows Server 2003 network has one specific DNS server being allowed to make queries to DNS servers outside of the firewall. This allows the firewall to be configured to allow DNS traffic only from this specific DNS server to leave the protected network, and allows only valid replies back to the DNS server to enter the protected network. Through this approach, all other DNS traffic—both inbound and outbound—can be dropped at the firewall, adding to the overall security of the network and the DNS service. Figure 3.6 illustrates this concept.

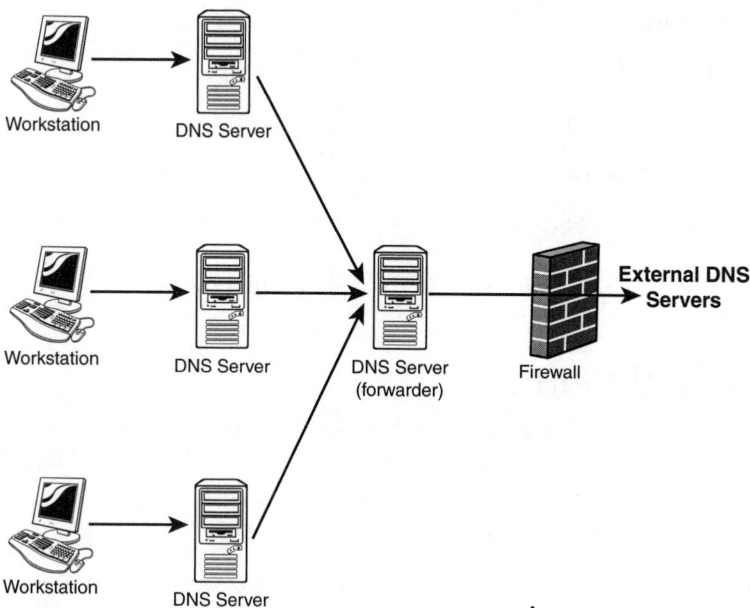

Figure 3.6 DNS forwarders can be implemented to control DNS traffic into and out of the protected network.

Forwarders can be used to ensure that DNS queries have the best possible chance of being answered with the requested information. As you have seen, they also can be implemented to increase security of the DNS service on your network. With security in mind, we examine other ways you can configure additional security on your DNS servers.

Configuring DNS Security

With the majority of your planning already accomplished, you now need to plan the security of the DNS service. Providing security for DNS is not a task that you can accomplish by performing one action or by configuring one item. DNS is a dynamic service that, by its very nature, must be capable of interacting with network clients on several different levels. Not only must clients be capable of retrieving information from a DNS server through queries, but authorized clients must also be capable of having their resource records entered or updated when they acquire a DHCP lease on the network. Thus, DNS security is a multifaceted area that takes some preplanning to implement properly.

Configuring DNS security can be broken into the following five general areas of concern:

- Dynamic updates
- Active Directory DNS permissions
- Zone transfer security
- DNS server properties
- DNS Security (DNSSEC)

Each of these concerns is addressed in the sections that follow.

Dynamic Updates

Dynamic updates occur when a DHCP server or a DNS client computer automatically updates the applicable DNS resource records when a DHCP leave is granted (or expires). Three types of dynamic updates exist in Windows Server 2003, each with its own security specifics.

Secure dynamic updates are available when Active Directory–integrated zones are in use. Using secure dynamic update, the DNS zone information is stored in Active Directory and thus is protected using Active Directory security features. When a zone has been created as or converted to an Active Directory integrated zone, Access Control List (ACL) entries can be used to specify which users, computers, and groups can make changes to a zone or a specific record.

If you are planning to use secure dynamic updates on your network and also plan to have multiple DHCP servers, you must ensure that all of your DHCP servers have been placed in the DnsUpdateProxyGroup group. Adding all of your DHCP servers to this group allows them to perform proxy updates for all of your network's DHCP clients.

The addition of the DHCP servers to the DnsUpdateProxyGroup is required to prevent records from being inaccessible to one DHCP server because a different DHCP server previously updated it, thus taking ownership of it. This process works the same as any other shared network resource, such as documents on a network file share.

Dynamic updates from DHCP can be configured to allow only specific DHCP servers to update DNS zone entries. The configuration takes place on the DHCP server by configuring it with the DNS zone that is responsible for automatically updating. It takes place on the DNS server by configuring it with the DHCP servers that are to be the only authorized computers to update the DNS entries. Dynamic updates from DHCP are best implemented when the DHCP client computers are not Windows 2000 or better—such as when the client computers are Windows 98 computers. Dynamic updates from DHCP can also be implemented if you determine that managing individual NTFS permissions for users, computers, and groups to update their respective DNS entries becomes an administrative burden. Finally, dynamic updates from DHCP can overcome the security risks that could potentially come from allowing unauthorized computers to impersonate authorized computers and populate the DNS zone file with bad information.

You should not configure the DHCP service on a computer that is also a domain controller to perform dynamic DNS updates. If a DHCP server exists on a domain controller, the DHCP server has full control over all DNS objects stored in Active Directory because the account it is running under (the domain controller computer account) has this privilege. This creates a security risk that should be avoided. You should not install the DHCP server service that is configured to perform dynamic DNS updates on a domain controller; instead, you should install it on a member server if you're performing dynamic DNS updates.

As an alternative, you can use a new feature in Windows Server 2003 DHCP, which allows for the creation of a dedicated domain user account that all DHCP servers will use when performing dynamic DNS updates.

DNS client dynamic updates are performed by clients running Windows 2000 or better. When these client computers start, their DNS client service automatically connects to the DNS server and registers the DNS client with the DNS server. Allowing DNS clients to perform dynamic updates is the least preferred method of dynamic updating and is hampered by manageability issues and potential security problems. You should typically plan to have DNS clients perform dynamic updates only when the computer has a static IP address and the assignment of the required permissions is manageable.

By default, dynamic updates are not enabled for standard zones, thus providing increased security by preventing an attacker from updating DNS zone information with bad entries. This is the most secure setting, but it offers the least functionality because all dynamic updates are disabled in this configuration. Dynamic updates are required for Active Directory–integrated zones and should be configured to allow secure dynamic updates or dynamic updates from DHCP instead of DNS client dynamic updates wherever possible, to increase security of the DNS zone data.

Active Directory DNS Permissions

If the zone is integrated with Active Directory, the Discretionary Access Control List (DACL) for the zone can be used to configure the permissions for the users and groups that may change or control the data in the DNS zone. Table 3.3 lists the default group and user permissions for Active Directory–integrated DNS zones.

Table 3.3 Default Group and User Permissions on Active Directory–Integrated DNS Zones

Group or User	Permissions
Administrators	Allow: Read, Write, Create All Child Objects, Special Permissions
Authenticated Users	Allow: Create All Child Objects
Creator Owner	Allow: Special Permissions
DnsAdmins	Allow: Full Control, Read, Write, Create All Child Objects, Delete Child Objects, Special Permissions
Domain Admins	Allow: Full Control, Read, Write, Create All Child Objects, Delete Child Objects
Enterprise Admins	Allow: Full Control, Read, Write, Create All Child Objects, Delete Child Objects
Enterprise Domain Controllers	Allow: Full Control, Read, Write, Create All Child Objects, Delete Child Objects, Special Permissions
Everyone	Allow: Read, Special Permissions
Pre–Windows 2000 Compatible Access	Allow: Special Permissions
System	Allow: Full Control, Read, Write, Create All Child Objects, Delete Child Objects

These default values can be modified to suit your particular needs.

Zone Transfer Security

You can use several methods to increase the security of zone transfers—and thus increase the security of your DNS servers overall. If attackers cannot capture your zone data from a zone transfer—once a very common method of gathering information about a domain (called *footprinting*)—they will not be able to easily determine the makeup of your network. In addition, this prevents the injection of unauthorized data into the zone files through zone transfer from an unauthorized DNS server.

By default, Windows Server 2003 DNS performs zone transfers only with the DNS servers that are listed in a zone's Name Server (NS) resource records. Even though this is a fairly secure configuration, you should consider changing this setting to allow zone transfers to be carried out only with specific IP addresses that you have explicitly configured. Figure 3.7 shows how you might make this configuration for a DNS server. Although you are still subject to IP address spoofing with this option configured, you have taken one more step toward a more secure DNS implementation. The task of identifying and defeating spoofed IP addresses lies at your perimeter security devices: firewalls, screening routers, and proxy servers.

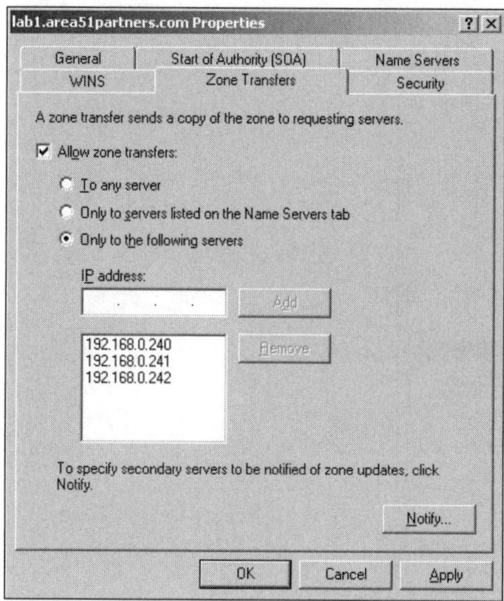

Figure 3.7 You can configure which DNS servers participate in zone transfers.

If you must perform zone transfers across an untrusted network, you should consider implementing and using a VPN tunnel between the two DNS servers. Encrypted zone information traveling inside the tunnel is safe from prying eyes, thus providing an uncompromised zone transfer. When using a VPN tunnel for zone transfer data, you should use the strongest possible level of encryption and authentication supported by both sides of the tunnel.

Your last option to secure zone data is to use only Active Directory–integrated zones. Because the DNS zone data is stored in Active Directory, it is inherently more secure. When Active Directory–integrated zones are in use, only Active Directory–integrated DNS servers participate in zone replication. In addition, all DNS servers hosting Active Directory–integrated zones must be registered with Active Directory. All replication traffic between Active Directory–integrated DNS servers is also encrypted, further adding to the level of security provided.

DNS Server Properties

By default, Windows Server 2003 DNS is configured to prevent unrequested resource records from being added to the DNS zone data, thus increasing zone security. From the Advanced tab of the DNS server Properties dialog box (see Figure 3.8), you can see the Secure Cache Against Pollution option, which is checked by default.

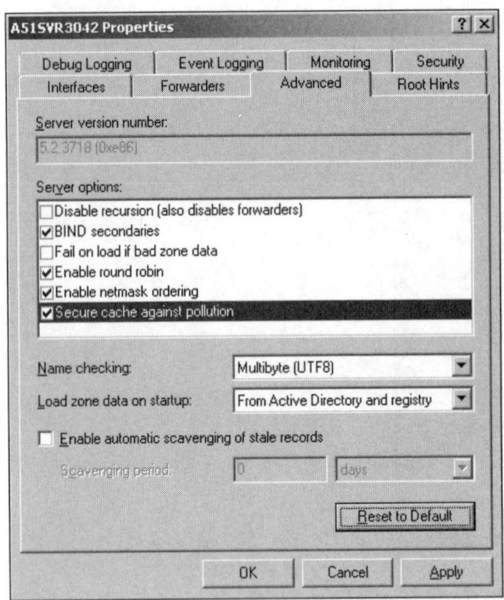

Figure 3.8 The Secure cache against pollution option prevents unrequested resource records from being added to the zone data.

By default, Windows Server 2003 DNS servers use a secure response option that eliminates the addition of unrelated resource records that are included in a referral answer to the cache. The server typically caches any names in referral answers, thus expediting the speed of resolving subsequent DNS queries. However, when this feature is in use, the server can determine whether the referred name is polluting or insecure and discard it. The server thus determines whether to cache the name offered in the referral depending on whether it is part of the exact DNS domain tree for which the original name query was made. As an example, a query made for `sales.bigcorp.com` with a referral answer of `smallcorp.net` would not get cached.

DNS Security (DNSSEC)

RFC 2535 provides for DNS Security, a public key infrastructure (PKI)–based system in which authentication and data integrity can be provided to DNS resolvers. Digital signatures are used and encrypted with private keys. These digital signatures can then be authenticated by DNSSEC-aware resolvers by using the corresponding public key. The required digital signature and public keys are added to the DNS zone in the form of resource records.

The public key is stored in the KEY Resource Record (RR), and the digital signature is stored in the SIG RR. The KEY RR must be supplied to the DNS resolver before it can successfully authenticate the SIG RR. DNSSEC also introduces one additional RR, the NXT RR, which is used to cryptographically assure the resolver that a particular RR does not exist in the zone.

DNSSEC is only partially supported in Windows Server 2003 DNS, providing basic support as specified in RFC 2535. A Windows Server 2003 DNS server could, therefore, operate as a secondary to a BIND server that fully supports DNSSEC. The support is partial because DNS in Windows Server 2003 does not provide any means to sign or verify the digital signatures. In addition, the Windows Server 2003 DNS resolver does not validate any of the DNSSEC data that is returned as a result of queries.

Integrating with Third-Party DNS Solutions

It's a fact of life that many organizations already have existing DNS solutions in place, such as Unix BIND. In some cases, these existing BIND servers might not meet the DNS requirements of Active Directory. Table 3.4 outlines the features of some of the more common versions of BIND in use.

Table 3.4 Features of Various BIND Versions

BIND Version	Features
4.9.4	Support for fast zone transfers
4.9.6	Support for SRV resource records
8.1.2	Support for dynamic DNS (DDNS)
8.2.1	Support for incremental zone transfers (IXFR) between DNS Servers
8.2.2	Full support for all Active Directory features

If you are faced with a situation in which you are dealing with other DNS systems, you have two basic choices of implementation:

- Upgrade existing DNS systems to meet the DNS requirements of Active Directory. For BIND, version 8.1.2 and later will be sufficient.
- Migrate existing DNS zones to Windows Server 2003 DNS.

Although it is recommended that you use only Windows Server 2003 DNS servers to ensure full support for Active Directory, you can use any DNS system that meets the following specifications:

- Support for SRV (Service) resource records
- Dynamic updates per RFC 2136

Although support for dynamic updates is highly recommended, it is not mandatory. Support for SRV resource records is mandatory, however, because they are required to provide DNS support to Active Directory.

If you have Unix BIND servers in you DNS infrastructure, you should consider placing them as secondaries instead of primaries. By default, Windows Server 2003 DNS servers use a fast zone transfer format whereby compression is used and multiple records can be sent in a single TCP message. BIND versions 4.9.4 and later support fast zone transfers. If you are using an earlier version of BIND or another third-party DNS system that does not support fast zone transfers, you must disable fast zone transfers. When you select the BIND Secondaries option (see Figure 3.9), fast zone transfers are disabled for that server.

In the TCP/IP network of today's connected world, DNS is no longer a nicety; it's a requirement. Originally created to replace the antiquated and difficult-to-maintain HOSTS.TXT file, the domain name system (DNS) has quickly seen its popularity rise as TCP/IP has become the king of all networking protocols. Microsoft had led the charge to make TCP/IP and DNS the defacto standards for all networks, small and large.

DNS is so critical to a Windows Server 2003 network that it is important that you prepare adequately before implementing your DNS solution. Only through proper planning can you be reasonably well assured of not having any problems down the road. The first decision you must make is what your DNS namespace will look like. You need to choose between an existing, a delegated, or unique namespace.

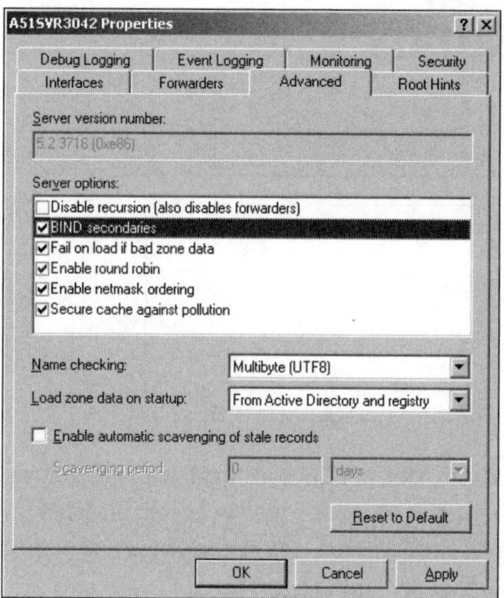

Figure 3.9 The BIND Secondaries option prevents fast zone transfers from occurring.

After choosing your namespace, you can determine what type of zones you will require, as well as how you will configure forwarding to occur. Of course, you also will want to look into securing your DNS infrastructure from attack and compromise. By choosing an Active Directory–integrated zone, you can ease administrative burden and increase DNS security.

Finally, if you have other DNS systems in use on your network, you need to decide on the roles that each DNS server will play in your Windows 2003 network. Will you upgrade these servers to a newer version that is compatible with and that supports the DNS requirements of Windows Server 2003? If not, you should consider migrating their DNS zones to your Windows Server 2003 DNS servers, and then retiring these legacy DNS servers or making them secondaries for improved redundancy.

Exam Prep Questions

Question 1

What type of organizational structure is the domain name system?

- ❍ A. Flat
- ❍ B. Circular
- ❍ C. Hierarchical
- ❍ D. Round-robin

Answer C is correct. The DNS namespace is a hierarchical one. At the top of the hierarchy is the root (.). Under the root are top-level domains, such as `.com` and `.net`. Under these top-level domains are the second-level domains, such as `microsoft` and `quepublishing`, that are then represented as `microsoft.com` and `quepublishing.com`, respectively. Answers A, B, and D are all incorrect because they don't represent the type of organizational structure used by DNS.

Question 2

What would be the FQDN of a workstation named **WKS042** located in the **Sales** subdomain of the **West** region domain of the **bigcorp.net** domain?

- ❍ A. **wks042.bigcorp.net**
- ❍ B. **wks042.west.bigcorp.net**
- ❍ C. **wks042.sales.bigcorp.net**
- ❍ D. **wks042.sales.west.bigcorp.net**

Answer D is correct. The FQDN (fully qualified domain name) would be `wks042.sales.west.bigcorp.net`. Answer A is missing the sales and west subdomains and is thus incorrect. Answer B is missing the sales subdomain and is thus incorrect. Answer C is missing the west subdomain and is thus incorrect.

Question 3

In the fully qualified domain name **wks042.sales.west.bigcorp.net**, what is the TLD?

❍ A. **wks042**

❍ B. **bigcorp.net**

❍ C. **.net**

❍ D. **west.bigcorp.net**

Answer C is correct. The TLD (top-level domain) in the FQDN `wks042.sales.west.bigcorp.net` is `.NET`. Other common TLDs include `.COM`, `.EDU`, `.GOV`, and `.MIL`. In addition, there are many country-specific TLDs, such as `.US`, `.CA`, `.MX`, `.UK`, `.DE`, `.IN`, and `.JP`. The `wks042` portion of the FQDN represents the hostname, so answer A is incorrect. The `bigcorp.net` portion of the FQDN represents the second-level and top-level domains, so answer B is incorrect. The `west.bigcorp.net` portion of the FQDN represents the third-level, second-level, and top-level domains, so answer D is incorrect.

Question 4

You are currently planning the DNS namespace for a new Windows Server 2003 deployment. The namespace will be used only for the internal network. There will be a separate public network located in a DMZ with a different DNS namespace. Which of the following DNS namespaces would be acceptable on the internal network, but not on the public network? (Choose all that apply.)

❑ A. **bigcorp.com**

❑ B. **bigcorp.corp**

❑ C. **bigcorp.local**

❑ D. **corp.bigcorp.com**

Answers B and C are correct. The `bigcorp.corp` and `bigcorp.local` namespaces are not allowable public DNS namespaces, per RFC 1123. However, they are perfectly acceptable for an internal namespace. Answers A and D represent valid external (public) namespaces and could thus be used internally or externally. Only answers C and D represent namespaces that are valid only on an internal network.

Question 5

You are a network consultant who has been hired by Carmen's Clown College, Inc. You have been given the task of designing a delegated DNS namespace for Carmen's new Windows Server 2003 network. Carmen's already owns the **clowncollege.com** domain, and its ISP is hosting its Web site. Which of the following options represents a valid delegated DNS namespace?

- ❍ A. **clowncollege.net**
- ❍ B. **corp.clowncollege.com**
- ❍ C. **clowncollege.corp.com**
- ❍ D. **clowncollege.com.corp**

Answer B is correct. The `corp.clowncollege.com` namespace represents a delegated DNS namespace. `corp.clowncollege.com` would thus become the root of the Active Directory forest and domain structure. Internal network clients should be allowed to resolve both internal and external domain names; however, external (Internet) clients should not be allowed to resolve internal hostnames. The namespace `clowncollege.net` represents a unique namespace, so answer A is incorrect. The namespaces `clowncollege.corp.com` and `clowncollege.com.corp` are not delegated namespaces of the `clowncollege.com` namespace, so answers C and D are incorrect.

Question 6

You are interviewing Chris, a candidate for an assistant administrator position in your company. When you ask her what a standard secondary zone is, what answer should she tell you?

- ❍ A. A zone that holds a writable copy of the zone data and that can transfer it to all configured servers
- ❍ B. A zone that holds a read-only copy of the zone data
- ❍ C. A zone that has its zone data held within Active Directory
- ❍ D. A zone that contains only those resource records necessary to identify the authoritative DNS servers for a zone

Answer B is correct. A standard secondary zone holds a read-only copy of the zone information in standard text format. Secondary zones are created to increase performance and resilience of the DNS configuration. Information is transferred from the primary zone to the secondary zones. A master zone is one that holds the only writable copy of the zone data, so answer A is incorrect. An Active Directory-integrated zone operates in a multimaster mode, whereby all name servers can make changes to the zone data; thus, answer C is incorrect. A stub zone contains only those resource records necessary to identify the authoritative DNS servers for a zone, so answer D is incorrect.

Question 7

A client computer that makes a DNS query to a DNS server for name resolution of a remote host is referred to as what?

❍ A. A recursive query

❍ B. An iterative query

❍ C. A DNS resolver

❍ D. A DNS forwarder

Answer C is correct. A DNS resolver is any system that has been configured with the IP addresses of one or more DNS servers and that performs name-resolution queries against these servers. Recursive and iterative represent the type of name-resolution queries that are performed. A recursive query is a DNS query that is sent to a DNS server from a DNS resolver asking the DNS server to provide a complete answer to the query, or an error stating that it cannot provide the information; thus, answer A is incorrect. An iterative query is a DNS query that is sent by a DNS server to another DNS server in an effort to perform name resolution; thus, answer B is incorrect. A DNS forwarder is a DNS server that has received a forwarded name-resolution request from another DNS server.

Question 8

You are a senior consultant for Legacy Systems, Inc., a leading consultancy that helps organizations integrate their existing networks with newer technologies, such as Windows Server 2003. You are currently working on getting the existing BIND DNS implementation working with the newer Windows Server 2003 DNS service. Eventually, you will be able to migrate the existing BIND DNS zones to Windows Server 2003, but the customer wants this to occur over a six-month period, to prepare for any troubles. There are several different BIND servers, all of different versions. You are not sure what the version is on each of them. What setting can you change in the Windows Server 2003 DNS configuration to ensure that zone transfers succeed between the Windows Server 2003 DNS servers and the BIND servers?

❍ A. BIND secondaries

❍ B. Enable round-robin

❍ C. Enable netmask ordering

❍ D. Secure cache against pollution

Answer A is correct. By selecting the BIND Secondaries option, you will disable fast zone transfers and ensure that zone transfers are compatible and can succeed with older DNS implementations that do not support fast zone transfers. BIND versions 4.9.4 and later do support fast zone transfers. Selecting the Enable Round Robin option configures the DNS server to use a round-robin rotation to rotate and reorder resource records if multiple records exist; thus, answer A is incorrect. The Enable Netmask Ordering option configures the DNS server to reorder its host records in the response that it sends to a query based on the IP address of the DNS resolver that the query came from; thus, answer C is incorrect. The Secure Cache Against Pollution option configures the DNS server to prevent the addition of resource records that are unrelated to the original query; thus, answer D is incorrect.

Question 9

You are a senior consultant for Legacy Systems, Inc., a leading consultancy that helps organizations integrate their existing networks with newer technologies, such as Windows Server 2003. You are currently working on getting the existing BIND DNS implementation working with the newer Windows Server 2003 DNS service. Eventually, you will be able to migrate the existing BIND DNS zones to Windows Server 2003, but the customer wants this to occur over a six-month period, to prepare for any troubles. There are several different BIND servers, all of different versions. You are not sure what the version is on each of them. What is the minimum version of BIND that you will require on these BIND servers to ensure that they meet the DNS requirements of Active Directory?

- ❍ A. 4.9.4
- ❍ B. 4.9.6
- ❍ C. 8.1.2
- ❍ D. 8.2.1

Answer C is correct. BIND 8.1.2 meets all of the DNS requirements to support Active Directory by adding support for dynamic DNS. BIND 4.9.4 introduces support for fast zone transfers and does not meet the requirements for Active Directory; thus, answer A is incorrect. BIND 4.9.6 introduces support for SRV resource records but does not meet all of the requirements for Active Directory; thus, answer B is incorrect. BIND 8.2.1 introduces support for incremental zone transfers—although this is not a requirement for Active Directory; thus, answer D is also incorrect.

Question 10

By default, what DNS servers will a Windows Server 2003 DNS server perform zone transfers with?

- ❍ A. Only those servers listed on the Zone Transfers tab of the zone properties dialog box
- ❍ B. Only those servers listed on the Name Servers tab of the zone properties dialog box
- ❍ C. All servers listed on the Name Servers and Zone Transfers tabs of the zone properties dialog box
- ❍ D. All servers not listed on the Name Servers and Zone Transfers tabs of the zone properties dialog box

Answer B is correct. By default, Windows Server 2003 DNS servers will perform zone transfers only with the DNS servers that are listed on the Name Servers tab of the zone properties dialog box; thus, answers A, C, and D are incorrect. All DNS servers that are considered to be authoritative for the DNS zone will be listed on the Name Servers tab. Although this is a fairly secure configuration, you can make it more secure by explicitly configuring DNS servers by IP address on the Zone Transfers tab that you want to allow zone transfers to occur with.

Need to Know More?

Davies, Joseph and Lee, Thomas. *Microsoft Windows Server 2003 TCP/IP Protocols and Services Technical Reference*, Redmond, Washington: Microsoft Press, 2003.

"Technical Overview of Windows Server 2003 Networking and Communications," `www.microsoft.com/windowsserver2003/techinfo/overview/netcomm.mspx`.

"Deploying Network Services," `www.microsoft.com/technet/prodtechnol/windowsserver2003/evaluate/cpp/reskit/netsvc/default.asp`.

Planning, Implementing, and Maintaining Server Availability

Terms you'll need to understand:

- ✓ Affinity
- ✓ Automated System Recovery (ASR)
- ✓ Backup
- ✓ Clustering
- ✓ Convergence
- ✓ Heartbeat
- ✓ Failback
- ✓ Failover
- ✓ Network load balancing
- ✓ Node
- ✓ Port rules
- ✓ Quorum disk
- ✓ Restoration
- ✓ Volume shadow copy

Techniques you'll need to master:

- ✓ Creating new network load balancing (NLB) clusters and adding new nodes
- ✓ Creating new Microsoft Clustering Service (MSCS) clusters and adding new nodes
- ✓ Performing backup and restoration operations using Windows Backup
- ✓ Using Automated System Recovery (ASR)
- ✓ Working with Volume shadow copy

What's all the buzz about high availability? Why is everyone so intent on achieving the Utopia of server availability: five nines? It really all comes down to one thing: economics. The economics of today's Internet-centric world demand that critical services and servers be available 100% of the time. In the absence of perfection (which no one has delivered yet), the bar for highly available solutions has been set at five nines: 99.999% uptime. What exactly does that equate to, though?

Five nines availability enables you to have critical services offline for 5.25 minutes per year. That's an unbelievably low number, no matter how you look at it. But that's the goal of highly available solutions. As you might know, 5 minutes per year is barely enough time to apply a hot fix, much less a service pack. The answer to this problem is highly available server solutions. When discussing highly available solutions, there are two distinctly different ways to look at the problem: one based on hardware and one based on software. Windows Server 2003 provides you with two types of software-based high availability: clustering and network load balancing (NLB), each of which is discussed in detail in the following sections.

Of course, having any solution in place—highly available or not—is of little use if disaster strikes and removes it from operation. Environmentally or intentionally caused disasters are a fact of life that you simply cannot afford to ignore. Although you might not be able to prevent your servers from experiencing a disaster condition, you can prevent extended downtimes and the temporary unavailability of the network by implementing a well-planned and practiced disaster-recovery plan.

Planning and Implementing High-Availability Solutions

As briefly mentioned previously, Windows Server 2003 provides support for two different types of high availability, or clustering, technologies. Of course, the capability to implement highly available solutions does not come without a price. In the case of Windows Server 2003, you must be using either the Enterprise or Datacenter Server versions to have this capability available to you. In this section, we first examine the types of clustering provided in Windows Server 2003. Next, we present key terms and operational modes that will be important as you plan and implement clustering solutions. Finally, we show you how to implement and manage clusters and network load balancing using Windows Server 2003.

High-Availability Solutions

Clustering is accomplished when you group independent servers into one large collective entity that is accessed as if it were a single system. Incoming requests for service can be evenly distributed across multiple cluster members or can be handled by one specific cluster member.

The Microsoft Cluster Service (MSCS) in Windows Server 2003 provides highly available fault-tolerant systems through *failover*. When one of the cluster members (node) cannot respond to client requests, the remaining cluster members respond by distributing the load among themselves, thus responding to all existing and new connections and requests for service. In this way, clients see little, if any, disruption in the service being provided by the cluster. Cluster nodes are kept aware of the status of other cluster nodes and their services through the use of heartbeats. A heartbeat is used to keep track of the status of each node and also to send updates in the configuration of the cluster. Clustering is most commonly used to support database, messaging, and file/print servers. Windows Server 2003 supports up to eight nodes in a cluster.

Windows Server 2003 also provides *network load balancing* (*NLB*), in which all incoming connection requests are distributed using a mathematical algorithm to members of NLB cluster. NLB clustering is best used when clients can connect to any server in the cluster, such as Web sites, Terminal Services servers, and VPN servers. You can configure how the client interacts with the NLB cluster as well, such as allowing the client to use multiple NLB cluster members during a single connection (acceptable for Web sites) or forcing the client to use the same cluster member for the entire connection period (a necessity for VPN and Terminal Services servers). Windows Server 2003 NLB clusters can contain as many as 32 nodes.

Although you can use both clustering and NLB in your final design (as in the case of an e-commerce site that uses NLB for front-end Web servers and clustering for back-end SQL servers), you cannot use both technologies on the same server

Network load balancing is available in all versions of Windows Server 2003. Clustering, however, is available only in the Enterprise and Datacenter editions of Windows Server 2003.

High-Availability Terminology

A good understanding of the following MSCS and NLB clustering terminology is key to successfully implementing and managing any clustered solution. Although the following list of terms is not all-inclusive, it represents some of more important ones you should understand:

- *Cluster*—A group of two or more independent servers that operate together and are viewed and accessed as a single resource.
- *Cluster resource*—A network application, service, or hardware device (such as a network adapter or storage system) that is defined and managed by the cluster service.
- *Cluster resource group*—A defined set of resources contained within a cluster. Cluster resource groups are used as failover units within a cluster. When a cluster resource group fails and cannot be automatically restarted by the cluster service, the entire cluster resource group is placed in an offline status and failed over to another node.
- *Cluster virtual server*—A cluster resource group that has a network name and IP address assigned to it. Cluster virtual servers are accessible by their NetBIOS name, DNS name, or IP address.
- *Convergence*—The process by which NLB clustering hosts determine a new, stable state among themselves and elect a new default host after the failure of one or more cluster nodes. During convergence, the total load on the NLB cluster is redistributed among all cluster nodes that share the handling of traffic on specific ports, as determined by their port rules.
- *Heartbeat*—A network communication sent among individual cluster nodes at intervals of no more than 500 milliseconds (ms); used to determine the status of all cluster nodes.
- *Failback*—The process of moving a cluster group (either manually or automatically) back to the preferred node after the preferred node has resumed cluster membership. For failback to occur, it must be configured for the cluster group, including the failback threshold and selection of the preferred node.
- *Failover*—The process of a cluster group moving from the currently active node to a designated, functioning node in the cluster group. Failover typically occurs when the active node becomes unresponsive (for any reason) and cannot be recovered within the configured failure threshold period.
- *Node*—An individual server within a cluster.

- *Quorum disk*—The disk drive that contains the definitive cluster-configuration data. Clustering with MSCS requires the use of a quorum disk and requires continuous access to the data contained within the quorum disk. The quorum disk contains vital data about the nodes participating in the cluster, the applications and services defined within the cluster resource group, and the status of each node and cluster resource. The quorum disk is typically located on a shared storage device.

Planning and Implementing NLB Clusters

As discussed previously, the NLB cluster is most often used to create distributed fault-tolerant solutions for applications such as Web sites, VPN servers, and Terminal Services servers. NLB clusters are composed of between 2 and 32 nodes, each of which must contain the same applications and content. Because NLB clusters do not replicate content among the member nodes, using applications that require users to save data locally on the node is not a good idea. In this instance, you would need to implement a clustered server environment on the back end, such as a SQL Server cluster.

Although it is beyond the capabilities of the normal NLB service, Application Center 2000 can be used to create NLB clusters that will replicate from a master node to all other member nodes, thus ensuring that changes made to the master node are kept current on all other member nodes.

The most critical part of deploying an NLB cluster is determining the operational mode to be used and the port rules that will be required. To plan for these items, you must know and understand what types of applications or services will be running on the NLB cluster. Certain applications, such as an e-commerce application, make extensive use of cookies during and between client connections. If an NLB cluster is configured to allow multiple requests to be sent to multiple servers during a single session, the client might experience application failures if the expected cookie is absent on other NLB cluster members. We discuss port rules, filtering mode, affinity, and cluster operation modes in the next sections. When you have a good understanding of these key NLB concepts, you will be ready to start implementing an NLB clustered solution in your organization.

Port Rules

When a network load-balancing cluster is created, port rules are used to determine what types of traffic are to be load-balanced across the cluster nodes. Within the port rule is the additional option to configure *port rule filtering*, which determines how the traffic will be load-balanced across each of the cluster nodes.

In an NLB cluster, every cluster node can answer for the cluster's IP address; thus, every cluster node receives all inbound traffic, by default. When each node receives the inbound request, it either responds to the requesting client or drops the packet if the client has an existing session in progress with another node. If no port rule is configured that specifically defines how traffic on the specific port is to be handled, the request is passed off to the cluster node with the lowest configured priority. This can result in decreased performance by the NLB cluster as a whole if the traffic is not meant to be or cannot be load-balanced.

Port rules enable you to change this behavior in a deliberate and controlled fashion. Think of port rules as the network load balancing equivalent of a firewall rule set. By configuring port rules to allow only traffic on the specific ports that you require to reach the NLB cluster and configuring an additional rule to drop all packets that do not meet any other port rules, you can greatly improve the performance of the NLB cluster by allowing it to drop all packets that are not allowed to be load-balanced. From an administrative and security standpoint, port rules allow for easier monitoring of the server due to the limited number of ports that must be monitored.

Filtering Mode and Affinity

As mentioned briefly in the previous section, you can configure how NLB clusters load-balance traffic across cluster nodes—this is referred to as *filtering*. By configuring filtering, you can specify whether only one node or multiple nodes within the NLB cluster are allowed to respond to multiple requests from the same client during a single session (connection).

The three filtering modes are as follows:

- *Single host*—When this filtering mode is configured, all traffic that meets the port rule criteria is sent to a specific cluster node. A typical example of when the Single host filter might be used is in a Web site that has only one SSL server. Configuring a port rule for TCP port 443 would specify that all traffic on this port must be directed to that one node.
- *Disable port range*—This filtering mode instructs the cluster nodes to ignore and drop all traffic on the configured ports without any further

action. This type of filtering can be used to prevent inbound traffic directed to these ports and port ranges from being load-balanced.

- *Multiple host*—This default filtering method specifies that traffic is allowed to be handled by all active nodes in the cluster. When implementing multiple host filtering, the host affinity must be configured. Affinity determines how clients interact with the cluster nodes and varies depending on the requirements of the applications that the cluster is providing. Three types of affinities can be configured:
  - *None*—This affinity type sends an inbound client request to all nodes within the cluster. This results in increased speed, but this affinity is suitable only for providing static content to clients, such as static Web sites and FTP downloads. Typically, this affinity type is configured when applications running on the cluster do not generate cookies.
  - *Class C*—This affinity type directs all inbound client requests from a particular Class C address space to a specific cluster node. This type of affinity allows the cluster to maintain a user's state but can be overloaded or fooled if all client requests are passed through a single firewall or proxy server.
  - *Single*—This affinity type maintains all client requests on the same node for the duration of the session (connection). This provides the best support for maintaining user state data and is often used when applications are running on the cluster that generate cookies.

NLB Cluster Operation Mode

The mathematical algorithm used by network load balancing sends inbound traffic to every host in the NLB cluster. The inbound client requests can be distributed to the NLB cluster nodes through one of two methods: unicast or multicast. Although both methods send all inbound client requests to all hosts by sending them to the MAC address of the cluster, they go about it in different ways.

When using the *unicast* method, all cluster nodes share an identical unicast MAC address. NLB overwrites the original MAC address of the cluster network adapter with the unicast MAC address that is assigned to all of the cluster nodes. When using the *multicast* method, each cluster node retains its original MAC address of the cluster network adapter. The cluster network adapter is then assigned an additional multicast MAC address, which is shared by all of the nodes in the cluster. Inbound client requests can then be sent to all cluster nodes by using the multicast MAC address.

The unicast method is usually preferred for NLB clusters unless each cluster node has only one network adapter installed in it. Recall that in any clustering arrangement, all nodes must be capable of communicating not only with the clients, but also among themselves. Recall that NLB modifies the MAC address of the cluster network adapter when unicast is used; thus, the cluster nodes will not be capable of communicating among themselves. If only one network adapter is installed in each cluster node, you must use the multicast method.

Switch Port Flooding

As discussed previously, the mathematical algorithm used by network load balancing sends inbound traffic to every host in the NLB cluster. This is accomplished by preventing the switch that the NLB cluster nodes are attached to from ever associating the NLB cluster's MAC address with a specific port on the switch. However, this leads to the unwanted side effect of switch port flooding, in which the switch floods all of its ports with all packets inbound to the NLB cluster.

This is both a waste of valuable network resources and a nuisance to you when implementing NLB clusters. In Windows 2000, you would need to place all nodes of an NLB cluster either on a dedicated switch or on a dedicated virtual LAN (VLAN) within the switch to get around the problems of switch port flooding. A new feature in Windows Server 2003 prevents switch port flooding from occurring.

To prevent flooding from occurring on the switch ports that do not have an NLB cluster node attached to them, Windows 2003 now provides Internet Group Management Protocol (IGMP) support for network load balancing. With this feature, non–NLB cluster nodes do not see inbound traffic that is intended for the NLB cluster. At the same time, all NLB cluster nodes continue to receive all inbound traffic, thus meeting the requirements of the NLB algorithm. IGMP support is available only when multicast mode is configured for the NLB cluster. Of course, that presents its own set of benefits and drawbacks. As an alternative, you can utilize the dedicate switch or VLAN methods to eliminate switch port flooding with the NLB cluster in unicast mode—unicast mode does not present the same drawbacks associated with multicast mode.

At this point, you are ready to move forward and create an NLB cluster. After creating your NLB cluster, you can join additional cluster nodes to it and begin managing the NLB cluster.

Creating an NLB Cluster

By now, you've gotten a good introduction to not only what network load balancing is, but also some of the key parts of it. But you might still not have a good idea of exactly what an NLB cluster solution might look like. Figure 4.1 shows a four-node NLB cluster arrangement.

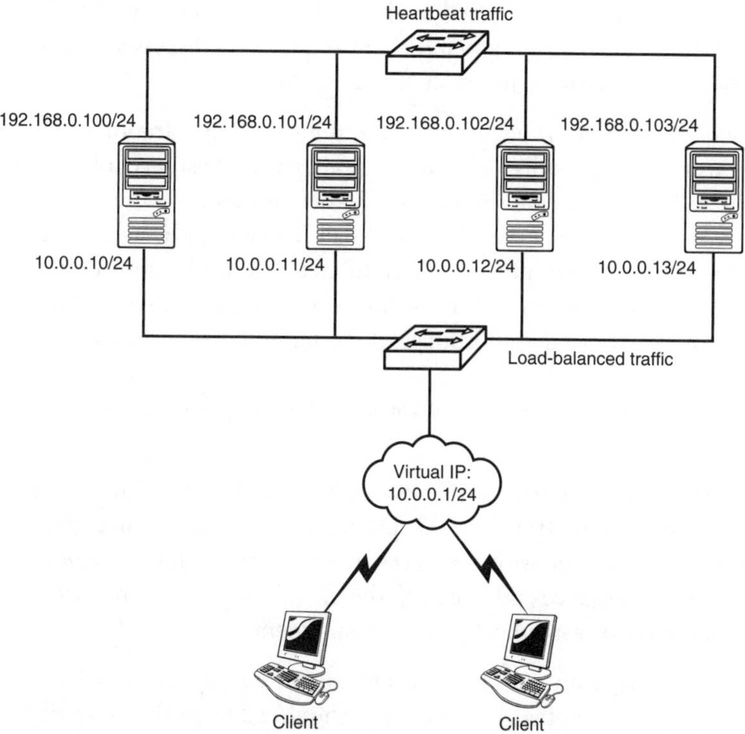

Figure 4.1 This four-node NLB cluster is providing highly available Web sites.

Any good implementation needs a good plan. To successfully implement your NLB cluster, you need to identify the key parameters that require you to have information ready ahead of time: cluster parameters and cluster host parameters. We examine each in the following paragraphs.

The following parameters are of interest when planning for the entire cluster:

- *Cluster virtual IP address*—The virtual IP (VIP) address that will be assigned to represent the entire cluster must be determined. This IP address must be in the same IP subnet as the IP addresses assigned to the cluster network adapters on all cluster hosts. In addition, these IP addresses should be in a different IP subnet from the IP addresses chosen for the administrative IP addresses.
- *Cluster FQDN*—A fully qualified domain name (FQDN) must be assigned to the cluster, just as with any host on the network. This FQDN will be registered in DNS and will enable clients to access the cluster as one unit. In addition, you need to designate an FQDN for each application and service that you are running on the cluster because they will be accessed by their FQDN by clients.

- *Cluster operation mode*—You need to choose between unicast and multicast mode for distributing inbound client requests, as discussed previously in the "NLB Cluster Operation Mode" section.
- *Cluster remote control settings*—By default, remote administration of the cluster using nlb.exe is disabled. To maintain the highest level of security for your NLB cluster, you should specify that all remote administration is to be performed using the Network Load Balancing Manager. You should also specify that all cluster administration must be done only from specified computers that are within your trusted and secured internal network, to prevent compromise of cluster administrative control.

The following parameters are of interest when planning for each of the cluster nodes:

- *Cluster host priority*—Each cluster node is identified by a unique host priority number ranging from 1 to 32. During cluster convergence, the remaining cluster node with the lowest numeric host priority triggers the end of convergence and becomes the default host. No two cluster nodes can have the same host priority assignment.
- *Administrative IP address*—These IP addresses are assigned to each non–load-balanced network adapter and should all be in the same IP subnet. In addition, these IP addresses should be in a different IP subnet from the IP addresses chosen for the cluster IP addresses.
- *Cluster IP address*—These IP addresses are assigned to each cluster network adapter and must be in the same IP subnet as the cluster VIP. They should also be in a different IP subnet from the IP addresses chosen for the administrative IP addresses.
- *Initial host state*—A Windows Server 2003 server configured to be an NLB cluster node starts the NLB service very early in the operating system startup process and joins the NLB cluster. If this occurs before clustered services and applications are started and available on the cluster node, clients might experience service disruptions. You must specify whether cluster nodes will automatically start the NLB service and join the NLB cluster upon operating system load or whether the NLB service will be manually started later.

When implementing either an NLB solution or a cluster, you should have two network adapters installed in each cluster node. The discussion and examples that follow assume that you have two network adapters installed in your cluster nodes.

With the required parameter information in hand, you are ready to create an NLB cluster and join additional nodes to the cluster. The process to create a new NLB cluster is as follows:

1. Open the Network Connections window by selecting Start, Settings, Network Connections. The Network Connections window opens, displaying all configured connections on the computer.
2. Double-click the network adapter that you will be using as the administrative network adapter to open the network adapter Status dialog box.
3. Click the Properties button to open the network adapter Properties dialog box.
4. On the General tab, select Internet Protocol (TCP/IP) and then click Properties. The Internet Protocol (TCP/IP) Properties dialog box opens, as shown in Figure 4.2.

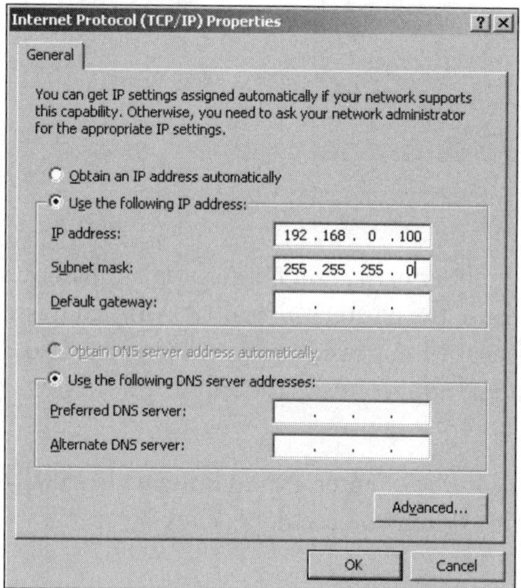

Figure 4.2 The Internet Protocol (TCP/IP) Properties dialog box is used to configure TCP/IP settings for a network connection.

5. Enter the IP address and subnet mask to be used for the administrative interface. In most cases, these interfaces will be connected only to each other, as shown in Figure 4.1, and thus will not require a default gateway or DNS server. You can configure this information if it is required, however.
6. Click Close to close the Local Area Connection Properties dialog box.
7. Open the Network Load Balancing Manager by selecting Start, Programs, Administrative Tools, Network Load Balancing Manager.

8. Right-click on Network Load Balancing Clusters and select New Cluster from the context menu. The Cluster Parameters dialog box appears (see Figure 4.3).

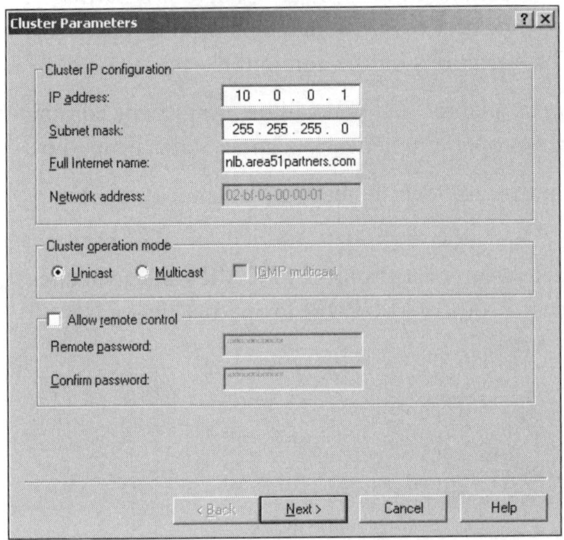

Figure 4.3 The Cluster Parameters dialog box enables you to create a new NLB cluster.

9. Enter the cluster's IP address, subnet mask, and cluster domain name. The IP address configured here is the cluster's virtual IP (VIP) address. Configure the cluster for unicast or multicast, as desired. You can also configure IGMP multicast and remote control, as desired. Click Next to continue.

10. In the Cluster IP Addresses dialog box, enter any additional virtual IP addresses using the Add button. When you are done, click Next to continue.

11. In the Port Rules dialog box, shown in Figure 4.4, configure any port rules that are appropriate for your NLB cluster installation. Clicking the Add button opens the Add/Edit Port Rule dialog box.

12. Configure your port rules, as discussed previously in the "Port Rules" and "NLB Cluster Operation Mode" sections of this chapter. Click OK to accept the new port rule. Click Next to continue creating the NLB cluster.

13. In the Connect dialog box, type the name of the first cluster node and click the Connect button. After a brief period, all available network adapters are displayed in the bottom half of the dialog box. Select the network adapter that is to be used for load balancing and click Next to continue.

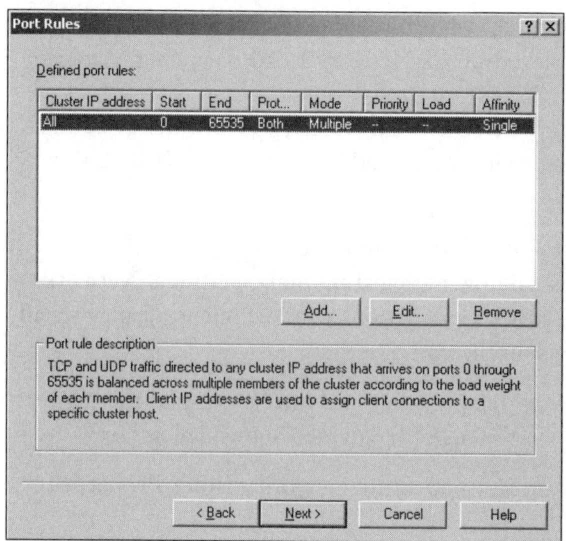

Figure 4.4 Port rules are used to quickly filter traffic from being load-balanced by the NLB cluster.

14. In the Host Parameters dialog box, shown in Figure 4.5, configure the host priority, the cluster node dedicated IP address, the subnet mask, and the initial state of the cluster node. The dedicated IP address is assigned to the cluster adapter and must be unique and in the same subnet as the cluster VIP. After entering all required information, click Finish to complete the NLB cluster-creation process.

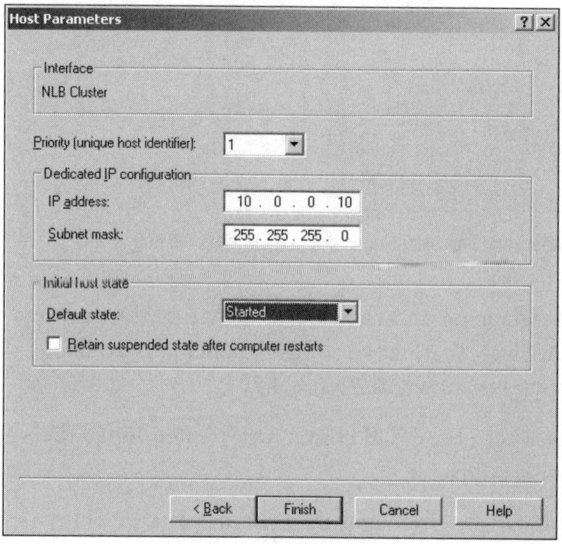

Figure 4.5 The Host Parameters dialog box contains critical configuration items that identify the specific cluster node.

15. After a brief period of time, you can see the newly created and fully converged cluster displayed in the Network Load Balancing Manager.

Of course, after you have created the NLB cluster, you will want to add at least one more cluster node to it. You can add nodes to the NLB cluster by following these steps:

1. On the server that is to be added to the NLB cluster, open the Network Connections window by selecting Start, Settings, Network Connections. The Network Connections window opens, displaying all configured connections on the computer.
2. Double-click the network adapter that you will be using as the cluster network adapter to open the network adapter Status dialog box.
3. Click the Properties button to open the network adapter Properties dialog box.
4. On the General tab, click the Install button to open the Select Network Component Type dialog box. Double-click on Service to open the Select Network Service dialog box shown in Figure 4.6.

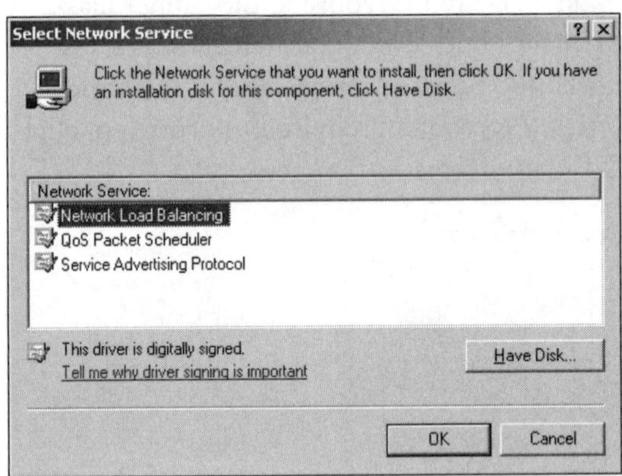

Figure 4.6 You must ensure that network load balancing is enabled for the clustering adapter.

5. Select Network Load Balancing and click OK. Verify that the network adapter properties now show that network load balancing is available for the clustering adapter, as shown in Figure 4.7.
6. From the cluster node where the NLB cluster was created, open the Network Load Balancing Manager.
7. If the Network Load Balancing Manager does not display the cluster, connect to it by right-clicking on Network Load Balancing Clusters and selecting Connect to Existing from the context menu.

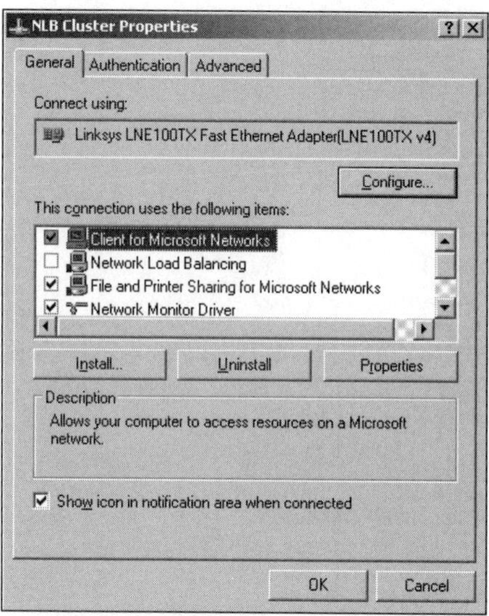

Figure 4.7 After network load balancing has been made available for the clustering adapter, you can quickly add the new cluster node.

8. Right-click on the NLB cluster and select Add Host to Cluster from the context menu.

9. On the Connect dialog box, type the name of the additional cluster node and click the Connect button. After a brief period, all available network adapters are displayed in the bottom half of the dialog box. Select the network adapter that is to be used for load balancing, and click Next to continue.

10. On the Host Parameters dialog box, configure the host priority, the cluster node dedicated IP address, the subnet mask, and the initial state of the cluster node. The dedicated IP address is the same as the cluster network adapter itself; it must be unique and in the same subnet as the cluster VIP. After entering all required information, click Finish to complete the NLB cluster creation process.

11. After a brief period of time, you see the updated and fully converged cluster displayed in the Network Load Balancing Manager, as shown in Figure 4.8.

With the discussion of creating NLB clusters behind us, we now move forward and examine MSCS clusters, commonly referred to as simply clusters.

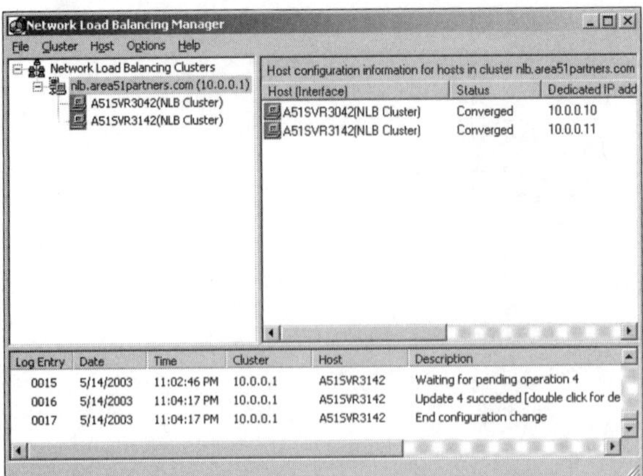

Figure 4.8 After a brief delay, the updated NLB cluster is fully converged.

Planning and Implementing MSCS Clusters

Earlier in this chapter, we said that NLB clusters were the "simpler of the two types to understand, deploy, and support." This is very much a true statement. As you've seen, NLB clusters require no special hardware. In fact, the only real additional requirement (beyond meeting those to install Windows Server 2003) is that each NLB cluster should have two network adapters installed. The services and applications installed on the NLB cluster might have additional requirements, but, for the most part, NLB clusters are less expensive and easier to implement and maintain.

However, MSCS clustering has its advantages—especially in applications that require uninterrupted access to data and services. Typically, you can expect to deploy MSCS clusters in support of Exchange Server, SQL Server, file shares, and printer shares—all services that businesses, clients, and users demand 24×7 access to.

So, what's the difference between MSCS clustering and network load balancing? As you saw in Figure 4.1, NLB uses a group of between 2 and 32 servers to distribute inbound requests to permit the maximum amount of loading with the minimum amount of downtime. Each NLB cluster node contains an exact copy of the static and dynamic content that each other NLB cluster node has. In this way, it doesn't matter which NLB cluster node receives the inbound request (except in the case of host affinity, in which cookies are involved). Heartbeats are used by the NLB cluster nodes to stay aware of the status of all nodes.

Clustering, on the other hand, uses a group of between two and eight servers that all share a common storage device. Recall that a cluster resource is an application, service, or hardware device that is defined and managed by the cluster service. The cluster service (MSCS) monitors these cluster resources to ensure that they are properly operating. When a problem occurs with a cluster resource, MSCS attempts to correct the problem on the same cluster node. If the problem cannot be corrected—such as a service that cannot be successfully restarted—the cluster service fails the resource, takes the cluster group offline and moves it to another cluster node, and restarts the cluster group. MSCS clusters also use heartbeats to determine the operational status of other nodes in the cluster.

Two clustering modes exist:

- *Active/Passive*—One node in the cluster is online providing services. The other nodes in the cluster are online but do not provide any services or applications to clients. If the active node fails, the cluster groups that were running on that node are failed over to the passive node. The passive node then changes its state to active and begins to service client requests. The passive nodes cannot be used for any other purpose during normal operations because they must remain available for a failover situation. All nodes should be configured identically, to ensure that when failover occurs, no performance loss is experienced.
- *Active/Active*—One instance of the clustered service or application runs on each node in the cluster. If a failure of a node occurs, that instance is transferred to one of the running nodes. Although this clustering mode enables you to make use of all cluster nodes to service client requests, it can cause significant performance degradation if the cluster was already operating a very high load at the time of the failure.

You must choose from three cluster models when planning for your new cluster. They are discussed in the next section.

Cluster Models

Three distinctly different cluster models exist for configuring your new cluster. You must choose one of the three models at the beginning of your cluster planning because the chosen model dictates the storage requirements of your new cluster. The three models are presented in the following sections in order of increasing complexity—and cost.

Single-Node Cluster

The single-node cluster mode, shown in Figure 4.9, has only one cluster node. The cluster node can make use of local storage or an external cluster storage device. If local storage is used, the local disk is configured as the cluster storage device. This storage device is known as a *local quorum resource*. A local quorum resource does not make use of failover and is most commonly used as a way to organize network resources in a single network location for administrative and user convenience. This model is also useful for developing and testing cluster-aware applications.

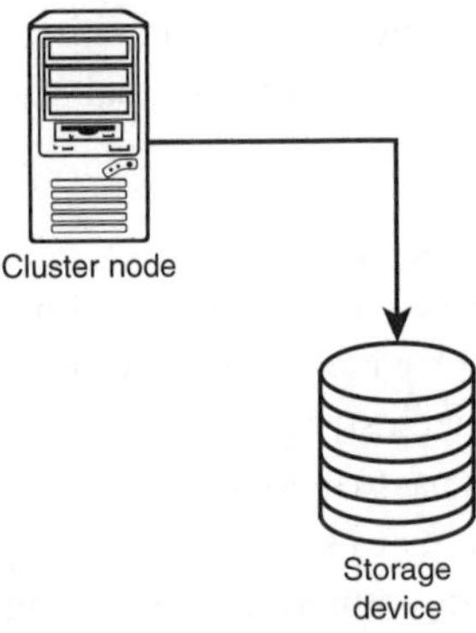

Figure 4.9 The single-node cluster can be used to increase service reliability and also to pre-stage cluster resource groups.

Despite its limited capabilities, this model does offer the administrator some advantages at a relatively low entry cost:

- The cluster service can automatically restart services and applications that might not be capable of automatically restarting after a failure. This increases the reliability of network services and applications.
- The single node can be clustered with additional nodes in the future, preserving the resource groups that you have already created. You simply need to join the additional nodes to the cluster, configure the failover, and move policies for the resource groups to ready the newly added nodes.

By default, the New Server Cluster Wizard creates the single-node cluster using a local quorum resource if the cluster node is not connected to a cluster storage device.

Single-Quorum Cluster

The single-quorum cluster model, shown in Figure 4.10, has two or more cluster nodes that are configured so that each node is attached to the cluster storage device. All cluster configuration data is stored on a single cluster storage device. All cluster nodes have access to the quorum data, but only one cluster node runs the quorum disk resource at any given time.

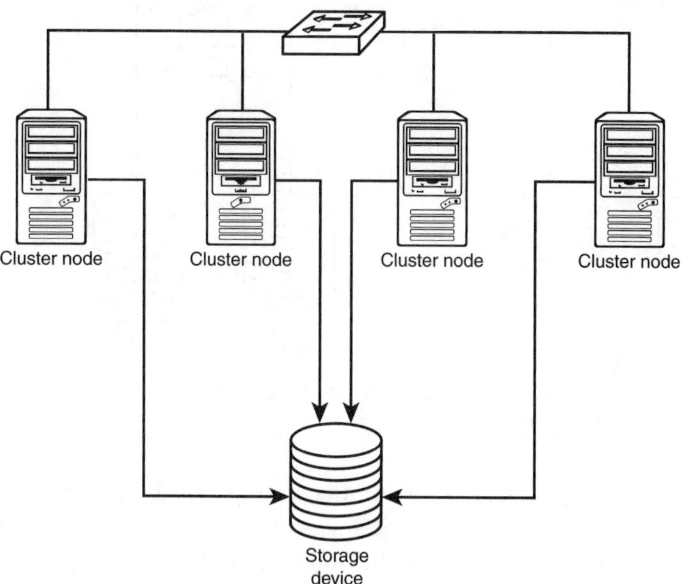

Figure 4.10 The single-quorum cluster shares one cluster storage device among all cluster nodes.

Majority Node Set Cluster

The majority node set cluster model, shown in Figure 4.11, has two or more cluster nodes that are configured so that the nodes might or might not be attached to one or more cluster storage devices. Cluster configuration data is stored on multiple disks across the entire cluster, and the cluster service is responsible for ensuring that this data is kept consistent across all of the disks. All quorum traffic travels in an unencrypted form over the network using Server Message Block (SMB) file shares. This model provides the advantage of being able to locate cluster nodes in two geographically different locations; they do not all need to be physically attached to the shared cluster storage device.

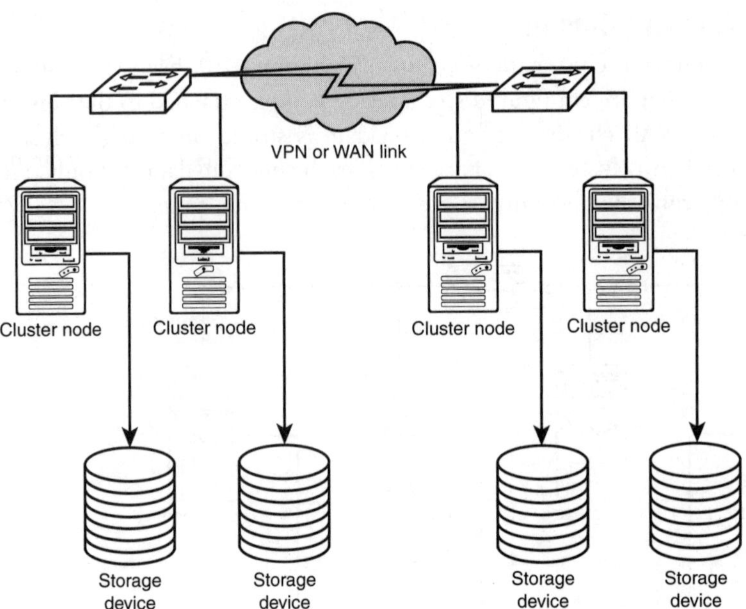

Figure 4.11 The majority node set cluster model is a high-level clustering solution that allows for geographically dispersed cluster nodes.

Even if all cluster nodes are not located in the same physical location, they appear as a single entity to clients. The majority node set cluster model provides the following advantages over the other clustering models:

- Clusters can be created without cluster disks. This is useful when you need to make available applications that can fail over, but you have another means to replicate data among the storage devices.
- If a local quorum disk becomes unavailable, it can be taken offline while the rest of the cluster remains available to service client requests.

However, you must abide by some requirements when implementing majority node set clusters to ensure that they are successful:

- A maximum of two sites can be used.
- The cluster nodes at either site must be capable of communicating with each other with less than a 500ms response time so that the heartbeat messages can accurately indicate the correct status of the cluster nodes.
- A high-speed, high-quality WAN or VPN link must be established between sites so that the cluster's IP address appears the same to all clients, regardless of their location on the network.

- Only the cluster quorum information is replicated among the cluster storage devices. You must provide a proven effective means to replicate other data among the cluster storage devices.

The primary disadvantage to this clustering model is that if a certain number of nodes fail, the cluster loses its quorum and it then fails. Table 4.1 shows the maximum number of cluster nodes that can fail before the cluster itself fails.

Table 4.1 Number of Failed Nodes to Fail the Majority Node Set Cluster

Number of Nodes in the Cluster	Number of Failed Nodes That Will Cause the Cluster to Fail
1	0
2	0
3	1
4	1
5	2
6	2
7	3
8	3

As shown in Table 4.1, the majority node cluster set remains operational as long as a majority—more than half—of the initial cluster nodes remains available.

Majority node set clusters most likely will be the clustering solution of the future because of their capability to geographically separate cluster nodes. This further increases the reliability and redundancy of your clustering solution. However, Microsoft currently recommends that you implement majority node set clustering only in very specific instances and only with close support provided by your original equipment manufacturer (OEM), independent software vendor (ISV), or independent hardware vendor (IHV).

Cluster Operation Modes

You can choose from four basic cluster operation modes when using a single-quorum cluster or a majority node set cluster. These operation modes are specified by defining the cluster failover policies accordingly, as discussed in the next section, "Cluster Failover Polices." The four basic cluster operation modes are listed here:

- *Failover pair*—This mode of operation is configured by allowing applications to fail over between only two specific cluster nodes. Only the two desired nodes should be placed in the possible owner list for the service of concern.
- *Hot standby (N+I)*—This mode of operation helps you reduce the expenses and overhead associated with dedicated failover pairs by consolidating the spare node for each failover pair into a single node. This provides a single cluster node that is capable of taking over the applications from any active node in the event of a failover. Hot standby is often referred to as active/passive, as discussed previously in this chapter. Hot standby is achieved through a combination of using the preferred owners list and the possible owners list. The preferred node is configured in the preferred owners list and designated as the node that will run the application or service under normal conditions. The spare (hot standby) node is configured in the possible owners list.
- *Failover ring*—This mode of operation has each node in the cluster running an instance of the application or service. If a node fails, the application or service on the failed node is moved to the next node in the sequence. The failover ring mode is achieved by using the preferred owner list to define the order of failover for a given resource group. This order should start on a different node on each node in the cluster.
- *Random*—This mode of operation allows the cluster to randomly determine which node will be failed over to randomly. The random failover mode is configured by providing an empty preferred owner list for each resource group.

Now that you've been introduced to failover, let's examine cluster failover policies.

Cluster Failover Polices

Although the actual configuration of failover and failback policies is discussed later in this chapter, it is important to discuss them briefly here, to properly acquaint you with their use and function. Each resource group within the cluster has a prioritized listing of the nodes that are supposed to act as its host.

You can configure failover policies for each resource group to define exactly how each group will behave when a failover occurs. You must configure three settings:

- *Preferred nodes*—An internal prioritized list of available nodes for resource group failovers and failbacks. Ideally, all nodes in the cluster will be in this list, in the order of priority that you designate.

- *Failover timing*—The resource can be configured for immediate failover if the resource fails, or the cluster service can be configured to try to restart the resource a specified number of times before failover actually occurs. The failover threshold value should be equal to or less than the number of nodes in the cluster.
- *Failback timing*—Failback can be configured to occur as soon as the preferred node is available or during a specified time, such as when peak load is at its lowest, to minimize service disruptions.

Creating a Cluster

Now that you have had a good introduction to what clustering is and how it works, you are ready to create the cluster and install the first node in the cluster. As with the NLB cluster, you should do a bit of preparation before actually starting the configuration process, to ensure that your cluster is created successfully.

To successfully implement your MSCS cluster, you need to determine and document the following pieces of information:

- All services and applications that will be deployed on the cluster.
- Failover and failback policies for each service or application that is to be deployed.
- The quorum model to be used.
- The configuration and operating procedures for the shared storage devices to be used.
- All hardware listed on the Hardware Compatibility List (HCL). MSCS clusters have higher hardware requirements than NLB clusters.
- The clustering and administrative IP address and subnet information, including the cluster IP address itself.
- The cluster name (no more than 15 characters long, to comply with NetBIOS naming requirements).

When you've configured and prepared your servers and shared storage device, you are ready to move forward with the creation of the MSCS cluster. Any installation and configuration required for the shared storage device must be completed in accordance with the manufacturer or vendor specifications to ensure successful deployment.

You can create a new MSCS cluster by performing the following steps:

1. Open the Active Directory User and Computers console and create a domain user account to be used by the MSCS service. Configure the password to never expire. Later, during the cluster-creation process, this user account will be given Local Administrator privileges on all cluster nodes and will also be delegated cluster-related user rights in the domain, including the Add Computer Accounts to the Domain user right.
2. Ensure that the load-balancing and administrative network adapters on the first cluster node are configured correctly, as discussed previously.
3. Open the Cluster Administrator by selecting Start, Programs, Administrative Tools, Cluster Administrator. You should be prompted with the Open Connection to Cluster dialog box shown in Figure 4.12. If not, click File, Open Connection.

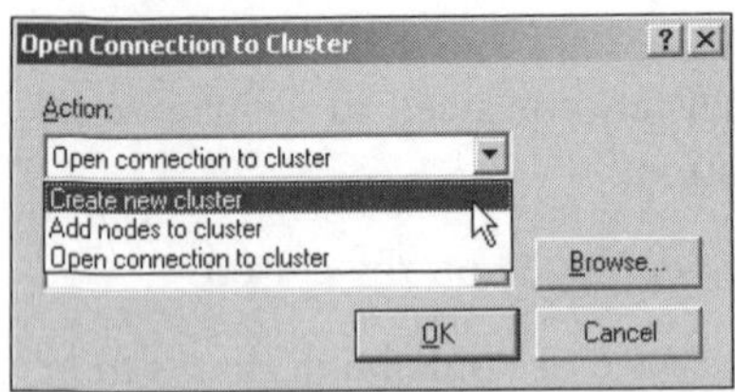

Figure 4.12 You need to create a new cluster because you don't have an existing one to open.

4. Click Next to dismiss the opening dialog box of the New Cluster Creation Wizard.
5. On the Cluster Name and Domain dialog box, select the cluster domain from the drop-down list. Enter the cluster name in the space provided. Click Next to continue.
6. In the Select Computer dialog box, select the computer that will be the first node in the new cluster. Click Next to continue.
7. The Analyzing Configuration dialog box, shown in Figure 4.13, appears and runs for a short period of time. You can continue with cautions as long as no errors or warnings occur. You can examine the log file by clicking the View Log button. Click Next to continue when you are done viewing the output.
8. In the IP Address dialog box, enter the IP address that is being assigned to the cluster. Click Next to continue.

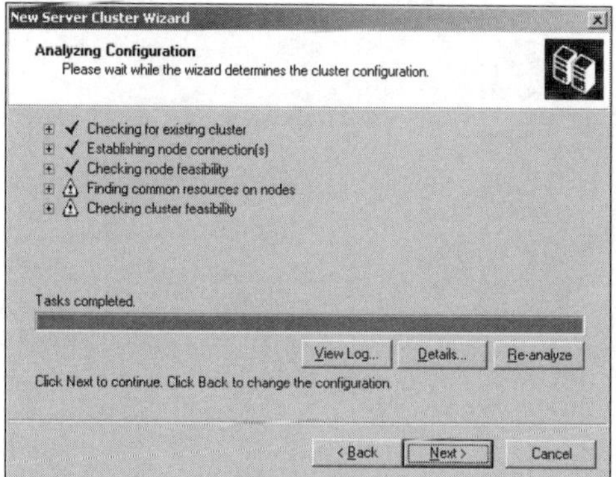

Figure 4.13 The Analyzing Configuration process alerts you to any showstoppers encountered with your selected node.

9. In the Cluster Service Account dialog box, shown in Figure 4.14, enter the proper credentials for the cluster domain user account you created previously. Click Next to continue.

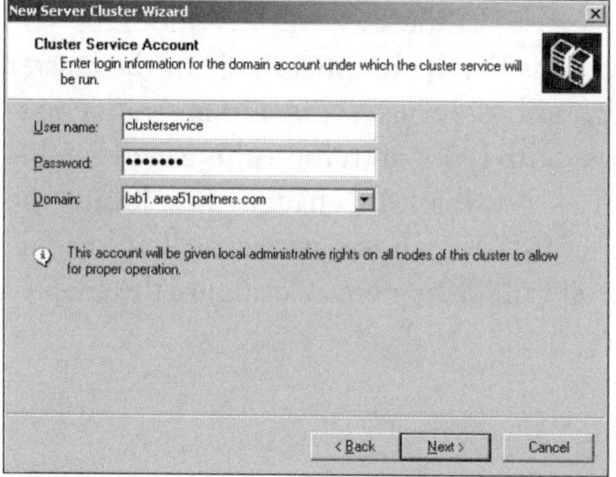

Figure 4.14 Supply the cluster domain user account name and password to continue the cluster-creation process.

10. In the Proposed Cluster Configuration dialog box, you can review the cluster configuration before continuing. Clicking the Quorum button enables you to change the type of quorum being used, as shown in Figure 4.15. When you are done, click Next to continue.
11. If all goes well—and, of course, it will—you should see results on the Creating the Cluster dialog box. Click Next to continue.
12. Click Finish to complete the Create New Cluster Wizard.
13. Your new cluster shows up in the Cluster Administrator.

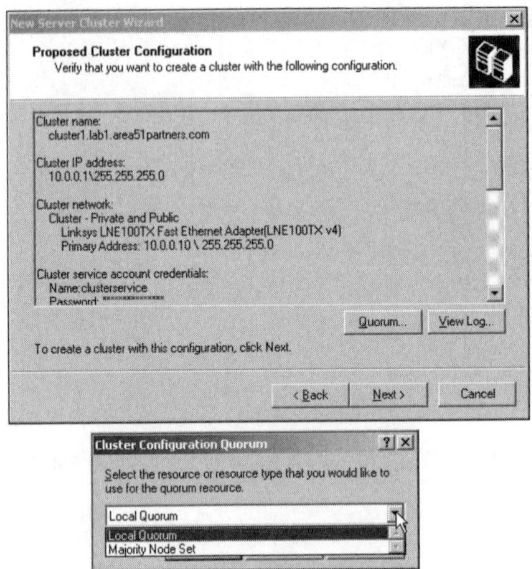

Figure 4.15 You can change the quorum type by selecting one of the available options, if desired.

Congratulations, you just created your first cluster! That wasn't so difficult when you got all of the preliminaries out of the way, was it? One thing you should change immediately, however, is the operational mode of the cluster node network adapters. By default, both the cluster and administrative network adapters are configured to pass both types of traffic—this is undesirable and should be corrected as soon as possible. To change this, locate the Networks node of the Cluster Administrator, shown in Figure 4.16. Right-click on each adapter to open its properties dialog box. Configure the adapter according to its role in the cluster.

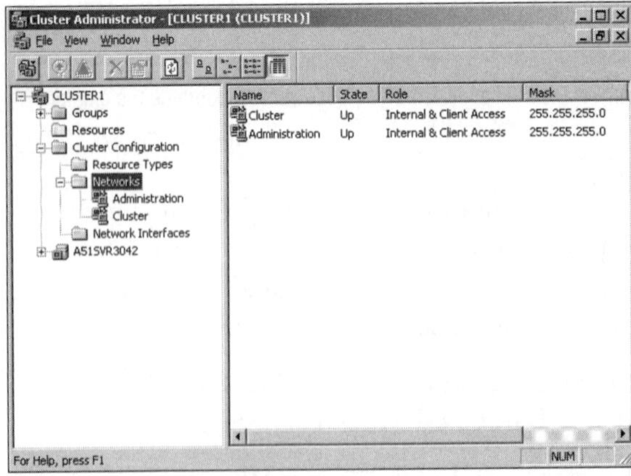

Figure 4.16 You should change the network adapter operational mode as soon as possible.

To add nodes to your cluster, perform the following steps:

1. Ensure that the load-balancing and administrative network adapters on the new cluster node are configured correctly, as discussed previously.
2. Open the Cluster Administrator. If the cluster does not appear in the Cluster Administrator, click File, Open Connection and supply the required information to connect to the cluster.
3. Right-click on the cluster name in the Cluster Administrator and select New, Node from the context menu.
4. Click Next to dismiss the opening dialog box of the Add Nodes Wizard.
5. In the Select Computers dialog box, enter the computer names that are to be joined to the cluster.
6. The Analyzing Configuration dialog box appears for the new node(s), providing information about their suitability to join the cluster. Click Next to continue.
7. In the Cluster Service Account dialog box, enter the correct password for the cluster service account. Click Next to continue.
8. In the Proposed Cluster Configuration dialog box, you can review the cluster configuration before continuing. Click Next to continue.
9. The Adding Nodes to the Cluster dialog box appears, detailing the status of the node addition. Click Next to continue.
10. Click Finish to complete the Create New Cluster Wizard.
11. Your new cluster node shows up in the Cluster Administrator, shown in Figure 4.17.

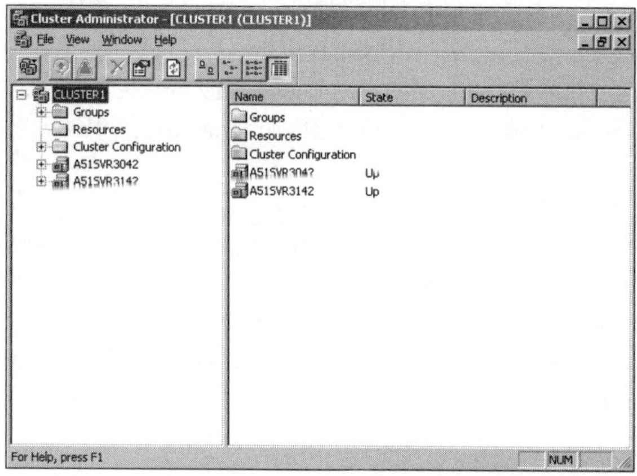

Figure 4.17 The Cluster Administrator displays the newly added cluster node.

Now that you know how to create NLB and MSCS clusters, let's examine disaster recovery in Windows Server 2003.

Planning and Implementing Backup and Recovery Solutions

Disasters happen. It's an administrator's worst nightmare, but it doesn't have to be. Even with the best hardware and most fault-tolerant design, nothing can replace a solid backup and restoration plan. The Backup utility provided in Windows Server 2003, `ntbackup.exe`, is actually a "light" version of the commercially available third-party product from Veritas Software. Although it is limited in its capability, when used properly, it can provide you with all of the functionality you should need for small networks or workgroups. If you have a larger network, you might want to put some serious thought into acquiring an enterprise backup solution, such as Backup Exec.

The following general points should be kept in mind when working with Windows Backup:

- You can back up to either a file or a tape drive.
- You can back up files from either the local machine or remote computers, provided that you have access to the files that you want to back up on the remote computer. The limitation of backing up a computer remotely is that system state information cannot be saved.
- To perform a backup, you must have Read access to the files or the user right of Backup and Restore Files, which is granted by default to the Administrators and Backup Operators groups.
- Special permissions are granted to the Administrators and Backup Operators groups to access all files for the purposes of doing backups. Even if members of these groups cannot access the data as users, they can back it up.

The Backup utility in Windows Server 2003 has undergone some changes from its predecessor in Windows 2000 Server. No longer will you be creating an emergency repair disk (ERD)—this has been replaced by the new and improved Automated System Recovery (ASR) function. Windows Server 2003 also introduces Volume Shadow Copy in the Backup utility. Each of these new functions is explained in more detail in the following section.

New Windows Server 2003 Backup Features

Using the volume shadow copy feature, an instant copy of the original volume is created at the time the backup is initiated. Data is then subsequently backed up to the backup medium from this shadow copy instead of the original files. This new technology provides a means for backing up open files that were in use at the time the backup was initiated. Using volume shadow copy, files that would normally be skipped during the backup are backed up in their current state (at the time of the shadow copy creation) and thus appear closed on the backup medium. Any applications that are running during the backup process can continue to run during the backup process. When the backup has been completed, the shadow copy is deleted. The volume shadow copy feature requires the NTFS file system to be in use and can be disabled, if desired.

You cannot disable the volume shadow copy option when performing a backup of the system state data.

Automated System Recovery (ASR) is an advanced restoration option of the Backup utility that can be used to restore your system if other disaster-recovery methods fail or are not available for use. Using ASR, you can restore the operating system to a previous state, which enables you to start Window Server 2003 if other methods do not work. You should always consider ASR your last resort for recovery, after Safe Mode, the Recovery Console, and Last Known Good Configuration (LKGC). You should make a point to keep your ASR media up-to-date as you make configuration changes to your computer, to minimize the amount of recovery required if you ever need to use ASR. To use the ASR Wizard to create a set of ASR media, click on the Automated System Recovery Wizard button on the main page of the Backup tool (which we examine later in this section).

Backup Methods

Windows Server 2003 supports five backup methods, as outlined in the following list:

- *Normal (full) backup*—Copies all selected files and marks each file as having been backed up (the archive attribute is cleared). Only the most recent copy of the backup file is required to perform restoration.

- *Incremental backup*—Copies only those files created or changed since the last normal or incremental backup; the archive attribute is then cleared. Using normal and incremental backups, you require the last normal backup and all incremental backups to perform restoration.
- *Copy backup*—Copies all selected files but does not mark each file as having been backed up (the archive attribute is not cleared). Copy backups have no effect on any other type of backup operation. Copy backups are most commonly used to create a full backup of data for a special purpose, such as a monthly backup of financial data that is to be archived at the corporate headquarters.
- *Daily backup*—Copies all selected files that have been modified the day the daily backup is performed; the archive attribute is not cleared in this case. Using normal and daily backups, you require the last normal backup and all daily backups to perform restoration. Unless your network has time every day in which the data you want to back up is not being used, such as between 6 p.m. and midnight, daily backups will almost certainly miss data to be backed up. For the most part, daily backups are not commonly used as part of a normal backup routine.
- *Differential backup*—Copies files created or changed since the last normal or incremental backup, but does not clear the archive attribute. Using normal and differential backups, you require the last normal backup and the last differential backup to perform restoration.

Using Windows Backup

Using the Backup utility consists of three distinct processes: creating one or more backup configurations, scheduling backups to occur automatically, and performing restorations.

Creating Backup Job Configurations

The Windows Backup utility makes it extremely simple to create a backup configuration. The basic steps to create the configuration are outlined next, although your options and decisions will vary depending on how your system and backup media devices are configured.

1. Open the Backup Wizard by selecting Start, Programs, Accessories, System Tools, Backup.
2. Click the Advanced Mode link to switch to Advanced mode of the Backup utility.

3. Start the Backup Wizard by clicking the Backup Wizard (Advanced) button from the main page of the Backup utility.
4. Click Next to dismiss the opening page of the wizard.
5. On the What to Back Up dialog box, shown in Figure 4.18, select the scope of the backup. Click Next to continue. If you choose to back up selected files and folders, proceed to step 6; otherwise, skip to step 7.

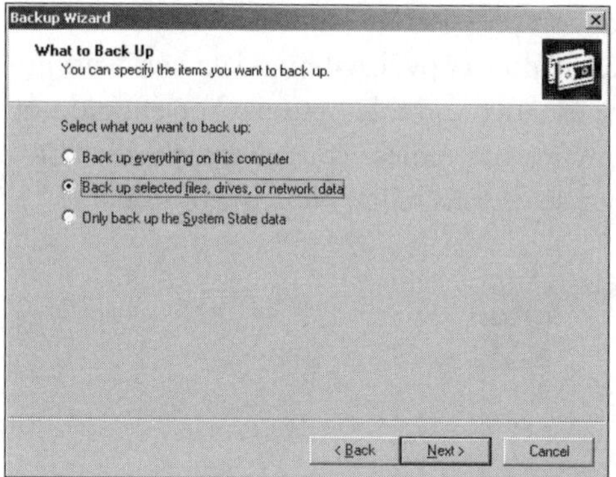

Figure 4.18 Select the scope of the backup that is to be performed.

The system state data contains information that is critical to the proper startup and operation of your Windows Server 2003 computer. The following items are included in the system state data:

- Registry
- COM+ class registration database
- Critical boot and system files
- System files that are protected by Windows File Protection
- Certificate Services database, if the server is a Certificate Authority
- Active Directory directory service, if the server is a domain controller
- SYSVOL directory, if the server is a domain controller
- Cluster Service information, if the server is a member of a cluster
- IIS metadirectory, if IIS is installed on the server

6. In the Items to Back Up dialog box, select the files and folders to back up. Click Next to continue.
7. In the Backup Type, Destination, and Name dialog box, choose the location to save the backup file (using the Browse button, if necessary) and enter the filename for the backup file. Click Next to continue.

8. The Completing the Backup Wizard dialog box appears. To configure advanced options, including scheduling and disabling volume shadow copy, click Advanced and proceed to step 9. If you want to perform this backup immediately, click Finish.
9. In the Type of Backup dialog box, select the type of backup you want. The default selection is Normal. Click Next to continue.
10. In the How to Back Up dialog box, shown in Figure 4.19, you can opt to verify data, enable hardware compression (if supported by your backup device), and disable volume shadow copy. Enabling data verification and hardware compression are usually desirable options. You should not disable the volume shadow copy feature, unless you have a specific reason to do so. After making your selections, click Next to continue.

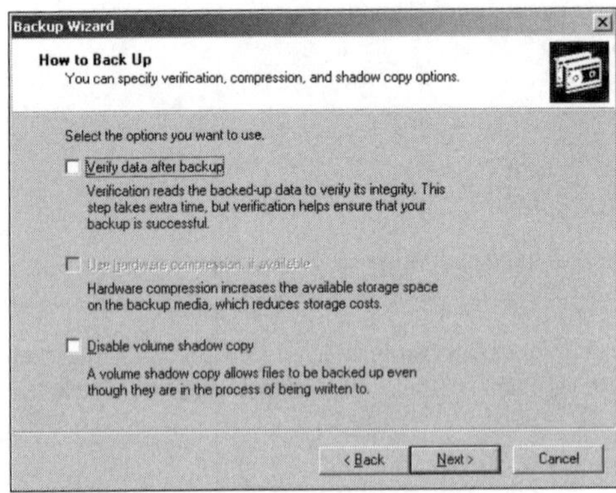

Figure 4.19 You should not disable the volume shadow copy feature without a valid reason to do so.

11. In the Backup Options dialog box, select whether to overwrite existing backup data on your media or to overwrite it. In the majority of cases, you simply overwrite the old data each night—especially if you are using one of the media-rotation methods discussed previously in this section. After making your selections, click Next to continue.
12. In the When to Back Up dialog box, shown in Figure 4.20, configure the data and time that you want to perform this backup job. Using the Set Schedule button enables you to configure the scheduling options for the backup; alternatively, you can run the backup immediately by leaving the Now radio button selected. After making your selections, click Next to continue.

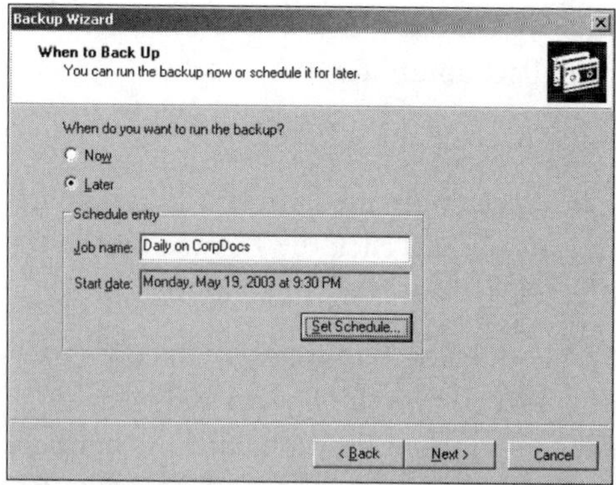

Figure 4.20 You can schedule backups to occur when your network will not be adversely affected.

13. If you selected Now, click Finish to complete the Backup Wizard and start the backup. If you selected Later, you are prompted for the username and password of a domain user account authorized to perform backups. Click Finish to complete the Backup Wizard—the backup will run at the date and time you selected.

Additionally, you can choose to create a backup configuration manually. However, you still must make all of the same decisions as when using the Backup Wizard.

Scheduling Backup Jobs

Managing a backup schedule is very easy in Windows Server 2003. In the Backup utility, simply switch to the Schedule Jobs tab. Each day on the calendar shows what type of backup is scheduled for that day. Holding the cursor over a backup displays the backup name. You can edit the backup properties, including rescheduling the backup by clicking it. You can also create new backup configurations by clicking the Add Job button.

Performing Restorations Using Windows Backup

If you ever need to put your backup system to the test, the actual process of performing the restoration is a relatively easy task in Windows Server 2003—as long as you are ready for the task. The basic steps to perform a restoration are outlined here, although your options and decisions will vary depending on how your system and backup media devices are configured:

1. Open the Backup Wizard by selecting Start, Programs, Accessories, System Tools, Backup.
2. Click the Advanced Mode link to switch to Advanced mode of the Backup utility.

3. Start the Restore Wizard by clicking the Restore Wizard (Advanced) button from the main page of the Backup utility.
4. Click Next to dismiss the opening page of the wizard.
5. In the What to Restore dialog box, select the medium and files that are to be restored. If your medium is not listed, click the Browse button to locate it. After making your selections, click Next to continue.
6. The Completing the Restore Wizard dialog box appears. To configure advanced options, including where to restore the files to and what to do with existing files found in the restoration location, click Advanced and proceed to step 7. If you want to perform this restoration immediately, click Finish.
7. In the Where to Restore dialog box, select the restoration location for the folders and files from the drop-down. Click Next to continue.
8. In the How to Restore dialog box, you decide what should occur if existing files are found in the restoration location. Click Next to continue.
9. In the Advanced Restore Options dialog box, shown in Figure 4.21, you can select from several advanced restoration options, as explained in the list following this procedure. The available options are determined by the data that has been backed up, the type of hardware installed in your server, and the role of the server. After making your selections, click Next to continue.

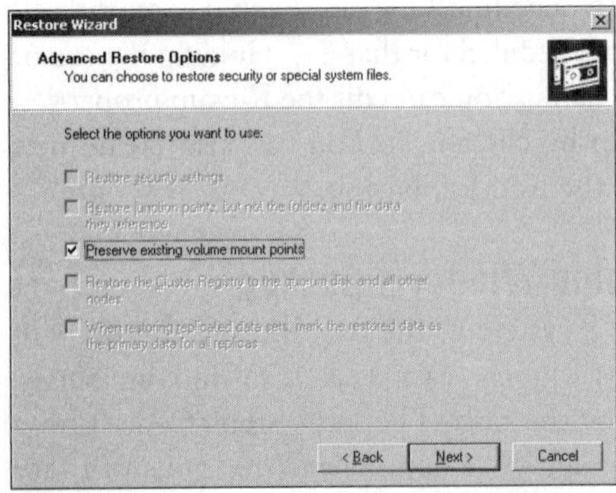

Figure 4.21 The Advanced Restore Options dialog box features several high-level configuration options.

10. Click Finish to start the restoration.
11. The Restore Progress dialog box appears, informing you of the status of the restoration.

The Advanced Restore Options are explained in the following list:

- *Restore security Settings*—Restores security settings for each file and folder. These include permissions, auditing entries, and ownership information. This option is available only for data that was backed up from an NTFS-formatted volume.
- *Restore Junction Points, and Restore File and Folder Data Under Junction Points to the Original Location*—Restores all junction points to your hard disks, along with the data that the junction points point to. If you are restoring a mounted drive and you want to restore the data that is on the mounted drive, you must select this check box. If you do not select this check box, you will restore only the folder containing the mounted drive.
- *Restore Junction Points, but Not the Folders and File Data They Reference*—Restores junction points only to your hard drive. It does not restore any folders or file data that reference the junction points.
- *When Restoring Replicated Data Sets, Mark the Restored Data as the Primary Data for All Replicas*—Performs a restoration and ensures that the restored File Replication Service (FRS) data is replicated to other configured servers.
- *Restore the Cluster Registry to the Quorum Disk and All Other Nodes*—Ensures that the cluster quorum database is restored and is also replicated on all nodes in the cluster.
- *Preserve Existing Volume Mount Points*—Prevents the restore operation from writing over any volume mount points that you have created on the partition or volume you are restoring data to.
- *Restore Removable Storage Database*—Restores the Removable Storage database and deletes the existing Removable Storage database. If you are not using Removable Storage to manage storage media, you do not need to select this option.

A junction point is a physical location on a hard disk that points to data located at another location on your hard disk or another storage device. Junction points are created when you create a mounted drive.

With the discussion of the Windows Backup utility behind us, we can move forward and examine a new feature in Windows Server 2003: Automated System Recovery.

Using Automated System Recovery

Making regular backups is an important task to accomplish, but those backups will be of no use to you if a server suffers a critical failure that prevents it from starting normally. Although you can use the `ntbackup.exe` command to create backups from the command line, you cannot perform restorations from the command line—a serious limitation if you cannot start a Windows Server 2003 computer normally.

As discussed previously, you can use ASR to restore the operating system to a previous state, which enables you to start Windows Server 2003 if other methods do not work. You should always consider ASR your last resort for recovery, after Safe Mode, the Recovery Console, and Last Known Good Configuration (LKGC).

ASR is a two-part process that uses a startup floppy disk and the original Windows installation CD-ROM to boot the Windows Server 2003 computer and a backup file (that must be accessible during ASR restoration) containing the system state, system services, and all disks associated with the operating system components. The startup disk contains information about the backup, the disk configurations, and how restoration is to be accomplished.

For an ASR recovery to be effective, you must keep it up-to-date. You should create a new ASR set after any configuration change to the server. In addition, you should create a new ASR set on a regular schedule, just as you would with a normal backup set.

Although you can create an ASR set without having a floppy drive installed in the server, you cannot perform the ASR restoration process without one.

To create a new ASR set, perform the following steps:

1. Place a blank, formatted 1.44MB 3-1/2 inch floppy disk in your server's floppy drive.
2. Open the Backup Wizard by selecting Start, Programs, Accessories, System Tools, Backup.
3. Click the Advanced Mode link to switch to Advanced mode of the Backup utility.
4. Start the Automated System Recovery Preparation Wizard by clicking the Automated System Recovery Wizard button from the main page of the Backup utility.

5. Click Next to dismiss the opening page of the Wizard.
6. In the Backup Destination dialog box, provide the path and filename of the backup file to be created. Click Next to continue.
7. Click Finish to close the Wizard and start the ASR set creation process.
8. Ensure that the blank, formatted floppy disk is inserted in your server's floppy drive when prompted. Click OK to create the startup floppy disk.

To perform an ASR recovery (after all other available methods to start the server normally have failed), perform the following steps. However, before starting the procedure, locate the following items and have them readily available:

- The correct (up-to-date) ASR startup floppy disk.
- The correct (up-to-date) ASR backup medium.
- The original Windows Server 2003 installation CD-ROM.
- Special drivers required for any mass storage controllers located in your server that are not available on the Windows Server 2003 CD-ROM. These will also need to be available on floppy disk.

Following are the steps for performing an ASR recovery:

1. Power on the server to be recovered using ASR.
2. Insert your original Windows Server 2003 CD into the CD-ROM drive.
3. When prompted to start from the CD-ROM, press the appropriate key.
4. If you need a special mass storage driver, press F6 when prompted to install it.
5. Press F2 when prompted to initiate ASR recovery.
6. Insert the ASR startup floppy disk
7. Follow the directions that are displayed.
8. If you need a special mass storage driver, press F6 when prompted to install it after the server restarts.
9. Follow the directions that are displayed.

That's all there is to using Automated System Recovery. Remember, however, that ASR is your last option and should not be used without attempting all other available methods to start the server.

Exam Prep Questions

Question 1

Christopher needs to back up the contents of a data folder on his server, but he does not have a tape drive. What other media can he use with Windows Backup?

- ❍ A. CD-ROM
- ❍ B. Floppy disk
- ❍ C. Text dump
- ❍ D. No other media can be used

Answer B is correct. In addition to tape drives, Windows Backup can store to any local or network drive. Answers A, C, and D are incorrect because only the floppy disk is a valid choice.

Question 2

Andrea is your newly hired assistant network administrator. She has been asking you recently about highly available solutions using Windows Server 2003. She tells you that she has heard of the phrase "five nines" but doesn't understand what it means. What is the correct answer that you should tell her regarding the meaning of the phrase "five nines"?

- ❍ A. "Five nines" means that servers must be up for at least 99,999 minutes per year.
- ❍ B. "Five nines" means that servers cannot ever have 99.999% CPU utilization.
- ❍ C. "Five nines" means that servers must be up for at least 99.999% of the time per year.
- ❍ D. "Five nines" means that all servers must have a minimum of five 90GB hard drives.

Answer C is correct. The phrase "five nines" refers to server (or service/application) availability and means that the server must be available for client requests at least 99.999% of the time—this equates to only 5.25 minutes of downtime per year. Answers A, B, and D are incorrect because they don't represent the standard of 5.25 minutes of downtime per year.

Question 3

Jean is the network administrator for a small company. Knowing that critical data must be recoverable, he has been doing normal backups every Friday night. Recently, he was forced to recover data lost on a Thursday from his last backup. Doing so has caused him to rethink the need for the frequency of backups. He has decided that he needs to back up his server every day. He does not care how long it will take to recover the data. However, he does want to minimize the time it will take to run the daily backup.

Required Result:

Data must be backed up at the end of every day.

Optional Desired Results:

Data must be recoverable in the shortest period of time possible (on average).

Data must be backed up in the shortest period of time possible (on average).

Proposed Solution:

Schedule a normal backup for each night.

Analysis:

Which result(s) does the proposed solution produce?

- ❍ A. This solution produces the required result as well as both optional results.
- ❍ B. This solution produces the required result and one of the optional desired results.
- ❍ C. This solution produces the required result but does not fulfill either of the optional desired results.
- ❍ D. This solution does not meet the required result.

Answer B is correct. Doing a full backup at the end of every day fulfills the required result. It also fulfills the optional result of being able to recover the data in the shortest period of time (on average). Because you need to consult only one tape to recover, this solution provides quick recovery. It does not provide quick backups, however, because Jean is saving all data every day. Answer A is incorrect because only one optional result is met. Answer C is incorrect because one of the two optional results are met. Answer D is incorrect because this solution produces the required result and one of the optional results.

Question 4

Austin is interviewing for the position of assistant server reliability administrator in your organization. You are asking Austin questions during the technical proficiency portion of his interview. You have asked him what types of highly available solutions Windows Server 2003 provides. What correct answers should Austin provide you? (Choose all that apply.)

- ❑ A. Network load balancing
- ❑ B. Windows File Protection
- ❑ C. Clustering
- ❑ D. Redundant power supplies

Answers A and C are correct. Windows Server 2003 provides network load balancing and MSCS clustering services to create highly available server solutions. Windows File Protection is a reliability feature, not an availability feature, so answer B is incorrect. Installing redundant power supplies makes servers more reliable as well, but not necessarily more available; thus, answer D is incorrect.

Question 5

Jean is the network administrator for a small company. Knowing that critical data must be recoverable, he has been doing normal backups every Friday night. Recently, Jean was forced to recover data lost on a Thursday from his last backup. Doing so has caused him to rethink the need for the frequency of backups. He has decided that he needs to back up his server every day. He would like the data to be recoverable in as short a period of time possible, but he would rather minimize the time it takes to do the daily backup.

Required Result:

Data must be backed up at the end of every day.

Optional Results:

Data must be recoverable in the shortest period of time possible (on average).

Data must be backed up in the shortest period of time possible (on average).

Proposed Solution:

Retain the Friday schedule for normal backups and add incremental backups Monday through Thursday.

Analysis:

Which result(s) does the proposed solution produce?

- A. This solution produces the required result as well as both optional results.
- B. This solution produces the required result and one of the optional desired results.
- C. This solution produces the required result but does not fulfill either of the optional desired results.
- D. This solution does not meet the required result.

Answer B is correct. By doing a normal backup once a week and incremental backups on all other days, Jean ensures that all the data is backed up. In addition, he ensures that daily backups are quick because an incremental backup records only changes made on the day it is invoked. An incremental backup will not recover data quickly (on average) because Jean will generally have to recover from a normal backup and an incremental backup (at least one) to recover data. Answer A is incorrect because only one of the two optional results is achieved. Answer C is incorrect because one of the two optional results is achieved. Answer D is incorrect because the required result and one of the optional results are achieved.

Question 6

Which of the following gives the best description of clustering?

- A. Clustering distributes all incoming client connection requests to its nodes via a mathematical algorithm.
- B. Clustering distributes all incoming client connection requests to its nodes via a round-robin system.
- C. Clustering allows multiple nodes to appear as a single system to clients.
- D. Clustering allows for the use of multiple CPUs in a server.

Answer C is correct. Clustering is accomplished when you group independent servers into one collective entity that is accessed as if it were a single system. Network load balancing distributes all incoming client requests using a mathematical algorithm, so answer A is incorrect. Neither clustering nor network load balancing uses a round-robin system, so answer B is incorrect. Clustering does not affect how many CPUs can be used in a server, so answer D is incorrect.

Question 7

Deanna needs to back up critical data on her server. However, she does not have enough backup tapes to back up everything on her server. She wants to make sure that, in addition to the user data she is backing up, she backs up the Registry on her server. What should Deanna select in addition to the data files that she wants to back up?

- ❍ A. C:
- ❍ B. System State
- ❍ C. My Documents
- ❍ D. My Computer

Answer B is correct. To back up (and, hence, recover) the Registry, you must back up the system state information for a local server. The only way to ensure that the Registry is backed up is to back up the System State data; thus, answers A, C, and D are incorrect.

Question 8

Which of the following gives the best description of network load balancing?

- ❍ A. Network load balancing distributes all incoming client connection requests to its nodes via a mathematical algorithm.
- ❍ B. Network load balancing distributes all incoming client connection requests to its nodes via a round-robin system.
- ❍ C. Network load balancing allows multiple nodes to appear as a single system to clients.
- ❍ D. Network load balancing allows for the use of multiple CPUs in a server.

Answer A is correct. Network load balancing (NLB) distributes all incoming connection requests using a mathematical algorithm to members of the NLB cluster. Neither clustering nor network load balancing uses a round-robin system; thus, answer B is incorrect. Clustering allows many servers to appear as a single server, so answer C is incorrect. Network load balancing does not affect how many CPUs can be used in a server, so answer D is incorrect.

Question 9

Wesley is the IT manager for a large Internet service provider. To make sure the Web servers (running Windows 2000 Server) are easily recoverable in case of a hardware failure, he wants to set a policy regarding the recovery tools available at each server. Each of these servers is running Windows 2000 Server and has a 4mm DAT drive attached. Wesley's bottom line is that each server must be fully recoverable. In addition, he wants to be able to easily recover small errors caused by mistakes that people sometimes make or by corruption in operating system files. Unfortunately, he does not have budgeted funds to purchase any additional software or hardware.

Required Result:

All Web servers must be fully recoverable with data loss of no more than 12 elapsed hours of work.

No third-party tools can be purchased.

Optional Desired Results:

In the case of service errors preventing restart, servers must be recoverable without reinstallation of operating system.

In the case of start file loss or corruption, servers must be recoverable without reinstallation of the operating system.

Proposed Solution:

Schedule a normal backup once a week for all servers. Configure all servers to boot to the Recovery Console when chosen.

Analysis:

Which result(s) does the proposed solution produce?

❍ A. This solution produces the required result as well as both optional results.

❍ B. This solution produces the required result and one of the optional desired results.

❍ C. This solution produces the required result but does not fulfill either of the optional desired results.

❍ D. This solution does not meet the required result.

Answer D is correct. Although he is on the right track, Wesley has missed an important requirement: Data loss (and downtime) must never last more than 12 hours. By scheduling a backup for once a week, he cannot come anywhere near that promise unless the data loss occurred late in the day on the day the backup was done. Answers A, B, and C are incorrect because neither the required result nor the optional results is produced by this solution.

Question 10

When referring to the process of convergence, what are you referring to?

- ❍ A. A network communication sent among individual cluster nodes at intervals of no more than 500ms that is used to determine the status of all cluster nodes
- ❍ B. The process of a cluster group moving back to the preferred node after the preferred node has resumed cluster membership
- ❍ C. The process by which NLB clustering hosts determine a new, stable state among themselves and elect a new default host after the failure of one or more cluster nodes
- ❍ D. The process of a cluster group moving from the currently active node to another still-functioning node in the cluster group

Answer C is correct. Convergence is the process by which NLB clustering hosts determine a new, stable state among themselves and elect a new default host after the failure of one or more cluster nodes. The heartbeat is used to determine the status of cluster nodes, so answer A is incorrect. Failback is the process of a cluster group moving back to its preferred node, so answer B is incorrect. Failover is the process of a cluster group moving to a functioning node within the cluster, so answer D is incorrect.

Need to Know More?

Windows Server 2003 Deployment Kit: Planning Server Deployments, `http://go.microsoft.com/fwlink/?LinkId=15309`.

Clustering Services Technology Center, `www.microsoft.com/windowsserver2003/technologies/clustering/default.mspx`.

Storage Services Technology Center, `www.microsoft.com/windowsserver2003/technologies/storage/default.mspx`.

Bixler, Dave and Will Schmied. *MCSE Training Guide 70-291: Implementing, Managing, and Maintaining a Microsoft Windows Server 2003 Network Infrastructure*. Indianapolis, Indiana: Que Publishing, 2003.

Scales, Lee. *MCSE Training Guide 70-290: Managing and Maintaining a Microsoft Windows Server 2003 Environment*. Indianapolis, Indiana: Que Publishing, 2003.

Planning and Maintaining Secure Networks

Terms you'll need to understand:

✓ 802.1x

✓ Extensible Authentication Protocol (EAP)

✓ IP Security (IPSec)

✓ Internet key exchange (IKE)

✓ Microsoft Management Console (MMC)

✓ RADIUS

✓ Remote Assistance

✓ Remote Desktop for Administration

✓ Remote Desktop Protocol

✓ Terminal Services

✓ Transport mode

✓ Tunnel mode

✓ Wireless LAN (WLAN)

Techniques you'll need to master:

✓ Create and configure Remote Assistance requests

✓ Configure Remote Assistance policies

✓ Create and configure Remote Desktop for Administration connections

✓ Configure Remote Desktop policies

✓ Create and configure wireless LAN security policies

✓ Create and configure IPSec policies

Network security—these two words make many administrators tremble. However, this does not have to be the case. As you've already seen, Windows Server 2003 is more secure than any version to precede it. You, the administrator, must take what Microsoft has given you and make it your own. You must take the tools and building blocks provided in Windows Server 2003 and create a working security solution for your network. But how do you do that in today's network environment, where you have clients connecting over wireless LANs (WLANs), clients at remote locations that need your expert assistance, servers at remote locations that require remote administration, and sensitive corporate data that must be protected from eavesdropping even when passed along your own internal network? The challenges are many, and the learning curve can be steep. Fortunately, you're up to the challenge.

Planning Secure Remote Administration Methods

Since Windows 2000 first appeared on the market, one of the great features that Microsoft has slowly been evolving is built-in remote administrative capabilities. You no longer have to purchase and install a costly third-party application to provide remote administrative access to your servers and workstations; Windows XP and Windows Server 2003 support it natively, as does the Windows 2000 Server line after installing Terminal Services in Remote Administration mode. Better yet, Windows XP and Windows Server 2003 also include the Remote Desktop Connection utility, which further takes advantage of the Remote Desktop Protocol (RDP) by allowing users to connect to a computer remotely as if they were actually using it locally.

Remote Assistance

Remote Assistance, first introduced in Windows XP, provides a built-in mechanism allowing an "Expert" to lend assistance to a "Novice" upon request. The Expert can be located on the same internal network or even somewhere else on the Internet. Remote Assistance allows the Expert to create a connection to the Novice's computer, view the desktop, communicate with the Novice, and even take remote control of the Novice's computer if the Novice allows. Remote Assistance can be performed only on computers running Windows XP or Windows Server 2003—a good reason to consider that desktop upgrade to Windows XP—and is an integral part of the operating system default installation. Before a computer is eligible to receive Remote Assistance, however, it must be enabled either locally or by Group Policy.

Assuming that Group Policy has not been configured from its default setting for Remote Assistance, you can enable it on the local computer by selecting Turn on Remote Assistance and Allow Invitations to Be Sent from This Computer. This command can be found on the Remote tab of the System Properties applet (located in the Control Panel).

Clicking the Advanced button opens the Remote Assistance Settings dialog box, which enables you to further configure Remote Assistance settings. From this dialog box, you have the option to allow the computer to be remotely controlled during the Remote Assistance session by selecting the option Allow This Computer to Be Controlled Remotely. You can also configure the length of time for which the Remote Assistance requests are valid.

Alternatively, you can configure Group Policy to control the Remote Assistance settings for your entire domain or by specific domains. The settings that you need to configure are located in the Computer Configuration, Administrative Templates, System, Remote Assistance node, shown in Figure 5.1. If settings are configured via Group Policy, the option to configure them locally using the System Properties applet will not be available. Recall that Group Policy is applied in the following order: local, site, domain, OU.

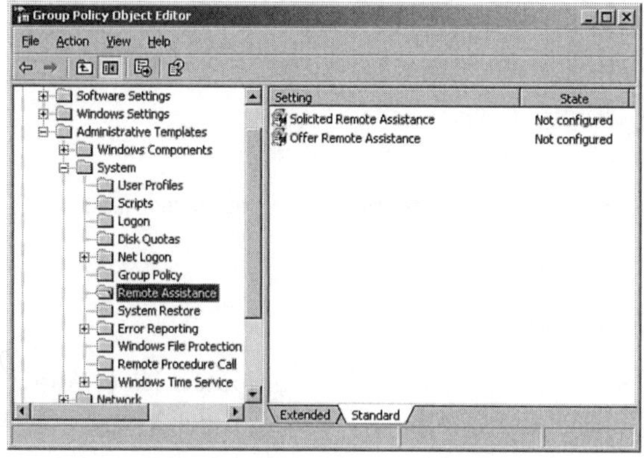

Figure 5.1 Remote Assistance can be configured using Group Policy.

The Solicited Remote Assistance setting, shown in Figure 5.1, is used to allow Remote Assistance requests to be sent from the computers to which the Group Policy Object (GPO) is applied. The Offer Remote Assistance setting shown in Figure 5.1 allows Remote Assistance to be offered without a previous request to computers to which the GPO is applied. The user (Novice) still has the option to allow or disallow the Remote Assistance offer.

Configuring Remote Assistance Policies

To configure Remote Assistance policies using Group Policy, which is always the preferred method, perform the following steps:

1. Locate the GPO for which you want to configure the Remote Assistance settings.
2. Expand the following nodes: Computer Configuration, Administrative Templates, System, and Remote Assistance.
3. Double-click the Solicited Remote Assistance setting to open its Properties dialog box (see Figure 5.2).

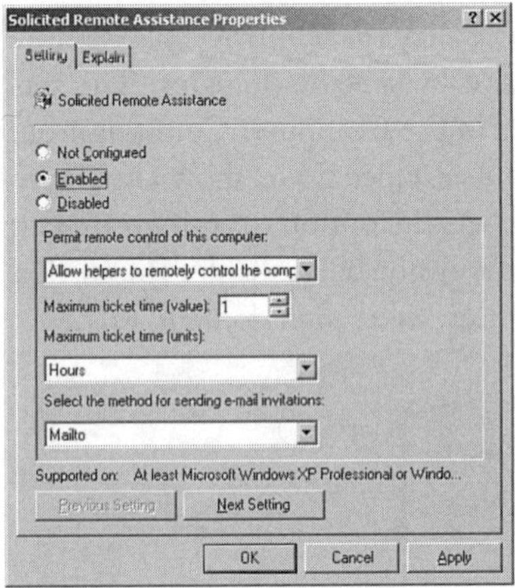

Figure 5.2 The Solicited Remote Assistance setting enables users of the computer to request Remote Assistance.

4. Select the Enabled radio button.
5. For the option Permit Remote Control of This Computer, select Allow Helpers to Remotely Control the Computer, to ensure that your Experts can fully offer Remote Assistance as needed. The Expert can take control only if the Novice allows it.
6. For the Maximum Ticket Time option, configure a reasonable lifetime for the Remote Assistance request, such as one hour. This gives the Expert a window in which to respond to the request without creating an overly large security risk.
7. For the option Select Method for Sending Email Invitations, your selection depends on the messaging client in use on your network. The Mailto option configures the Remote Assistance request to be sent as

an Internet link and works in virtually all situations. The SMAPI (Simple Messaging Application Program Interface) option configures the request to be attached to the message.

8. Click OK to close the Solicited Remote Assistance Properties dialog box.
9. Double-click the Offer Remote Assistance setting to open its Properties dialog box, shown in Figure 5.3.

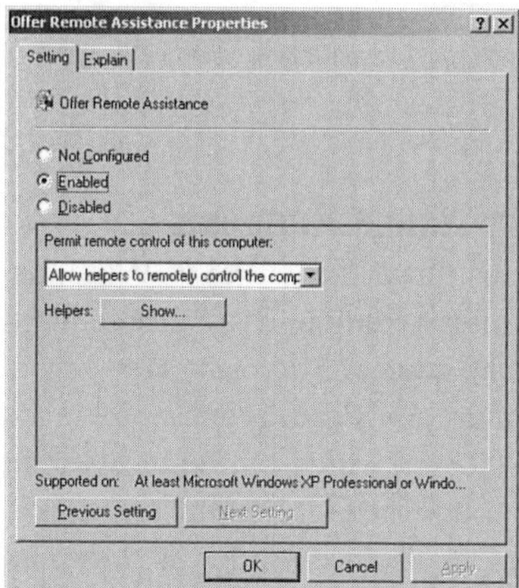

Figure 5.3 The Offer Remote Assistance setting enables Experts to offer unsolicited Remote Assistance to users.

10. To allow Experts to offer unsolicited Remote Assistance to users, select the Enabled radio button.
11. For the option Permit Remote Control of This Computer, select Allow Helpers to Remotely Control the Computer, to ensure that your Experts can fully offer Remote Assistance as needed. The Expert can take control only if the Novice allows it.
12. Click the Show button to open the Show Contents dialog box, shown in Figure 5.4.
13. To add users and/or groups, click the Add button. You can add only one object at a time, and you must use one of the following formats:

    <Domain Name>\<User Name>

    <Domain Name>\<Group Name>

14. Click OK to close the Offer Remote Assistance Properties dialog box.

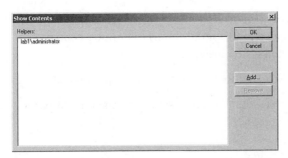

Figure 5.4 You must manually add the selected users and groups to which you want to offer unsolicited Remote Assistance.

Sending and Managing Remote Assistance Requests

Users can request Remote Assistance in three basic ways: Windows Messenger, email (sends a URL), or file (creates a Remote Assistance request file). Note that Windows Messenger is not the same as Microsoft Messenger, although both use similar technologies. Remote Assistance requests are most easily sent by using the Help and Support Center, which can be accessed at Start, Help and Support. On the main page, click the Get Remote Assistance link under the Support column. The Remote Assistance window is shown in Figure 5.5.

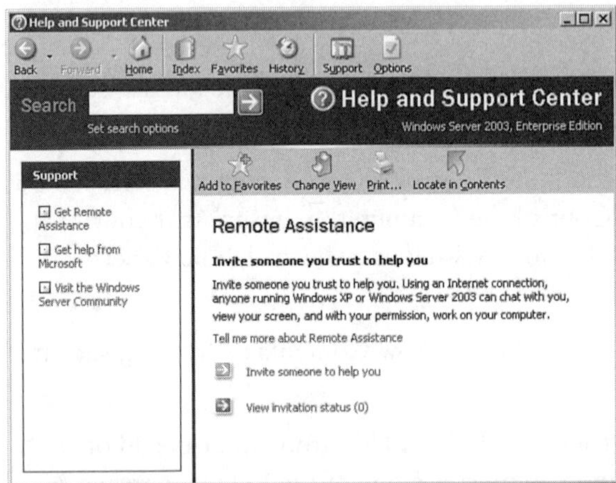

Figure 5.5 Remote Assistance requests can be easily sent and managed from within the Help and Support Center.

To send a Remote Assistance request, perform the following steps:

1. Open the Help and Support Center by clicking Start, Help and Support.
2. Click the Get Remote Assistance link under the Support column.

3. On the Remote Assistance window, shown in Figure 5.5, click the Invite Someone to Help You link.
4. The easiest way to ask for Remote Assistance is to use Windows Messenger. Note that Windows Messenger is not installed in Windows Server 2003. You can download the Windows XP version (which works perfectly in Windows Server 2003) from `www.microsoft.com/windows/messenger/download.asp`.
5. The Remote Assistance window changes, enabling you to pick how to contact the assistant (the Expert). Windows Messenger, email, and file methods are available.
6. Selecting a Windows Messenger user and clicking Invite This Person causes the Windows Messenger window to open on the Expert's computer with the Remote Assistance request. The Expert can then accept or decline the invitation, thus beginning the Remote Assistance session.
7. Alternatively, you can opt to send an email request using your MAPI-compliant messaging application, such as Outlook or Outlook Express, by entering the Expert's first name and clicking Continue.
8. The next window enables you to enter a password and duration for the request to remain valid. Click the Create Email Invitation button to proceed.
9. A new email message opens. You must enter the correct email address and add any other notes that you want before sending the message. The Expert can initiate the Remote Assistance request by clicking on the URL in the message and is required to download and install an ActiveX applet from the Microsoft Web site as part of the process.
10. Your last option is to create a Remote Assistance file and either give the file to the Expert or place it where the Expert can access it, such as on a file share. You can create the Remote Assistance file by clicking Send Invitation as a File (Advanced). You can configure the name of the Expert, the duration for which the request should remain valid, and the password when creating the saved file. Remote Assistance request saved files have the *.msrcincident file extension.

Remote Assistance requests can be viewed and managed by clicking the View Invitation Status (*x*) link, shown in Figure 5.5. The *x* represents the number of Remote Assistance requests that you have to manage; in Figure 5.5, this number is 0. Clicking this link changes the window so that you can manage your Remote Assistance requests.

For each Remote Assistance request, the following options are available:

- *Details*—Enables you to view details about the request, including to whom it was sent, when it was sent, when it will expire, the current status, and whether it is password protected.
- *Expire*—Enables you to force an open request to expire immediately, regardless of its configured duration.
- *Resend*—Enables you to resend an expired request. Resending expired requests is an easy way to send the same request again without needing to re-enter all of the required details.
- *Delete*—Enables you to permanently delete the request.

Using Remote Assistance

Regardless of how the Remote Assistance request has been sent, the end result is the same. After the Expert has accepted the request, a direct connection is made between the Expert's computer and the Novice's computer that allows the Expert to communicate directly with the Novice and to see the Novice's desktop in Screen View Only mode, as in Figure 5.6.

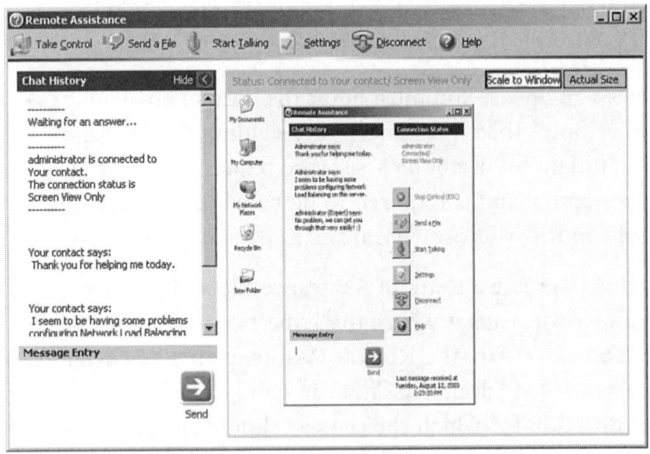

Figure 5.6 The Expert is initially limited to a Screen View Only connection.

The following control buttons are available to the Expert:

- *Take Control*—Sends a request to the Novice to allow the Expert to take control of the Novice's computer.
- *Send a File*—Allows the Expert to transmit a file from the Expert's computer to the Novice's computer. This is useful in sending updates and such.

- *Start Talking*—Establishes an audio connection between the Expert and the Novice similar to that offered in Windows Messenger or Net Meeting.
- *Settings*—Allows the Expert to configure the Remote Assistance settings for the computer.
- *Disconnect*—Terminates the Remote Assistance session and closes the direct connection between the two computers.
- *Help*—Displays Remote Assistance help.

The following control buttons are available to the Novice:

- *Stop Control*—Terminates the Expert's ability to remotely control the computer.
- *Send a File*—Allows the Novice to transmit a file from the Novice's computer to the Expert's computer.
- *Start Talking*—Establishes an audio connection between the Expert and the Novice similar to that offered in Windows Messenger or Net Meeting.
- *Settings*—Allows the Expert to configure the Remote Assistance settings for the computer.
- *Disconnect*—Terminates the Remote Assistance session and closes the direct connection between the two computers.
- *Help*—Displays Remote Assistance help.

Remote Assistance Security Concerns

As with all the Terminal Services– and Remote Desktop Protocol–based applications, Remote Assistance requires that TCP port 3389 be available to make a connection. This raises the question of whether you want to leave this port open on your external firewalls. Logic says no. By closing this port on your external firewalls, you can instantly prevent the largest security risk associated with Remote Assistance: compromise by unauthorized external entities. There is really no reason why any person outside of your protected, private internal network should be tasked with providing Remote Assistance. If this situation arises, consider implementing leased WAN links directly between sites or using permanent VPN connections to give some extra security measure.

But what do you do about the Remote Assistance request itself? The email is sent by default as a standard email message and is thus subject to capture and viewing. In addition, the Remote Assistance files are simply XML files that are easily taken apart. Email messages can and should be digitally signed and encrypted. If your network is using Exchange 2000 or later with Outlook 2000 or later, this is an easy fix. If you are not, consider acquiring a personal email certificate, or using Pretty Good Privacy (PGP) or some other message encryption and signing utility. You should protect the Remote Assistance files by whatever means are available, including NTFS permissions, Encrypted File System (EFS) encryption, or other third-party methods. Windows XP and Windows Server 2003 give multiple EFS users access to the same file.

Remote Desktop for Administration

Remote Desktop for Administration, previously referred to as Remote Administration mode in Windows 2000, provides a built-in method to remotely administer and control servers. If you have the correct credentials, you can even remotely restart or shut down a server—of course, you should probably warn any users who might be connected to it before doing so!

You can use Remote Desktop for Administration in one of two ways. The first—and simplest (although less feature rich)—is to use the Remote Desktop Connection utility, which can be found by clicking Start, Programs, Accessories, Communications, Remote Desktop Connection. After you have clicked the Options button, the Remote Desktop Connection dialog box opens (see Figure 5.7).

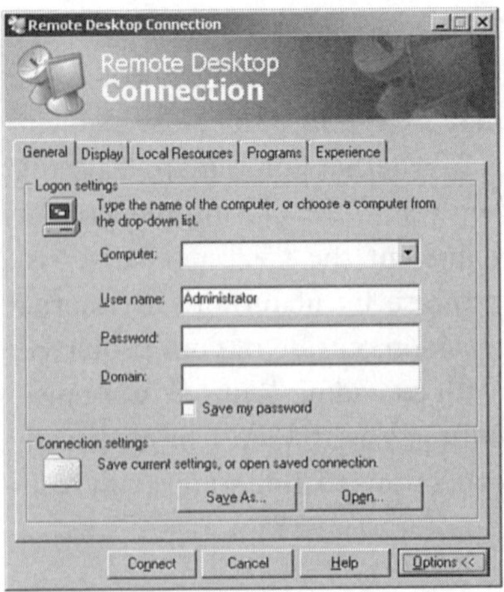

Figure 5.7 The Remote Desktop Connection utility enables you to quickly and easily create a connection to a remote computer.

By entering the computer's name or IP address and clicking Connect, you can make a Remote Desktop for Administration connection. You might be required to supply your network credentials to complete the connection and logon process.

You can also create Remote Desktop for Administration connections using the new Remote Desktops Microsoft Management Console (MMC). This method offers the following two fantastic features, for which Windows administrators have been clamoring since the introduction of Terminal Services:

- Multiple connection profiles can be created. You can configure multiple connections in the Remote Desktops MMC console and then switch through them quickly and easily, all within the confines of a single window. The multiple windows required when using the Remote Desktop Connection utility or the Terminal Services client are not required.
- Connections are made directly to the console session. In the past, Terminal Services connections could not be made to the console session, preventing many administrators from using Terminal Services for remote administration or prompting the use of third-party applications such as PC Anywhere or VNC. Windows Server 2003, using the Remote Desktops console, now creates connections to the console session, allowing administrators to view messages and pop-ups that are not redirected to any other session. In addition, you can use the `/console` switch on the Remote Desktop Client to create a console connection.

Figure 5.8 shows the Remote Desktops console with a connection in progress.

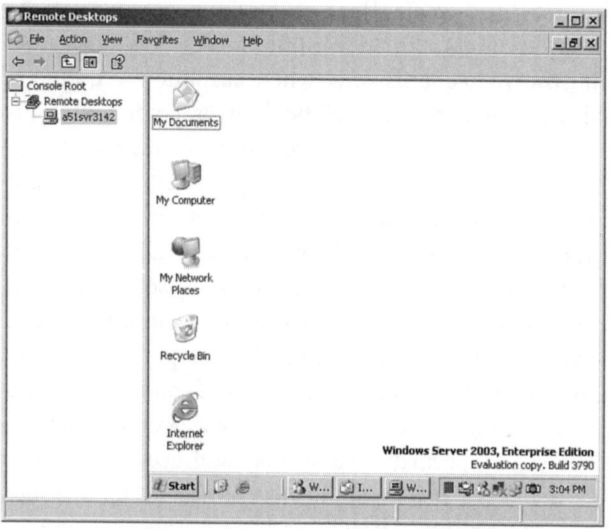

Figure 5.8 The Remote Desktops console is the best way to manage multiple servers remotely.

It's important to note that the Windows 2000 Terminal Services Web Client is still around in Windows Server 2003, although with a new name and many improvements. It is now known as the Remote Desktop Web Connection utility.

Remote Desktop for Administration Security and Management Issues

Remote Desktop for Administration, like the Terminal Services Administration mode before it, is fairly restrictive with regard to who can use it and how it can be used:

- Only administrators can create Remote Desktop for Administration connections, by default—this is a good thing. You want the number of users with this power to be as small as possible, to minimize the risk of an attacker gaining complete control over your network. Access control is provided through membership in the Remote Desktop Users group.
- Only two Remote Desktop sessions can exist on a computer, and *both* active and disconnected (but still running) sessions count toward this number. This is done so that the number of concurrent changes being made to a computer is minimized to prevent configuration errors and conflicts. However, this does present a potential for a denial-of-service (DoS) attack against a computer—or, at least, the Remote Desktop portion. In addition to these two connections, one other connection to the server's console session can exist.

Because only administrators can create Remote Desktop connections by default, the use of these accounts should be minimized. Administrators should use their administrative accounts only when absolutely required—and, even then, should make judicious use of the Run As command. This simply makes good network security sense and is part of the principle of least privilege. Using the principle of least privilege, a compromised user account has a smaller impact on the network's overall security than if you were to blanket-assign permissions to users that they did not need. Ideally, all normal user operations should be carried out in the context of a user account. If additional privileges are required for a specific reason, the administrator can either log in to the network with a special account for the purpose of performing those actions, or use the Run As command to perform those actions within the context of the account that has the additional privileges. In addition, you will want to enforce strong security precautions and account-lockout policies on all accounts that have the capability to connect using Remote Desktop—Chapter 8, "Managing and Maintaining User Authentication and the Active Directory Infrastructure," explores these topics in more detail.

Although the Remote Desktop Connection utility offers the capability to create and save connection configurations on a local computer, this practice should be avoided, if at all possible. Connection configurations are saved to a computer that contains all of the Remote Desktop Connection settings in a plain-text file with the file extension of *.RDP. Although the password (if entered) is encoded, it is only a matter of time before an application is written that will be capable of quickly decoding this information. Even if an attacker does not decode the password, all required information is available to establish the Remote Desktop connection and begin wreaking havoc on your network.

A question that often arises with Remote Desktop is, what do you do about disconnected sessions? How long should the timeout value be for these disconnected sessions? There is no hard, fast answer for these questions. Consider the situation in which an administrator has made a Remote Desktop connection to a server and begun the process of applying a service pack. After starting the installation, the administrator disconnects from the server and begins working on another server. Would you really want to impose a timeout limit or manually terminate the session? You must spend some time considering the requirements of your network and how you will meet them to avoid problems down the road. Session timeout values can be configured as granular, as by specific users, so this is an option that you might want to configure. A special shared administrative account can be used that has no timeout values configured on it—when this account is used to create a Remote Desktop connection, all operations can proceed without danger of automatically timing out. This also allows individual administrators to make connections to the server, as required to perform other tasks, provided that the Log Off of the Server When Completed option is selected. Remember that shutting down or restarting a server from a Remote Desktop session causes that action to occur on the server if the user has the required permissions—be careful when using the Shut Down Windows dialog box.

On test day, be aware of the various means that Windows Server 2003 provides to establish connections to remote computers. Remote Assistance and Remote Desktop for Administration each include several smaller parts that you will want to know about.

Planning Wireless LAN (WLAN) Security

It's an inescapable fact of today's computing environment that users want to be connected while on the move. For users, the use of a wireless local-area network (WLAN) translates to the power to move freely about an office or even an entire building without being wired to the wall. For administrators, this usually means headaches, heartaches, and visions of hackers silently sifting through the network. Fortunately, the latter doesn't have to be the case.

Although the WLAN security functionality provided in Windows Server 2003 is in no way intended to replace a dedicated solution that is available from a company that specializes in WLAN technologies, it is a good start for smaller organizations and a nice addition to existing security measures in larger organizations.

In Windows Server 2003, administrators can now use Group Policy to design and implement security policies to secure 802.11 WLANs. It supports the use of both Wired Equivalent Privacy (WEP) and 802.1*x* authentication. The Group Policy options that are configured in a GPO and applied to a computer then take precedence over any user-configured settings, thus ensuring that your configuration is applied. You can create policies for the following three types of WLANs:

- *Access point (infrastructure)*—The most common type of wireless LAN, the infrastructure mode WLAN consists of wireless clients communicating directly with wireless access points (APs). No direct client-to-client communications exist. This is considered the most secure type of WLAN.
- *Computer-to-computer (ad hoc)*—Ad hoc WLANs consist of wireless clients communicating directly with each other without using an AP in the middle. This type of communication does not provide a direct path to the wired network.
- *Any available network access point preferred*—This option configures the policy to attempt a connection to an AP first, if one is available. If an AP is not available, the client attempts to create an ad hoc connection, if possible. This method is least preferred and usually most problematic over time.

As shown in Figure 5.9, the WLAN Group Policy options can be located in the Computer Configuration, Windows Settings, Security Settings node. By default, no policies are defined, meaning that you must create and configure them as your network requires. We examine this process later in this section.

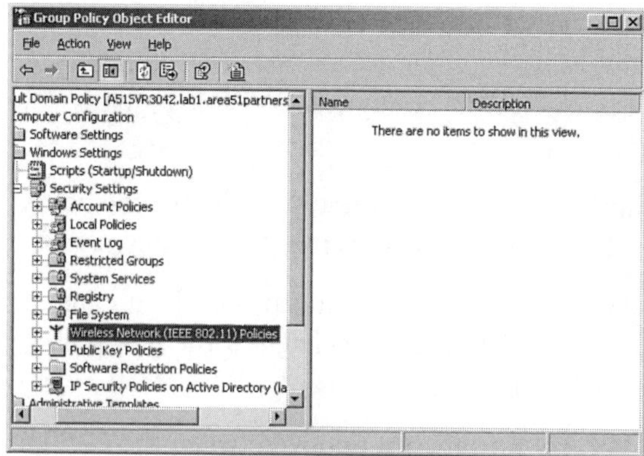

Figure 5.9 You can now configure WLAN policies for your Windows Server 2003 and Windows XP Professional computers.

Before creating a policy, you should spend some time planning for it. WLANs can greatly increase business productivity when implemented and secured properly. If you fail to plan properly for the security of your WLAN, you might just as well plan to fail. Consider the following key items with regard to authentication issues:

- Your APs must support the authentication method that you intend to use, such as 802.1*x*.
- Your clients and RADIUS servers must all support the same authentication method, such as Extensible Authentication Protocol–Transport Level Security (EAP-TLS) or Protected Extensible Authentication Protocol (PEAP) over 802.1*x*.
- Computers should always be authenticated; this option is enabled by default.
- If using EAP-TLS (as recommended), you should consider allowing the autoenrollment of certificates for users and computers. This makes the process much simpler.

When configuring and implementing WLAN security policies via Group Policy, you need to consider the following points with regard to their behavior:

- Configurations made in GPOs take precedence over user-configured settings, with the exception of the preferred networks list. The preferred networks lists are merged from the GPO settings and the user-configured settings to form a composite list. When the network list is merged, infrastructure networks always have higher precedence than ad hoc networks. Also, the user can change the configured WEP key that is assigned per Group Policy.

- As with all GPOs, nonadministrators cannot remove or disable the policy so that it will not apply to them. This also holds true for administrators.
- When GPO-configured WLAN settings are changed, the client connection is momentarily broken (the client is disassociated) if the new policy takes precedence over the old policy.
- When GPO-configured WLAN settings are removed (when the GPO is deleted or the link is removed), the client is disassociated while the Wireless Configuration Service performs a soft reset and clears its cache. When the service restarts, the client reverts to any existing client-configured settings in place.
- When a client is subject to multiple GPOs at various levels that assign WLAN settings, the normal Group Policy processing order applies. The GPO that is closest to the computer object takes precedence and overrides the settings that are assigned to a higher-level Active Directory (AD) container.

With your initial planning completed, you can begin the process of creating WLAN security policies using Group Policy, as follows:

1. Using either the Group Policy Management Console (GPMC) or the Group Policy Editor (GPE), locate the GPO in which you want to create the WLAN security policy.
2. Expand the Computer Configuration, Windows Settings, Security Settings nodes in the GPO to locate the Wireless Network (IEEE 802.11) Policies node. Right-click on it, and select Create Wireless Network Policy from the context menu. The Wireless Network Policy Wizard starts.
3. Click Next to dismiss the opening page of the wizard.
4. Enter a name and description for the new policy on the Wireless Network Policy Name dialog box. Click Next to continue.
5. The Completing the Wireless Network Policy Wizard dialog box appears. Ensure that the Edit Properties option is selected, and click Finish to exit the wizard and start configuring the policy properties.

6. As discussed in Table 5.1, the policy properties dialog box opens with the options available. Configure your selections as desired per the information in Table 5.1, and switch to the Preferred Networks tab.
7. Click the Add button to open the New Preferred Setting Properties dialog box.
8. On the Network Properties tab, configure the selections as you require, per the information in Table 5.2. When you are done, switch to the IEEE 802.1*x* tab.
9. On the IEEE 802.1*x* tab, configure the selections as you require, per the information in Table 5.3. When you are finished, click OK to commit the preferred network to the policy.
10. Returning to the Preferred Networks tab of the policy properties dialog box, you can add another preferred network, if desired. You can also remove or edit existing preferred network entries, as well as change their relative order by using the Move Up and Move Down buttons.
11. Click OK to close the WLAN Policy dialog box.

Table 5.1 outlines the configuration options that are available on the General tab of the Wireless LAN Properties dialog box, as discussed in step 6 of the Wireless Network Policy creation process.

Table 5.1 Options Available on the General Tab of the WLAN Properties Dialog Box

Option	Description
Name	Enables you to specify a descriptive name of the policy.
Description	Enables you to enter a longer description of the policy.
Check for Policy Changes Every	Configures how often Active Directory should be polled to check for changes to this security policy. The default value is 180 minutes and is acceptable in most instances.
Network to Access	Specifies the types of WLANs to which you want to allow clients to make connections. You have the following available options: ➤ Any available network (access point preferred) ➤ Access point (infrastructure) networks only ➤ Computer-to-computer (ad hoc) networks only

(continued)

Table 5.1 Options Available on the General Tab of the WLAN Properties Dialog Box *(continued)*

Option	Description
Use Windows to Configure Wireless Network Settings for Clients	Configures whether client settings are automatically configured for clients' 802.11 WLAN connections by the Wireless Configuration Service.
Automatically Connect to Nonpreferred Networks	Configures whether clients can connect to other 802.11 WLANs for which they are in range.

Table 5.2 outlines the configuration options that are available on the Network Properties tab of the New Preferred Setting Properties dialog box, as discussed in step 8 of the Wireless Network Policy creation process.

Table 5.2 Options Available on the Network Properties Tab of the New Preferred Setting Properties Dialog Box

Option	Description
Network Name (SSID)	Specifies the Service Set Identifier (SSID) of the WLAN. This value must exactly match the SSID value being used by your access points and wireless clients.
Description	Enables you to enter a longer description of the WLAN.
Wireless Network Key (WEP)	Specifies that a WEP key is required for the available options: ➤ *Data Encryption (WEP Enabled)*—This option specifies that a WEP key must be used to encrypt data sent over the WLAN. ➤ *Network Authentication (Shared Mode)*—This option specifies that a WEP key must be used to perform authentication to the WLAN. ➤ *The Key Is Provided Automatically*—This option specifies that the WEP key must be provided automatically to wireless clients by a key server of some sort—typically, a RADIUS server.
This is a computer-to-computer (ad hoc) network; wireless access points are not used.	When selected, configures this network as an ad hoc network. If not selected, configures this network as an infrastructure network.

Table 5.3 outlines the configuration options that are available on the IEEE 802.1*x* tab of the New Preferred Setting Properties dialog box, as discussed in step 9 of the Wireless Network Policy creation process.

Table 5.3 Options Available on the IEEE 802.1*x* Tab of the New Preferred Setting Properties Dialog Box

Option	Description
Enable Network Access Control Using IEEE 802.1X	Specifies that 802.1*x* authentication is to be used when connecting to the WLAN.
EAPOL-Start Message	Specifies how Extensible Authentication Protocol over LAN (EAPOL) start messages are to be transmitted. Options include these: ➤ Do not transmit ➤ Transmit ➤ Transmit per IEEE 802.1X
Max Start	Has a default value of 3 seconds.
Held Period	Has a default of 60 seconds.
Start Period	Has a default of 60 seconds.
Authentication Period	Has a default of 30 seconds.
EAP Type	Specifies what EAP type is to be used from the following options: Smart Card or Other Certificate and PEAP. Clicking the Settings button enables you to configure additional options, including the following: ➤ Using a smart card or certificate on the computer ➤ Validating server certificate ➤ Specifying which servers to connect to ➤ Trusted Root Certification Authorities ➤ Viewing certificates ➤ Selecting and configuring an authentication method
Authenticate as Guest When User or Computer Information Is Unavailable	Specifies that wireless clients are to attempt to authenticate to the WLAN as a guest when user or computer information is not available.
Authenticate as Computer When Computer Information Is Available	Specifies that wireless clients must attempt to authenticate to the WLAN even if a user is not logged on.
Computer Authentication	Specifies how the computer is to authenticate to the WLAN. The following options are available: ➤ With User Authentication ➤ With User Reauthentication ➤ Computer Only

(continued)

Table 5.3 Options Available on the IEEE 802.1*x* Tab of the New Preferred Setting Properties Dialog Box *(continued)*

Option	Description
	The recommended setting is With User Reauthentication. This setting forces the computer to authenticate before a user is logged on, and then performs authentication using the user's credentials when the user logs on. When the user logs off, authentication is performed again using the computer's credentials.

When it comes to WLAN security on exam day, the most important thing to do is make sure that you understand the options and methods that Windows Server 2003 provides. This is not a WLAN-specific exam, so don't expect any difficult or complex WLAN exam questions to show up.

Planning Data Transmission Security Using IP Security (IPSec)

IP Security (IPSec) is a framework of open standards for ensuring private, secure communications over IP networks. This protocol is rapidly becoming the underlying framework for secure communications using VPNs and will likely replace the Point-to-Point Tunneling Protocol (PPTP) as Microsoft's VPN protocol of choice. IPSec takes advantage of many of the most popular encryption protocols that are in use today. IPSec is based on an end-to-end security model, which means that only the sending and receiving computers must know about IPSec. The packets travel the network without being affected by any of the intervening network devices. Each IPSec device handles its own security and functions, with the assumption that the transport medium is not secure. The Internet is an excellent example of a transport medium that is not secure.

The Microsoft Windows Server 2003 implementation of IPSec is based on standards developed by the Internet Engineering Task Force (IETF) IPSec working group. However, it is important to note that Microsoft uses two implementations of IPSec: the IETF version, also known as Pure IPSec Tunnel mode or just tunnel mode, and the Microsoft variant on IPSec, which Microsoft calls L2TP/IPSec mode or transport mode. An IPSec VPN configured to use transport mode secures an existing IP packet from source to destination, using the encryption and authentication methods discussed later in this section. Tunnel mode puts an existing IP packet inside a new IP packet that is sent to a tunnel endpoint in the IPSec format. Both transport and tunnel mode can be encapsulated in Encapsulating Security Payload (ESP) or Authentication Header (AH) headers. The original IETF Request for Comments (see RFC 2401 at `www.ietf.org/rfc/rfc2401.txt`) IPSec tunnel protocol specifications did not include mechanisms suitable for remote-access VPN clients and instead focused on site-to-site VPN implementations. For that reason, Microsoft's implementation of tunnel mode relies on the use of the L2TP protocol developed jointly with Cisco to provide this additional packet format. It is worth noting that a new RFC (see RFC 3193 at `www.ietf.org/rfc/rfc3193.txt`) in late 2001 discussed using L2TP with IPSec.

The exam includes questions and scenarios on IPSec. Although you don't need to memorize the minutiae surrounding the encryption protocols used by IPSec, you should be familiar with what the components of IPSec are, how to implement an IPSec tunnel, and especially how to work with IPSec policies.

The Windows Server 2003 IPSec implementation supports the following new features:

- IPSec in Windows Server 2003 now supports User Datagram Protocol (UDP) encapsulation of IPSec packets to allow Internet Key Exchange (IKE) and ESP traffic to pass through a Network Address Translation (NAT) device—something that was not previously possible in Windows 2000 Server. It is now possible for Windows 2000 and Windows XP clients to establish IPSec connections with a Windows Server 2003 server that is located behind one or more NAT devices.

- The IP Security Monitor is now implemented as an MMC snap-in instead of a standalone executable (as in Windows 2000). In addition, you can now monitor information about local and remote computers, as well as several other enhancements.

- IPSec now supports the use of a 2048-bit Diffie-Hellman key exchange. As a result, the secret key resulting from the Diffie-Hellman exchange has a longer key length and, therefore, a greater strength, which increases the difficulty that an attacker faces when trying to determine a secret key.

- You can administer and control IPSec from the command line with new extensions to the `netsh` command. Using the `netsh ipsec` context, you can configure static or dynamic IPSec main mode settings, quick mode settings, rules, and configuration parameters. The `netsh ipsec` context replaces the Ipsecpol.exe tool that was provided with the Windows 2000 Server Resource Kit.

- IPSec now provides stateful filtering of network traffic during computer startup. Any outbound traffic initiated by the computer upon startup is permitted, as is any inbound reply traffic. The Dynamic Host Configuration Protocol (DHCP) is exempt from this new protection provided by IPSec and is thus allowed during startup. You can also specify other types of traffic that you want to exempt. Computer startup security can be configured only by using the `netsh` command with the `ipsec` context.
- Windows Server 2003 (Enterprise Edition) and Windows Server 2003 (Datacenter Server Edition) provide improved support for integration of IPSec with network load balancing (NLB). This enables a group of NLB servers to better provide highly available IPSec-based VPN services to clients. NLB can now accurately track IPSec-secured sessions, and the IPSec IKE protocol can now detect when an IPSec-secured session is being established with a cluster server and quickly recover from a failover.
- IPSec provides an extension to the Resultant Set of Policy (RSoP) snap-in (another new addition to Windows Server 2003) that can be used to view IPSec policy assignments of computers or other Active Directory objects.

The following are the standard features of the Windows Server 2003 IPSec implementation:

- IPSec in Windows Server 2003 is policy based. It cannot be configured without an IPSec policy in place, thereby allowing an administrator to more easily apply settings to groups of objects, such as computers or users.
- IPSec on Windows Server 2003 can use Kerberos v5, a digital certificate, or a shared secret (string) for user authentication.
- IPSec mutually authenticates computers before any data is exchanged.
- IPSec establishes a security association (SA) between the two host computers involved in the data transfer. An SA is the collection of a policy and keys that defines the rules for security settings.
- IPSec encrypts data using Data Encryption Standard (DES) or Triple DES (3DES).
- IPSec uses the MD5 or SHA1 algorithm for data hashing.
- IPSec is invisible to users. IPSec operates at the network level of the Open Systems Interconnect (OSI) model; therefore, users and applications do not directly interact with the protocol. After an IPSec tunnel has been created, users can connect to applications and services as if they were on the local network and not on the other side of a public network.

IPSec operates at the network layer; therefore, it is invisible to applications and computers. Understanding the following features, however, will help you troubleshoot connectivity problems that might arise.

- IPSec policies are part of the local and group policies within Active Directory. This built-in feature allows changes and management to be centralized. Settings for IPSec are enforced on the computer as the policy is enforced.
- The Internet Security Association and Key Management Protocol (ISAKMP) monitors the negotiations between the hosts and provides the keys to use with security algorithms.
- The installed IPSec driver secures traffic between the two hosts.

Enabling IPSec

Before enabling IPSec on your local computer or domain, you'll want to configure IPSec through policies. An IPSec policy is a set of rules that defines how and when communication is secured between two endpoints. This is done through the configuration of various rules. Each rule contains a collection of actions and filters that begin when they encounter endpoints that match.

Policies enable you to quickly and easily configure IPSec based on the settings that are required within your organization. Windows Server 2003 comes with three preconfigured IPSec policies that might or might not meet your needs:

- *Client (Respond Only)*—This policy requires IPSec-provided security only when another computer requests it. This policy allows the computer to attempt unsecured communications first and switch to IPSec-secured communications if requested. This policy contains the default response rule, which creates dynamic IPSec filters for inbound and outbound traffic based on the requested protocol and port traffic for the communication that is being secured. This policy, which can be used on workstations and servers alike, provides the minimum amount of IPSec security.
- *Server (Request Security)*—This policy requests security from the other computer and allows unsecured communication with non–IPSec-aware computers. The computer will accept inbound unsecured traffic, but it always attempts to secure further communications by requesting IPSec security from the sending computer. If the other computer is not IPSec-enabled, the entire communication is allowed to be unsecured. This

policy, which can be used on workstations and servers alike, provides a medium level of IPSec security.

- *Secure Server (Require Security)*—This policy is implemented on computers that require highly secure communications, such as servers that transmit sensitive data. The filters in this policy require all outbound communication to be secured, allowing only the initial inbound communication request to be unsecured. This policy has a rule to require security for all IP traffic, a rule to permit Internet Control Message Protocol (ICMP) traffic, and the default response rule to respond to requests for security from other computers. This policy, which is typically used only on servers, provides the highest level of IPSec security on a network. It can also be used on workstation computers, if desired. Non–IPSec-enabled computers cannot establish any communications with computers that use this policy.

You can opt to either use one of the preconfigured policies that comes with Windows Server 2003 or to create your own policy. You can also modify the preconfigured policies to suit your needs, if desired. Before we discuss IPSec further, we must first create the tools that enable you to manage IPSec on a local computer, as outlined in the following steps:

1. Open a blank MMC console by clicking Start, Run and then typing **MMC**.
2. In your new console, click the File menu and select Add/Remove Snap-in. The Add/Remove Snap-in dialog box opens.
3. Click the Add button to open the Add Standalone Snap-in dialog box.
4. Scroll down the list and select IP Security Monitor. Click the Add button.
5. Select IP Security Policy Management and click the Add button. You are prompted to choose the scope that the snap-in will manage.
6. For this example, choose Local Computer from the Select Computer or Domain page. Notice that you have the option to select the Active Directory domain that this computer is part of, another AD domain, or another computer. Click Finish to complete the addition of the IP Security Policy Management snap-in to your console.
7. Click Close on the Add Standalone Snap-in dialog box.
8. Click OK on the Add/Remove Snap-in dialog box. Your completed IPSec console will look something like Figure 5.10.

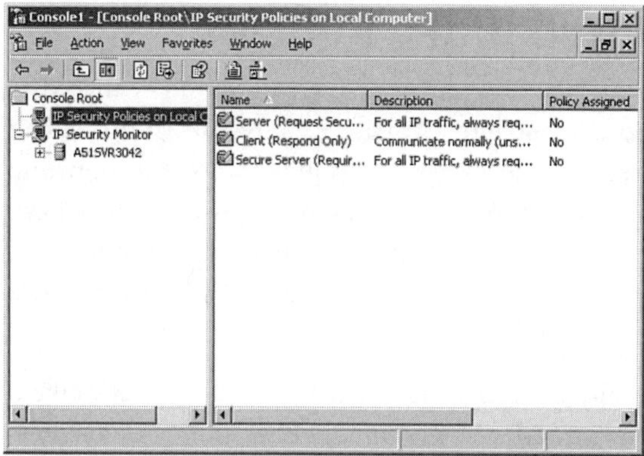

Figure 5.10 Your completed IPSec management console contains the tools you need for managing and monitoring IP Security.

9. Save your newly created console by clicking File, Save. Enter a suitable name, such as Local IPSec Management Console, and click Save. By default, the console is saved in the Administrative Tools folder of the currently logged-in user.

Armed with your newly created IPSec management console, you can now configure and manage IPSec. At this point, you might want to implement a preconfigured IPSec policy or create one of your own. The following list explores the latter. The former can be accomplished by right-clicking on the desired policy in the right pane of the console window and selecting Assign from the context menu. Note that you can have only one IPSec policy assigned at a time.

You can verify that the policy is now assigned to the computer by examining the Active Policy node of the IP Security Monitor, as shown in Figure 5.11.

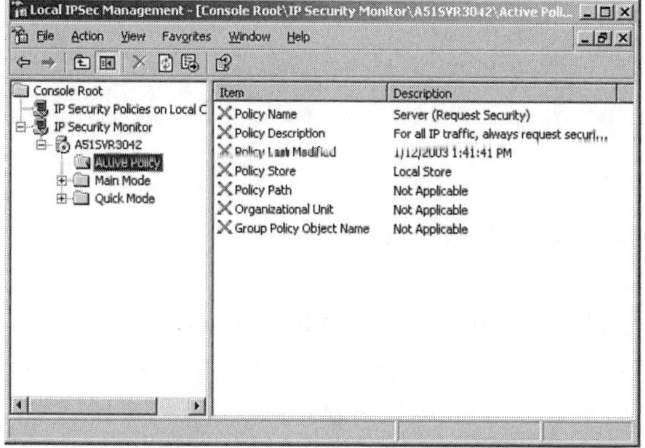

Figure 5.11 The IP Security Monitor can be used to display many bits of useful information about IPSec.

Creating Customized IPSec Policies

When you've decided to use IPSec on your network, you might realize that the preconfigured IPSec policies do not provide exactly the solution you need. You can opt to either customize an existing policy or create a new one from scratch. I prefer to create policies from scratch, to ensure that I have complete control over every piece of the puzzle—and that's exactly what IPSec can turn out to be if not treated with caution and respect: one large puzzle that you are left to piece together.

Before getting down to actually creating your own IPSec policy, let's take a few moments to examine the parts that make up an IPSec policy by dissecting the Secure Server (Require Security) policy. From within your IPSec management console, double-click on this policy to open its properties page. There are two tabs: Rules and General.

Let's look at the Rules tab first. The IP Security Rules window lists all IP security rules that are active for that policy. Selecting a rule and clicking the Edit button opens the Edit Rule Properties dialog box, shown in Figure 5.12. The five tabs within the dialog box contain the configuration settings for this particular rule.

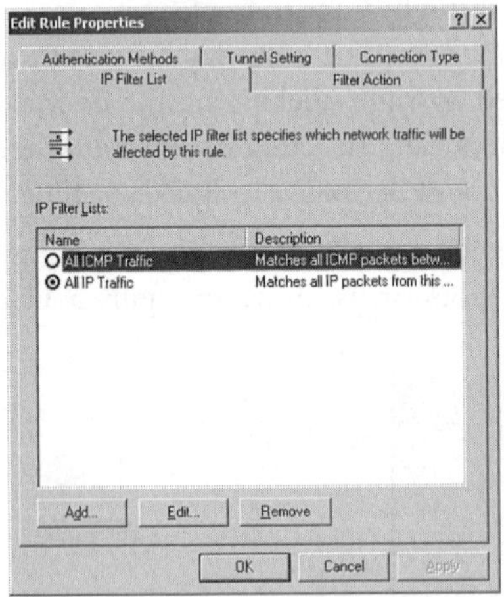

Figure 5.12 The IP Filter List tab of the Edit Rule Properties dialog box.

The IP Filter List tab shows all IP filters configured for the selected rule. An IP filter contains source and destination IP addresses that apply to this rule. These IP addresses can be those of an individual computer or of a network subnet. If a network communication is identified that has a participant listed in an IP filter, a particular filter action that is specific for that connection is applied. Selecting the All IP traffic filter for editing opens the dialog box (shown in Figure 5.13) from which you can specify many items, including the source and destination IP addresses to which this filter applies.

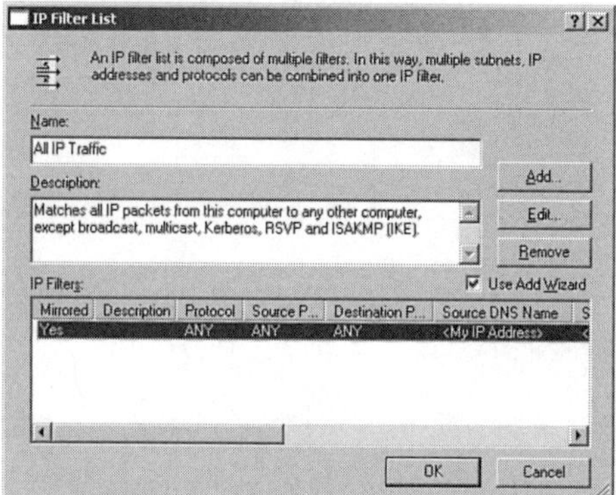

Figure 5.13 You can edit the filter properties to specify the source and destination computers to which it applies.

The Filter Action tab contains actions that specify the type of security and the methods by which security is established.

Filter actions (see Figure 5.14) define the type of security and the methods by which security is established. The default methods are Permit, Block, and Negotiate Security. The Permit option passes the traffic without the requirement for security. This action is appropriate if you never want to secure traffic to which a rule applies. The Block action silently blocks all traffic from computers specified in the IP filter list. The Negotiate Security action specifies that the computer is to use a list of security methods to negotiate the appropriate security for the communication.

If the Negotiate Security option is selected, both computers must agree on the security parameters to be used—meaning that they both must support at least one common set of security parameters from those in the list. The list entries are processed in order of preference, from top to bottom. The first security method shared by both computers is used.

From the Authentication Methods tab you can configure what method will be used to authenticate both sides of the communication. You can choose from Kerberos (the default setting), a digital certificate, or a shared secret (string) that will be used to protect the key exchange process. You can configure more than one method and also choose the order of precedence for your configured methods. Using the shared secret option is not recommended because this is a static entry that can be compromised.

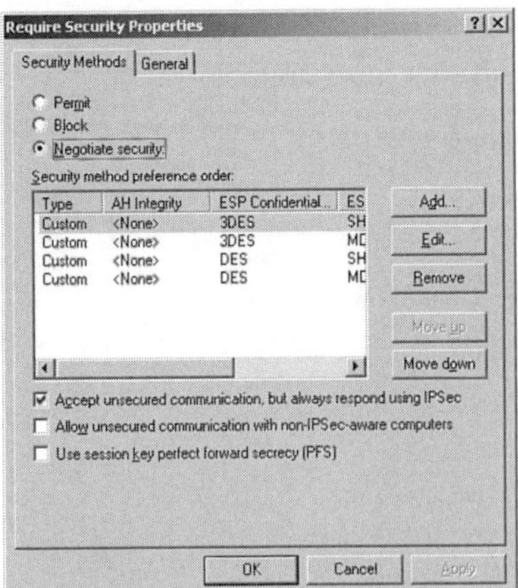

Figure 5.14 You can specify exactly what the computer will do when a filter action is processed.

From the Tunnel Setting tab, shown in Figure 5.15, you can either have the rule apply to a tunnel by specifying an endpoint, or have it not apply to a tunnel (transport mode).

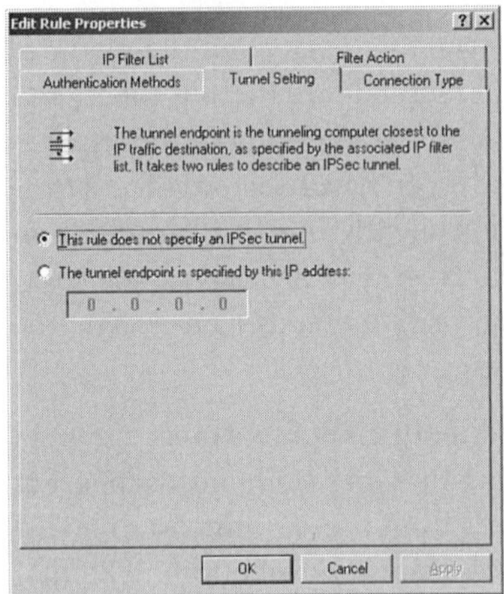

Figure 5.15 The Tunnel Setting tab enables you to configure a tunnel endpoint, if required.

The Connection Type tab determines the types of connections the rule will be applied for: All Network Connections, LAN, or Remote Access.

You can create two basic types of IPSec policies: those that specify a tunnel and those that do not specify a tunnel. Tunneling is commonly used in the creation of a VPN and is called tunnel mode. Transport mode, which does not use a tunnel, is commonly used between subnets or computers on an Intranet. The following steps examine the process of creating a new IPSec policy that operates in transport mode between two subnets (192.160.11.0 and 192.168.12.0) in the same intranet of a company. These two subnets represent the Accounting and Payroll departments, respectively, and they need to pass only secured traffic between their subnets.

1. Open the IPSec management console that you previously created.
2. Right-click on IP Security Policies, and select Create IP Security Policy from the context menu.
3. You can dismiss the opening dialog box of the IP Security Policy Wizard by clicking Next.
4. In the IP Security Policy Name dialog box, enter a descriptive name for your new policy. Use the name Accounting to Payroll Security Policy for this example. Click Next after entering the required information.
5. On the Requests for Secure Communication dialog box, ensure that you deselect the option Activate the Default Response Rule. You will be configuring this policy entirely by yourself. Click Next to continue.
6. You are now at the end of the wizard portion of the creation process. Ensure that the Edit Properties option is selected, and click Finish to begin editing the policies properties.
7. Now you are presented with the Accounting to Payroll Security Policy Properties dialog box.
8. On the Rules tab, ensure that the Use Add Wizard option is selected; click the Add button to start the Security Rule Wizard to create a new filter list and action.
9. Click Next to dismiss the opening dialog box of the Security Rule Wizard.
10. On the Tunnel Endpoint dialog box, select the This Rule Does Not Specify a Tunnel option (recall that this IPSec policy is being created to secure communications between two subnets on the same intranet). Click Next to continue.
11. On the Network Type dialog box, select the network connections to which this rule applies. Select All Network Connections, and click Next to continue.
12. The IP Filter List dialog box shows that no IP filters have been configured for this rule. Click the Add button to create a filter that meets your requirements.

13. From the IP Filter List dialog box, configure the IP filter properties for this rule. Enter a descriptive name, such as Accounting to Payroll Security, in the Name box, and enter a description, if desired. Ensure that the Use Add Wizard option is selected, and click the Add button.

14. The IP Filter Wizard opens to start the IP filter configuration process. Click Next to dismiss the wizard's opening dialog box.

15. In the IP Filter Description and Mirrored Properties dialog box, enter a description of the filter. Ensure that the Mirrored option is selected. This allows the rule to automatically match packets with the exact opposite source and destination addresses to ensure that machines from the destination subnet are also included in the incoming filter. Click Next to continue.

16. In the IP Traffic Source dialog box, select the option A Specific IP Subnet, and configure the IP address and subnet mask as required. Recall that you are creating a policy between the 192.168.11.0 and 192.168.12.0 subnets. Enter **`192.168.11.0`** and the subnet mask of **`255.255.255.0`**, and click Next to continue.

17. In the IP Traffic Destination dialog box, select the option A Specific IP Subnet, and configure the IP address and subnet mask as required. Enter **`192.168.12.0`** and the subnet mask of **`255.255.255.0`**, and click Next to continue.

18. In the IP Protocol Type dialog box, you can configure which IP protocol types you want to include in the filter. You want the filter to apply to all types, so leave the default selection of Any and click Next to continue.

19. You should now see the Completing the IP Filter Wizard dialog box. Ensure that the Edit Properties option is deselected, and click Finish.

20. Return to the IP Filter List dialog box, where you can see your newly created IP filter. Click OK to close the filter and complete the creation process. If you click Cancel, your newly created filter will be lost, so be careful here.

21. Select the Accounting to Payroll Security filter from the list on the IP Filter List dialog box, and click Next to continue with the Security Rule Wizard.

22. On the Filter Action dialog box, select a filter action. Ensure that the Use Add Wizard option is selected, and click Add to start the Filter Action Wizard.

23. The Filter Action Wizard starts. Dismiss its opening dialog box by clicking Next.
24. On the Filter Action Name dialog box, enter a descriptive name and description for the filter. Click Next to continue.
25. On the Filter Action General Options dialog box, select Negotiate Security and click Next to continue.
26. In the Communicating with Computers That Do Not Support IPSec dialog box, you are asked whether you want to allow unsecured communications. In this case, this is not allowed because all communications must be secured. Ensure that the option Do Not Communicate with Computers That Do Not Support IPSec is selected, and click Next to continue.
27. On the IP Traffic Security dialog box, select Custom to specify what security methods are to be used. Click Settings to edit the security settings.
28. The Custom Security Method Settings dialog box opens, enabling you to specify the settings you want. Ensure that both the AH and ESP check boxes are selected. Configure the desired integrity and encryption algorithms. Do not configure settings for the session key at this time. Click OK to accept your settings.
29. Back at the IP Traffic Security dialog box, click Next to continue.
30. In the Completing the IP Security Filter Action Wizard dialog box, ensure that the Edit Properties option is selected and click Finish.
31. Back at the Filter Action Properties dialog box, ensure that the option Use Session Key Perfect Forward Secrecy (PFS) is selected, and click OK. Selecting session key PFS ensures that the master key keying material cannot be used to generate more than one session key; this adds both security and overhead to the connection. Do not click Cancel unless you want to scrap your newly configured filter action.
32. Back at the Filter Action dialog box, select the newly created filter and click Next to continue.
33. On the Authentication Method dialog box, select the primary authentication method that this rule will use. The default selection of Kerberos v5 should be used in most cases. You can add additional authentication methods after the rule has been configured. Click Next to continue.

34. From the Completing the Security Rule Wizard dialog box, ensure that the Edit Properties option is deselected, and click Finish to complete the rule-creation process.

35. Finally, you are back to the policy properties dialog box. You still have some additional configuration that you can complete, however.

36. On the General tab, you can configure the interval at which the computer will check for updates and changes to the security policy. The default setting of 180 minutes is usually acceptable.

37. You can modify the settings used for the IKE process by clicking the Settings button at the bottom of the General tab.

38. In the Key Exchange Settings dialog box, you can configure for master key perfect forward secrecy, which improves security of the keying process. Additionally, you can change the defaults that are provided for key generation.

39. If you want to configure the methods that are used to protect the identities, click the Methods button. The Key Exchange Security Methods dialog box opens. Note that, by default, the new 2048-bit Diffie-Hellman key exchange method is not used. You can select it by adding or editing a security method.

40. Click OK as required to return to the policy properties page. Your new IPSec policy is now configured and ready to use. Assign it as previously discussed.

IPSec can be deployed at any level within your organization. Thus far, you have examined it only from the point of view of a local computer. You can just as easily apply it via Group Policy using the Active Directory Users and Computers console, shown in Figure 5.16.

Troubleshooting IPSec

If you have problems with IPSec, you should first verify that any routers or firewalls that traffic might be passing through are configured to support IPSec traffic. You need to allow the following traffic:

- Protocol ID 50 and 51 or ESP and AH traffic
- UDP port 500 for IPSec negotiation traffic

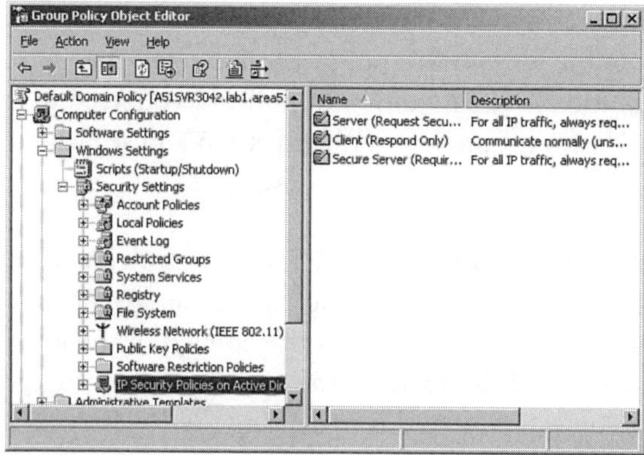

Figure 5.16 You can easily apply IPSec at the domain or OU level using Group Policy.

Some other basic problems and troubleshooting tips are outlined here:

- *You cannot establish any communications with a computer.* In this case, you should first verify that basic network connectivity exists between the computers in question by using the `ping` command. You should also ensure that all required network services, such as DHCP and the domain name system (DNS), are operating properly for both computers.
- *You cannot establish any communications with a computer.* This might be a result of a computer having been removed from the domain. Whatever the reason, it causes IPSec communications to fail.
- *Communications are occurring, but not as expected.* You need to ensure that you have the correct (and compatible) IPSec policies assigned on both computers.
- *No hard associations are being formed.* If there are currently soft associations in place, a hard association will not be formed. You need to completely stop all communications between the computers for approximately 5–10 minutes to allow the soft associations to time out. The easiest way to do this is to disable the network connection. After you have allowed the soft associations to time out, you should check to see that a hard association has been formed. If a hard association still has not been formed, you need to examine the IPSec policy to verify that unsecured communications are not allowed.
- *IPSec communications are failing after you configure a digital certificate for authentication.* You must make sure that the required digital certificate is installed on the computers that are using that IPSec policy to communicate. This can also be a result of specifying an incorrect Certificate Authority (CA).

- *Some computers can create IPSec connections, and some cannot.* This is most likely caused by not having the same IPSec policy applied to all the computers. If you are intentionally using different policies, you need to ensure that they share at least one common authentication and security method.

IPSec-related problems can be found in the security log. You can view IKE events (negotiation success and failure) by enabling success and/or failure auditing for the Audit Logon Events audit policy for the domain or the local computer. The IKE event category is also used for the auditing of user logon events in other services, but you can disable this by editing the Registry.

When success and/or failure auditing for the Audit Logon Events audit policy is enabled, IPSec records the success and/or failure of each main mode and quick mode negotiation. The establishment and termination of each negotiation is logged as a separate event, for easier analysis and troubleshooting. Be aware, however, that when you enable audit logon events, the security log will likely quickly fill up with IKE events unless you opt to disable auditing of those events. You can find more information about this at `www.microsoft.com/technet/prodtechnol/windowsserver2003/proddocs/entserver/sag_ipsec_tools.asp`.

The Network Monitor included in Windows Server 2003 can also be used to view IPSec traffic between the computer it is installed on and other network computers. Network Monitor includes parsers for the ISAKMP (IKE), AH, and ESP protocols. The parsers for ESP can parse inside the ESP packet only if null encryption is being used and the full ESP packet is captured. Network Monitor cannot parse the encrypted portions of IPSec-secured ESP traffic when the encryption is being performed in Windows. However, if the encryption is being performed by an IPSec hardware offload network adapter, the ESP packets have already been decrypted when Network Monitor captures them; as a result, they can be parsed and interpreted into the upper-layer protocols. If you need to diagnose ESP Windows-encrypted communication (that is, software-encrypted communication), you must first disable ESP encryption and use ESP null encryption by changing the IPSec policy on each computer.

Exam Prep Questions

Question 1

You are the network administrator for Joe's, a regional restaurant chain. You have recently begun to implement IPSec to secure communications on the internal network segments. You have just completed the configuration and implementation of the Richmond office network segment. Users in Richmond are now reporting to you that they can connect to their network resources from some computers, but not from others. What do you suspect is the most likely cause of this problem?

❍ A. The computers do not have basic network connectivity.

❍ B. More than one IPSec policy is in place.

❍ C. The domain controller (DC) is not responding.

❍ D. The Kerberos key distribution center (KDC) is not responding.

Answer B is correct. More often than not, when you have some computers that can create IPSec connections and others that cannot, you have more than one IPSec policy in place. If you are intentionally using multiple policies, you need to ensure that you have at least one common authentication and security method between them, or communications will fail. Although basic network connectivity is always a potential problem, it does not appear to be the problem here; thus, answer A is incorrect. The status of the DC is not an issue here; thus, answer C is incorrect. The status of the KDC is also not an issue here; thus, answer D is incorrect.

Question 2

You are the network administrator for Jeff's Jeep Tours, an Australian tour company. You have a central office in Sydney with 20 other smaller remote offices located all over the country. You have recently completed your rollout of Windows Server 2003 for all servers and Windows XP Professional for all clients in the corporate network. Some of the remote offices have only three or four employees, and they do not have an IT staff. The IT management responsibility for these offices is shared among all of the IT staff in other locations. When users in remote locations with no IT staff have problems with their Windows XP Professional computers, what feature should they use to get help for their problems?

❍ A. Terminal Services

❍ B. Remote Desktop for Administration

❍ C. Remote Desktop Protocol

❍ D. Remote Assistance

Answer D is correct. If configured to allow it, Windows XP and Windows Server 2003 computers can send Remote Assistance requests to an Expert asking for help with problems. The Novice requesting the Remote Assistance can choose from Windows Messenger, email, or a file to ask for Remote Assistance, and can control the level of interaction and control that the Expert has on the Novice's computer when the Remote Assistance connection has been made. Terminal Services is used in Windows Server 2003 to provide the Terminal Server role, thereby allowing users to make connections to a terminal server to execute applications that are not available on their local computer. This does not provide a means for users to get help with problems on their computers; thus, answer A is incorrect. Remote Desktop for Administration is used to create administrative connections to computers and does not require a request to be sent; thus, Answer B is incorrect. The Remote Desktop Protocol is used to power Remote Assistance and Remote Desktop for Administration, but it does not directly provide the solution required; thus, answer C is incorrect.

Question 3

You are the network administrator for Jeff's Jeep Tours, an Australian tour company. You have a central office in Sydney with 20 other smaller remote offices located all over the country. You have recently completed your rollout of Windows Server 2003 for all servers and Windows XP Professional for all clients in the corporate network. Some of the remote offices have only three or four employees, and they do not have an IT staff. The IT management responsibility for these offices is shared among all of the IT staff in other locations. You need to install a service pack on one of the Windows XP computers located in an office that does not have an IT staff. What Windows Server 2003 features will you use?

❍ A. Terminal Services

❍ B. Remote Desktop for Administration

❍ C. Remote Desktop Protocol

❍ D. Remote Assistance

Answer B is correct. The Remote Desktop for Administration feature replaces what was previously known as the Remote Administration mode of Terminal Services in Windows 2000 Server. Remote Desktop for Administration allows for a maximum of two concurrent connections to a server for the purposes of managing and maintaining it. Unlike Remote Assistance, Remote Desktop for Administration sessions do not start with a user request—an administrator can initiate a Remote Desktop for Administration connection whenever desired. Terminal Services is used in Windows Server 2003 to provide the Terminal Server role, thereby allowing users to make connections to a Terminal Server to execute applications that are not available on their local computer. It does not provide a means for users to get help with problems on their computers; thus, answer A is incorrect. The Remote Desktop Protocol (RDP) is the protocol used by Terminal Services, Remote Desktop, and Remote Assistance, and is not the solution in and of itself; thus, answer C is incorrect. Remote Assistance allows a Novice to request help from an Expert if the Novice's computer is configured to allow Remote Assistance; thus, answer D is incorrect.

Question 4

You are the network administrator for Widgets and Hammerstein, LLC. Andrea, one of your users, has called you and says that she cannot connect to one of the network servers that requires secured communication. What can you do to quickly verify the IPSec policy that computer uses?

- ❍ A. Use the IP Security Monitor snap-in to see what IPSec policy the computer uses.
- ❍ B. Use Network Monitor to see what IPSec policy the computer uses.
- ❍ C. Use the IP Security Policies snap-in to see what IPSec policy the computer uses.
- ❍ D. Use the **ipconfig/all** command to see what IPSec policy the computer uses.

Answer A is correct. You need to use the IP Security Monitor snap-in to examine what IPSec policy, if any, is currently assigned to the computer. Network Monitor and the IP Security Policies snap-in will not show you what IPSec policy is assigned, and neither will the `ipconfig/all` command; therefore, answers B, C, and D are incorrect.

Question 5

You are the network administrator for Joe's Crab Shack, a regional restaurant chain. While at a standards-setting meeting in Redmond, Washington, you are informed that one of your newly installed Windows Server 2003 DHCP servers has stopped leasing addresses. Rick, the president of the company, has asked you to make a Remote Desktop for Administration connection to the server via your VPN connection. After you have connected to your internal network via VPN, you attempt to create a Remote Desktop for Administration connection to the affected DHCP server and cannot. The DHCP server is located on the same IP subnet as the VPN server. You can create Remote Desktop for Administration connections to other Windows Server 2003 computers, however. What is the most likely reason for this problem?

❍ A. Remote Desktop is not enabled on the server.

❍ B. Your VPN server is not functioning correctly.

❍ C. TCP port 3389 is being blocked at your firewall.

❍ D. Remote Desktop is not enabled on your portable computer.

Answer A is correct. Because you can create a connection to your network via the VPN server, the most likely problem is that Remote Desktop is not enabled on this server. The VPN server is obviously functioning correctly because you are able to VPN into the network; thus, answer B is incorrect. Because you are connecting directly to your internal network via a VPN tunnel, the status of the firewall configuration is not an issue; thus, answer C is incorrect. Remote Desktop does not need to be enabled on your portable computer; thus, answer D is incorrect.

Question 6

You are the network administrator for Roger's Rockets, a manufacturer of toy rocket kits. You are preparing to configure a new WLAN policy for your network. You want your wireless clients to connect only to access points and to create no other connections. What type of network will you configure in the new WLAN security policy?

❍ A. Ad hoc

❍ B. Infrastructure

❍ C. Central

❍ D. Core

Answer B is correct. Infrastructure networks are those in which wireless clients create connections only to access points. Ad hoc networks are those in which wireless clients can create connections directly to each other without an access point; thus, answer A is incorrect. Central and core are not network types; thus, answers C and D are incorrect.

Question 7

You are the network administrator for the Sunny Day, Inc., company. You are creating a new IPSec policy for your internal network's financial subnet. When creating your new policy, what items can you specify as part of the IP filter? (Check all correct answers.)

- ❑ A. Source IP address
- ❑ B. Destination IP address
- ❑ C. Network protocol
- ❑ D. Operating system

Answers A, B, and C are correct. You can specify the source IP address, destination IP address, source port, destination port, and network protocol in your IP filters. The operating system is not part of the filters; thus, answer D is incorrect.

Question 8

You are the network administrator for Roger's Rockets, a manufacturer of toy rocket kits. You have configured four different WLAN security policies for your network: one at the domain level, one on the Graphics OU, one on the Engineering OU, and one on the Manufacturing OU (which is a child object inside the Engineering OU). All users and computers in each department are located in the corresponding OU. Which security policy will be implemented for a computer located in the Manufacturing OU?

- ❍ A. The domain WLAN security policy
- ❍ B. The Engineering OU WLAN security policy
- ❍ C. The Graphics OU WLAN security policy
- ❍ D. The Manufacturing OU WLAN security policy

Answer D is correct. WLAN security policies are applied using the normal Group Policy processing order; thus, the security policy that is closest to the computer object takes precedence. Answers A, B, and C are, therefore, incorrect.

Question 9

You are the network administrator for Roger's Rockets, a manufacturer of toy rocket kits. You have one WLAN security policy in place for your network that is configured in the Default Domain GPO. When you make a change to this WLAN security policy that changes the list of preferred networks, what will any currently connected wireless clients do?

❍ A. The client connection will be momentarily broken if the new policy takes precedence over the old policy.

❍ B. The client connection will be momentarily broken. When the Wireless Configuration Service restarts, the client will revert to any existing client-configured settings in place.

❍ C. The client connection will be momentarily broken. When the Wireless Configuration Service restarts, the client will revert to the client settings that are configured in the next higher-level WLAN security policy.

❍ D. The client connection will be broken until the radio on the wireless client has been restarted.

Answer A is correct. When a WLAN security policy is changed, the client connection is momentarily broken if the new policy takes precedence over the old policy—that is, if the new policy changes something such as the authentication method. Thus, answers B, C, and D are incorrect.

Question 10

You are the network administrator for Herb's Happenings, a public relations firm. You want to create a new IPSec policy for traffic on your private network that provides the strongest secret key possible. In Windows Server 2003, what is the maximum Diffie-Hellman value that can be used?

❍ A. 512 bit

❍ B. 768 bit

❍ C. 1024 bit

❍ D. 2048 bit

Answer D is correct. Windows Server 2003 provides the increased Diffie-Hellman option of 2048 bits; thus, answers B, C, and D are incorrect. The Diffie-Hellman Group is used to determine the length of the base material that is actually used to generate the IPSec secret key. This increased length increases the secret key strength and, thus, makes it more difficult for an attacker to break.

Need to Know More?

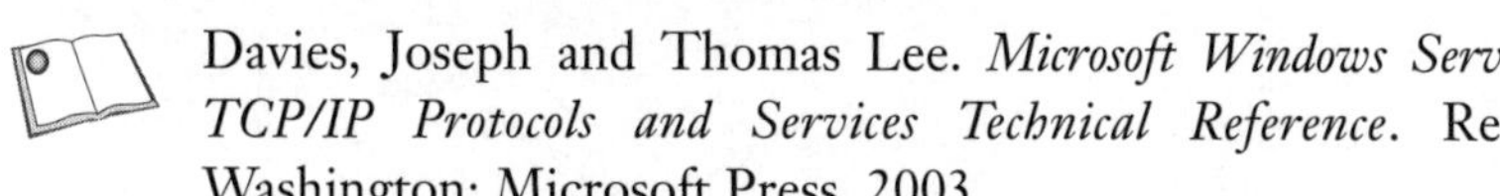

Davies, Joseph and Thomas Lee. *Microsoft Windows Server 2003 TCP/IP Protocols and Services Technical Reference*. Redmond, Washington: Microsoft Press, 2003.

Microsoft Corporation. *Microsoft Windows Server 2003 Resource Kit*. Redmond, Washington: Microsoft Press, 2003.

Microsoft Corporation. *Microsoft Windows Server 2003 Deployment Kit*. Redmond, Washington: Microsoft Press, 2003.

Technical Overview of Windows Server 2003 Security Services: `www.microsoft.com/windowsserver2003/techinfo/overview/security.mspx`.

Internet Protocol Security Overview: `www.microsoft.com/technet/prodtechnol/windowsserver2003/proddocs/standard/sag_IPSECintroduct.asp`.

Planning, Implementing, and Maintaining Security Infrastructure

Terms you'll need to understand:

- ✓ Auditing
- ✓ Automatic Updates
- ✓ Certificate
- ✓ Certificate Authority (CA)
- ✓ Certificate Revocation List (CRL)
- ✓ Change management
- ✓ CRL Distribution Point (CDP)
- ✓ DumpEL
- ✓ Enterprise CA
- ✓ EventCombMT
- ✓ Group Policy Editor
- ✓ Group Policy Object (GPO)
- ✓ Microsoft Baseline Security Analyzer (MBSA)
- ✓ Principle of least privilege
- ✓ Revoked certificate
- ✓ Root CA
- ✓ Software Update Services (SUS)
- ✓ Standalone CA
- ✓ Subordinate CA
- ✓ Validity period

Techniques you'll need to master:

- ✓ Planning for a Windows Server 2003 PKI implementation
- ✓ Installing and configuring a Windows Server 2003 CA
- ✓ Requesting certificates from a CA through various methods
- ✓ Planning for a smart card implementation
- ✓ Planning and implementing a security update and inventory infrastructure
- ✓ Planning and implementing a security-monitoring policy
- ✓ Planning and implementing a change- and configuration-control policy

As you might realize, networks today keep growing and intermingling with other networks. This growth presents a challenge for Microsoft Certified Systems Engineers, in that it increases network exposure to users and other individuals who seek to penetrate its defenses and gain entry. What makes it possible for all these networks to be vulnerable to attack? They share a common protocol.

The common protocol used in the exchange of data is Transmission Control Protocol/Internet Protocol (TCP/IP), as discussed in previous chapters of this book. Data sent via TCP/IP is broken up and sent over various routes to the final destination. Because of the very design of TCP/IP, data can be intercepted easily without the sender or the receiver knowing that the data has been intercepted. Certainly, as data passes through networks around the globe, it is susceptible to interception or forgery, and users are often the recipients of data whose content might jeopardize their own data.

We need a way to protect our outgoing data and ensure that our incoming data has not been compromised. We also need a way to verify that people and machines we communicate with are who they say they are. Enter the digital certificate. This chapter introduces the fundamentals of certificates and then discusses installing and configuring CA Services.

Maintaining a secure network is not a one-step or one-day event; it is a daily, ongoing event that requires you to not only implement an initial solution, but also monitor it and massage it over time to ensure that new threats and required changes are being taken into account. Too many times in the past, administrators have tried to treat server and network security as a "set it and forget it" type of thing—but that's just not possible today. To help the Windows Server 2003 administrator keep computers and the network secure, Microsoft has provided a relatively pain-free method of identifying and installing required updates and security fixes through the Microsoft Baseline Security Analyzer (MBSA) and Software Update Services (SUS).

Of course, as you might have guessed, at the heart of all your security plans must lie a solid plan to not only implement and control security, but also monitor and manage it. Planning is key in network administration, and Windows Server 2003 networks are no different.

What's New in Windows Server 2003 Certificate Services?

Windows Server 2003, when combined with a Windows XP Professional client computer in a Windows Server 2003 Active Directory-based network, features several enhancements and improvements to Certificate Services.

These features will make more sense to you as you work your way through this chapter's discussion of PKI and Certificate Services:

- *Version 2 Certificate Templates*—Version 2 templates extend the range of properties that you can configure from those provided in Version 1 templates. You now have the capability to create new certificate templates (an option sorely lacking from Windows 2000), copy existing certificate templates, and supercede certificate templates that are already in use. You need a Window Advanced Server 2003 functioning as the enterprise root CA.
- *Integrated and enhanced key recovery*—Windows 2000 Server relied on a Data Recovery Agent (DRA) to decrypt files following the loss of or damage to an encryption key. Additionally, the Exchange 2000 Server Key Management Service (KMS) ran on top of Windows 2000 Certificate Services and did not fully integrate. Windows Server 2003 allows the archival and recovery of private keys, and also enables the administrator to access data encrypted with a lost or damaged private key. Now Key Recovery Agents (KRAs) are used to recover lost or damaged private keys across Windows Server 2003 and Exchange Server 2003.
- *Delta Certificate Revocation Lists*—Windows Server 2003 supports RFC 2459–compliant Delta Certificate Revocation Lists (CRLs) that contain only the certificates whose status has changed since the last full (base) CRL was compiled. This results in a much smaller CRL that can be more frequently published with no adverse effects on the network or client computers. Additionally, this provides more accurate CRLs due to reduced latency periods. In Windows 2000, CRLs were typically published once per week (the default setting). Delta CRLs enable you to publish one or more times daily, as required.
- *CA Qualified Subordination*—Another part of RFC 2459, qualified subordination, allows a parent CA to granularly configure what a subordinate CA is allowed to do. Examples include preventing the subordinate CA from signing a certificate for another subordinate CA.
- *Common Criteria role separation*—By separating common CA-related tasks into several different levels of administration, Common Criteria requirements can be met in addition to enhancing task delegation. Because roles are separated, no one individual should possess the capability to compromise the services or operation of the CA.
- *Enhanced auditing*—Windows Server 2003 provides for more detailed auditing of Certificate Services by adding two new types of events: access check and system events. System events come from seven critical areas: CA service, backup and restoration, certificate requests, certificate revocations, CA security, key archival and key recovery, and CA configuration.

Planning a Windows Server 2003 Public Key Infrastructure (PKI)

So you want to install a Windows Server PKI on your network to issue and validate digital certificates? Great idea! But what exactly is a PKI, and what is it made up of? Before getting around to the planning and implementation of the often misunderstood PKI, you should first have a good idea of what it is and how it all works. After you've gotten an introduction to PKI, you can then plan for and subsequently implement your PKI solution more efficiently.

Introduction to the Public Key Infrastructure (PKI)

To combat the openness of TCP/IP without losing the functionality of the protocol, PKI has been developed in tandem with TCP/IP as a means of offering security for data sent between hosts—on an intranet or on the Internet.

Using encryption, network administrators and security experts can ensure that the data is read only by the intended recipient and that data received has not been tampered with. The analogy of a physical signature and envelopes sealed with wax is an excellent parallel to how PKI is used today. In lieu of your "John Hancock" and sealing wax, you use a digital signature.

A digital signature ensures that the message is from the source it says it's from and that the message hasn't been digitally "steamed open." In addition to digital signatures, you can implement digital identifications—thus, the digital certificate.

Certificates

What exactly is a digital certificate? Essentially, it's your electronic version of your password or employee identification. It proves that you are who you say you are. This certificate is what ultimately allows you to access resources and data.

Certificates are issued not only to individuals, but also to organizations, businesses, routers, and other entities as a way of controlling and securing data. A digital certificate contains the following information:

- The user's name
- The user's public key

- Serial number
- Expiration date
- Information on the certificate itself
- Information on the entity (called a Certificate Authority) that issued the certificate

When transferring secure data, an electronic seal is inserted into the data through cryptography. When the recipient opens the data, the electronic seal is verified to ensure that it exists and that it has not been tampered with. In addition, the recipient can be assured that the sender of the data is accurate.

Traditionally, when you want to send encrypted data to other users, you use your key to encrypt and secure the data. When the recipients want to open the encrypted data, they use their copy of the key to unlock the data. If others without the key intercept the packets, they can't decrypt the information. This method of security is not really all that secure. The problem is that when unauthorized users gain access to the key, they gain access to the data—not unlike discovering your house keys in the outside lock of your door.

Digital certificates, however, use a slightly different method of locking and unlocking the data. With digital certificates, you no longer have to make copies of keys for others to unlock your data. Digital certificates use a private key to lock the data and then a different key, the public key, to unlock the data. No longer is the same key used to lock and unlock data.

With this two-key technology, your private key remains private. No one but the rightful owner should ever have access to it. However, by means of the digital certificate, you can disperse the public key to whoever needs it.

When Dick wants to send a private message to Jane, for example, Dick uses Jane's public key to encrypt the message. No one other than Jane can decrypt the message, but now the private key, Jane's key, is required to unlock the contents. When Jane responds to Dick, she can use Dick's public key to encrypt the response. Dick then uses his own private key to unlock the message.

Certificate Authorities (CAs)

All certificates are issued by a CA, such as VeriSign or one internal to your own network. The CA verifies that the owner of the certificate is who he says he is. A CA is a trusted third party that is responsible for physically verifying the legitimacy of the identity of an individual or organization before issuing a digital certificate. A CA is also responsible for issuing certificates, revoking certificates, and publishing a list of revoked certificates.

With Windows Server 2003, you can use a third-party CA, or you can create your own CA through Microsoft's Windows Server 2003 Certificate Services, which offers four distinct types of CAs: enterprise root CA, enterprise subordinate CA, standalone root CA, and standalone subordinate CA. We take a closer look at these types of CAs throughout the chapter.

If you elect to create an internal CA for your organization, you'll want to establish some rules and guidelines to verify that users are employees. You can use social security numbers, employee badges, or an even more secure method—*smart cards*, which are physical, portable devices that enable users to log in and access and send data, such as email and data on a network.

The Enterprise CA

A Windows Server 2003 enterprise CA provides certificates for the internal security of an entire organization, whereas an external CA (such as VeriSign) provides security for external security needs. Microsoft provides support for both, and you can mix and match to fit your business needs.

If users request a certificate in a Windows Server 2003 environment, their user account acts as the credentials for the user because they are logged on and recognized in the Active Directory.

A Windows Server 2003 enterprise CA has five key characteristics:

- The CA server can run on any Windows Server 2003 server in the domain. Plan for activity, network load, and physical placement of the server for best implementation.
- Because the CA name is integrated into the certificates it assigns, the name of the server should be determined before implementing CA services.
- The Enterprise CA Authority is integrated into the Active Directory.
- When you've installed an enterprise CA, a policy module is created. An administrator can edit the policy.
- Because the CA is crucial for the successful implementation of the PKI, it must have a fault-tolerance scheme and a schedule of regular secure backups.

The Standalone CA

Another type of CA that Windows Server 2003 enables you to install is a *standalone CA*. The standalone CA doesn't require the interaction of Active Directory, but it can use Active Directory, if it's available.

A standalone CA is useful in issuing certificates and digital signatures, and it supports secure email (S/MIME) and Secure Sockets Layer (SSL) or Transport Layer Security (TLS).

A typical standalone CA has these key characteristics:

- It doesn't require Active Directory interaction.
- It can be used with extranets.
- It doesn't verify the requests for certificates. (All requests are pending until an administrator approves them.)
- Users requesting a certificate from a standalone CA must supply all user account information. This is not required within an enterprise CA because the user is recognized by the logon account in the Active Directory.
- No certificate templates are used.
- Windows Server 2003 logon credential certificates are not stored on smart cards. Other certificates can be, however.
- An administrator must distribute the standalone CA certificate to the Trusted Root Certificate Store.

If Active Directory exists on the network and a standalone CA can access it, additional options are available:

- If a domain administrator with write access to Active Directory installs the standalone CA, the standalone CA is added to the Trusted Root Certification Authorities Certificate Store. In this situation, make certain that the default action of pending requests isn't changed to allow the standalone CA to automatically approve all requests for certificates. Do not change the default action of pending certificate requests on a standalone CA.
- If a domain administrator group member of the parent domain (or an administrator with write access to Active Directory) installs the standalone CA, the standalone CA publishes the certificate and the Certificate Revocation list to Active Directory.

With this brief PKI introduction out of the way, we can move forward into the planning stages for your Windows Server 2003 PKI implementation.

Initial Planning for the PKI

When you are preparing to install a CA, you should start by planning how to configure your PKI. As we've discussed, certificates and CAs are a means to prove an identity. But what if a user discovers Bob's password and logs on to the domain as Bob? As far as the system is concerned, the unauthorized user must be Bob because, after all, it is Bob's username and password.

The most popular solution to securing a network is, of course, physical security. Next is the implementation of a strong policy: strong passwords that change frequently. Finally, another secure choice is the implementation of smart cards because they allow users to carry their digital credentials with them from home to office or anywhere they need to go.

Windows Server 2003 Group Policy can allow you to publish and revoke certificates directly to user accounts. This feature enables you to change a user's digital information and enforce it for accessing and retrieving data. Finally, your PKI scheme should include measures for your enterprise to secure email using Secure/Multipurpose Internet Mail Extensions (S/MIME), Secure Sockets Layer (SSL), and Transport Layer Security (TLS).

Before you can install the PKI and your first CA, you need to have a plan that addresses these additional questions:

- What type of CA or CAs do you require?
- How many total CAs will you require?
- How long will certificates be valid for?
- Who will manage the security?
- Will administrative duties be delegated?
- How will the CA be monitored? Who will monitor it?
- What kind of auditing should be in place for the CA?
- Where will the CA be located?
- Will you be using smart cards?

After you've answered these questions and have documented your answers to formulate a plan, you're ready to move into the next stages of planning.

Planning the CA Hierarchies

Windows Server 2003 PKI allows for and encourages a dispersed hierarchy of CAs. Building a tree of CAs allows for scalability with other organizations and with internal and external resources, and compatibility with third-party CA implementations.

Ideally (for ease of administration), an enterprise would have one CA; this is not usually a reality, however. Each CA hierarchy begins with the root CA, and multiple CAs branch from this root CA in a parent-child relationship. The child CAs are certified by the parent CA, all the way back to the root CA. The parent CAs bind a CA public key to the child CA's identity.

In this parent-child relationship, child CAs are trusted by the parent. That parent, in turn, is trusted by its parent CA, all the way back to the originating root CA. Also, in this model, when an organization trusts a CA by adding its certificate in the Trusted Root Certification Authorities Certificate Store, the organization therefore trusts every subordinate CA in the hierarchy. If a subordinate CA has its certificate revoked by the issuing CA, the revoked CA is no longer trustworthy.

Hierarchies serve many purposes. Some of the reasons for creating a CA hierarchy include these:

- *Varying usages*—Certificates can be issued for a number of purposes, such as secure email, SSL, and TSL. Different CAs can be responsible for different areas of security.
- *Politics*—A hierarchy allows for various departments within an enterprise to use unique policies.
- *Geography*—In a wide area network (WAN) environment, a different CA might be needed in each physical location to save network resources.
- *Security*—The root CA requires a very secure environment with fault-tolerant devices. Subordinate CAs do not require the same amount and type of security as the root.
- *Revoking*—Most organizations need to have the capability to revoke individual CAs rather than be forced to revoke an entire enterprise.

As you're planning your hierarchy, remember that a root CA is a CA from which all subordinate CAs branch. This CA should be the most secure and should probably be taken offline (in the case of a standalone CA) after the installation to ensure the security of the originating certificate and keys. Figure 6.1 illustrates the concept of multiple branching CAs in an organization.

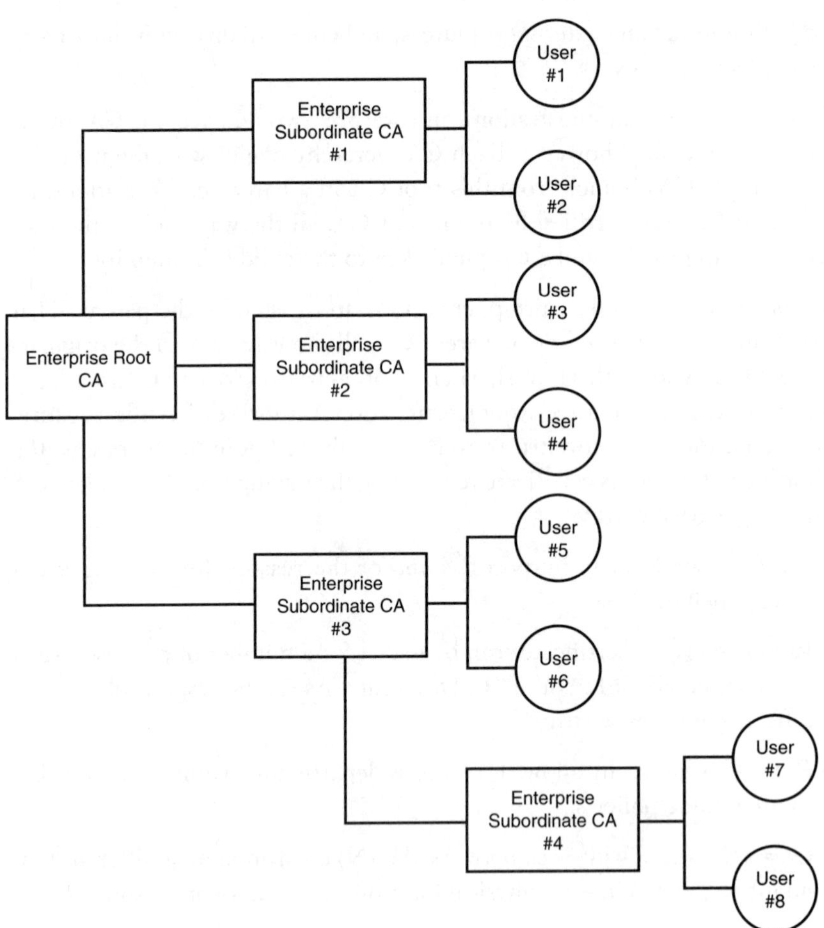

Figure 6.1 You can have Certificate Authorities arranged in any hierarchical order you require.

Planning Certificate Revocation and Renewal

CAs are not only responsible for issuing and signing digital certificates; they are also responsible for maintaining an accurate and up-to-date listing of those certificates that are no longer valid and thus should not be trusted. This listing of invalid certificates is known as a Certificate Revocation List (CRL) and is itself digitally signed by the issuing CA to verify its authenticity.

When a certificate is issued, it has a set lifetime attached to it—typically two years, by default. Under normal circumstances, the certificate can be used for this period of time and ceases to be valid automatically if it is not renewed before the expiration date has been reached. Thus, it is necessary to place only certificates that have been revoked early for some reason on the

CRL—certificates that have expired (those that have passed their expiration date) are automatically considered invalid and do not need to be placed on a CRL.

The real decisions that you must make in relation to certificate revocation, in most cases, are limited to determining what circumstances require a certificate revocation and how to publish the CRL. Some organizations might require a certificate to be revoked only when an employee leaves the company, whereas other organizations might require a certificate to be revoked for Acceptable Use Policy (AUP) violations and the like. In addition, you might need to change the interval and location to which CRLs are published. You can publish the CRL as often as once per day to any combination of the following locations: Active Directory (the default), a URL for access via a Web browser, or a CRL file that can be transported to a different location.

In direct contrast to certificate revocation, certificate renewal is just as important to your PKI implementation. Will you allow certificates to be renewed after their initial lifetime? When will you allow certificates to be renewed—how much of their lifetime must have passed before they can be renewed? Will you be using the same key pair for the renewed certificate, allowing a user to extend the usable life of their key, or will you require a new key pair to be created for the renewal, making any previously encrypted information unreadable?

Renewing CAs

In a parent-child relationship between CAs, the parent CA issues a certificate as part of the relationship to designate the child CA. Just like the certificate to a client, the certificate to a subordinate CA includes a validity period.

When the validity period expires for a CA, its own certificate must be renewed before it can grant any certification requests from client computers. When organizing your PKI, take into account the time a certification in a parent-child relationship should last.

As a safety and security measure, Windows Server 2003 PKI is set up so that a CA cannot issue certificates to requestors that last beyond its own certificate's expiration date. This is handy because it ensures, for example, that a CA scheduled to expire this October cannot issue a certificate that expires later than October.

Even the Root CA's own certificate eventually expires. Because of this, certificates that it issues to subordinates are staggered from its own expiration date. In other words, when the root CA expires, all subordinate CAs will have expired as well. No subordinate CAs are valid beyond the date of the originating CA.

Planning Certificate Template Usage

Windows Server 2003 comes with a wide range of preconfigured certificate templates that can be used to issue a variety of digital certificates. Although it is not mandatory to decide before beginning your PKI implementation, you need to be aware of the certificate templates that are available and what purpose they serve. Certain applications—Exchange Server, for example—cannot be installed with full functionality unless certain optional certificate templates are made available first. Table 6.1 outlines the certificate templates that are available for use in Window Server 2003.

Table 6.1 The Windows Server 2003 Certificate Templates

Template	Purpose
Administrator	Provides for trust list signing and user authentication
Authenticated Session	Allows the user to authenticate to a Web server
Basic EFS	Allows the user to encrypt data using the Encrypting File System (EFS)
CA Exchange	Provides for key storage that is configured for private key archival
CEP Encryption	Allows the computer to act as a registration authority (RA) for simple certificate enrollment protocol (SCEP) requests
Code Signing	Provides a means to digitally sign software
Computer	Provides a means for a computer to authenticate itself on the network
Cross-Certification Authority	Used for cross-certification and qualified subordination of CAs
Directory Email Replication	Provides a means to replicate email within Active Directory
Domain Controller	A general-purpose certificate used by domain controllers
Domain Controller Authentication	Allows computers and users to authenticate to Active Directory
EFS Recovery Agent	Allows the user to decrypt files that have been encrypted with EFS
Enrollment Agent	Allows a user to request certificates on behalf of another subject
Enrollment Agent (Computer)	Allows a computer to request certificates on behalf of another computer subject
Exchange Enrollment Agent (Offline request)	Allows Exchange Server to request certificates on behalf of another subject and supply the subject name in the request

(continued)

Table 6.1 The Windows Server 2003 Certificate Templates *(continued)*

Template	Purpose
Exchange Signature Only	Allows the Microsoft Exchange Key Management Service (KMS) to issue certificates to Exchange users for digitally signing email
Exchange User	Allows the KMS to issue certificates to Exchange users for encrypting email
IPSec	Provides a means for a computer to use IP Security (IPSec) to digitally sign, encrypt, and decrypt network communication
IPSec (Offline Request)	Allows IPSec to digitally sign, encrypt, and decrypt network communication when the subject name is supplied in the request
Key Recovery Agent	Provides a means to recover private keys that are archived on the Certificate Authority
RAS and IAS Server	Provides a means for Remote Access Service (RAS) and Internet Authentication Service (IAS) servers to authenticate their identity to other computers
Root Certification Authority	Allows the root CA to prove its identity
Router (Offline request)	Allows a router to request a certificate when requested through Simple Certificate Enrollment Protocol (SCEP) from a certification authority that holds a CEP Encryption certificate
Smartcard Logon	Allows the user to authenticate to the domain using a smart card
Smartcard User	Provides a means for the user to authenticate and protect email using a smart card
Subordinate Certification Authority	Provides a means to prove the identity of the root certification authority
Trust List Signing	Allows the user to digitally sign a trust list
User	Provides for users for email, EFS, and client authentication to Active Directory
User Signature Only	Provides a means for users to digitally sign data
Web Server	Allows a Web server to prove its identity
Workstation Authentication	Allows client computers to authenticate their identity to servers

With your basic PKI planning out of the way, you are ready to move forward into more specific planning and implementation of your PKI solution.

Planning Appropriate Certificate Authority Types

What exactly are the certificate requirements for your network? Will you be issuing certificates solely for use on your internal private network, or will you need to issue code-signing certificates used to digitally sign applications that can be downloaded or otherwise distributed? The uses for digital certificates that you have will ultimately determine the type of Certificate Authorities that you need to implement. Just as a note, CA types and certificate uses are directly related: The type of CA that you install determines what your users and computers will be able to do.

As a general review, let's examine each of the four basic CA types again briefly as you plan the needs for your network.

Enterprise Root CA

Recall that the root CA is at the top of the CA chain, as seen previously in Figure 6.1—this holds true both for enterprise and standalone hierarchies. The enterprise root CA, then, is at the top of an enterprise—Active Directory—certificate chain and is at the top of the hierarchy. In short, all other CAs trust this root CA.

The enterprise root CA can issue any type of certificate desired, including those for subordinate CAs, users, and computers. However, it is usually best (and most commonly implemented) to have the root CA issuing certificates only to its subordinate CAs; this preserves the hierarchical nature of the certificate chain and specifies a single point that is "all knowing."

The subordinate CAs are then charged with the responsibility of issuing certificates directly to users and computers within the organization. By implementing this parent-child relationship, you can segregate different levels of authority, providing for an overall more robust and secure CA infrastructure.

Because the enterprise root CA sits at the top of the certificate chain, it must sign its own certificate, asserting that it is the root of the certificate chain and that all other CAs are to trust it as such.

Enterprise Subordinate CA

The enterprise subordinate CA is the child in the parent-child relationship of CAs, as discussed previously. The enterprise subordinate CA does require Active Directory to function and can issue certificates to other (lower-level) subordinate CAs, users, and computers, as shown previously in Figure 6.1.

Enterprise subordinate CAs can be implemented in various locations through the network to provide for increased performance and better load-balancing among CAs. Theoretically, you can have as many enterprise subordinate CAs as you desire, although practicality dictates that you should have only enough to ensure that all users can connect to a CA that is relatively nearby. Having unnecessary CAs on the network causes a security weakness, in that a compromised CA might lead to further network compromises.

Standalone Root CA

Just as the enterprise root CA is at the top of the certificate chain in an Active Directory network, the standalone root CA is at the top of the chain in a network that might not be using Active Directory. However, the standalone root CA can make use of Active Directory, if it is available. Being independent from Active Directory gives the standalone Root CA the advantage of being removed physically from the network, thus greatly increasing its security.

You can actually use a standalone root CA very effectively to increase the security of your network by issuing from it certificates that are very important, such as those for subordinate CAs and those used by developers for digitally signing applications for distribution.

Standalone Subordinate CA

The standalone subordinate CA behaves in a similar fashion as the enterprise subordinate CA—with one major difference. The standalone subordinate CA does not require the presence of Active Directory. Standalone subordinate CAs are used to issue certificates directly to users—without Active Directory, you have no reason to issue certificates to computers.

It Matters Not What Type of CA You Implement...

...for you must still take the required precautions to ensure that it is as secure as can be. You must ensure, first and foremost, that all of your CAs are secure from physical access by unauthorized personnel. It is a commonly held belief among security administrators that physical access is the most dangerous threat to any critical server in the network. Place your CAs in a locked and access-controlled server room. Place them inside locked server cabinets as an added layer of protection.

Of course, physically securing your CAs is of little use if they experience a disaster situation. As with any critical business data, you must ensure that CAs are being backed up regularly using an approved and effective backup plan. The most important part of any CA is the CA's private key—without this, the entire CA is useless and every certificate that it has issued must be reissued.

Finally, you should ensure that your network is providing adequate protection for the CAs against both internal and external threats. Viruses and other malicious code run rampant today on the Internet, and you must ensure that your network is protected against these threats. In addition, access controls must be implemented to prevent unauthorized access to a CA.

Although you won't explicitly see it listed in the objectives to install and configure a CA, it's very difficult for you to understand the points made in the following sections without having seen a CA installed and configured first.

Installing and Configuring an Enterprise Root CA

You should be aware that you must provide the following information during the installation of your first CA:

Unlike IIS 5.0 in Windows 2000 Server, IIS 6.0 is not installed by default in Windows Server 2003 (with the exception of Windows Server 2003 Web Edition). If you have not previously installed IIS before you install the enterprise root CA, you must install it from the Windows Component Wizard under the Application Server option group.

For best results, you should install IIS before starting the installation of Certificate Services. Installing IIS before Certificate Services allows the installation of Certificate Services to properly configure IIS to support the Web Enrollment pages.

You should be aware of the fact that you must provide the following information during the installation of your first CA:

- *CA type*—What type of CA will this be? Options include an enterprise root CA, enterprise subordinate CA, standalone root CA, or standalone subordinate CA.
- *Advanced options*—If you enable advanced options during the install of your CA, you have to provide the following:
  - *Cryptographic Service Provider (CSP)*—This is necessary to generate the public and private keys.
  - *Key length*—The longer the key is, the more secure it is.
  - *Hash algorithm*—This is a computation to produce a hash value of some piece of data. The default is Secure Hash Algorithm (SHA)-1, which is a 160-bit hash value.
- *CA name*—You can use just about any character you want. The name you assign the CA will also be the common name (CN) of the CA's distinguished name in Active Directory. Special characters (non–American Code for Information Interchange ASCII and ASCII punctuation) are stripped out in a sanitized name. Also remember that Active Directory is limited to 64 characters before it truncates names.
- *Organization*—This is the name of your organization as it is known throughout its community.

- *Organizational Unit*—This is the division that this CA manages.
- *City and state or province*—This is the location of the organization.
- *Country*—This is the X.500 two-character code for your country.
- *Location of the database*—By default, it's stored in \%systemroot%\system32\certlog.
- *Shared folder*—You can create a shared folder for CA information if the CA is not participating in an Active Directory (such as a standalone server) .

The following steps outline the procedure to install an enterprise root CA in Windows Server 2003:

1. Log into a Windows Server 2003 that is a member of the Active Directory domain with administrative permissions.
2. Select Start, Settings, Control Panel, Add or Remove Programs to open the Add or Remove Programs dialog box.
3. Click the Add/Remove Windows Components button located on the left side of the Add or Remove Programs dialog box to open the Windows Components Wizard.
4. Select the Certificate Services option.
5. You are presented with a warning dialog box informing you that you cannot rename the server after installing Certificate Services on it. Click Yes to continue.
6. Click Next on the Windows Components Wizard dialog box to commence the installation process.
7. On the CA Type dialog box, shown in Figure 6.2, you must select the type of CA you are installing. For this example, select Enterprise Root CA and click Next to continue. If you want to customize the key pair settings, you can do so by selecting the Use Custom Settings to Generate the Key Pair and CA Certificate option.

If you selected to customize your key settings, the Public and Private Key Pair dialog box appears. You have the opportunity to customize the installation by selecting the CSP and the key length. In addition, you can use and import an existing certificate and key. Selecting the Allow This CSP to Interact with the Desktop option allows system services to interact with the desktop of the user who is currently logged on. Click Next to continue.

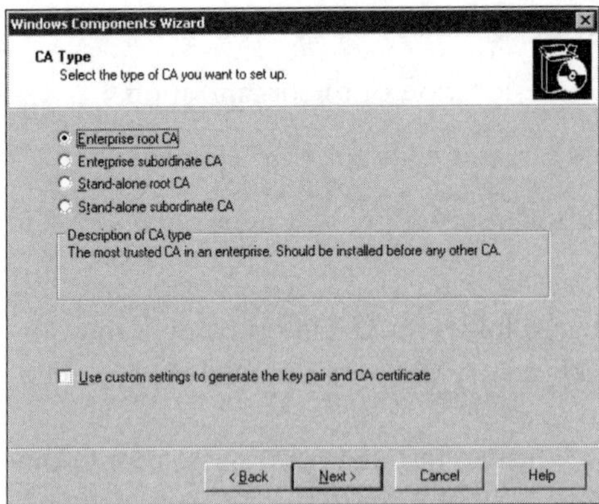

Figure 6.2 You must select one of the four available types of CAs.

8. On the CA Identifying Information dialog box, you must enter the common name of the CA. This should be something descriptive but should not contain any special characters. You also need to configure the validity period—the default value is 5 years. After entering your selections, click Next to continue.

9. In the Certificate Database Settings dialog box, shown in Figure 6.3, you must enter the database and log locations or simply use the default selections—usually the best option, in most cases. If you have clients that are not using Active Directory, you might want to specify that the CA maintain a shared folder in which newly created certificates are placed. This can be done by selecting the Store Configuration Information in a Shared Folder option and entering the path of the shared folder. (As a note, if you were reinstalling Certificate Services onto a server that has already been a CA, the Preserve Existing Certificate Database option would become available.) Click Next to continue.

10. If IIS is running on the server, you are prompted to acknowledge that it will be stopped to perform the configuration of the CA. If IIS is not installed, you are prompted to install it before Web Enrollment can be used. Click Yes to acknowledge the warning. Click Next to continue. You may be prompted to supply the location of the Windows Server 2003 installation files.

11. Click Finish to close the Windows Component Wizard. Close the Add or Remove Programs window. The CA is now ready and available for immediate usage.

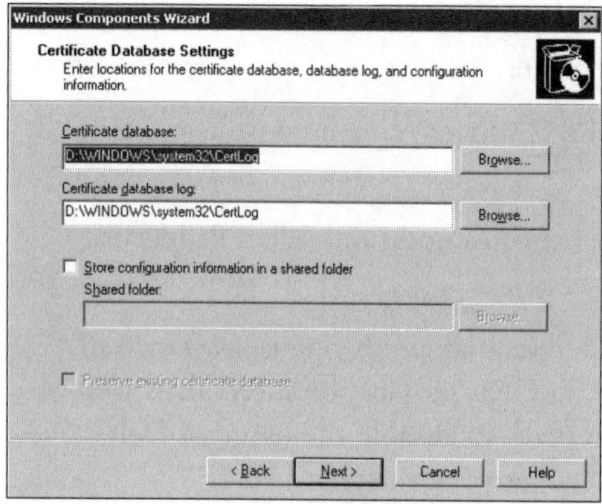

Figure 6.3 You can specify the location of the database and log files, if desired.

When creating the root CA, you also need to ensure a long lifetime for the public and private key of this CA by using a long key length as a deterrent to hackers who make brute-force attacks. The longer the key is, the longer you can use the private and public keys with confidence that the keys have not been compromised.

Microsoft recommends using a key length of at least 2048 bits. However, there is a trade-off between key length and CA server performance: Longer key lengths require more system resources.

With the knowledge of how to install the first CA in hand, you can move forward to configuring Active Directory for certificate publication.

Configuring Active Directory for Certificate Publication

By default, the enterprise CA automatically publishes all certificates directly into Active Directory. As such, there really is no need for additional configuration in that regard. However, you can configure two other parts of Certificate Services that deal with the publication of Certificate Revocation Lists (CRLs) and which certificates a user is allowed to submit a new certificate request for.

Recall that a CRL is used to identify all certificates that have been revoked (cancelled) before their normal end of lifetime. The default behavior of an enterprise root CA is to publish the CRL to Active Directory—as you might well expect. However, you can perform some modification of the CRL publishing configuration to suit the needs of your network. The following outlines the process to modify the CRL publishing configuration:

1. Select Start, Programs, Administrative Tools, Certification Authority to open your CA management console.
2. Locate the CA of concern in the CA management console and expand its nodes.
3. Right-click on the Revoked Certificates node and select Properties from the context menu.
4. The Revoked Certificates Properties dialog box opens, as shown in Figure 6.4. You can configure the CRL publication interval, as well as the Delta CRL publication interval—or disable the usage of Delta CRLs completely. Click Apply to set your changes.

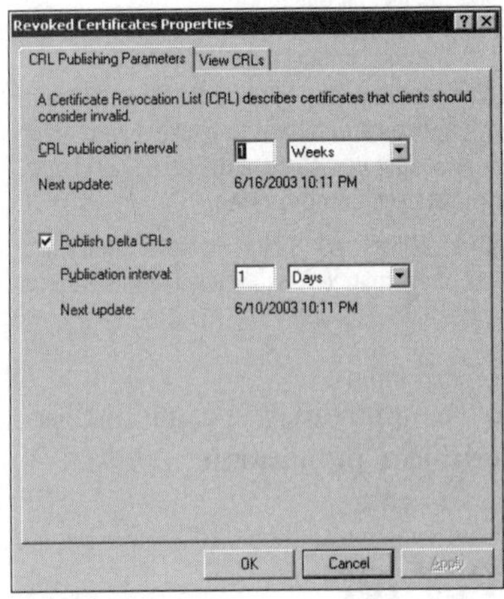

Figure 6.4 The default values for CRL publication can be changed, if desired.

5. You can view CRLs that have been published by switching to the View CRLs tab. You can examine the contents of a specific CRL by selecting it and clicking the View CRL or View Delta CRL buttons, as applicable. When you have finished, click OK to close the Revoked Certificates Properties dialog box.
6. To change the CRL publication location, right-click on the CA name and select Properties from the context menu.
7. When the CA Properties dialog box opens, switch to the Extensions tab, shown in Figure 6.5. You can publish to Active Directory, a file system location, and an FTP or HTTP location. Note that not all options are available for each location. After making your configuration change, click OK. You are prompted to stop and restart Certificate Services to make the changes live.

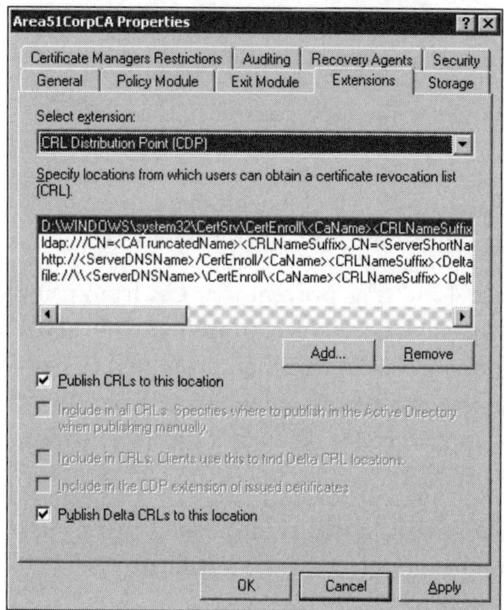

Figure 6.5 You can modify the locations to which the CRL is published from the Extensions tab of the CA Properties dialog box.

8. After you've configured the CRL publication schedule and location to your liking, you might want to immediately manually publish the CRL. To manually publish the CRL, right-click again on the Revoked Certificates folder and select All Tasks, Publish. You are asked what type of CRL you want to publish; select either A New CRL or A Delta CRL and click OK to publish it as you've previously configured.

The only other configuration you might want to undertake regarding certificate publication involves modifying the default configuration of the allowed certificate templates. You might want to perform the following additional actions from within the Certification Authority management console:

- Specify the types of certificates that are allowed to be issued by each of your CAs. This is done by deleting or adding (as required) certificate templates in the Certificate Templates node of the CA.
- Configure the Access Control List (ACL) for each template to limit its use to those users you specifically allow. To request a new certificate using a specific template, the user must have the Enroll permission enabled on the certificate template ACL.

The following steps outline the process by which you can manage the certificate templates your CA is allowed to issue to your users:

1. Open the Certification Authority management console and expand the nodes under your CA.
2. Click on the Certificate Templates node, which enables you to examine the certificate templates that are currently available for your CA.
3. To remove a certificate template—and thus prevent that CA from using it to issue new certificates—right-click on the certificate template and select Delete from the context menu. Click Yes when prompted to confirm that you really want to remove the certificate template from the CA. Note that the certificate template is not deleted; it's just removed from use at that time.
4. To add a new certificate template that is not currently listed, right-click on the Certificate Templates node and select New, Certificate Template to Issue from the context menu.
5. The Enable Certificate Templates dialog box opens, enabling you to select the certificate template you want to make available for use. Select the certificate template and click OK. The selected certificate template now shows up in your Certificate Templates node.
6. If you want to configure the ACL for a certificate template, you need to first open the Certificate Templates console by right-clicking on the Certificate Templates node and selecting Manage.
7. The Certificate Templates console, new to Windows Server 2003 and shown in Figure 6.6, opens, enabling you to configure the properties of all certificate templates installed on your CA.
8. To modify the ACL of a certificate template, right-click it from within the Certificate Templates console and select Properties from the context menu.
9. The certificate template properties dialog box opens. Switch to the security tab, seen in Figure 6.7, and configure Allow—Enroll Permission for Your Users and Groups Are Required. Click OK to close the properties dialog box when you are done.

With the discussion of CRL publication and certificate template configuration behind us, we now move on to certificate enrollment and distribution planning.

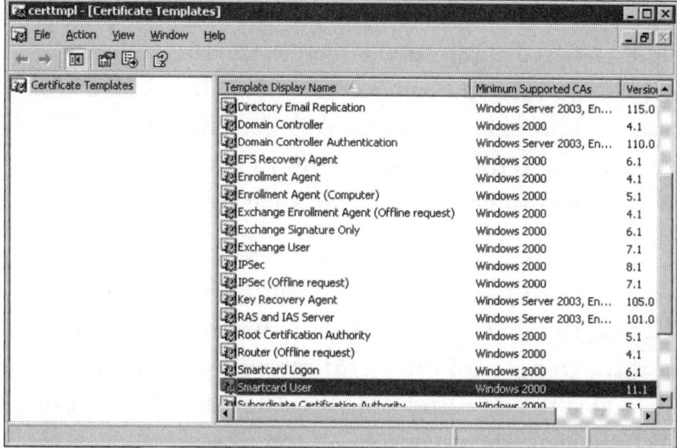

Figure 6.6 The Certificate Templates console enables you to manage the properties of your certificate templates from a centralized location.

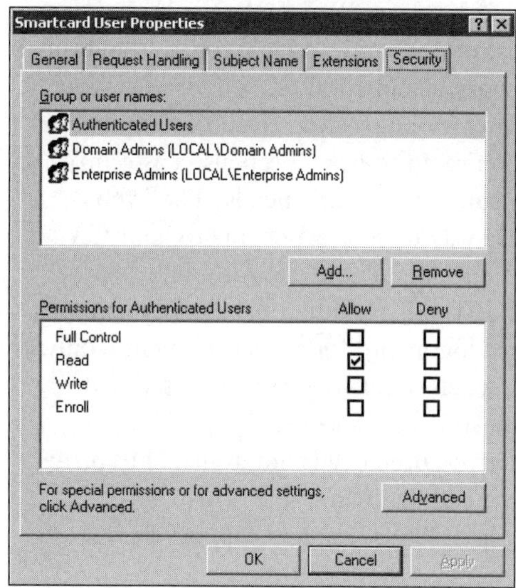

Figure 6.7 You can control who can request a certificate using a specific template by configuring the ACL.

Planning Certificate Enrollment and Distribution

With your CA installed and configured, now comes the question of how you will be enrolling and distributing (installing) the newly requested certificates. Depending on the configuration of your network, you have four different certificate enrollment options.

- *Certificate autoenrollment and renewal*—You can automatically issue certificates that enable PKI-based applications, such as smart card logon, EFS, SSL, and S/MIME to user and computers within your Active Directory environment. Through a combination of certificate template properties and Group Policy settings, you can opt to enroll computers when they start up and users when they log into their domain on the network.
- *Certificate Request Wizard/Certificate Renewal Wizard*—Users of Windows 2000, Windows XP, and Windows Server 2003 computers can manually request certificates through usage of the Certificates MMC snap-in. This snap-in can be added to any custom MMC. Alternatively, you can launch the Certificates management console by entering `certmgr.msc` at the command prompt.
- *Web Enrollment Web pages*—You can connect to a CA by entering `http://`*`CAServerName`*`/certsrv` in your browser. By default, the Web Enrollment pages—which consist of ASP and ActiveX controls and thus could be considered dangerous—are installed on a CA. However, you can install these pages on any other Windows Server 2003 computer running IIS that you desire. If you're up to it, you can also customize these Web Enrollment pages to suit your specific needs. The Web Enrollment pages provide an easy way to connect clients to your CA without using the Certificates management console. Although standalone CAs also make usage of the Web Enrollment pages, they cannot provide certificates for smart card logon and for autoenrollment—only enterprise CAs can. In addition, when standalone CAs are used with Web Enrollment pages, the requestor must specifically specify all required information because Active Directory is not available to provide the information for the certificate template. Windows 2000, Windows XP, and Windows Server 2003 computers support the use of Web Enrollment pages.
- *Smart Card enrollment station*—This is an advanced form of the Web Enrollment pages that enables trusted administrators to request and enroll smart card logon certificates for smart card users on the network. Only Windows XP and Windows Server 2003 computers support this form of enrollment.

Configuring Certificate Autoenrollment and Renewal

As already mentioned, one of the new features of Windows Server 2003 Certificate Services is the concept of autoenrollment for new certificates and automatic renewal for those approved certificates. Through the combination of Version 2 certificate templates and Group Policy settings, Windows XP and Windows Server 2003 computers and their users can automatically request and enroll new and newly renewed certificates at every Group Policy refresh—upon computer startup, upon a user login event, or per the configured refresh interval for the network.

If you've ever been responsible for managing a PKI infrastructure, you can quickly appreciate the value in user and computers being allowed to automatically enroll and renew the most commonly used certificate types, such as those for EFS, SSL, smart cards, and S/MIME. Although users must still request the certificates manually, the task of distributing (also referred to as enrolling or installing) an approved certificate occurs automatically—thus saving the PKI administrator time and effort, as well as cutting down on the number of mistakes and errors made.

The following steps outline the process to configure Group Policy for autoenrollment:

1. On a domain controller or domain workstation running the Administration Tools, select Start, Programs, Administrative Tools, Active Directory Users and Computers to open the Active Directory Users and Computers console.
2. Expand the nodes of your Active Directory forest until you locate the specific site, domain, or Organizational Unit (OU) that you want to configure certificate autoenrollment for.
3. Right-click on the desired location and select Properties from the context menu.
4. Switch to the Group Policy tab of the properties dialog box, shown in Figure 6.8.
5. Either select an existing GPO to be edited for certificate autoenrollment options or create a new one, as desired.
6. Within the Group Policy Editor, expand the nodes as follows to configure certificate autoenrollment for computers: Computer Configuration, Windows Settings, Security Settings, Public Key.
7. Double-click the Autoenrollment Settings option and configure computers for autoenrollment as desired, as shown in Figure 6.9.
8. Click OK to close the Autoenrollment Settings option dialog box.
9. If you want to configure certificate autoenrollment settings for users, do so from the User Configuration, Windows Settings, Security Settings, Public Key Policies node of the Group Policy editor.

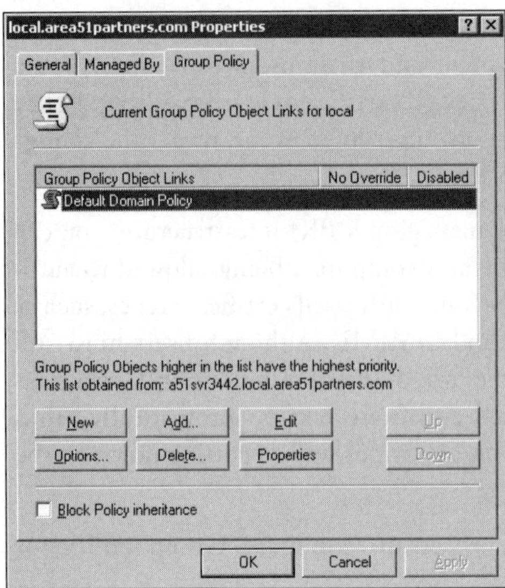

Figure 6.8 Select the GPO to be edited, or create a new one.

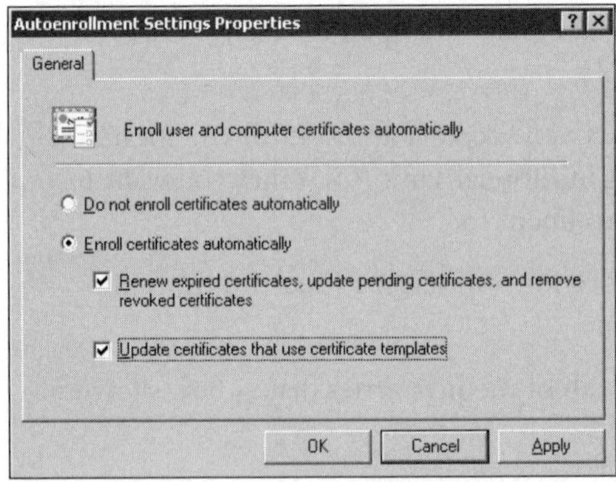

Figure 6.9 Select the Enroll Certificates Automatically option to enable autoenrollment.

10. To refresh Group Policy immediately, run the `gpupdate` command from the command prompt. Figure 6.10 shows the update in action as the domain controller has received an autoenrollment certificate, as evidenced by Event ID 19 in the application log of the Event Viewer.

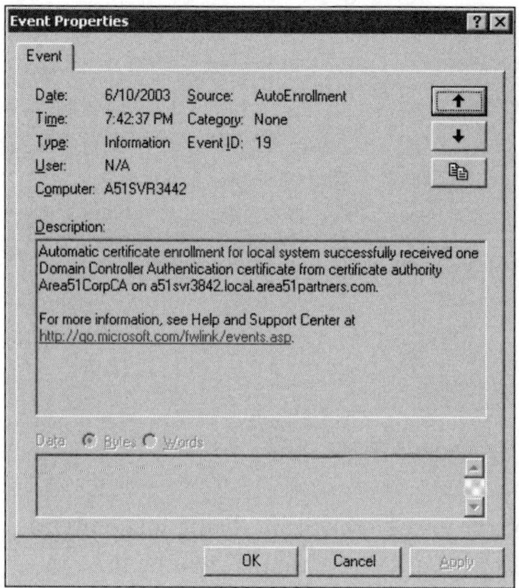

Figure 6.10 Computers will begin using certificate autoenrollment immediately after the next Group Policy refresh.

Using the Certificate Request Wizard and Certificate Renewal Wizard

Although not as new or as fancy as certificate autoenrollment, the Certificate Request Wizard and the Certificate Renewal Wizard are effective ways for Windows 2000 computers (as well as Windows XP and Windows Server 2003) to quickly request and renew certificates. The following steps outline the usage of the Certificate Request Wizard to request a new certificate from the CA:

1. Open the Certificates console by adding it as a snap-in to a custom MMC console or by entering `certmgr.msc` at the command prompt.
2. Right-click on the Personal node and select All Tasks, Request New Certificate to start the Certificate Request Wizard.
3. Click Next to dismiss the opening page of the Certificate Request Wizard.
4. On the Certificate Types dialog box, shown in Figure 6.11, you are asked to select the type of certificate being requested. In addition, you can configure advanced options, including the CSP to be used, by selecting the Advanced check box. Click Next to continue.

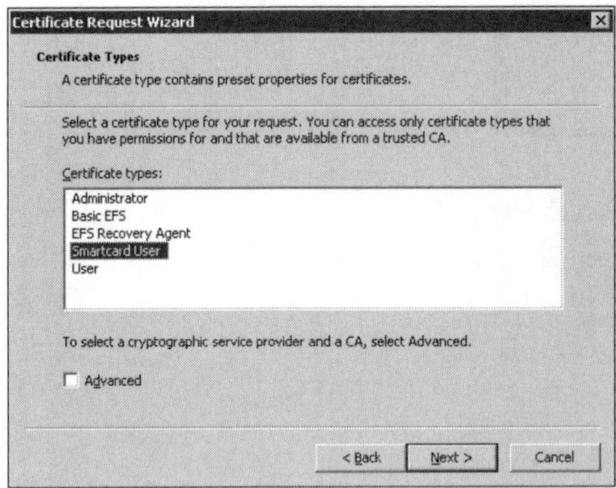

Figure 6.11 You are limited in your request by what certificate templates are available.

5. On the Certificate Friendly Name and Description dialog box, enter a friendly name and description for your certificate that will be used to identify it more easily in the future. Click Next to continue.
6. Click Finish on the Completing the Certificate Request Wizard dialog box to complete the process. If your request was approved, the dialog box informs you of this fact. Click OK.

Using the Web Enrollment Web Pages

As an alternative, and sometimes more useful, means to request certificates, you can very easily allow your clients to use the Certificate Services Web Enrollment pages. Assuming that you have IIS installed on the CA—which you should do before installing the CA itself—you can use Web Enrollment by connecting to the CA using the local Internet Web address of `http://`*`CAServerName`*`/certsrv` in your Web browser. It is recommended that you use a current version of Internet Explorer because strange things have been known to happen with other browsers or older versions.

The following steps outline the use of the Web Enrollment pages to request a new certificate from the CA:

1. Open a new Internet Explorer window and enter `http://`*`CAServerName`*`/certsrv` in the address bar, where CAname represents the name or IP address of your CA. Note that you might be asked to add this IP address to IE's trusted locations. Additionally, you might be prompted to supply your network credentials for authentication.
2. Click Request a Certificate Link to request a new certificate. If desired, you can also check the status of a previous certificate request or download the current CRL from this CA.

3. To request a basic user certificate, click the User Certificate link, shown in Figure 6.12. If you want to request any other type of certificate, click the Advanced Certificate Request link. For this example, you want to request a smart card certificate, so click Advanced Certificate Request.

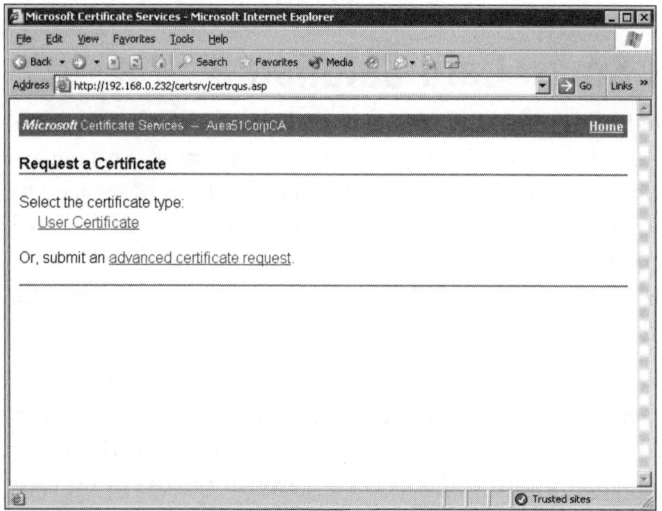

Figure 6.12 Click the Advanced Certificate Request link to request any certificate type other than a user certificate.

4. On the Advanced Certificate Request page, click the Create and Submit a Request to This CA link to continue.
5. On the Advanced Certificate Request page you can select the type of certificate being requested, as well as configure its properties as you require. After you have configured your certificate request as desired, click the Submit button located at the bottom of the page.
6. As part of the enhanced security of Windows Server 2003 (and Windows XP), you are notified that a Web page is requesting a certificate on your behalf—not a problem unless you see this warning while surfing the Internet! Click Yes to allow this certificate to be requested.
7. If the request was successfully approved, you are next presented with the Certificate Issued page. Click Install This Certificate to install your new certificate.
8. Again, Windows alerts you that the Web page is attempting to perform some action related to a digital certificate—in this case, the Web page

is attempting to install the certificate for you. Click Yes to allow the certificate to be installed.

9. Your certificate is now installed and the Web Enrollment pages reflect this fact.

Planning a Smart Card Solution

Introduced for the first in Windows 2000, smart cards provided an alternative—and secure—means for user authentication. Smart cards are tamper-resistant hardware tokens that can be used to add another layer of security to the network. Although smart cards might at first be confused with standard credit cards, they have metallic contacts on them instead of the magnetic stripe found on a credit card. In addition, smart cards require specially designed readers that are attached to the computer being used for login.

Smart cards are used to provide the highest level of user authentication available in Windows Server 2003 networks. A user enters a password or PIN to access the digital certificate on the smart card, thus protecting the user's identity from rogue applications and attackers. Through the use of on-card digital signatures, smart cards can ensure that a user's private key is never exposed. Perhaps the single best feature of smart cards is that they, unlike software-based private keys, can easily be moved, at will, from one computer to another. Smart cards can be prevented from being used to access the network after a preconfigured number of incorrect login attempts, protecting them further from dictionary attacks—a type of password-guessing attack in which a password is guessed from a list, or dictionary, or common words and phrases.

When implementing a smart card system, consider making the following certificate templates available for usage. Bear in mind that none of these certificate templates is made available for use by default—you must manually add each to the Certificate Templates node of the Certification Authority, as discussed earlier in this chapter in the section "Configuring Active Directory for Certificate Publication."

- *Enrollment Agent*—Used to allow authorized users to request smart card certificates on behalf of other users
- *Smartcard User*—Used to allow a smart card user to log on to the network and digitally sign email
- *Smartcard Logon*—Used to allow a smart card user to log on to the network.

Smart cards can provide you with a great benefit—if they are implemented properly in your network. As you might have guessed, this means more planning for you! The following sections discuss smart card planning issues.

Smart Card Distribution Requirements

This is often the most difficult aspect of implementing a new smart card system: How will the smart cards be distributed? What happens if a user has a lost, damaged, or stolen smart card? What about when common issues such as name changes, job changes, or department changes arise? All of these items need to be addressed in your smart card issuance and distribution plan. How do you handle these situations for your Windows user accounts? Perhaps you can model your smart card solution in part after your network password solution.

Another critical question that must be answered for smart cards to be a valid solution is, how you will you ensure that you are giving the correct credentials to the correct person? Will you require users to present validated photo identification, such as corporate employee badges or drivers licenses, to ensure that users really are who they claim to be? What will you do if some users are geographically distant from your location? An ideal solution might be to issue blank smart cards to authorized users and then let them autoenroll (and thus install) the certificate to their smart card. In this way, only the authorized user has access to the smart card and the PIN required to access it. Your smart card distribution solution will be unique to the needs and organization of your company, but, in any case, it must ensure that the security of the smart card program is maintained at all times.

Although it might not seem like it should be part of the distribution planning, you must also ensure that you have adequately planned for things such as public key length values, certificate lifetimes, and certificate renewal policies. Be aware, however, that the memory capacity of the smart card you use can dictate the length of the public key—larger, more secure public keys require larger amounts of storage space, as you might imagine.

Smart Card Enrollment Options

As briefly mentioned previously, you must ensure that you have a method in place to actually enroll the smart card certificates that will be required. You have two basic options to chose from when it comes to enrolling smart card certificates:

- *Use an enrollment agent*—An enrollment agent enables a trusted administrator to process all smart card certificate requests and ensures that smart cards and their certificates are created and installed properly.

Although this can be a good thing from a user's point of view, it can quickly become an overwhelming task if too few enrollment agents are designated. The other disadvantage to using enrollment agents becomes apparent if one of the enrollment agents is later deemed to be untrustworthy—what do you do with all of the smart cards that the agent previously enrolled?

- *Allow self-enrollment by smart card users*—Although enrollment agents are usually the best (and, by far, the most secure) method to enroll smart cards, in some cases you might need or want to have users perform this task themselves. When you cannot physically (and safely) distribute fully ready smart cards, you might want to consider issuing blank smart cards and allowing the user to self-enroll. If you think that self-enrollment is completely insecure, recall that you can configure your CA to hold all new requests pending a manual administrative approval, thus giving you a chance to examine and validate the request before allowing the smart card to be enrolled with its certificate.

Smart Card User Education

What would any security plan be without a good dose of user education? Smart cards are still a rather esoteric thing in the majority of networks today, so you should take steps to ensure that your users thoroughly understand what the smart card is, how it works, and what it provides for the network. Although not an all-inclusive listing, the following points should definitely be in your user education plan for a new smart card implementation:

- Ensure that users understand what special hardware and software they will need to use their smart cards properly.
- Ensure that users know where to get this hardware and software. Additionally, ensure that users know who to contact when they run into problems with their smart card.
- Ensure that users understand that smart cards need to be protected from scratching, chipping, denting, and other forms of damage on the external chip area. These sorts of damages can prevent the card from being read properly, rendering it unusable.
- Ensure that users understand that the card should not be exposed to temperature extremes, direct sunlight, or magnetic sources—as with any form of magnetic media.
- Ensure that users are instructed not to fold, spindle, or mutilate (yes, I had to say this!) their smart cards. Smart cards are fairly rugged, but they contain several internal components that can be broken by slipping

the smart card into a back pocket, using the smart card to open a locked door (yes, this happens), or doing other abusive actions.

- Ensure that users understand that a smart card is a form of identity and, as such, they should not loan it out to anyone else to use. In addition, users must report any loss or theft of a smart card immediately.

Smart Card Group Policy Options

When using smart cards for increased security of your network, you can configure several Group Policy options to further enhance the security of your smart card implementation.

- *Interactive Logon: Require Smart Card*—This option, located in the Computer Configuration, Windows Settings, Security Settings, Local Policies, Security Options node of the Group Policy editor, can be used to prevent users from logging into the domain by using a standard Windows username and password. Although this setting provides enhanced security, it can leave users without network access if their smart cards become unavailable for any reason. You should apply this policy at the OU level, making all smart users members of a domain local group and placing that group within the OU. Mistakenly applying this setting to non–smart card users will have disastrous effects.
- *Interactive Logon: Smart Card Removal Behavior*—This option, also located in the Security Option node, can be used to define what Windows should do when a smart card is removed from its reader with the user logged in. Possible options include No Action, Lock Workstation, and Force Logoff. This option again presents both benefits and dangers. A user who mistakenly removes her smart card with open documents could well lose any changes made since the document was last saved. On the other hand, for computers located in kiosks or other insecure areas, this setting can greatly increase the security of the computer and your network. This Group Policy setting requires training on your part to ensure that your smart card users understand the consequences of their actions. Again, this setting should be configured on a OU containing only those users who have been issued smart cards.
- *Do not allow smart card device redirection*—This option, located in the Computer Configuration, Administrative Templates, Windows Components, Terminal Services, Client/Server Data Redirection node of the Group Policy editor can be used to prevent users from logging into a Terminal Server with a smart card. This can increase security and decrease loading on your Terminal Servers.

- *Account Lockout Policy*—The Account Lockout Policy node, located at Computer Configuration, Windows Settings, Security Settings, Account Policies, Account Lockout Policy in the Group Policy Editor, contains three useful Group Policy settings that you can use to enhance both smart card login and standard Windows login. The Account lockout threshold setting can be configured to specify how many failed logon attempts should be allowed before that user account is locked out. The Account lockout duration setting specifies how long the account is to be locked out (barring an administrator unlocking the account early). The Reset account lockout counter after option specifies how much time must pass before failed logon attempts are no longer counted against the Account lockout threshold setting. These policies are typically applied at a high level in your organization, such as the root of a domain, so that they apply to all users within the domain.

Remember that account policies can be applied only at the domain level.

Planning and Implementing a Security Update Infrastructure

As administrators, we constantly strive to maintain a secure and functional computing environment for our users. In the perfect world, administrators would never have to update an installation of Windows—unfortunately, this is just not the case. Between weaknesses that are inherent to Windows (through coding mistakes or other issues) and the insatiable desire of attackers to find new and more devious ways to open up your network like a can of sardines, you will soon have your hands full trying to keep your network's security stance up-to-date with the latest patches and hot fixes.

Realizing that it needed to become more proactive in helping Windows network administrators understand and correct the issues associated with the various security flaws that occur in the Windows operating systems, Microsoft has provided you with several tools that you can use to identify, categorize, and correct security-related issues on your network. The choice of what tool you use really depends on how you want to go about keeping your network updated. The following options are available for you to use in identifying and installing required security updates on your network's computers:

- *Microsoft Baseline Security Analyzer (MBSA)*—MBSA is an enhanced GUI version of the popular command-line HFNetChk application that can be used on Windows 2000, Windows XP, and Window Server 2003 computers to look for missing security updates, missing service packs, and weak security configurations in the supported Windows operating systems, Office, IIS, SQL Server, and several other popular Microsoft applications. Even though MBSA cannot be run on a Windows NT 4.0 computer, it can be used remotely to scan a Windows NT 4.0 computer. MBSA does a good job of identify and categorizing missing updates and security problems that it finds, but it does not provide any direct means to update required patches. The real strength of MBSA is that it can be used to scan many computers, even remote ones, at a time, providing a quick and easy way to interpret graphical output.
- *Windows Update*—Windows Update has been around since Windows 98 arrived and provides an easy-to-use (although not always accurate) Web-based tool for determining the need to install newly available updates on a local computer. Automatic Updates works in conjunction with Windows Update when SUS has not been installed and provides automatic downloading and installation of required updates
- *Software Update Services (SUS)*—Introduced for Windows 2000 and improved for Windows Server 2003, SUS enables you to provide one or more Windows Update servers that run inside your protected internal network. SUS enables an administer to exercise very granular control over which updates get installed (and which don't) by allowing only "approved" updates to be installed on network computers configured to use a SUS server for updating. After they are installed, all management and configuration of SUS is performed from within your Web browser, for ease of administration.
- *Automatic Updates*—Automatic Updates is a new component of Windows XP SP1 and Windows 2000 SP3 that can download and install required updates from either the Windows Update Web servers or your internal SUS servers, depending on how it has been configured—the default configuration is to use the Windows Update Web servers. Automatic Updates is included in the default installation of Windows Server 2003. To configure Automatic Updates to use an internal SUS server, you must first install and configure at least one SUS server, and then you must configure the appropriate Group Policy settings to require clients to use the designated SUS servers.
- *Systems Management Server*—SMS 2.0 has been in use by a large number of organizations well before the release of Windows 2000 and its

IntelliMirror and Active Directory technologies—the heart of software installation via Active Directory. SMS has been updated recently with the SMS 2.0 Software Update Services Feature Pack to allow it to integrate into a SUS implementation without changing the configuration of the network clients. For many years, administrators have used SMS to manually push updates to clients—the feature pack allows this to become a more automatic function. SMS is due for a new version in late 2003 that will be Active Directory–integrated and promises many new features for software management and maintenance.

Planning for Software Update Services

Although Windows Server 2003 provides native support for SUS, it does not, by default, include SUS. It's easy enough, however, to acquire the SUS installation package and get to work configuring and implementing SUS on a network. But what, really, is SUS? SUS is nothing more than a locally controlled and managed Windows Update server. Instead of configuring the Automatic Updates client on your client workstations to download updates directly from the Microsoft Windows Update servers, you can install and configure one or more SUS servers on your internal network and point your client workstations toward those servers.

As you might imagine, the capability to have your client workstations use an internal server for Windows Update can be a tremendous benefit to you because it means decreased bandwidth use. As important as bandwidth savings might be, there is actually a larger benefit to be realized by implementing a SUS solution on your internal network: the capability to approve specific updates that are to be installed on your clients. When you use Windows Update, your client computers install any available update that matches their needs. With SUS, you can specify which of the available updates are authorized to be pushed to the clients after you are satisfied that the update will pose no problems for the systems. This is a tremendous benefit that often goes unrealized.

As previously implied, SUS is actually one part of a two-part system. The other part, the Automatic Updates client, runs on the servers and client workstations that you want to download updates. Although the Automatic Updates client was included in Windows XP (before Service Pack 1), it was not the correct version to participate in SUS. You need to install Windows 2000 Service Pack 3 (or higher) or Windows XP Service Pack 1 (or higher) on client workstations to get the updated version that can interact with

SUS. Alternatively, you can install the updated version of the Automatic Updates client, which you can download from `www.microsoft.com/windows2000/windowsupdate/sus/default.asp`.

You can also download the SUS installation package from this location. Unlike the previously released version of SUS, this one can be installed on a domain controller, which provides a great benefit to small organizations in which only one server is in use at some locations. The requirements to install SUS on a Windows Server 2003 computer are as follows:

- Pentium III 700MHz or higher CPU.
- 512MB RAM.
- 6GB free disk space on an NTFS partition for storage of update files.
- The system partition on the SUS server must also be formatted with NTFS.

The actual process for installing and configuring SUS and Automatic Updates is covered in Exam 70-291, "Implementing, Managing, and Maintaining a Microsoft Windows Server 2003 Network Infrastructure" and is not discussed here.

Using the Microsoft Baseline Security Analyzer

MBSA is very straightforward and quick to learn. After you download the most current version from `www.microsoft.com/technet/security/tools/tools/mbsahome.asp` and install it, you are just a few mouse clicks away from performing security analysis of your network's computers.

When you launch the MBSA utility, you are presented with the option to scan one computer, scan multiple computers, or review previous scan reports, as shown in Figure 6.13.

By clicking the Scan More Than One Computer link, you can enter the NetBIOS domain name or IP address range that you want scan. When the scan is complete, you can see the results of each computer's scan, as shown in Figure 6.14. As you can see, the computer in this figure is in a *severe risk* situation because it is missing one or more critical security updates.

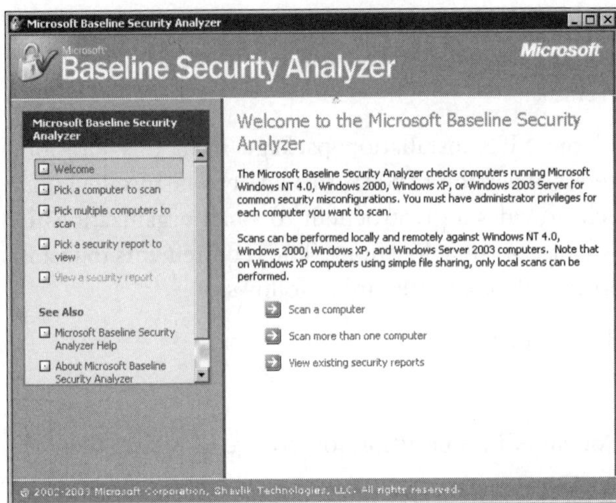

Figure 6.13 You can quickly scan multiple computers with just a few clicks of the mouse using MBSA.

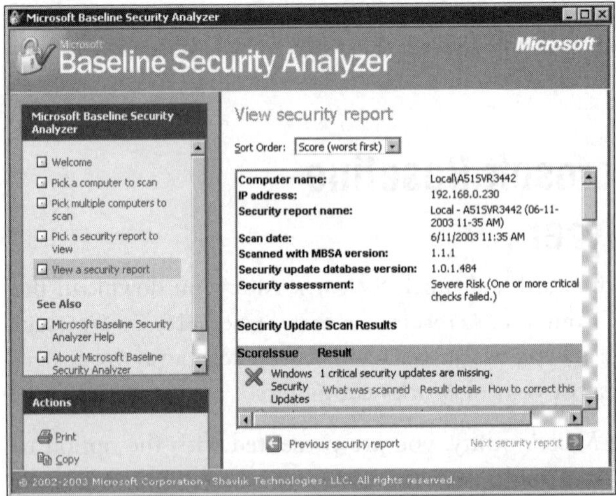

Figure 6.14 This computer is at severe risk due to a missing security update.

As mentioned previously, MBSA scans your computers not only for Windows security updates, but also for updates associated with other Microsoft products. MBSA 1.1.1 (the current version as of this writing) scans for security updates in the following products:

- Windows NT 4.0
- Windows 2000
- Windows XP

- Windows Server 2003
- Internet Explorer 5.01 and later
- Windows Media Player 6.4 and later
- IIS 4.0 and later
- SQL Server 7.0 and 2000 (including Microsoft Data Engine)
- Exchange 5.5 and 2000 (including Exchange Admin Tools

Maintaining a Security Update Infrastructure

In newly implemented Windows Server 2003 Active Directory networks, implementing a SUS solution to download and install approved security updates most likely is the best bet. If you have an existing security update architecture in place, such as SMS or some other third-party solution, you might need to evaluate the benefits and costs of changing to SUS. If you are relying only on Windows Update or Automatic Updates (without SUS) to keep your systems up-to-date, you need to seriously look into rolling out SUS.

One possible scenario for using SUS and MBSA on your network to monitor and maintain security goes like this: You install and configure one or more SUS servers on your network, as determined by the number of clients that will be accessing them (each server can handle approximately 15,000 clients) and the geographical dispersion of your network. You configure SUS to automatically synchronize content nightly when network traffic is at its lowest. You also configure Automatic Updates via a GPO to download, install, and restart computers as required nightly—thus installing any newly approved updates. You make it a habit to review, test, and approve new security updates one or more times a week to keep your systems up-to-date. Finally, you could run MBSA against your network computers twice monthly to spot-check the effectiveness of SUS in keeping your computers updated with the patches you have approved.

Planning a Security Framework

As the old adage goes, if you fail to plan, you plan to fail. Nowhere does this ring more true than when dealing with network security and change and configuration management. By now, you've undoubtedly performed quite a bit of work on your network in an attempt to increase its security. But two questions need to be asked at this point:

1. How will you verify whether your security implementation is functioning as desired?
2. How will you ensure that the security of your network is not reduced or compromised through changes made to the network?

Although the topics of monitoring and change and configuration management are an inch deep and mile wide, we briefly examine both of them here.

Planning for Security Monitoring

So your network is complete. You've rolled out all of your servers and clients, network links are 100% available, and all Group Policy Objects are working properly. Your network is in a utopian state—or is it? How would you know if things weren't really as good deep down as they appeared to be on the surface? If you can't see any problems, does that mean that they do not exist? Unfortunately, no.

You must include in your administrative plan for the network a plan to perform routine regular security monitoring of all parts of the network—from the most high-profile server to the seemingly least important client workstation sitting in the lobby kiosk. But how will you go about monitoring security? It can be a big job that only increases exponentially as the number of computers on a network goes up. Although many very good third-party products exist that you can use (and might want to at a later time) to centrally monitor security for your network, you can do a fair bit of monitoring yourself using only the tools provided within Windows or made available as an add-on download by Microsoft.

First and foremost, before you even start to monitor security, you should strive to always enforce the principal of least privilege for your users. This principle dictates that users are given only the minimum privileges required to perform the specific set of tasks that they have been assigned.

If you use the principle of least privilege, a compromised user account has a smaller impact on the overall security of the network than if you blanket-assigned users permissions that they did not need. Ideally, all normal user operations should be carried out in the context of a user account. If additional privileges are required for a specific reason, the administrator can either log in to the network with a special account for the purpose of performing those actions or use the Run As command to perform those actions within the context of the account that has the additional privileges.

When you have completely implemented the principle of least privilege, the task of monitoring network security will be greatly simplified: You can more easily determine what types of events are normal and what types of events are abnormal, indicating a possible security flaw or breach in your network.

The first part of your security-monitoring plan should be to implement a well-thought-out and carefully configured auditing program. Windows Server 2003 enables you to perform auditing of the following areas:

- *Audit account logon events*—This option configures auditing to occur for user logons. A successful audit generates an audit entry when a user successfully logs in, and a failed audit generates an entry when a user unsuccessfully attempts to log in.
- *Audit account management*—This option configures auditing to occur for each event of account management on a computer. Typical account-management events include creating a user, creating a group, renaming a user, disabling a user account, and setting or changing a password. A success audit generates an audit entry when any account-management event is successful, and a failure audit generates an entry when any account-management event fails.
- *Audit directory service access*—This option configures auditing to occur when a user accesses an Active Directory object that has its own system Access Control List (SACL). This setting is only for Active Directory objects, such as GPOs, not for file system and Registry objects. A success audit generates an audit entry when a user successfully accesses an Active Directory object that has a SACL specified, and a failure audit generates an entry when an unsuccessful access attempt occurs.
- *Audit logon events*—This option configures auditing whenever a user logs on or off a computer. The audit events are generated on domain controllers for domain account activity and on local computers for local account activity. When both the Audit Logon Events and Audit Account Logon Events options are configured, logons and logoffs that use a domain account generate logon or logoff audit events on the local computer as well as the domain controller. A success audit generates an audit entry when a logon attempt succeeds, and a failure audit generates an audit entry when a logon attempt fails.
- *Audit object access*—This option configures auditing to occur whenever a user accesses an object, such as a file, folder, printer, or Registry key that has its own SACL configured. To configure auditing for object access,

you also need to configure auditing specifically on each object that you want to perform auditing on. A success audit generates an audit entry when a user successfully accesses an object, and a failure audit generates an audit entry when a user unsuccessfully attempts to access an object.

- *Audit policy change*—This option configures auditing to occur whenever user rights assignment policies, audit policies, or trust policies are changed. A success audit generates an audit entry when a change to one of these policies is successful, and a failure audit generates an audit entry when a change to one of these policies fails.
- *Audit privilege use*—This option configures auditing to occur whenever a user exercises a user right. A success audit generates an audit entry when the exercise of a user right succeeds, and a failure audit generates an audit entry when the exercise of a user right fails.
- *Audit process tracking*—This option configures auditing to occur for events such as program activation, process exit, handle duplication, and indirect object access. A success audit generates an audit entry when the process being tracked succeeds, and a failure audit generates an audit entry when the process being tracked fails.
- *Audit system events*—This option configures auditing to occur when certain system events, such as computer restarts and shutdowns, occur. A success audit generates an audit entry when a system event is executed successfully, and a failure audit generates an audit entry when a system event is attempted unsuccessfully.

Auditing is configured through Group Policy and is covered by Exam 70-291, "Implementing, Managing, and Maintaining a Microsoft Windows Server 2003 Network Infrastructure."

The second part of your security-monitoring plan should be to collect, filter, and examine the event logs for all network computers in a centralized location. Several third-party applications provide this type of utility, often with many other nice features as well, but you can get good results by using the EventCombMT utility, which is part of the Windows Server 2003 Resource Kit. You can download the Resource Kit tools from `www.microsoft.com/windowsserver2003/downloads/default.mspx`.

Figure 6.15 shows the EventCombMT utility after the completion of a log-gathering session. Note that text files are created with the output results in tab-delimited format.

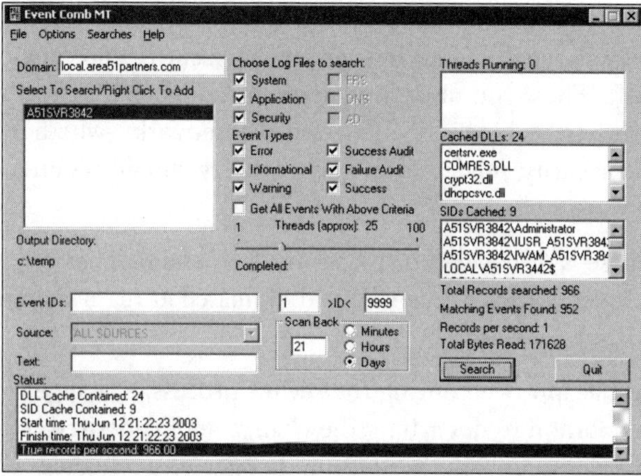

Figure 6.15 The EventCombMT utility provides a quick, easy, and free method of gathering event logs from the network.

Planning for Change and Configuration Management

It's fair to say in today's networking environment that you can no longer just make changes to the configuration of the network or its computers without having documentation in hand. More often than not, this documentation is twofold: One set of documents details exactly what you are going to be doing and how you will back out of it if problems arise. The second set you create as you work, documenting the new configuration that you have set in place.

The first document just detailed—the one outlining exactly what will be done, how it will be done, and what will happen if things do not work out correctly—is in itself derived using yet another document: the change- and configuration-management policy for your network. Use the change- and configuration-management policy document to create all future plans for making security and configuration changes on your network. The key thing that you must realize—and make all members of your organization realize—is that even the smallest change to the network can turn out to be the largest security problem you've ever seen. A good example of this is a (routine) routing table change that caused PPTP traffic to take the tunnel in one direction and the regular IP subnet on the return path so that only half of the conversation was encrypted.

As you can see from this very simple example, even the smallest, most routine administrative tasks can have a large impact on the security and functionality of your network. Thus, you must implement a change and control policy that will be used when making any change to the network—whether or not it appears to be a security-related one! Such a policy should require, at a minimum, the following steps:

1. As the need for change is discovered or recognized, a pending change request is filed. Such requests are reviewed and evaluated at regular intervals.

2. If the change request is approved during the review process, a change order is created. In addition to describing the change and its desired results, the change order might specify staffing, budget, and schedule requirements.

3. When the change order schedule indicates that work to incorporate the requested change is to begin, a change job or work order is enacted. Normally, such changes apply to a copy of the system being changed and do not affect changes to production environments until later in this process. The implementation group must also document its changes and file proposed changes to security policy documents at this time.

4. During the implementation process, module and unit tests make sure that the change, as implemented, meets the requirements of the change as specified. When the implementation team decides that the change is complete, it is turned over to a test group for change testing as an external check.

5. If the external testing group agrees that the change meets the specifications, that the change has no adverse effects on overall system behavior or capability, and that the documentation changes properly reflect resulting security policy, change enactment is authorized. Only at this point are changes introduced into a production environment, so only at this point do real, visible changes occur.

As you can see, this process can become lengthy and time consuming, but no amount of planning is ever wasted. Fortunately, you do not have to reinvent the wheel to implement a good change- and configuration-control plan—many high-quality resources can be found both in print and on the Internet. Some of the more useful ones on the Internet include these:

- Change Management Learning Center: www.change-management.com
- Change Management Resource Library: www.change-management.org
- Kentucky Governor's Office for Technology: http://gotcm.ky.gov

As you have seen, proper prior planning is the single most important key to success when implementing a network security plan. No effective security plan consists of only one security solution—the concept of defense in depth states that multiple, layered security solutions should be implemented to increase network security as much as possible. An example of the defense in depth principle is a network that requires a username and password to gain access to the network. To further protect sensitive information, data on file servers is encrypted using EFS. Finally, IPSec is implemented to secure network communications as they cross the network cabling itself.

Digital certificates come into play with many of these security solutions—digital certificates can be used for smart cards to authenticate and verify the identity of the user, digital certificates are required for the use of EFS, and digital certificates can be used to provide security and authentication for IPSec communications on your network. The scope and type of PKI infrastructure that you implement will be specified, in large part, by the requirements of your network's users.

Two basic types of CAs are available for use in Windows Server 2003. Enterprise CAs are completely integrated with Active Directory and provide some features not otherwise available in a standalone CA. Standalone CAs do not require the presence of Active Directory, but if AD is in use, they can make use of it. Standalone CAs can be used to issue certificates and then can be removed from the network to increase their physical security. Each type of CA has two child types: root and subordinate. There is only one root CA within a PKI implementation; all other CAs are subordinate (or child) CAs. The root CA signs its own CA certificate, as well as the CA certificate of all subordinate CAs directly below it. Subordinate CAs issue and sign certificates for network users, computers, and other subordinate CAs.

Microsoft introduced Software Update Services in Windows 2000 to provide an easy-to-administer way for network administrators to keep the network up-to-date with required security updates. In Windows Server 2003, SUS has been integrated into Windows Server 2003. Using SUS and Automatic Updates enables you to have approved updates automatically installed on client computers on the schedule you have configured. By allowing only administratively approved updates to be installed on client computers, SUS and Automatic Updates help you protect your network from problems caused by required updates that are not compatible with your network or network applications.

When you've gotten a security solution planned and implemented for your network, ensure that your network stays secure. Microsoft has a two-step network security plan: Get Secure, Stay Secure. The Stay Secure portion requires you to maintain security after you have gotten it in place. To maintain security, you must monitor security. Security monitoring can be accomplished in many ways, but the most common include auditing and event logs. In addition, you must have a functional and well-thought-out change- and configuration-plan in place to prevent mistakes from being made that can compromise the security of your network.

Exam Prep Questions

Question 1

You are the network administrator for Flagston Enterprises, a developer of Windows applications. The Windows Server 2003 network consists of 8 domain controllers, 4 member servers, and 592 Windows XP Professional workstations. You have created a plan to implement CA solution. You report to your supervisor that the first CA will be an enterprise root CA. Your plans then call for an enterprise subordinate CA and a standalone subordinate CA. Your supervisors want to know why the standalone CA is required. Of the following, what is a valid reason for adding this standalone CA?

- ❍ A. Having a standalone subordinate CA allows you to provide code-signing certificates and then take the CA off the network for increased security.
- ❍ B. Windows XP workstations cannot contact the enterprise subordinate CA; thus, you need the standalone subordinate CA.
- ❍ C. Having a standalone subordinate CA allows you to take the enterprise root CA off the network to increase security.
- ❍ D. Having the standalone subordinate CA provides an extra measure of availability for your CA solution.

Answer A is correct. The only real reason why you would implement the standalone subordinate CA in this instance would be to provide code-signing certificates for your developers and then be able to take the CA off the network, thus increasing security. Windows XP workstations can contact the enterprise subordinate CA, so answer B is incorrect. You would not normally take an enterprise CA off the network, so answer C is incorrect. The reliability improvement by adding a standalone subordinate CA is questionable and certainly not the best reason for adding one; thus, answer D is incorrect.

Question 2

You are the network administrator for Nebuchadnezzar Furnaces. The Windows Server 2003 domain consists of domain controllers, 2 member servers, and 765 Windows XP Professional workstations. Daniel, your supervisor, reports to you that he suspects that Sam is still accessing the network through the Internet, although he has been fired from the company 12 days ago. He asks you to resolve the matter so that Sam cannot access the network remotely. Of the following, which remedy would ensure that Sam cannot access the network?

❍ A. Delete Sam's previously assigned certificate.

❍ B. Revoke Sam's previously assigned certificate.

❍ C. Force Sam's certificate to expire early.

❍ D. Publish the CRL.

Answer B is correct. You should revoke Sam's certificate to prevent him from accessing any network resources. Certificates are revoked, not deleted, so answer A is incorrect. Forcing Sam's certificate to expire early, although not an option, is the same as revoking it, so answer C is incorrect. Publishing the CRL is something that you will need to do after you revoke a certificate, but it does not solve your problem by itself; thus, answer D is incorrect.

Question 3

You are the network administrator for Fast Sloth Enterprises. After increasing the security of your network client computers, you need to implement an auditing system to keep track of when computers are restarted and shut down. Which of the following options should you configure to track these events?

❍ A. Audit Process Tracking

❍ B. Audit System Events

❍ C. Audit Object Access

❍ D. Audit Privilege Use

Answer B is correct. The Audit System Events option configures auditing for certain system events, such as computer restarts and shutdowns. Answer A is incorrect because the Audit Process Tracking option configures auditing for events such as program activation, process exit, handle duplication, and indirect object access. Answer C is incorrect because the Audit Object Access option configures auditing to occur whenever a user accesses an object, such as a file, folder, printer, or Registry key that has its own SACL configured. Answer D is incorrect because the Audit Privilege Use option configures auditing to occur whenever a user exercises a user right.

Question 4

Andrea is the network administrator for the Think Pink Bike Company. She has recently finished implementing an auditing solution for her Windows Server 2003 network. Andrea wants to track unauthorized access attempts to the company network. After two weeks, she has not found any unauthorized access attempts, even though she tried password-guessing several users' accounts just this morning. What is the most likely reason for the problem that Andrea is experiencing?

- ❍ A. Andrea has not configured success audits for the Audit account logon events option.
- ❍ B. Andrea has not configured failure audits for the Audit account management option.
- ❍ C. Andrea has not configured failure audits for the Audit logon events.
- ❍ D. Andrea has not configured success audits for the Audit policy change option.

Answer C is correct. To track failed logon attempts, Andrea needs to configure failure auditing to occur for the Audit logon events option. Answer A is incorrect because Andrea needs to configure auditing for failure events, not success events.Answer B is incorrect because the Audit Account Management option does not track user logon and logoff. Answer D is incorrect because the Audit Policy Change option also does not track user logon and logoff.

Question 5

You are the network administrator for the Sunbrew Dairy Farms, Inc., corporate network. You have just completed the installation and configuration of SUS for your network. Your client computers are all running Windows 2000 Professional Service Pack 2, and your servers are all Windows Server 2003 computers. After a week has passed, you notice that none of your clients has received any updates that are available from your SUS server. What is the most likely reason for this problem?

- ❍ A. Your SUS server has lost network connectivity to the Internet and has not downloaded any updates from the Windows Update Web servers.
- ❍ B. You have not correctly configured the Group Policy options for Software Update Services.
- ❍ C. The GPO in which you configured the Automatic Updates changes has not been replicated to the rest of the network.
- ❍ D. Your client computers are not using the correct version of the Automatic Updates client software.

Answer D is correct. To participate in SUS, the Windows 2000 computers need to be updated to at least Service Pack 3, and any Windows XP computers need to be updated to Service Pack 1. Alternately, you can install an updated version of the Automatic Updates client, to achieve the same effect. Although a network connectivity issue would prevent your SUS server from acquiring new updates, your SUS server does have updates available on it as stated, so answer A is incorrect. Group Policy does not contain settings for SUS; it contains settings for Windows Update, which is where you will perform the configuration of the Automatic Updates settings. Thus, answer B is incorrect. Although it is possible that an Active Directory replication problem could be at fault here, the most likely reason is that your clients do not have the required version of the Automatic Updates client software; thus, answer C is incorrect.

Question 6

You are the network administrator for the Wing Walkers, Inc., corporate network. You are configuring SUS for your network's client computers, which are all running Windows XP Professional Service Pack 1. You want all client computers to automatically download from your SUS server and install any required updates each night at 11:30 P.M. After the updates have been installed, you want the client computers to restart so that the updates can fully install and the computers will be ready for work the next morning. What must you do to ensure that updates will be installed each night and the computers will be restarted after the updates are installed? (Choose all that apply.)

- ❑ A. You must configure the Automatic Updates client options on each of your Windows XP Professional Service Pack 1 client computers to download and install updates nightly.
- ❑ B. You must set the Configure Automatic Updates option in Group Policy to Enabled and set option 4. You then need to configure a schedule for nightly updates at 11:30 P.M.
- ❑ C. You must set the No Auto—Restart for Scheduled Automatic Updates Installations option in Group Policy to Disabled.
- ❑ D. You must set the Specify Intranet Microsoft Update Server Location option in Group Policy to Enabled and enter the URL of your SUS server.

Answers B, C, and D are correct. For SUS to operate, the SUS server must be provided to the Automatic Updates client computers via the Specify Intranet Microsoft Update Server Location option. In addition, you need to configure the schedule by using the Configure Automatic Updates option and configure for restarting by using the No Auto—Restart for Scheduled Automatic Updates Installations option. In a large environment, you would configure the Automatic Updates configuration settings by using Group Policy instead of performing the configuration locally on each computer, so answer A is incorrect.

Question 7

Andrea is the network administrator for Purple Pony Wear, Inc., a leading supplier of novelty clothing items. The Purple Pony network consists of 2 Windows Server 2003 computers and 34 Windows XP Professional client computers, 30 of which are laptops that are in use in various remote locations by sales personnel. Andrea wants to create and implement a PKI solution so that her users can use smart cards to log on to their laptop computers, thus increasing the security of the laptop and the Purple Pony network. The Purple Pony network does not use Active Directory at the current time. What type of CA must Andrea create as her first CA?

- ❍ A. Enterprise root CA
- ❍ B. Enterprise subordinate CA
- ❍ C. Standalone root CA
- ❍ D. Standalone subordinate CA

Answer C is correct. Because the Purple Pony network does not use Active Directory currently, Andrea needs to install and configure a standalone CA as her first CA. Andrea cannot install an enterprise root CA or an enterprise subordinate CA without having Active Directory, so answers A and B are incorrect. The first CA that is installed is always a root CA, so answer D is incorrect.

Question 8

Austin is the network administrator for Captain Bob's Ocean Fantasies, a retailer specializing in hard-to-find ocean-related collectible items. As part of his smart card solution, Austin has decided to limit the number of incorrect logon attempts that users can make within a specified amount of time. Within the Group Policy Editor, where would Austin be able locate the settings that he needs to configure?

- ❍ A. Computer Configuration, Windows Settings, Security Settings, Account Policies, Account Lockout Policy
- ❍ B. Computer Configuration, Windows Settings, Security Settings, Local Policies, Security Options
- ❍ C. Computer Configuration, Administrative Templates, Windows Components, Terminal Services, Client/Server Data Redirection
- ❍ D. Computer Configuration, Windows Settings, Security Settings, Public Key Policies

Answer A is correct. The Account Lockout Policy node contains three items that can be used to limit the number of incorrect logon attempts over a specified amount of time. The Account Lockout Threshold setting can be configured to specify how many failed logon attempts should be allowed before that user account is locked out. The Account Lockout Duration setting specifies how long the account is to be locked out (barring an administrator unlocking the account early). The Reset Account Lockout Counter After option specifies how much time must pass before failed logon attempts are no longer counted against the Account Lockout Threshold setting. These policies are typically applied at a high level in your organization, such as the root of a domain, to cause them to apply to all users within the domain. Only the Account Lockout Policy node contains the settings Austin needs to configure his solution, so answers B, C, and D are incorrect.

Question 9

Austin is the network administrator for Captain Bob's Ocean Fantasies, a retailer specializing in hard-to-find ocean-related collectible items. Captain Bob's network currently has about 500 remote traveling users who connect to the network via Terminal Services using their smart cards for authentication. A new change in company policy requires that all remote users will no longer make Terminal Services connections to the network, but instead will create and use VPN tunnels to one of the available RRAS servers. In addition to announcing this policy change, what can Austin to do ensure that his remote smart card users do not make Terminal Services connections?

- ❍ A. Interactive Logon: Require Smart Card
- ❍ B. Interactive Logon: Smart Card Removal Behavior
- ❍ C. Do Not Allow Smart Card Device Redirection
- ❍ D. Account Lockout Policy

Answer C is correct. The quickest way to configure Captain Bob's network to prevent smart cards from being used to log on to Terminal Services servers is to configure the Do Not Allow Smart Card Device Redirection option, located in the Computer Configuration, Administrative Templates, Windows Components, Terminal Services, Client/Server Data Redirection node of the Group Policy editor.

Question 10

Christopher is the network administrator for the Heron Woods Resort Cottages company. Heron Woods rents vacation cottages at several locations along the eastern shores of Virginia and Maryland. Christopher needs to implement a solution that will keep the Windows Server 2003 and Windows XP Professional computers at all of his locations up-to-date with the latest security updates, while at the same time installing only those updates that he has specifically approved of. Heron Woods has a main office in Chincoteague, Virginia, connected to the Internet by a fractional T1 line. All other locations are considered remote locations and have a dedicated ISDN link connecting them to the main office. What solution can Christopher implement that will allow him to meet his goals of providing available updates and allowing only approved updates to be installed without adding any unnecessary extra burden on his already saturated WAN links? Christopher has received authorization from the CEO of Heron Woods to add additional servers as required to provide the best solution meeting the requirements.

❍ A. Christopher should configure all servers and client workstations to connect directly to the Microsoft Windows Update Web servers weekly to download and install any new security updates that are required.

❍ B. Christopher should install a SUS server at each of his locations, including the remote offices, that is configured to automatically synchronize each night with the Windows Update Web servers. Additionally, he should configure Automatic Updates to download and install any new security updates that are required on a nightly basis from the local SUS server.

❍ C. Christopher should install a SUS server at each of his locations, including the remote offices. The SUS server at the main office should be configured to automatically synchronize each night with the Windows Update Web servers. The SUS servers at each of the remote offices should be configured to synchronize each night using the SUS server at the main office as its source. Additionally, he should configure Automatic Updates to download and install any new security updates that are required on a nightly basis from the local SUS server.

❍ D. Christopher should install a SUS server at his main office that synchronizes nightly with the Windows Update Web servers. Automatic Updates for all clients, local and remote, should be configured to download and install all approved updates from the main office SUS server on a nightly basis.

Answer C is correct. By configuring a SUS server at the main office that synchronizes nightly from the Windows Update Web servers, Christopher can ensure that all available updates are ready for his testing. By configuring the remote office SUS servers to point to the main office SUS server,

Christopher can ensure that the remote offices are getting only the updates he has approved, while at the same time using only the required amount of bandwidth to perform the data transfer. Configuring Automatic Updates to install updates nightly using the local SUS server also ensures that all computers are up-to-date and that WAN bandwidth usage is minimized. Having client computers download updates directly from the Windows Update servers does not allow Christopher to control what updates are applied, so answer A is incorrect. By configuring each SUS server to download all updates, Christopher is wasting bandwidth, so answer B is incorrect. By configuring all clients to download updates from the main office SUS server, Christopher will be putting an undue load in it, so answer D is incorrect.

Need to Know More?

Bixler, Dave and Will Schmied. *MCSE Training Guide 70-291: Implementing, Managing, and Maintaining a Microsoft Windows Server 2003 Network Infrastructure.* Indianapolis, Indiana: Que Publishing, 2003.

Chapple, Mike, Debra Littlejohn Shinder, and Shawn Porter. *TICSA Training Guide.* Indianapolis, Indiana: Que Publishing, 2002.

Microsoft Windows Server 2003 Administrator's Companion. Redmond, Washington: Microsoft Press, 2003.

Microsoft Windows Server 2003 Deployment Kit, Designing a Managed Environment, www.microsoft.com/windowsserver2003/techinfo/reskit/deploykit.mspx.

Microsoft Windows Server 2003 Deployment Kit, Designing and Deploying Directory and Security Services, www.microsoft.com/windowsserver2003/techinfo/reskit/deploykit.mspx.

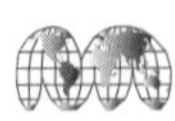

SUS home page, www.microsoft.com/windows2000/windowsupdate/sus.

Windows Server 2003 online help "Auditing Security Events," www.microsoft.com/technet/prodtechnol/windowsserver2003/proddocs/entserver/AuditTN.asp.

Windows Server 2003 online help "Security Configuration Manager," www.microsoft.com/technet/prodtechnol/windowsserver2003/proddocs/entserver/SEconcepts_SCM.asp.

Planning and Implementing an Active Directory Infrastructure

Terms you'll need to understand:

- ✓ Application data partitions
- ✓ `dcpromo`
- ✓ Domain
- ✓ Domain controller
- ✓ Forest
- ✓ Forest and domain functional levels
- ✓ Forest root
- ✓ Global Catalog (GC)
- ✓ Member server
- ✓ SYSVOL
- ✓ Trust relationship
- ✓ Workgroup
- ✓ Universal group

Techniques you'll need to master:

- ✓ Implementing an Active Directory forest and domain structure
- ✓ Creating the forest root domain
- ✓ Creating a child domain
- ✓ Installing and configuring an Active Directory domain controller
- ✓ Setting forest and domain functional levels
- ✓ Establishing trust relationships, including external trusts, shortcut trusts, and cross-forest trusts
- ✓ Planning a strategy for placing Global Catalog servers
- ✓ Evaluating network traffic considerations when placing Global Catalog servers
- ✓ Evaluating the need to enable universal group caching

After the installation of Windows Server 2003 Server, the system exists in one of two settings: a member server (or standalone server) of a workgroup or a member server of an existing domain. In either state, the server can hold several roles. For example, a standalone server can share folders and files, Web services through IIS, media services, database services, print services—the list of functional uses is long. However, directory services are not part of a member server's functionality. For that reason, you might need to consider implementing a "domain" environment.

What are some of the immediate advantages of a domain environment? Perhaps your company requires a single point of logon, centralized management of resources, or scalability. Or, your network and directory infrastructure might need to grow with your company over time. Making that first move toward a domain begins with establishing your first domain controller (DC). To accomplish this with Windows Server 2003, you need to install the Windows Server 2003 Active Directory (AD) service and configure it properly to suit your company's needs. This endeavor requires some forethought and planning to allow for a smooth domain deployment.

The Windows Server 2003 Domain

The term *domain* is not new to the networking vernacular. The way Windows Server 2003 utilizes the concept, however, is quite advanced. The Windows Server 2003 domain is defined as being a boundary for security that provides an organized means of structuring users, resources, and directory information. It also provides a method for replicating that information, and it provides the core administrative services in a Windows Server 2003 network. In Windows Server 2003, only one directory database, called the *Active Directory (AD)*, stores all the user accounts and other resources for the directory. This centralized structure means that users need only one account that provides access to all resources for which they are given permission.

In the actual creation of a domain, you identify a domain name system (DNS) name for the domain. This requires some planning, in harmony with the material in Chapter 3, "Planning, Implementing, and Maintaining a Network Infrastructure," to choose a name that is appropriate from both a corporate and a legal standpoint. Windows Server 2003 domains utilize the DNS naming convention to maintain an organized structure. Because the first domain created is the top-level domain in your directories' infrastructure, this domain is the most crucial, especially if you will be implementing additional domains in the network. Another term for the first domain is the *root domain*, so named because it is the root of the entire forest tree and, by extension, the entire forest.

Even though it is small, a single domain without child domains is considered its own domain tree. In addition, this single domain is called the *forest root* because it becomes the first tree of a possible new forest. The forest root can be likened to the foundation of a building, which holds up the rest of the structure. The foundation of a domain must be solid, and it begins by the promotion of a member server to be a domain controller. You accomplish this promotion by installing AD. Before installation can proceed, however, you must ensure that certain requirements have been met on the server that will be your DC.

Requirements for AD

Whenever you implement a new feature within a Windows product, minimum hardware and software requirements must be met so that the feature works adequately. The first requirement to run Active Directory is fairly obvious: You must have a computer running Windows Server 2003. Meeting this AD requirement ensures that your system meets the minimum hardware for your operating system.

Actually four versions of Windows Server 2003 exist—Standard Edition, Enterprise Edition, Datacenter Edition, and Web Edition (in addition to the 64-bit versions of the Enterprise and Datacenter editions for Intel Itanium processors). Some of the key differences in versions relate to number of processors supported, the amount of RAM supported, and clustering/load balancing support. For this book and exam, the Standard Edition and the Enterprise Edition of Windows Server 2003 are interchangeable.

The following list identifies the minimum requirements for the installation of Windows Server 2003:

- *CPU*—Pentium 133 MHz or higher (550 MHz or better recommended)
- *Memory*—128MB minimum (256 MB or more is recommended)
- *Hard disk space*—1.5 GB of free space
- *Display*—VGA resolution or higher

After the operating system is installed, the following requirements are necessary to install AD:

- Depending on the partition of the hard disk where you plan to install your AD database and transaction log files, you will need 200MB for the database and 50MB for the transaction log. The files can reside on a partition that is formatted with the file allocation table (FAT), FAT32, or NT File System (NTFS) file systems. These files will grow over time as more objects are added, so you need to ensure that the space is sufficient. Additional space is required if your DC is also configured to be a Global Catalog server.

- Along with the database and transaction logs, a special folder structure is installed during the installation, and the root folder is called SYSVOL. This folder must reside on an NTFS partition. If your system doesn't have an NTFS partition, the AD installation will fail.

If you would like to install your SYSVOL folder on a partition that you already have allocated as FAT and you cannot reformat the partition without losing critical data (as in the case of your boot and system partition), you need to use the **convert** command. Go to a command prompt and type **convert.exe c: /fs:ntfs**, where **c:** should be replaced with the drive letter you require.

- Another requirement is that your system be functioning under TCP/IP and utilizing a DNS server. If you've forgotten to establish a DNS server, this will be provided as an option during AD installation.

When you've established that your server meets the requirements to install AD and you have invested the necessary time in planning your first DC, it's time to kick off the installation.

The AD Installation Wizard

The actual creation of the first domain of your network is not a difficult task. You are simply promoting a Windows Server 2003 server to be a domain controller by using the AD Installation Wizard. You are creating your forest root as the first DC of your new domain.

Unlike some wizards, the AD Installation Wizard does not have an icon or shortcut to execute. It requires that you select Start, Run. In the box, type `dcpromo.exe` (or just `dcpromo`, for short) and press Enter.

This wizard offers the following directory service installation options:

- Create a domain controller for a new domain. You have the option to create a new forest, a new child domain, or a new parent domain.
- Add an additional domain controller for an existing domain.

Installing Your First Domain

To install the first DC by promoting a member server, follow these steps:

1. Begin the promotion by selecting Start, Run, and typing **`dcpromo.exe`**. Press Enter.
2. After your AD Installation Wizard has initialized, a welcome screen appears. Select Next.
3. The first screen is a warning telling you that Windows 95 and Windows NT 4.0 SP3 and earlier computers cannot log on to Windows Server 2003 domain controllers. If this is a consideration on your network, you must address this before implementing a Windows Server 2003 domain controller.
4. As shown in Figure 7.1, you are presented with two options: creating a DC of a new domain (either a child domain, new domain tree, or new forest) or creating an additional DC for an existing domain (which takes on the account information of the domain joined). Because this is the first domain of a new forest, select the first radio button and click the Next button.

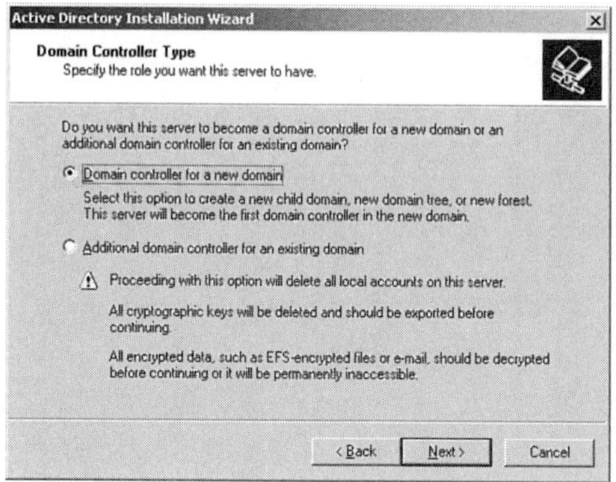

Figure 7.1 Domain Controller Type screen.

5. You are now asked whether you want to create a new domain tree in a new forest, a new child domain in an existing domain tree, or a new domain tree in an existing forest. In the case of creating a new domain in a new forest, you select the first radio button and click the Next button.
6. You will next be asked to supply the full DNS name of your domain. If you've planned your naming strategy and registered a name for your company's domain, use that name. If you are implementing your directory

structure in a test environment without a registered domain name, use a fictitious DNS name. Click the Next button. (Refer back to Chapter 3 for more information about DNS namespace planning.)

7. You next are asked for the NetBIOS name. This name is used for clients running earlier versions of Windows or NT that utilize NetBIOS for the location of their DCs. It is usually the same as the first part of your domain name. Enter the name and click the Next button. Note that this name must be less than 15 characters in length.

8. The next screen, shown in Figure 7.2, specifies the location of the AD database and log files. These files can exist on any of the supported files systems for Windows Server 2003. Remember, the minimum requirement for AD is 200MB for the database and 50MB for the log files. Also remember that minimum requirements should usually be exceeded to allow for flexibility and growth. Choose your location and then click the Next button.

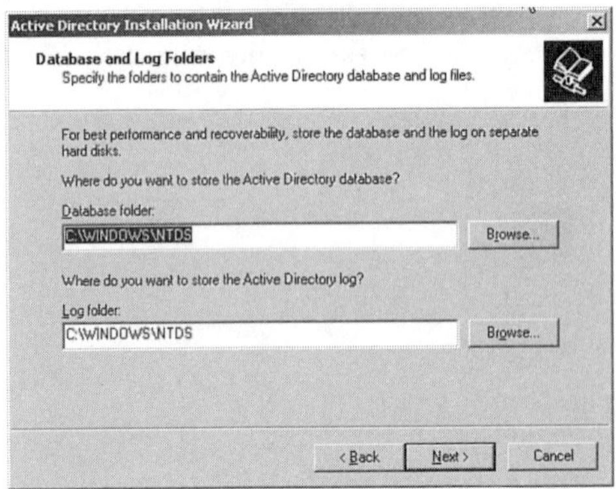

Figure 7.2 Location of database and log files.

Placing your database files and your log files on separate hard drives is recommended. Your database holds your directory, whereas your log file holds your temporary database changes before they are written to the actual database. This creates a conflict of interest for your hard drive as information is written back and forth. Placing the files on different drives (not partitions) will ensure equal time to both files.

9. The next screen, shown in Figure 7.3, is quite important and necessary to your AD installation. Here you specify the location for the SYSVOL folder. This folder, which is shared, allows the DCs to receive replicas of the information within. Therefore, it must be on an NTFS partition. Indicate the location of this folder and then click the Next button.

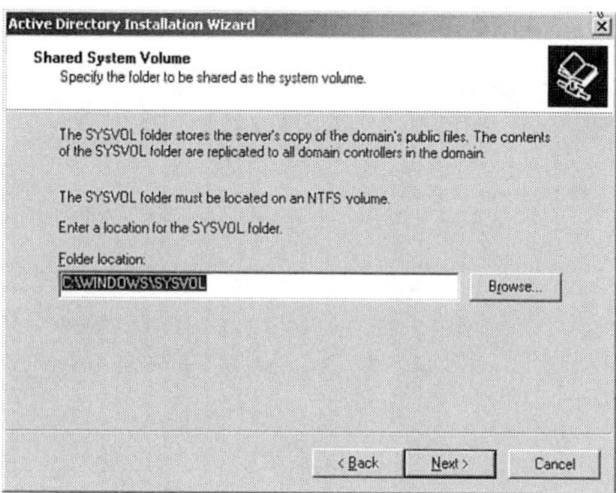

Figure 7.3 The placement of the SYSVOL folder.

10. The next step in the installation process is the DNS Registration Diagnostics, as shown in Figure 7.4. The purpose of this is to determine whether an existing DNS server has already been configured or whether the Active Directory Installation Wizard needs to install and configure the DNS service as part of the installation. Figure 7.4 shows a DNS server that has already been set up for use by AD. If no DNS server was located, the installation wizard would install it behind the scenes as part of the actual installation.

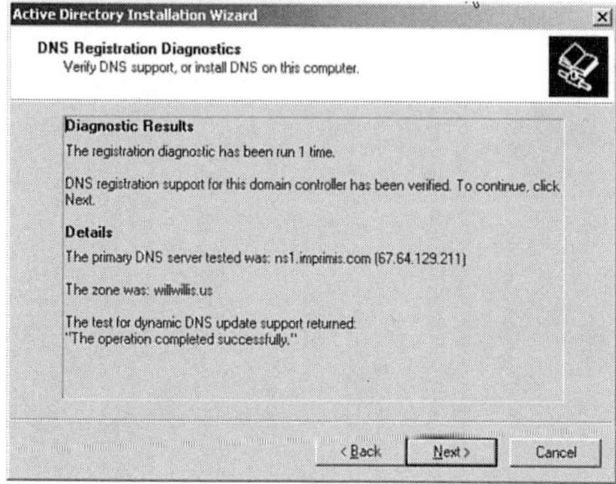

Figure 7.4 The AD Installation Wizard needs to determine the status of DNS before installation.

11. The next step in the installation process asks whether you want to allow permissions to be compatible with pre–Windows 2000 servers or whether you want to allow Windows 2000– and 2003–compatible permissions only. The first selection comes with a warning. If you enable this option, anonymous users will be able to read information on the domain. This can be beneficial in some cases—for example, if you are

migrating toward Windows Server 2003 from an NT 4.0 platform and will have a mixed environment of remote access servers. With this type of situation, your users dialing in from home will have difficulty logging in to the domain if they contact a Windows Server 2003 DC, unless the permissions are oriented toward a pre–Windows 2000 or 2003 system. Select your choice and then click the Next button.

12. Next, you specify the password for the administrative account that is used during Directory Services Restore mode. Because the AD service is not started when entering this mode, you must be authenticated by the server through another means. A non-AD database containing the administrator's name and password allows authentication under these circumstances. Specify your administrative password and then click the Next button.

13. When all your information is complete, you get the final screen, shown in Figure 7.5, which is customized to your choices. Look them over before clicking the Next button. After you do, the installation will follow through until you see a final screen of completion, where you should click Finish.

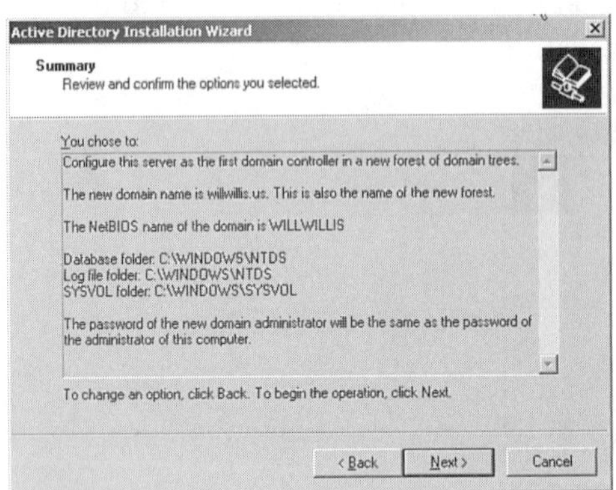

Figure 7.5 The final promotion screen.

Your installation now proceeds by establishing your system as the first DC for your new domain tree under a new forest root.

Deciding Which Type of DNS to Use

As already mentioned, having a DNS server for your AD installation is a prerequisite. However, you can determine which type of DNS server you will use. Although your choices are limited, they do exist. Let's assume that you haven't made your decision by the time you install AD. Not a problem—Windows Server 2003 makes the decision for you.

After you've indicated the location of the SYSVOL folder, the wizard begins a search for the DNS in the IP stack to see whether it exists and whether it supports dynamic updates. In our scenario, a DNS server already existed, so it was unnecessary for the installation wizard to install and configure DNS. However, if DNS was not located, you would receive an informative prompt that it will be created for you. Click OK at this point.

The screen that follows asks whether you want the DNS configured and installed on this computer or whether you want to install it yourself.

When the DNS service is configured and supports dynamic updates (which is automatically done during the installation), the rest of your installation proceeds.

Active Directory installation does not automatically set the DNS to allow automatic updates unless you tell the wizard to do so. Microsoft recommends that you set this or allow the AD Installation Wizard to set it for you if the wizard is also installing DNS as part of AD installation. However, AD will work without enabling dynamic updates. If you do not allow dynamic updates, you must manually synchronize the SRV resource records when you add or remove additional domain controllers.

Fault-Tolerant Replicas

The concept of fault-tolerant replicas is simple: It refers to creating additional DCs within a single domain tree. Additional DCs in a domain help share the load and improve performance. They also provide fault tolerance because, if one DC goes down, the other DCs can authenticate the users and provide normal operations while the damaged DC is repaired.

When adding more DCs to a domain, keep the following factors in mind:

- The more DCs you have in a domain, the greater the availability of logon authenticity is because when users log on to the domain, they can gain authentication from any one of the DCs.
- Each of the DCs will replicate or share its copy of the AD database with the other DCs in the domain. Adding more DCs to a domain also increases the following, thereby degrading network performance:
    - The amount of replication that takes place within the domain
    - The amount of bandwidth that is used on the network

When deciding how many DCs will be in the domain, you must consider both of these factors. You must balance increased speed of logon authenticity against bandwidth usage due to directory replication.

Adding DCs to a domain is not a difficult task. Starting with a Windows Server 2003 server, you promote it using the `dcpromo.exe` command, which executes the AD Installation Wizard. Instead of selecting the option Domain Controller for a New Domain, you select Additional Domain Controller for an Existing Domain (refer back to Figure 7.2).

Additionally, you could create a child domain under an existing domain by doing much the same as you've already done. The main difference in the process is selecting the option to create a child domain at the first part of the installation wizard. An example of child domains would be to take the `willwillis.us` domain created during the previous installation and create `marketing.willwillis.us`, `support.willwillis.us`, and `sales.willwillis.us` child domains underneath it. Child domains are useful for delegating administrative roles to a particular division without giving permissions over the parent domain, as well as controlling replication.

After you have created the first domain, how do you know that your installation was a successful one? This topic is discussed in the next section.

Troubleshooting Your AD Installation

Any number of things can cause your AD installation to fail. Here are a few scenarios:

- *You get an Access Denied error message when creating or adding domains.* These types of error messages usually indicate an incorrect user account. Perhaps you have logged on with an account that doesn't have permissions in the Local Administrators group of the server on which you are trying to create a new domain. Or, as in the case of adding a DC to a pre-existing domain, it's possible that you are not a member of the Domain Administrators group or the Enterprise Administrators group.

Be conscious of questions or scenarios on the exam in which you are not a member of the Domain Administrators group, especially if you are asked about the accounts needed to install AD on a system. Group membership and the rights granted are important aspects of troubleshooting many scenarios.

- *Your DNS Fully Qualified Domain Name is not unique.* You don't have much of a choice here; you must have unique names, so you need to change them to names that are unique. The only exception to this rule is in the case of a testing/training situation in which you are testing the various options for the domain structure in a lab environment (not a production environment, we hope), and you've added systems to the domain and then failed to remove them correctly, perhaps by merely formatting the drive. Now your AD domain tree might still see these nonexistent names as being present. To resolve this problem, you need to edit AD with some additional tools that Microsoft provides, such as ADSI Edit, a snap-in for the Microsoft Management Console (MMC) that acts as a low-level AD Editor. A potential gotcha is that NetBIOS names are limited to 15 characters (plus 1 hidden hex character assigned by the operating system). DNS domain names don't have that limitation. If you had a domain called `WINDOWSNETWORK1.COM` and tried to create `WINDOWSNETWORK2.com`, the NetBIOS name creation for the second would fail if you left it at the default. This is because only the first 14 characters of the DNS name would be used for the NetBIOS name.
- *The DC cannot be contacted, and you are sure that there is a DC up and running.* This situation might indicate that DNS is not set up correctly. Several areas of concern with DNS have already been discussed, but you should ensure that SRV resource records are present for the domain being contacted. Check your DNS server first to make certain that these records exist. If they do exist, use the NSLOOKUP tool to determine whether you can resolve DNS names on the computer where you are installing AD.
- *You have an insufficient amount of disk space, or you don't have an NTFS partition.* You must have a minimum disk space of 250MB for the database and transaction logs. You must also have an NTFS partition for the SYSVOL folder. If you can't free enough space, consider using another volume or partition to store these files. If you do not have an NTFS partition and cannot create one, you need to convert your existing partition. If you are running Windows Server 2003 Server in a dual-boot situation with Windows 98 on a FAT32 partition, you will not be able to make the move toward a DC and retain your Windows 98 operating system under FAT32; you must convert your partition or remain a member server with FAT32.

Microsoft does not recommend having a Windows Server 2003 server in a dual-boot configuration outside of a testing environment.

Verifying Your AD Installation

When your installation is complete and the system has rebooted, you might want to verify your installation. Verification can be accomplished in a number of ways, the easiest being a check of your newly acquired Administrative Tools. However, you have a few other options to ensure a valid install.

File Verification

One way to verify that your installation is complete is to ensure that the AD files are located where you've specified. The following is a list of files that are necessary for AD:

- *NTDS.DIT*—The directory database file.
- *EDB.LOG and EDB.CHK*—The EDB files are the transaction logs and the checkpoint files. Transaction logs temporarily hold transactions before they are written to the directory. The checkpoint file is a pointer file that tracks transaction logs after they have been committed to the database. These files work in harmony to ensure an accurate database with multiple points of strength.
- *EDB.LOG*—The transaction log file temporarily holds transactions before they are written to the directory. It works in harmony with the EDB.CHK file to ensure an accurate database with multiple points of strength.
- *RES1.LOG and RES2.LOG*—RES files are reserved files that are used for low-disk-space situations. These two files are 10MB in size, as are all transaction logs. Because these are permanent, there is always a way to write to a file, even when disk space is low.

SYSVOL

Another way to make sure you've had a successful install is to ensure that the SYSVOL folder structure is on an NTFS partition and contains a server copy of all shared files, including Group Policy and scripts. The SYSVOL folder should include several subfolders, including these:

- Domain
- Staging
- Staging Areas
- Sysvol

The Sysvol folder within should be shared out as, you guessed it, SYSVOL. Another necessary folder that should be shared is the Scripts folder under the Domain folder, which is under the SYSVOL folder. The Scripts folder is shared out as NETLOGON and is used for backward compatibility with NT systems that search for scripts during logon in the NETLOGON share.

Final Checkpoints

You can investigate many avenues to ensure that your AD install was successful, but the most direct method is to check within the event logs. Event logs retain several different types of logs that help you quickly pinpoint a failure, whether on the system itself or with one of the services, such as DNS.

If DNS doesn't seem to be functioning properly, you'll have to troubleshoot your DNS installation (such as verifying records with the `nslookup` tool and monitoring your DNS forward and recursive queries within the DNS properties on the Monitoring tab). Even if your DNS is working properly, you might benefit from running `nslookup` in interactive mode and querying for the zone SVR resource records.

AD Removal

At times, you might want to remove your AD, especially if you've done some restructuring of your accounts and find that some domains require unnecessary administrative overhead, or if certain DCs are simply not required and are creating a strain on the network because of an overabundance of replication. You remove AD with the same tool you used to install it—the AD Installation Wizard. Logically, not just any user can remove AD from the DC. If you are removing the last DC in the forest, you must be logged on as a member of the Domain Administrators group. If you are not removing the last DC in the forest, you must be a member of either the Domain Administrators group or the Enterprise Administrators group.

What Removing AD Entails

When you remove AD, the following actions occur (which are reversals of what took place when you installed AD):

- Group Policy security settings are removed, and Local Security is re-enabled for local security settings.
- Any Flexible Single Master Operations (FSMO) roles are transferred over to other DCs, if any exist.

- The SYSVOL folder hierarchy is removed, along with any related items within, including the NetLogon share.
- The DNS is updated to remove DC Locator service records.
- The local Security Accounts Manager (SAM) is now used for user authentication.
- Services that related to AD are stopped and configured not to start automatically.
- If there is another DC, final changes are replicated to that controller before AD is shut down. The system that is removing AD notifies the remaining DCs to remove it from the DC's OU.

Troubleshooting AD Removal

Sometimes removing AD is a problem; for whatever reason, the removal doesn't work. In most cases, there are reasons, such as data not having finished replicating to other domain controllers. However, in a production environment, you can't always wait and must do a removal immediately; or, in a lab environment, you might not need to wait. In such cases, you can force the removal of Active Directory. You must be running Windows 2000 SP4 or later (or, at minimum, have SP3 and the Q332199 hotfix installed), or Windows Server 2003 to forcibly remove AD. Simply run `dcpromo /forceremoval` to get the process to go through.

Post-AD Installation Options

When AD is installed and running correctly, you might want to investigate several different options.

Integrated Zones

Now that AD is installed, perhaps you want to implement AD-integrated zones within your DNS structure. Integrated zones allow the DNS zone files to be replicated by the AD replication engine instead of being replicated through DNS zone transfers; the zone database files are included within AD rather than stored in their usual systemroot/System32/DNS folder.

When your server is supporting AD-integrated zones, you can configure your zones for secure dynamic updates with the DNS Secure Update Protocol. This allows a greater level of security on your DNS updates.

Domain Mode Options

Windows Server 2003 supports three different types of domain modes: Windows 2000 mixed mode, Windows 2000 native mode, and Windows Server 2003 mode. Upon first installing or upgrading your domain to Windows Server 2003, you will be running in Windows 2000 mixed mode, which supports having NT 4.0, Windows 2000, and Windows Server 2003 domain controllers in your domain. This mode does not allow for all of the functionality of Active Directory, though, so you might decide to change to Windows Server 2003 mode to take advantage of added functionality that becomes available. The differences among the three modes are described in the following sections.

Windows 2000 Mixed Mode

Mixed mode is used for supporting DCs that are NT 4.0 controllers. While moving your current structure toward Windows Server 2003, you might continue to use NT 4.0 backup domain controllers (BDCs) for some time; by running in mixed mode, the Windows Server 2003 DCs will be capable of synchronizing information. Although there is no timetable for how long you must run in mixed mode, Microsoft recommends that you switch to native mode when you no longer have NT 4.0 DCs in your domain so that you can take advantage of native mode's additional functionality.

You can continue to run in mixed mode even if there are no NT 4.0 DCs in the domain. Also, you can make the move toward native mode even if you still have remaining NT 4.0 member servers present in your domain because they do not require the synchronization between the servers.

Windows 2000 Native Mode

If you are installing Windows Server 2003 in an environment with no preexisting NT 4.0 DCs but one that had Windows 2000 domain controllers, you should consider native mode. Native mode provides several enhancements, including the following:

- *Group nesting*—Enables you to place groups within other groups to allow permissions to flow through
- *Universal security groups*—Enables another level of group possibilities, allowing for forest-wide group implementations
- *Security ID (SID) history*—Used during migrations to retain the original SID of the objects that are moved. (Note that this is a short-term migration option, and these fields should be cleared after security on related objects has been updated.)

Windows Server 2003 Mode

If you have only Windows Server 2003 domain controllers in your domain, and after you've upgraded any pre-existing NT 4.0 and Windows 2000 domain controllers, you can convert your domain to a Windows Server 2003 *functional level.* The term *functional level* is used in Windows Server 2003 in place of *mode*. As with changing from Windows 2000 mixed mode to Windows 2000 native mode, raising the functional level to Windows Server 2003 is irreversible.

Windows Server 2003 goes further than Windows 2000, though: There are *domain functional levels* and *forest functional levels*. As you would expect, the differences between the two relate to functionality at the domain or forest levels.

You cannot raise the functional level of the forest until all domains in the forest are operating at the Windows Server 2003 functional level.

When you raise the domain functional level of a domain, you get the benefits of going from Windows 2000 mixed mode to Windows 2000 native mode, plus the following:

- *Domain controller renaming*—Allows you to rename domain controllers without having to remove and reinstall AD
- *Update Logon Timestamp*—Enables you to track a user account's logon history
- *User password on* `InetOrgPerson`—Used in some LDAP and X.500 directory services to represent people within an organization. The `InetOrgPerson` object class enables you to set the password just like you would any other user account and makes migrating from other directory services to AD more efficient.

If all of your domains are raised to the Windows Server 2003 functional level, you can then raise your forest functional level from the default Windows 2000 to Windows Server 2003. As with raising the domain functional level, when you raise the forest functional level, you cannot revert back to the Windows 2000 level without rebuilding your forest from scratch (not a pleasant thought in a production environment). The Windows Server 2003 functional level gains you the following forest-level functionality:

- Improved Global Catalog replication, such as the preservation of the synchronization status of the GC, which reduces the amount of data to be replicated
- Defunct Schema objects, or the capability to deactivate schema classes and attributes, and then reactivate them later, if desired
- Forest-level trust relationships
- The capability to rename domains without removing them and reinstalling
- Linked value replication, to improve AD replication efficiency
- Dynamic auxiliary classes, to support the linking of dynamic auxiliary classes directly to individual objects and not just classes of objects

It is important to remember that although you can raise functional levels, you cannot lower them. So, if you are going to make the move, make sure that you're ready. You can change functional levels in one of two ways:

- Through AD Users and Computers
- Through AD Domains and Trusts

In either tool, the options are the same. Open either AD Users and Computers or AD Domains and Trusts. To raise the domain functional level, open either AD Users and Computers or AD Domains and Trusts, right-click the domain, and then select Raise Domain Functional Level. The dialog box shows you the current domain functional level, with a drop-down list to choose any higher levels that you can raise the domain to. In the scenario shown in Figure 7.6, we're in Windows 2000 mixed mode still and have the choices of Windows 2000 native mode and Windows Server 2003 on the drop-down list. When you select a higher level and click the raise button, you cannot go back to the previous level without removing the domain and reinstalling it.

Raising the forest functional level is very similar. The only difference is that, instead of right-clicking on the domain to select the option, you right-click on the root container of the Active Directory Domains and Trusts console and select Raise Forest Functional Level.

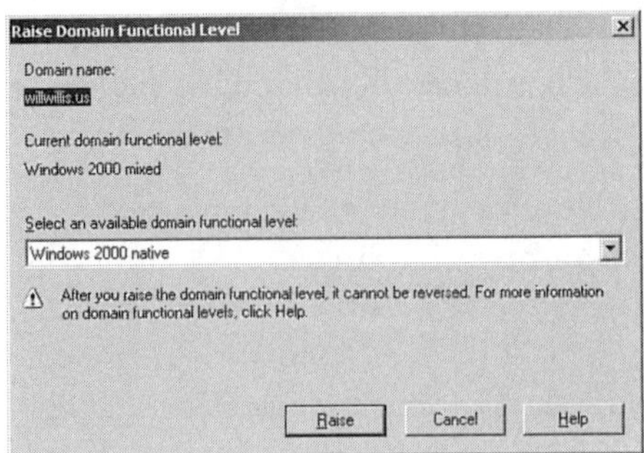

Figure 7.6 Raising the domain functional level is easy, but there is no going back.

Trust Relationships

On a small network, you might have only a single Active Directory forest and domain. However, larger companies often divide their networks into multiple forests and domains. This can be for delegation of administration, for political boundaries, or for any number of other reasons. As a network grows more complex, so does the administration of the network. To facilitate network useability and management, Windows Server 2003 uses the concept of *trust relationships* between domains and forests.

At its basic level, a *trust relationship* is simply a configured link that allows a domain to access another domain, or a forest to access another forest. A typical use is to allow users in one domain or forest to access resources in another domain or forest without needing a separate user account in the other domain or forest. When a trust relationship is established, permission can be granted to a resource, such as a shared folder, in domain1 for a user account in domain2. This simplifies the management of the network, in that administrators don't have to duplicate accounts. It also simplifies network useability from an end user's standpoint because users don't have to keep track of multiple accounts and passwords to access the resources they need.

The following sections examine the various trust relationships available in Windows Server 2003.

Transitive Trusts

Transitive trusts were first introduced in Windows 2000 and were a great improvement over the older Windows NT–style trusts that required explicitly defining each and every trust relationship (something that could be unwieldy in a large enterprise environment). For example, before Windows

2000, if Domain1 trusted Domain2, and Domain2 trusted Domain3, there was no implicit relationship between Domain1 and Domain3. That is, a trust would also need to be manually configured between Domain1 and Domain3, if needed.

With Windows 2000 and 2003, transitive trusts simplify administration. In the previous example, if Domain1 trusted Domain2 and Domain2 trusted Domain3, then Domain1 would automatically trust Domain3. Two-way transitive trusts are automatically configured by Windows Server 2003 whenever a new domain is added to an existing domain tree. For instance, if you added a child domain `texas.studio.willwillis.us`, there would automatically be a two-way transitive trust created between the new child and the parent domain (`studio.willwillis.us`), and also with its parent (`willwillis.us`). Likewise, when a new domain tree is added to an existing forest, two-way transitive trusts are created automatically between the new domain tree and each tree in the forest.

Parent-child transitive trusts are created automatically by Windows Server 2003 and do not require administrative management. The other four types of trust, discussed next, require the administrator to configure them manually. Windows Server 2003 provides the command-line tool *netdom* and a graphical *New Trust Wizard* application. For the exam, you don't need to know the specifics of netdom, so in this chapter we focus on using the New Trust Wizard. After discussing each type of trust, we look at the process of actually creating a trust relationship.

Forest Trusts

As the name suggests, forest trusts are used to share resources between forests. The trust relationship can either be one-way or two-way and is transitive in nature. It is important to note that forest trusts must be created between the forest root domains in each Windows Server 2003 forest; trusts created between nonforest root domains in different forests are not forest trusts, but rather *external trusts*, which are discussed in the next section.

A one-way forest trust enables users in one forest to access resources in another forest (assuming that permission is given to the desired resources), but not the other way around. A two-way forest trust enables users in domains in both forests to access resources in the trusting forest. Because forest trusts are transitive, child domains in a forest receive the benefit of the trust relationship between forest root domains. That is, if a trust relationship is established between `willwillis.us` and `virtual-realm.com`, users in the child domain `studio.willwillis.us` would automatically be a part of the trust through the transitive nature of forest trusts.

It is important to note that, to create a forest trust, both forests must be operating at the Windows Server 2003 forest functional level.

External Trusts

External trusts are similar to forest trusts, in that they must be explicitly configured by an administrator, but that's where the similarity ends. External trusts are nontransitive, meaning that you use them to explicitly define a one-to-one relationship between domains. They are commonly used when you still have NT 4.0 domains on your network because NT 4.0 did not support transitive trust relationships and used a flat domain structure rather than the hierarchical tree structure of Active Directory. You would therefore use an external trust to set up a trust relationship between a Windows Server 2003 domain and an NT 4.0 domain.

External trusts have another use as well. With forest trusts, we noted that they needed to be configured between forest root domains and were transitive. If you didn't want that, but you still wanted to create a trust relationship between domains in different forests, you would use an external trust. For example, if you wanted only the Windows Server 2003 domains `studio.willwillis.us` and `design.virtual-realm.com` to have a trust relationship, without involving the parent domains, you would configure external trusts between the two.

External trusts can either be configured as one-way or two-way. The New Trust Wizard, discussed later, enables you to specify at the time of creating the trust whether it is two-way, one-way outgoing, or one-way incoming.

Realm Trusts

One of the most exciting new features of Windows Server 2003 is the capability to create realm trusts, which allows for interoperability between a Windows Server 2003 Active Directory forest and any non-Windows realm that supports Kerberos 5 (such as Unix). In the past, Microsoft has taken the approach of closing off domains to being able to enter into trust relationships only with other Windows domains. Now, if you have a heterogeneous environment that can utilize Kerberos 5, you can exploit the benefits of trust relationships.

Realm trusts have extra flexibility: You can define them as either transitive or nontransitive, depending on your needs. When you use the New Trust Wizard, you have the choice of transivity as well as whether to make the trust one-way or two-way.

Shortcut Trusts

Shortcut trusts are useful administrative trusts that help speed up the time it takes for user authentication. For example, consider a situation in which a forest contains the domain trees `willwillis.us` and `virtual-realm.com`. Users in the child domain `texas.studio.willwillis.us` regularly access a shared folder in `texas.design.virtual-realm.com` to collaborate on projects. When a user attempts to access the resource, the authentication request must travel the path of the trust relationship. That means the authentication token passes through `texas.design.virtual-realm.com`, `design.virtual-realm.com`, `virtual-realm.com`, `willwillis.us`, `studio.willwillis.us`, and, finally, `texas.studio.willwillis.us`. Because that could become cumbersome, especially in an even more complex forest, shortcut trusts were created.

In the preceding scenario, a shortcut trust could be configured between `texas.studio.willwillis.us` and `texas.design.virtual-realm.com` to speed up the authentication processing. This trust results in the shortening of the path necessary for authentication to travel, speeding up performance. Shortcut trusts are transitive in nature and, like other manually configured trusts, can be configured as either one-way or two-way.

It is important to note the difference between external trusts and shortcut trusts. Shortcut trusts are used to connect domains in domain trees within the same forest. External trusts are used to connect domains in different forests.

New Trust Wizard

In the following example, we configure a forest trust between two distinct Windows Server 2003 Active Directory forests, `willwillis.us` and `virtual-realm.com`. To complete the task on your end, you need a lab environment with two domains configured in their own forests. If you have that, just substitute the names of your domains for what we have here.

Plan a Strategy for Placing Global Catalog Servers

A Global Catalog (GC) contains location information for every object created, whether it was created by default upon installation or manually with the AD. It is also responsible for several other important features, such as the following:

- Logon validation of universal group membership
- User principal name logon validation through DC location
- Search capabilities for every object within an entire forest

The GC retains only some of the more frequently searched-for attributes of an object. There is no need—nor would it be very practical, from a replication standpoint—for the GC to retain every single detail of every single object. Then the GC would be, in fact, a DC.

Several factors should be considered regarding the GC and how it functions to enhance logon validation under a Windows 2000 native mode and Windows Server 2003 functional level situation.

GC and Logon Validation

Universal groups are centrally located within the GC. The universal groups that a user belongs to are quite important in the creation of an access token that is attached to that user and is needed to access any object, to run any application, and to use system resources. The access token literally holds the SID and the group IDs, which indicate what groups the user belongs to. Those access tokens are necessary for logon validation as well as resource access, so each token must include a user's universal group membership. When a user logs on to a Windows 2000 native mode or Windows Server 2003 functional level domain (these are the only ones to include universal groups), the GC updates the DC on the universal group information for that particular user's access token.

Evaluate Network Traffic Considerations When Placing Global Catalog Servers

Because GC servers are prominent in logon validation and in locating AD resources, it is important to plan for their placement on a complex LAN. Ideally, you would have a GC server at each AD site, but this may not always be practical, especially for small branch offices. GC traffic increases the burden on WAN links, so there is a trade-off between making remote sites contact a GC across a WAN link and dealing with the additional replication traffic that a GC server generates across the WAN link. Microsoft recommends having a GC server at each site if your server hardware supports it.

If you are using UPN logon and a GC cannot be contacted, users will not be able to log in using their UPN login information.

Evaluate the Need to Enable Universal Group Caching

With Windows 2000 native mode, a GC server must be available at all times to verify universal group membership. If you have sites separated by slow or unreliable WAN links, the practice is to place a GC server at each local site. The downside to this is that replication traffic is increased. If the domain is operating at the Windows Server 2003 functional level, you can enable the caching of universal group membership so that users can log in even if no GC server is available.

Universal Group Caching is most practical for smaller branch offices with lower-end servers where it might be problematic to add the additional load of hosting a GC, or for locations that have slower WAN connections. To enable caching, use the Active Directory Sites and Services utility. Navigate down the left side of the console and click on the site where you want to enable caching. On the right side (the contents pane), you'll see NTDS Site Settings. Right-click this and choose Properties, which brings up the window shown in Figure 7.7.

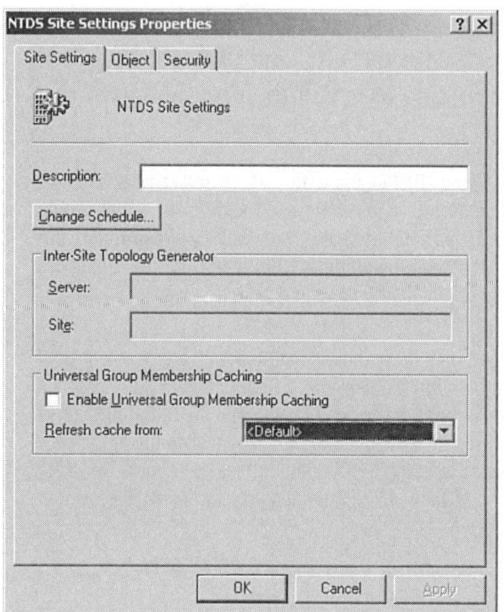

Figure 7.7 Check the box to enable Universal Group Caching, and select a cache server, if desired.

To enable Universal Group Caching, simply check the box on the property sheet. You have the option of choosing a specific server to refresh the cache from or leaving it as <default>, which causes Windows Server 2003 to attempt to refresh the cache from the nearest GC server that it can contact. By default, Windows Server 2003 attempts to refresh the cache every eight hours.

When caching has been enabled, a user must log in once for the information to be cached. On the initial logon, a GC server must be contacted to obtain the group membership information; after the initial logon, the information is cached. As a result, logon times are faster because a GC server doesn't need to be contacted, and network bandwidth utilization is improved without GC replication taking place.

Pay keen attention to the functionality of a GC. Your knowledge of GCs will enable you to determine whether possible solutions will solve the presented problems.

User Principal Names and Logon Validation

Normally, an individual might log on to a domain with a common name and password. For example, suppose that the user's common name is DonnaD and that her password is Duncan1968. Now suppose that Donna attempts to log on to the system using her principal name—for example, `donna@virtual-realm.com`. If Donna is attempting to log on from a system that is in the accounting domain, the DC in `acct.virtual-realm.com` will not know her account. However, the DC will check with the GC, and that will lead to the DC for the `virtual-realm.com` domain. The user will then be validated.

One of the major reasons for using UPN logins is to mask the user's domain. For example, all employees at Microsoft have an **@Microsoft.com** email, which would be part of their UPN logon. Ed Jones could have a UPN of **EdJ@Microsoft.com**, but his logon domain might be **Windows.development.Microsoft.internal** (because the **Microsoft.com** suffix could be an additional registered suffix (without a matching domain).

This means that all employees can have their email address act as their UPN (because both require unique names), the user has a shorter UPN than the actual domain name is, and the user will not necessarily know what the logon domain is if he is taught only the UPN. This gives you a situation that makes the GC access critical during logon. The benefit to using UPN logins is that you can move users from one domain to another, and they will still be able to seamlessly log on that same way in the morning.

Adding GC Servers

Not all DCs are GC servers. Following are several thoughts to keep in mind:

- The first DC in a forest is a GC server.
- Any DC can be a GC server if set up to assume that function by the system administrator.
- Usually one GC is helpful in each site.
- You can create additional GCs, if necessary.
- Except when all DCs are GCs, the server that has been assigned the Infrastructure Master role should not also be a GC server.

To add another GC, perform the following tasks from AD Sites and Services:

1. Within the tree structure on the left pane, expand the DC that will be the new GC.
2. Right-click NTDS Settings and select Properties.
3. In the NTDS Settings Properties dialog box, under the General tab, select the Global Catalog check box, shown in Figure 7.8.

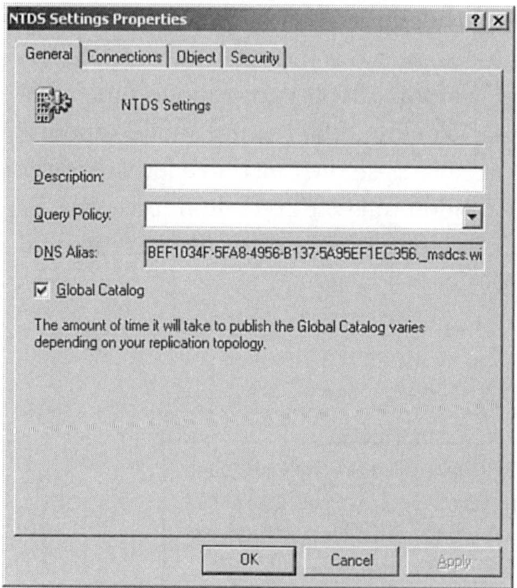

Figure 7.8 Adding a Global Catalog server.

Exam Prep Questions

Question 1

You are attempting to create a universal group in a child domain, but the option is unavailable. Several child domains under a single parent domain all have the capability to create universal security groups, with the exception of this one. What would be a valid reason for such a dilemma?

❍ A. The domain is still residing in Windows 2000 mixed mode.

❍ B. The domain is not running at the Windows Server 2003 functional level.

❍ C. The domain is still in Windows 2000 native mode and needs its functional level raised.

❍ D. You are attempting to create the group on a backup domain controller (BDC).

Answer A is correct. If you are still residing in a Windows 2000 mixed-mode scenario, your groups will be only domain local and global. Universal groups exist only in Windows 2000 native mode and at the Windows Server 2003 functional level. It is perfectly legitimate for one domain in a tree to be at the default Windows 2000 mixed mode, while other child domains in the tree have had their functional levels raised. Answer B is incorrect because universal groups are also available at the Windows 2000 native mode functional level. Answer C is incorrect because Windows 2000 native mode supports universal groups, so you would not need to raise the functional level. Answer D is incorrect because domains in Windows Server 2003 do not use BDCs, nor would it matter which DC you tried to implement a security group on if the domain was not in native mode.

Question 2

Pete Umlandt is attempting to log on to a domain called **research.corp.com**, although his user account is located in **corp.com**. Pete is using his user principal name, **pete@corp.com**. What feature of an Active Directory network will most assist him in logging on to the system?

❍ A. Universal groups

❍ B. Global Catalog servers

❍ C. Additional domain controllers

❍ D. Operations masters

Answer B is correct. Global Catalog servers search for the domain information necessary during logon when an individual uses a user principal name. Answer A is incorrect because, although universal groups can ease administration in domains that have had their functional levels raised, they don't help with logging in through a child domain. Answer C is incorrect because, although additional domain controllers will add fault tolerance, they are not necessarily GC servers and do not assist in logon validation. Answer D is incorrect because, although Kerberos is used to verify authentication to the resources, it doesn't assist in the location of the GC domain controller that will validate a user.

Question 3

Miriam Haber is performing a review of the installation plan for her new Windows Server 2003 domain in a multidomain Windows Server 2003 Active Directory forest. Her staff has detailed the placement of all DCs and operations masters. The administrators are in a small building on a single subnet. There are 10 administrators. The network design team proposes that two DCs be placed in its site. Because there are only 10 people, 1 server would be fairly slow. A more powerful server would be a Global Catalog server and the Infrastructure Master. Miriam rejects this plan and asks the network design team to reconsider. What did she not like about this design?

- ❍ A. Although two DCs are reasonable in other circumstances, the role of the administrators is too important not to have at least three.
- ❍ B. The Infrastructure Master will not operate on a server that is functioning as a Global Catalog server. Either one of these tasks should be moved to the second DC.
- ❍ C. The Infrastructure Master role does not need to be close to the administrators. Because this role is used only for schema updates, it would be better to move this elsewhere and to replace the role with something more pertinent to the administrators' jobs.
- ❍ D. Miriam wants the help desk team to be moved to another site. Having it in a separate site will cause performance issues.

Answer B is correct. Although some of the other answers sound good, only answer B has it completely right. Two DCs should give enough redundancy, but three would not be going overboard. However, answer A is incorrect because not having three would not cause the plan to be rejected. Answer C is incorrect because other roles could be close to the administrators, but depending on what types of tasks are performed most commonly, it might make sense to make the Infrastructure Master closest. Answer D is incorrect because, although the administrators are in a different site, that does not necessarily mean that they have a slow connection to the rest of the network.

Sites are also sometimes used to manage replication. Regardless of any of this, the Infrastructure Master will not operate correctly on a server that is also a Global Catalog server, unless all domain controllers are also Global Catalogs.

Question 4

Sandy Garrity is the design analyst that determines the AD structure for W&W, Inc. The structure takes into account the physical distribution of the company, with the headquarters in Lewisville, Texas, and three branch offices located in Omaha, Seoul, and Barcelona. She determines a need to create a headquarters domain root called **w-w.com** with three child domains beneath. By default, how many Global Catalog servers will be initially created for this widely dispersed solution?

- ❍ A. One
- ❍ B. Three
- ❍ C. Four
- ❍ D. Zero

Answer A is correct. The first DC for the entire forest will contain the role of Global Catalog. By default, this is the only GC in the entire forest. It is recommended that the administrator manually create additional GCs in remote locations and do so when it will be the most convenient for network traffic between the two GCs. GCs hold a copy of every object in the entire forest and a subset of attributes for each of those objects. Answers B and C are incorrect because they provide for too many. Answer D is also incorrect because there is always at least one GC for the forest.

Question 5

You install Active Directory on a server, and you want it to be a separate domain that is part of an existing tree structure. What is this type of domain called?

- ❍ A. A replica
- ❍ B. A parent domain
- ❍ C. A child domain
- ❍ D. A forest root

Answer C is correct. A child domain is one that exists below a parent domain and uses a contiguous namespace. Answer A is incorrect because a secondary domain controller, as a replica, would not be a "separate domain." Answer B is incorrect because there is already an existing domain in the domain tree. As a result, it cannot have another parent created above it. Answer D is incorrect because the forest root would have been established first to add a child domain.

Question 6

You are giving a presentation to executive management on upgrading your Active Directory domains from Windows 2000 to Windows Server 2003. A question is asked of you: "How will this upgrade improve connectivity with our Unix users?" Which of the following features would you describe for the executive committee?

- ❍ A. Realm trusts
- ❍ B. Forest trusts
- ❍ C. Shortcut trusts
- ❍ D. External trusts

Answer A is correct. Realm trusts in Windows Server 2003 enable you to create trust relationships between Windows Server 2003 and any outside realm that supports the Kerberos 5 protocol. As a result, you could establish trust relationships between your Unix environment and the Windows Server 2003 domains, improving administrative efficiency and end-user useability. Answer B is incorrect because forest trusts can be established only between Windows Server 2003 forests, which doesn't meet the needs of the question. Likewise, answer C is incorrect because shortcut trusts are for connecting domains in different trees within the same Windows Server 2003 forest. Answer D is incorrect because external trusts are used for connecting Windows Server 2003 domains to NT 4.0 domains and for connecting Windows Server 2003 domains from separate forests that are not connected by a forest trust.

Question 7

You have recently purchased a new rack-mounted server from a top-level hardware vendor. As you are installing Active Directory on the server, the process halts because the SYSVOL folder cannot seem to be placed where you've specified. What is the most likely cause of the problem?

- ❍ A. You've requested that it be placed on a partition that doesn't have enough space.
- ❍ B. You've formatted the partition with NTFS.
- ❍ C. The drive letter you've specified doesn't exist.
- ❍ D. The partition you are specifying is FAT or FAT32.

Answer D is correct. The SYSVOL folder structure must be on an NTFS partition. Answers A and C are incorrect because, although they are possible causes, the question asks for the "most likely" cause. Answer B is incorrect because putting the SYSVOL folder on an NTFS partition would have actually been the correct thing to do.

Question 8

In selecting the locations of your database and log files, which two of the following options would enhance the performance of these files?

- ❑ A. Placing them on the same NTFS partition
- ❑ B. Ensuring plenty of hard disk space for these files to expand
- ❑ C. Placing them on separate physical disks
- ❑ D. Restricting them to small partitions, for additional control over their size

Answers B and C are correct. Plenty of room and separate physical disks will make for a healthy database and log file configuration. Answer A is incorrect because, although placing the files on an NTFS partition isn't a bad idea, it doesn't enhance performance. Answer D is incorrect because you don't want to prevent your database and log files from growing. This is a normal part of the directory service.

Question 9

Which of the following is not a valid domain functional level for a Windows Server 2003 domain?

- ❍ A. Windows 2000 mixed mode
- ❍ B. Windows 2000 native mode
- ❍ C. Windows Server 2003 functional level
- ❍ D. Windows Server 2003 native mode

Answer D is correct. When domain functional levels are discussed, the term *native mode* refers to Windows 2000 native mode. In Windows 2000, this was the highest mode the domain could run at. In Windows Server 2003 the "native mode" is simply called the Windows Server 2003 functional level. Answers A, B, and C are all valid functional levels in Windows Server 2003 and are therefore incorrect.

Question 10

You are the senior network administrator for an enterprise that has 4 Windows Server 2003 forests consisting of 15 domains. A junior administrator is struggling with some concepts and asks if you can explain why you have trust relationships configured between some domains when they are in the same forest?

❍ A. Shortcut trusts improve the efficiency of user authentication.

❍ B. Shortcut trusts are required to connect child domains in different domain trees, even in the same forest.

❍ C. External trusts are required to connect child domains in different domain trees, even in the same forest.

❍ D. Transitive trusts allow for automatic trusting within a domain tree but not across trees in the same forest.

Answer A is correct. By establishing shortcut trusts between domains that are already connected with transitive trusts, you can improve authentication times. This is especially true in complex forest/domain environments. Answer B is incorrect because shortcut trusts are not required in the strictest sense; authentication would still take place over the transitive trust paths (albeit slower). Answer C is incorrect because, within a forest, you would not use external trusts. Answer D is incorrect because transitive trusts apply to all domains within the same tree, not just within an individual domain tree.

Need to Know More?

Mulcare, Mike and Stan Reimer. *Active Directory for Microsoft Windows Server 2003 Technical Reference*. Redmond, Washington: Microsoft Press, 2003.

Microsoft Corporation. *Microsoft Windows Server 2003 Resource Kit*. Redmond, Washington: Microsoft Press, 2003.

Microsoft Corporation. *Microsoft Windows Server 2003 Deployment Kit*. Redmond, Washington: Microsoft Press, 2003.

Managing and Maintaining User Authentication and the Active Directory Infrastructure

Terms you'll need to understand:

- ✓ Application data partition
- ✓ Authoritative restore
- ✓ Built-in account
- ✓ Domain user account
- ✓ Garbage collection
- ✓ Local user account
- ✓ Nonauthoritative restore
- ✓ Schema
- ✓ Single sign-on
- ✓ User logon name
- ✓ User principal name (UPN)
- ✓ UPN suffix

Techniques you'll need to master:

- ✓ Planning a user authentication strategy
- ✓ Creating a password policy for domain users
- ✓ Planning a smart card authentication strategy
- ✓ Performing an authoritative restore and a nonauthoritative restore
- ✓ Managing schema modifications
- ✓ Adding or removing a UPN suffix
- ✓ Creating and configuring application data partitions

Active Directory (AD) is essentially a database that stores data about network resources and other objects. Two of the most common types of objects stored within AD are users and groups. Having these objects stored within AD enables people to log on to the network and gain access to a range of network resources. Because all objects are stored within AD along with access permissions, you can achieve a *single sign-on*, which is a feature in Windows Server 2003 that enables users to log in to the network with a single username and password and to receive access to a host of network resources. The user does not need to enter any additional usernames or passwords to gain access to network shares, printers, or other network resources.

Generally, *groups* are collections of user accounts (although they can also include computers) that ease administration. Because you can create a group and assign permissions for a resource to this single entity, using groups is far easier than assigning permissions to individual user accounts. In Windows Server 2003, you can also nest groups, which allows groups themselves to contain other groups, further simplifying network administration. In this chapter, we examine users and groups and how they can be used in a Windows Server 2003 environment.

For the most part, Active Directory is self-sufficient after you've done the initial installation and configuration. Sometimes, however, you might need to perform some additional administrative tasks. In this chapter, we examine two of the more common ones: creating UPN suffixes and creating application data partitions. In addition, we look at domain controller backup and restoration-crucial knowledge for any Active Directory administrator.

Introducing Users and Groups

Obviously, if a user cannot log on to a Windows Server 2003 network, that user cannot gain access to the data and resources—such as files and folders, email accounts, and printers—that are stored there. User accounts are the fundamental building blocks of your network. Because they are so important, you will likely spend a lot of time working with user accounts in your environment.

A Windows Server 2003 network has three different types of user accounts:

- *Domain user account*—This account is used to gain access to a Windows Server 2003 domain and all its associated resources. This is the most common type of logon you will experience on a Windows Server 2003 network. A logon that exists on one domain can be given permissions in other Windows Server 2003 domains.

- *Local user account*—This account exists on a standalone server or a Windows 2000 or XP Professional system. It enables a user to log on to a specific computer and gain access to the local resources that it offers. By definition, a standalone computer is not acting as part of a Windows Server 2003 network. Therefore, a local user account cannot grant access to resources in a domain.
- *Built-in user accounts*—These accounts have been created for specific administrative tasks to ease the burden of administration. They define special accounts up front that have permissions to both resources and AD itself.

Because your enterprise network might have a few hundred user accounts (perhaps even hundreds of thousands), creating accounts can be an arduous process. To ease this burden, you can bulk-import accounts using tools provided with Windows Server 2003. In this chapter, we take a closer look at these tools. Creating user accounts in bulk fashion saves the administrator a great deal of time.

The most commonly used network resources include files, folders, and printers. You might have to deal with several hundred or thousand user accounts, so granting access to resources based solely on individual user accounts would be time-consuming and hugely repetitive. Instead, you can use groups. The concept of groups is very simple: You create a single object within AD and grant (or deny) access permissions to this single entity. User accounts are then added as members of the group and inherit the permissions assigned to the group. If these permissions must be changed, you can then simply modify them on the group object a single time. Any changes to the group permissions are applied to all the user accounts that are members of the group.

In addition, Windows Server 2003 enables you to build a hierarchy of groups and assign different permissions to each level of the hierarchy. This is achieved by nesting groups. Nesting groups further simplifies your security model.

Plan a User Authentication Strategy

User logon names are also known as *user account names*. However, be careful with your use of terminology in Windows Server 2003; a user can have more than one type of logon name because Microsoft has provided the capability to use older-style usernames in a Windows Server 2003 network along with a new type of logon name.

Types of Logon Names

When logging in to a Windows Server 2003 network, users can use one of the two types of names they have been assigned: their user principal name or their user logon name. The end result is the same, although the older-style logon names should slowly be phased out. Domain controllers (DCs) can authenticate the users regardless of what method they use. Let's look at these two types of usernames.

User Principal Name

The *user principal name (UPN)* is the new-style logon name on Windows Server 2003 networks. A user principal name is made up of two parts. One part uniquely identifies the user object in AD; the other part identifies the domain where the user object was created. A user principal name looks like this:

```
WWillis@Inside-Corner.com
```

As you can see, the two parts of the user principal name are divided by the "at" sign (`@`). This tells Windows Server 2003 which part of the name is the user object name and which is the domain name. These two parts can further be defined as the following:

- *User principal name (UPN) prefix*—In the preceding example, this is `WWillis`.
- *User principal name (UPN) suffix*—By default, the suffix is derived from the root domain name on your Windows Server 2003 network. You can create additional user principal names by using other domains on your network, although doing so increases the administrative overhead of your network. Windows Server 2003 administrators who have deployed Exchange Server commonly use the email address as the user principal name suffix. In the preceding example, the user principal name suffix would be `Inside-Corner.com`.

User Logon Name

The *user logon name* is used to describe backward-compatible usernames. It is used by clients logging on to a Windows Server 2003 network from an older operating system, such as Windows 9*x* or Microsoft Windows NT 4.0. In our example, the user logon name would simply be `WWillis`.

Logging on to a Windows Server 2003 domain using the user logon name means that users must provide two distinct pieces of information. First, they must enter their username; second, they must enter the name of the domain where their account exists. This can be somewhat confusing to users who might not understand why they need to supply a domain name to logon. Thus, user principle names (UPNs) are usually the easiest way to go when implementing a new solution.

Rules for Logon Names

Because user accounts are used to gain access to a Windows Server 2003 network, a username must be unique. The scope of this uniqueness varies depending on the type of logon name you intend to use. Such uniqueness enables single sign-on. The administrator must ensure that user accounts follow a set of rules so that they are unique within a Windows Server 2003 forest.

User principal names must be unique within a forest. This can make coming up with a naming strategy more difficult, especially when you have tens of thousands of users, but the benefits outweigh the difficulties. You should come up with a naming strategy that allows for usernames that are easy to remember yet easily distinguishable.

The username suffix (in our case, `Inside-Corner.com`) is derived from the domain in which the user account is created by default. However, this can be changed. By adding additional suffixes, you ensure that users have a standard and easy-to-understand user principal name. Before an additional suffix can be used, it must be added to AD, as discussed later in the "UPN Suffixes" section of this chapter.

User logon names must be unique within the domain in which they are created. If you think you will use these logon types exclusively, you have a little more flexibility in naming conventions because, in effect, you can share a single username across multiple domains. However, using a single name exclusively is discouraged. Over time, this will undoubtedly cause additional administrative overhead.

Administering User Accounts

Many of the ongoing administrative tasks performed on a Windows Server 2003 network are based on user accounts. This includes the creation and maintenance of these accounts. In this section, we look at the common administrative tools you will use, as well as how to search AD for specific data.

The most common administrative tool is AD Users and Computers. To access this utility, select Start, Programs, Administrative Tools, Active Directory Users and Computers.

AD Users and Computers provides you with all the day-to-day functionality you need. In this section, we look at some of the most common functions you are likely to perform. Being familiar with the interface of AD Users and Computers helps you be more efficient at administering user accounts in your environment. The common administrative tasks we look at include the following:

- Resetting passwords
- Unlocking user accounts
- Deleting user accounts
- Renaming user accounts
- Copying user accounts
- Disabling and enabling user accounts

Because these are common tasks, Microsoft has provided an easy method to perform them. To perform each of these tasks, simply select the Users container in the left panel of AD Users and Computers, and then right-click the user object you want to change in the panel on the right. When you do this, you are presented with the context-sensitive menu shown in Figure 8.1.

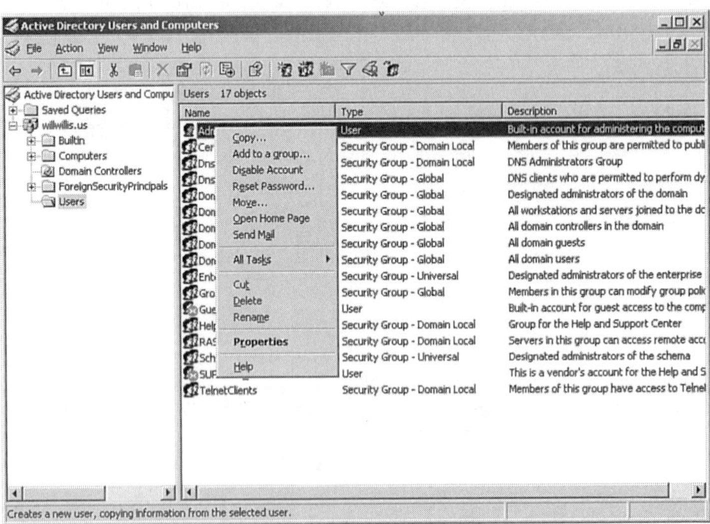

Figure 8.1 AD Users and Computers context-sensitive menu.

As you can see, this menu offers you a wealth of functionality. Note that it is possible to perform some tasks on multiple user accounts. For instance, if you highlight five user accounts and then right-click them, you will see a context-sensitive menu with a subset of functions. One of these functions is the capability to disable an account, which, in this case, lets you disable several accounts simultaneously.

Resetting Passwords

Passwords are at the heart of the security of your network. They should be secure, should be changed often, and should be hard to crack (for instance, you should not use the name of your spouse or family pet as your password).

You might also find that users sometimes forget their password and request that you change it for them. As an administrator, you do not need to know the user's old password to change it. If you make a change to a user's password, don't forget to check the User Must Change Password at Next Logon check box. This is a best practice that allows the user to log on once with the password you set, and then the user creates a new one.

You access this function by selecting Reset Password from the context-sensitive menu.

Unlocking User Accounts

User accounts are subject to the security settings that have been defined in Group Policy. One of the most common settings is for an account to be locked out after three failed login attempts. This typically occurs when a user has forgotten a password and makes several consecutive attempts, guessing wrong each time. Another reason user accounts can become locked out is due to password guessing on user accounts by unauthorized users. We discuss creating a password policy later in this chapter.

To unlock an account, select Properties from the context-sensitive menu. You are then presented with the User Properties dialog box. Click the Account tab and uncheck the Account Is Locked Out check box, as shown in Figure 8.2.

Don't confuse locked-out accounts with disabled accounts. Accounts that are locked out are in that status as a result of your domain's password policy. Locked-out accounts can be easily unlocked and made available for usage again. Disabled accounts are accounts that have been disabled (and thus cannot be used) by an administrator for one of various possible reasons. Reasons why an account might typically be disabled include users being on vacation or accounts created for users who do not yet require the account.

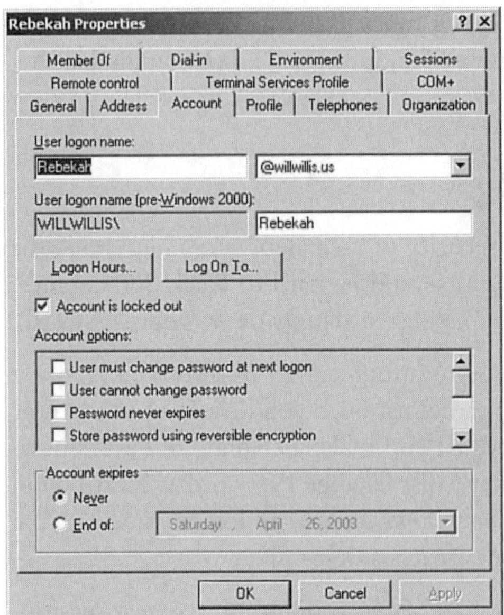

Figure 8.2 The User Properties dialog box.

Deleting User Accounts

If a user leaves your organization, you have two choices: You can delete the account, or, if the user is being replaced, you can simply rename the account for use by the replacement person. The choice here should be based on security, not just convenience. If the user is being replaced immediately, it is easier to rename the account. Otherwise, you should delete the account to maintain the integrity of security on your network.

To delete a user account, select Delete from the context-sensitive menu. When prompted with the message "Are You Sure You Want to Delete this Object?", click Yes to delete the object or No to abort the deletion.

The key point to keep in mind when deleting and subsequently re-creating a user account is that even if the name of the account is the same, the account will not be the same. Every object in Active Directory has a unique security identifier (SID) and/or globally unique identifier (GUID), thus preventing any two objects from ever being the same.

Renaming User Accounts

Renaming a user account is convenient when a user's function is being taken over by someone else. A user account is not simply a name and password; it is also a set of permissions and group memberships. Sometimes it is easier to rename a user account so that this data is maintained rather than re-creating it from scratch—this maintains the same SID or GUID, but it changes the properties of the object.

When renaming a user account, remember to take every object property into account. At a minimum, you should change the first name, last name, and logon name fields. However, several optional attributes will likely need to be changed, such as telephone number and description.

To rename an account, select Rename from the context-sensitive menu. Simply type the new name and press Enter when you are done.

Copying User Accounts

You can also create an account and use it as a template for other accounts. For instance, you might have a standard set of group memberships that all users are assigned upon creation of the account. Let's say, for example, that you have a member of the Finance group who has already been configured with all necessary group memberships. When a new employee joins the finance department, you can just copy a current account rather than create one from scratch.

When copying an account, you are prompted to enter a new first name, last name, and user logon name. You are also prompted to assign a new password. To copy a user account, simply select Copy from the context-sensitive menu. You are then presented with the Copy Object-User Wizard.

By using the **%username%** variable in the home directory and profile path entries when user accounts are created, the paths automatically change as the account is renamed. Any files that existed in the old location are not moved, however.

Disabling and Enabling User Accounts

As a variation on locking out an account, disabling an account temporarily prevents a user from logging in to the network. This is commonly performed when the user will be gone for an extended period of time. For the account to become active again, you must enable the account.

To disable an account, select Disable Account from the context-sensitive menu. The account is immediately disabled, and the username is displayed with a red X through it. To enable the account, select Enable Account from the context-sensitive menu (the Disable Account option will be grayed out).

Create a Password Policy for Domain Users

We have talked about general guidelines for setting up password policies, but we have not yet discussed how to actually do it. As shown in Figure 8.3, configuring password options is done through the Group Policy snap-in for the Microsoft Management Console (MMC).

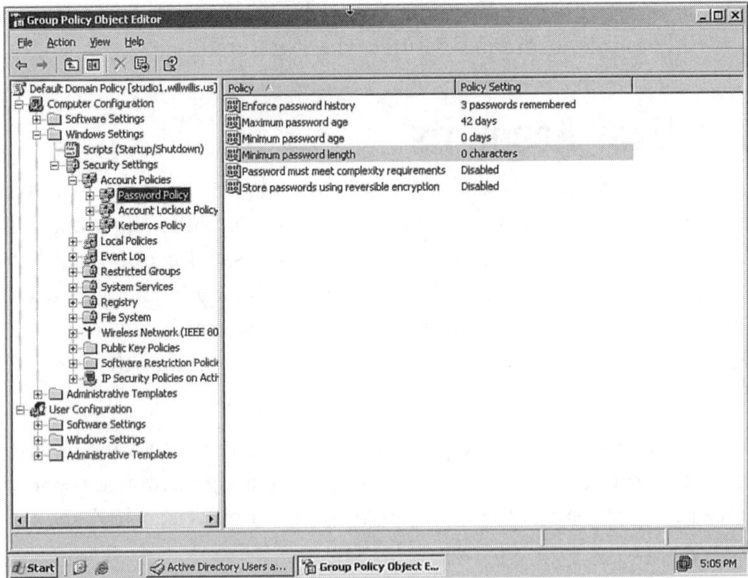

Figure 8.3 The Group Policy MMC snap-in enables you to configure your password options for all user accounts in the Active Directory.

Password policies are comprised of the six items outlined in Table 8.1.

Table 8.1 The Password Policy Options

Policy Item	Description
Enforce Password History	Keeps a history of users' passwords, preventing them from using the same password more than one time until it has left the history.
Maximum Password Age	Specifies the maximum amount of time that a user's password can remain in use without being changed.
Minimum Password Age	Specifies the minimum amount of time that a user's password must remain in use before it can be changed again by the user.

(continued)

Table 8.1 The Password Policy Options *(continued)*

Policy Item	Description
Minimum Password Length	Specifies the minimum number of characters that the user's password must contain.
Passwords Must Meet Complexity Requirements	Specifies that the user's password must have a mix of uppercase and lowercase letters, numbers, and standard keyboard symbols.
Store Password Using Reversible Encryption for All Users in the Domain	Specifies that a copy of the user's password is to be stored in Active Directory using reversible encryption. This setting is required for digest authentication to be used.

You can start the Group Policy snap-in in several ways. You can start an empty MMC and add the Group Policy snap-in to the console. However, for our purposes, start Group Policy as follows:

1. Click Start, Programs, Administrative Tools, Active Directory Users and Computers.
2. An Active Directory Users and Computers console appears. When it does, right-click on your domain and click Properties. Figure 8.4 illustrates this.

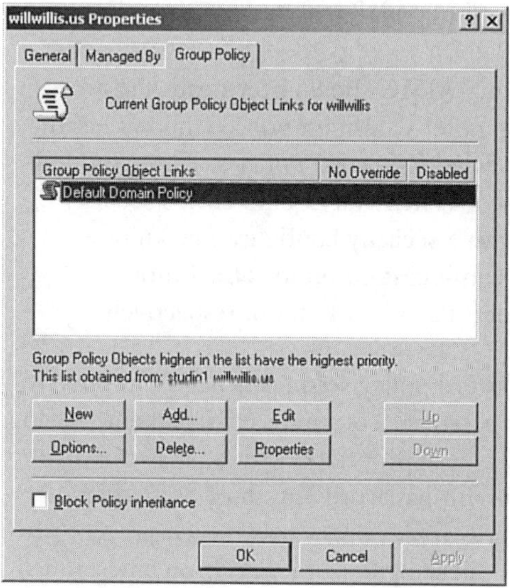

Figure 8.4 Opening the Domain Properties sheet.

3. Click on the Group Policy tab, where you will see the Default Domain Policy link. This is the only option, by default, although you can add additional Group Policy links or create new ones. With Default Domain Policy highlighted, click Edit. The screen shown in Figure 8.5 appears.

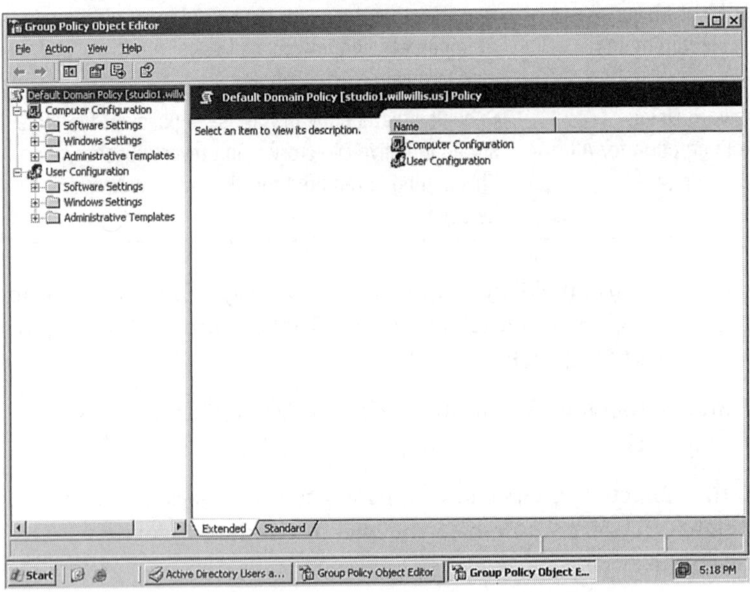

Figure 8.5 Editing the default domain policy within Domain Properties.

4. You are now in the Group Policy MMC shown previously. Password options are located under Computer Configuration, Windows Settings, Security Settings, Account Policies, Password Policies. Here you find the options previously discussed. When you double-click a security attribute, you are presented with a security configuration window. Figures 8.6 and 8.7 show the configuration options for Enforce Password History and Minimum Password Length, respectively.

How strict you are with these password policy settings depends on the environment in which you work. In a typical corporate environment, having passwords expire every 90–120 days is appropriate, with a password history of up to 10 passwords and a minimum password length of 8–12 characters. You should also consider enforcing complex passwords, which prevent people from using passwords that are easier to guess or crack. In an environment with high employee turnover or a lot of contractors going in and out, you would want passwords to expire more frequently.

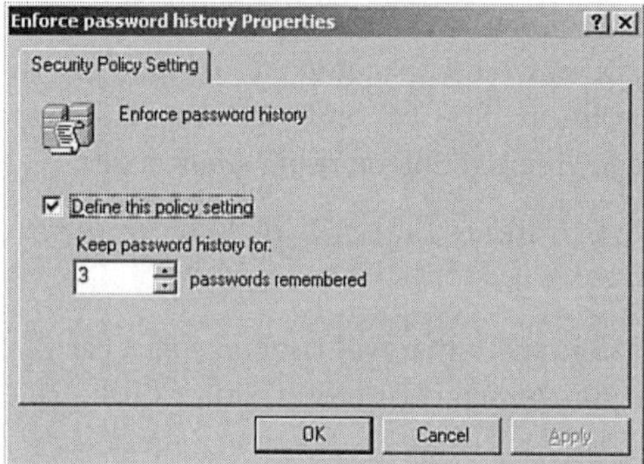

Figure 8.6 The Enforce Password History security attribute configuration.

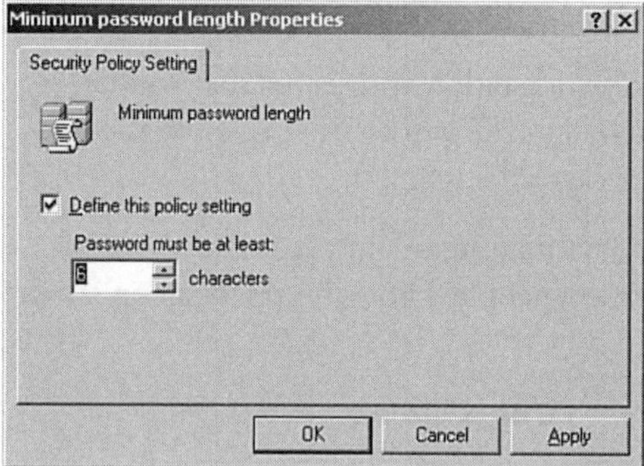

Figure 8.7 The Minimum Password Length security attribute configuration.

Plan a Smart Card Authentication Strategy

To combat the hassle and lack of security of passwords, organizations are increasingly turning toward alternative methods for user authentication. One such method that is natively supported in Windows Server 2003 is smart cards. As a result, we will simply give a brief overview of what is involved in deploying smart cards without supplying much detail, and then use that as a lead-in to a discussion on strategy planning.

It isn't within the scope of this particular exam to know all of the intricacies of deploying smart cards, but you will be expected to know the fundamentals of planning an authentication strategy for smart cards. Refer to Chapter 6, "Planning, Implementing, and Maintaining Security Infrastructure," for additional information on smart cards.

Setting up Windows Server 2003 to use smart cards involves a series of steps, some of which you might or might not have to complete, depending on whether you are already running Certificate Services on your network. These required elements must be in place for users to log on using smart cards:

- Install and configure at least one Certificate Authority (CA) on your Windows Server 2003 network.
- Configure the permissions in each domain that will contain smart card users with the enroll permission for the smart card user, smart card logon, and Enrollment Agent certificate templates. This way smart card users will be able to enroll for the required certificates.
- Configure the CA to issue smart card certificates.
- Configure the CA to issue Enrollment Agent certificates.
- Install smart card readers at each workstation and server that will be used with smart card logons, including the workstation used by the person who will be setting up smart cards for users.
- Prepare a smart card enrollment station, including getting an Enrollment Agent certificate for the people who will be setting up smart cards for users.
- Set up each required smart card to be used for user logon.
- Distribute the smart cards and train users on how to log on with them.

It is important to note that Windows Server 2003 smart card support requires that the workstation or server being logged into be a member of a domain. Smart cards are not supported on standalone computers.

When you are planning to deploy smart cards for logon use on your Windows Server 2003 network, a few considerations must be taken into account. One of the first considerations is with respect to how smart cards will be issued. The Enrollment Agent certificate is very powerful, and whoever has one can issue smart cards on behalf of anyone in the domain. By default, only members of the Domain Admins group can request a certificate, but this permission can be delegated in Active Directory Sites and Services if a specific nonadministrator is chosen to issue the smart cards. Microsoft recommends that after you have issued the necessary Enrollment Agent certificates to the people who will be enrolling users, you administer the CA and disable the issuance of Enrollment Agent certificates until they are needed. This prevents someone from being able to get an Enrollment Agent certificate and create fraudulent smart cards on behalf of legitimate users.

If you have a mixed environment of Windows 2000 and Windows XP workstations, or Windows 2000 and Windows Server 2003 servers, there is another planning consideration. Windows 2000 systems can use only smart cards that were enrolled on a Windows 2000 enrollment station. Windows XP and Windows Server 2003 computers can log on with smart cards that were enrolled on Windows 2000 Professional or Server, Windows XP Professional, or Windows Server 2003.

From Passwords to Smart Cards, and Back Again

When you issue smart cards to users, you need to set up their user account to use the smart card. To do this, use the Active Directory Users and Computers utility. Navigate to the user account that you want to configure, right-click on it, and click Properties. As you can see in Figure 8.8, when you navigate to the Account tab, you have a number of configuration options, including Smart Card Is Required for Interactive Logon. By selecting this option, you disable password logon and force the user to use the smart card.

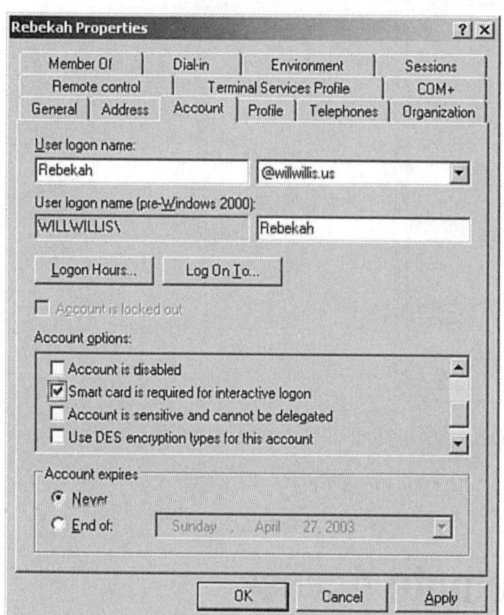

Figure 8.8 Forcing the user account to log on with a smart card rather than a password.

If a user loses a smart card, or the card or reader becomes defective, you can easily revert the user back to password logon by unchecking that box in the user's account properties. If you do that, you should assign the user account a temporary password and require the user to change the password at the next logon. When the problem with smart card logon is resolved, you can disable password logon again.

What if you need to configure hundreds or thousands of user accounts to use smart cards? Fortunately, you do not have to open each individual account and check the box to require smart card logon. Active Directory Users and Computers enables you to perform certain tasks on multiple accounts simultaneously. One of these tasks is configuring smart card usage. Simply select as many user accounts as desired in the console, right-click, and select Properties. Go to the Accounts tab, where you see a number of options such as those in Figure 8.9. Scroll down to Smart Card Is Required for Interactive Logon and select the left check box to enable the option; then select the right check box to set the option itself. Likewise, you can uncheck the box for multiple users, if necessary.

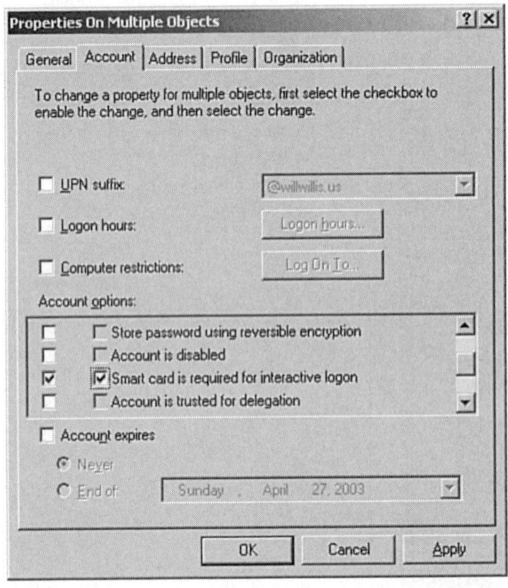

Figure 8.9 Active Directory Users and Computers allows you to enable the smart card requirement for user logon for multiple accounts at once.

Smart Cards and Remote Access

As an administrator, you likely must support remote users on your network. If you are using smart cards on Windows Server 2003, you can extend this functionality to your remote users as well. For instance, if you have mobile salespeople who log on through virtual private network (VPN) or dial-up connections across the Internet, you can support them as smart card users just like regular domain users. Issue these individuals their smart cards and readers as normal, and set up their VPN or dialup connection as normal to log on to the network. When you're done, go into the Properties dialog box for the connection and to the Security tab, as shown in Figure 8.10.

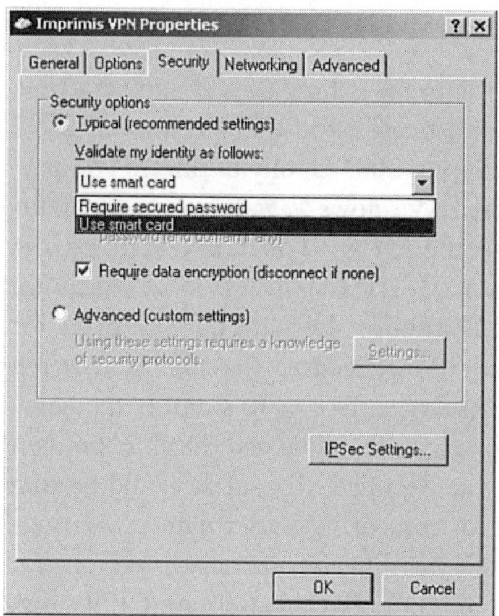

Figure 8.10 Configuring a remote access connection to use a smart card.

By default, the connection is set up to require a secure password. Simply click the drop-down menu under Validate My Identity as Follows and choose Use Smart Card. After you've done that, click OK to return to the logon dialog box. You'll notice, as in Figure 8.11, that the password entry has been removed. Insert your smart card into its reader and click Connect; you should be able to log on to your remote access server.

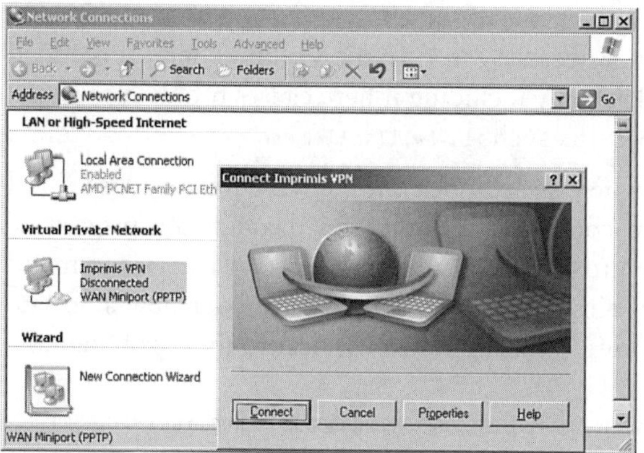

Figure 8.11 After you configure the connection security to use a smart card, the option to enter a password is removed.

Using smart cards is an effective way to overcome the limitations and inherent weaknesses of passwords.

UPN Suffixes

One of the tasks you must know for the exam is how to add and remove a user principal name (UPN) suffix. In most cases, the UPN is the full DNS domain name of the object. Windows Server 2003 is fully backward compatible, so you can still use the traditional Windows *domain\user* format for logon authentication, or you can use the UPN. The UPN suffix is the domain portion of the UPN, such as `@willwillis.us` in `user1@willwillis.us`. Windows Server 2003 enables you to configure alternate UPN suffixes for logon, which can be used to provide additional security (having the user log in with the alternate rather than the primary suffix), or to simplify the naming in multiple-level child domains. For example, if you had the child domain `lewisville.texas.studio.willwillis.us`, the default UPN suffix would be that same lengthy name with an `@` symbol in front of it. A user named `Meli` logging in to that domain would have a UPN of `Meli@lewisville.texas.studio.willwillis.us`. As an administrator, you might create an alternate UPN suffix for logon purposes called lewisville, whereby the user's UPN would instead just be `Meli@Lewisville`. This is much easier to work with and more secure if someone is trying to authenticate using the default UPN. In addition, this makes it easy to move user accounts between domains because users never really need to know what child domain actually contains their user accounts—they need only know their UPN.

To create an alternate UPN suffix, open the Active Directory Domains and Trusts administrative console, right-click on the root container, and select Properties. This brings you to the UPN Suffix dialog box, illustrated in Figure 8.12. Simply type in the name of the UPN suffix you want to add, and click Add. Note that it is not necessary to type the `@` symbol here. It is added for you automatically, and actually including it here causes problems because you'll end up with a UPN suffix such as `@@willwillis.us`.

To test the results of your new suffix, open the Active Directory Users and Computers administrative console, and either go through the process of creating a new user or go into the properties of an existing user account and go to the Account tab. In either case, you should have your new alternate UPN available as an option in the drop-down list next to the logon name.

If you remove a suffix that is in use, user accounts that reference that suffix will not be capable of authenticating.

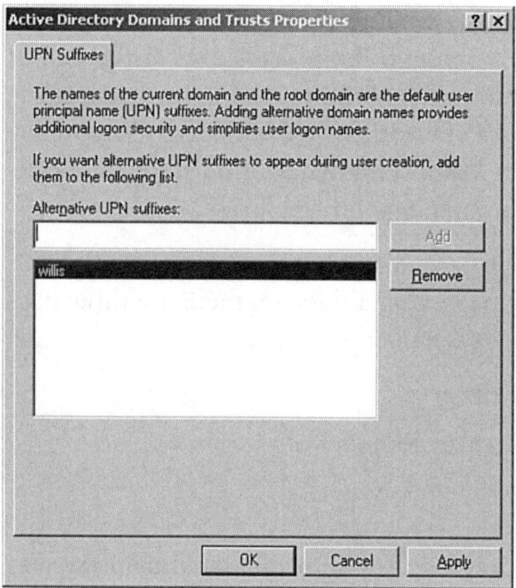

Figure 8.12 You can easily add or remove alternate UPN suffixes for your domain.

Application Data Partitions

Another new feature in Windows Server 2003's version of Active Directory that wasn't available in Windows 2000 is the concept of application data partitions. An *application data partition* is a partitioned section of Active Directory that is replicated only to specified domain controllers. The data partition is used by applications such as the DNS service and can contain Active Directory objects. The most common use of the data partition is to create specialized DNS zones that are to be replicated only among certain domain controllers. The advantage of such a configuration is that replication traffic is reduced and, therefore, more efficient. Application data partitions can be hosted only on Windows Server 2003 domain controllers. In addition to supplying replication efficiency, application data partitions provide fault tolerance by storing replicas on specified domain controllers in the forest. In this sense, they differ from the domain directory partitions that AD uses because AD directory partitions are replicated to all domain controllers in a domain.

Application data partitions are typically created by applications that can use them because they store application-specific data. As an administrator, you might never have to manually create or configure an application data partition, but Microsoft gives you the capability to do so anyway through the NTDSUTIL command-line utility (there are a couple of other ways as well, which we'll discuss a bit later). Because you'll likely be tested on configuring application data partitions, we walk through the process of it at the end of this section. Furthermore, replication of application data partitions is managed automatically through Active Directory's Knowledge Consistency Checker (KCC), which is a built-in AD process that runs on all domain controllers and manages the replication topology for the forest.

As far as naming goes, an application data partition is part of the overall DNS namespace in your forest. Similar to creating a domain, there are three possible ways you can place your application data partition:

- Child of a domain directory partition
- Child of another application data partition
- A new tree in a forest

Naming an application data partition requires following the same rules and conventions as naming DNS domains. One thing to note is that you cannot create a domain directory partition as a child of an application data partition. For example, if you had an application data partition named `app1.quepublishing.com`, you could not create a domain that had a DNS name of `domain1.app1.quepublishing.com`.

Previously, we mentioned that although applications typically handle the management of their own application data partitions while the KCC handles replication, Windows Server 2003 provides administrators with the capability to manually create and manage application data partitions. Application data partitions can be created, deleted, and managed in four ways:

- Application-specific tools supplied by software vendors
- NTDSUTIL command-line utility
- LDP utility
- Active Directory Service Interfaces (ADSI)

Using ADSI typically involves some level of programming. For the exam, you will need to concern yourself only with the `NTDSUTIL` utility, discussed next.

Creating an Application Data Partition

You can use the `NTDSUTIL` command-line utility to manually create application data partitions. Simply open a command prompt, type **`NTDSUTIL`**, and press Enter. When you do so, you are presented with a cryptic prompt that just says `NTDSUTIL:` and a flashing cursor. If you press the ? key and press Enter, you will see a menu like that in Figure 8.13.

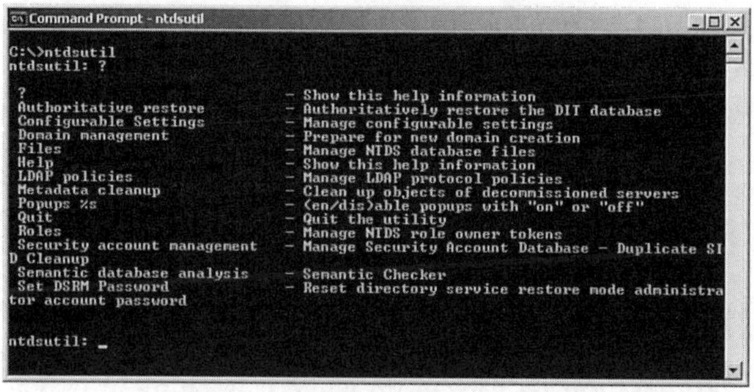

```
Command Prompt - ntdsutil
C:\>ntdsutil
ntdsutil: ?

 ?                             - Show this help information
 Authoritative restore         - Authoritatively restore the DIT database
 Configurable Settings         - Manage configurable settings
 Domain management             - Prepare for new domain creation
 Files                         - Manage NTDS database files
 Help                          - Show this help information
 LDAP policies                 - Manage LDAP protocol policies
 Metadata cleanup              - Clean up objects of decommissioned servers
 Popups %s                     - (en/dis)able popups with "on" or "off"
 Quit                          - Quit the utility
 Roles                         - Manage NTDS role owner tokens
 Security account management   - Manage Security Account Database - Duplicate SI
D Cleanup
 Semantic database analysis    - Semantic Checker
 Set DSRM Password             - Reset directory service restore mode administra
tor account password

ntdsutil: _
```

Figure 8.13 **NTDSUTIL** provides a number of options for managing your server.

To create an application data partition, the user account that you use must be a member of the Domain Admins or Enterprise Admins groups. The following steps outline the process to create an application data partition.

1. To begin the process of creating an application data partition, type **`domain management`** and press Enter. You will see the prompt change from `NTDSUTIL:` to `domain management`.
2. Next, you will need to connect to the domain controller you will be creating this partition from. At the domain management command prompt, type **`connection`**.
3. At the Connection command prompt, type **`connect to server`** ***`server_name`***. Type **`quit`** at the connection command prompt to back out to the domain management prompt.
4. Next, type the following:

   ```
   create nc ApplicationDataPartition DomainController
   ```

   In the preceding code, you would substitute *`ApplicationDataPartition`* with the distinguished name of the partition that you want to create, and substitute *`DomainController`* with the fully qualified domain name (FQDN) of the domain controller you want to create the application data partition on. Putting it together, if you wanted to create an application data partition named `adptest1.willwillis.us` on a domain controller `studio1.willwillis.us`, you would type the following line at the prompt:

   ```
   create nc dc=adptest1,dc=willwillis,dc=us studio1.willwillis.us
   ```

5. At this point, assuming that you substituted names that were valid on your network, you will see a message that the object is being added to Active Directory. When the process has completed, you are returned to the `domain management:` prompt.

Deleting an application data partition follows the same procedure; you simply substitute `create` with `delete` in the preceding syntax. When you remove the last replica of an application data partition, any data that it contained is lost.

Active Directory Backup and Restoration

A Windows Server 2003 DC can be backed up while it is online, thereby minimizing disruption. It is not enough to back up only the database and log files. Instead, you must back up the system state data.

System state data is a collection of data that makes up a functioning AD infrastructure. It includes the AD database, along with other folders and files. These files collectively can be used to recover from even the most catastrophic failure. System state data includes the following:

- AD database files
- SYSVOL folder
- Registry
- System startup files (Ntdetect.com, Ntldr, and Bootsect.dat)
- Class Registration database
- Certificate Services database

All these items might not exist on your server; for instance, the Certificate Services database is an optional component. You need all these folders because, in some way, they support the server.

The SYSVOL folder is a shared folder that exists on all DCs. This folder is used to replicate Group Policy Object (GPO) data and logon scripts. The Class Registration database is composed of component services that are installed on a system.

Active Directory Data Files

Active Directory uses the Extensible Storage Engine (ESE), which was first pioneered in Microsoft Exchange Server. It uses the concept of transactions to ensure that the database does not become corrupted by partial updates and that it can recover in the case of a power failure. Each transaction is a call to modify the database. A modification can be the addition of new data or a change made to data that is already stored.

For the transactional system to work, the AD database must have associated log files. These log files are used to store modifications before the data is written to the physical database file. We will look at how this works in a moment. Before we do, however, we must define which files are used by the database. Five files make up the AD database system:

- ntds.dit
- edb*.log
- ebd.chk
- res1.log
- res2.log

Each of these files has a role to play in ensuring that data can be written to the directory in a safe and recoverable fashion. You should note that these files exist on every DC in your environment. The AD database is not centralized in any way; it exists on each server that is promoted to the role of DC. Each instance must be maintained separately.

ntds.dit

This is the single file that holds all the AD data, including all objects and the schema information. This file is stored by default in the <systemroot>\NTDS folder, although it can be moved. The ntds.dit file works in conjunction with the log files. The .dit extension stands for directory information tree.

edb*.log

The edb*.log file is the transaction log for ntds.dit. The file that is currently being used is called simply edb.log. When that file reaches a specified size (10MB, by default), the file gets renamed edb*****.log, where the asterisks are incremented from 1 upward. When the files are no longer needed, they are deleted by the system.

edb.chk

Two copies of changes to AD data exist. The first copy is kept in log files; these changes occur as data is accepted from an administrative tool, such as Active Directory Users and Computers. The second copy is the database file itself. This checkpoint file keeps track of which entries in the log file have been written to the database file. In the case of failure, Windows Server 2003 uses this file to find out which entries in the log file can safely be written out to a database.

res1.log and res2.log

Essentially, res1.log and res2.log are two placeholders that exist to simply take up space. If a DC runs out of disk space, the AD replica can become inoperable. It is far better for the DC to shut down gracefully. These two files, each 10MB in size, exist to prevent a DC from being capable of writing to the log files. If a DC runs out of disk space, AD can be sure that it has at least 20MB of space to write out any necessary log data.

Garbage Collection

Garbage collection is the process by which old data is purged from the AD. Because all DCs in a Windows Server 2003 network act as peers, deleting objects is a little more difficult than it might first appear. If an administrator wants to delete a user object from the network, he can simply hit the Delete key. However, how will Windows Server 2003 make sure that all DCs in the enterprise are aware that this deletion is taking place? If the deletion happens in real time, it can't. Hence, the use of *tombstoning*.

Data is never immediately deleted from AD. Instead, the object's attributes are deleted, and the object is moved to a special container called Deleted Objects. The object is then assigned a tombstone. By default, this tombstone expires in 60 days, although this parameter can be changed. The tombstone means that the physical deletion of the object occurs by the configured interval. This gives AD time to replicate this change to all DCs. It also means that the deletion can take place at around the same time, no matter how distant the DCs may be.

Garbage collection also defragments the database by using the online defragmentation process.

To change the interval for garbage collection, you must use the ADSIEdit tool included with Windows Server 2003. Connect to the Configuration container and edit the **garbageCollPeriod** and **tombstoneLifetime** attributes. By default, the period is 60 days. This is displayed in ADSIEdit as **<not set>**. Be careful about setting the value too low; this can prevent your restores from working. Microsoft recommends leaving the value set at the default. You will not be able to restore Active Directory data from backup sets that are older than the tombstone value, so keep this in mind when changing the tombstone value.

Backing Up System State Data

You can back up the system state data without buying third-party utilities. To do this, simply use the built-in backup utility and follow these steps:

1. Select Start, All Programs, Accessories, System Tools, Backup. When you do this, an informational screen appears. The introductory screen is shown in Figure 8.14. Click the Advanced Mode link.

Figure 8.14 The built-in backup utility.

2. This displays the Advanced Mode Backup/Restore window, shown in Figure 8.15.

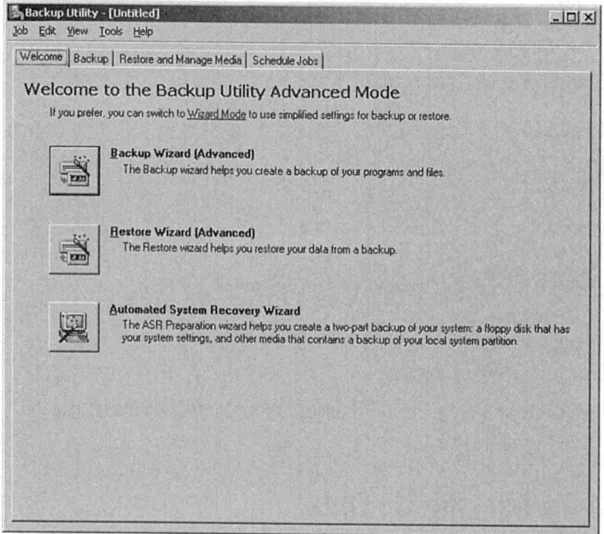

Figure 8.15 The Backup Utility is your one-stop backup and restoration location.

3. Next, change to the backup options. Click the Backup tab. Then select System State, as shown in Figure 8.16.
4. You will see an informational screen next (see Figure 8.17). When you have read this screen, click Start Backup.

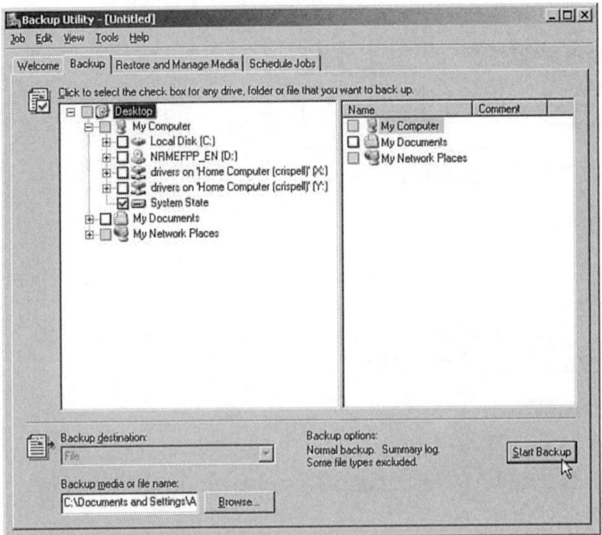

Figure 8.16 Selecting System State.

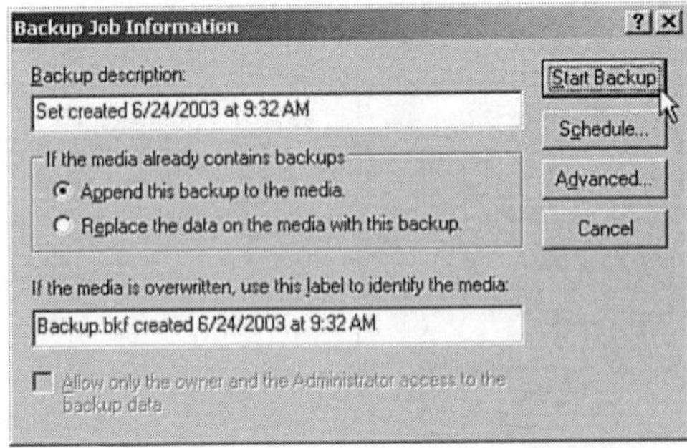

Figure 8.17 You can configure additional backup options immediately before starting the backup job.

Recommendations for Backing Up Data

You can't restore a DC fully if you do not have a backup of the system state data. However, even having that data might not be enough if an entire server has been lost in, say, a flood. Make sure you are also backing up all other folders and disk drives on the server periodically. To do this, you can use the built-in backup tool or a third-party utility.

You must be a member of the Administrators, Backup Operator, or Server Operators groups before you can back up data. These are built-in groups; if you do not want to use them, you must assign permissions yourself.

The backup utility built in to Windows Server 2003 can be used only to back up data that is local to the computer (although it can store the backup files in remote locations). This means that it cannot be configured from a single server to back up system data on all DCs in your enterprise. For this reason alone, you might want to consider purchasing a utility that offers more features.

Restoring AD

Depending on the backup options you have implemented in your environment, you might have three methods to choose from when restoring a Windows Server 2003 DC. If you have performed a backup by following the steps outlined in the previous section, you could simply perform a restore operation with the built-in backup tool.

When you perform a restore, you have two options: You can perform a nonauthoritative restore or an authoritative restore. We take a closer look at these two options in a moment.

Be careful about performing restores when utilizing external trusts. Windows Server 2003 renegotiates the password on an external trust every seven days. If a restore is performed that is older than this (say, 14 days), you will have to re-establish the trust.

Alternatively, you can simply rely on AD replication to take care of updating a new DC. In this scenario, a failed DC is simply reinstalled from scratch. When the DC is online, it updates itself via normal replication techniques. This occurs automatically and does not require any additional administrative tasks.

To perform a restore at a DC, you must be capable of logging on with the Active Directory restore password. This password is stored in the local SAM, not within Active Directory. In Windows Server 2003, it is now possible to change the local Administrator password from within **NTDSUTIL**. Because the local Administrator password allows for AD restores, it should be kept confidential.

Nonauthoritative Restore

The nonauthoritative restore is the simplest form of restore when you are using backup media. A nonauthoritative restore is simply a restore of data from backup. Because the data will probably be outdated (presumably, some changes were made to the data in AD after the last backup), normal AD replication processes make sure that the missing data elements are updated.

This is a common practice if a hard disk failure occurs. If a hard disk fails, the server might become inoperable. You simply replace the failed hardware, perform a nonauthoritative restore, and then wait for AD replication to bring the DC up-to-date. This process is faster than simply reinstalling the server and promoting it to a DC with dcpromo.exe because less data must be replicated to the restored DC.

Performing a nonauthoritative restore is fairly simple. However, you cannot restore AD data while it is in use. For this reason, the server must be taken offline before a restore can happen. To do this, follow these steps:

1. Restart the server, pressing F8 during startup. The Advanced Startup Options are displayed.
2. Select Directory Services Restore Mode. This starts the server but does not start AD.
3. Log in to the server using the Administrators account. This is stored locally on each DC and can be different for each DC in your enterprise.
4. Use the backup tool to restore system state data.
5. Restart the DC.

After the server has been restarted, it is updated by its replication partners. An integrity check also takes place, and various indexes on AD data are rebuilt. This places a temporary additional load on the server during boot time.

Restore operations are highly dependent on the tombstone period discussed previously. If you leave the default tombstone lifetime (60 days) in place, you won't be able to restore system state data from tapes that have backups on them older than 60 days. This is because data is deleted when the tombstone lifetime has expired, and introducing a DC with older data that has now been erased from other DCs causes database inconsistencies. Be careful not to set the tombstone lifetime for too short of a time period.

Authoritative Restore

The authoritative restore can be used to restore individual pieces of AD. This is useful if an error has taken place and an object has been deleted by mistake. Let's look at an example to clarify this process. Imagine that an administrator is working with the AD Users and Computers tool and accidentally deletes an Organizational Unit (OU). The OU contained user objects, and they are deleted as well. A DC accepted this change, so it is replicated to all AD replicas in the enterprise. Because there is no way to turn off this process, the mistake will soon be widespread on the network.

If the OU contained a small number of accounts, it might not be a problem to simply re-create it; however, if a large number of user objects were involved, re-creating the data could take some time. An authoritative restore allows an administrator to restore the deleted OU from backup. When an authoritative restore takes place, the update sequence number (USN) of the object is, by default, incremented by 100,000 per day since the last update to the Active Directory database. Because the PVN is higher than that of the copy currently held by the DC's replication partners, the restored object is assumed to be the most up-to-date copy. This change is then forced out to all other DCs via normal AD replication processes.

It is assumed that more than 100,000 changes have not been made to the restored data since the backup took place.

The process for performing an authoritative restore is somewhat different from the process outlined for a nonauthoritative restore. After you have restored the system state data, you must not restart the computer. Instead, perform these additional steps:

1. Open a command prompt. Type **`NTDSUTIL`** and press Enter.
2. Type **`authoritative restore`** and press Enter.
3. Type **`restore subtree`** ***`<distinguished name>`***, where *`<distinguished name>`* is the full path to the object. For an OU called Finance in a domain called MCSEWORLD.COM, this would be `OU=finance,DC=MCSEWORLD,DC=COM`.
4. Type **`quit`**. Type **`quit`** again and press Enter to exit NTDSUTIL.
5. Restart the DC.

The one exception to the capability to do authoritative restores arises when you want to restore objects stored in the Schema partition. The Schema is "owned" by the Schema Master Operations Master. To restore the Schema, you must restore the Schema Master. Any changes made since the backup was performed are lost.

Exam Prep Questions

Question 1

AD is made up of several files. Which of the following represents part of the file set used by AD?

❍ A. NTDS.DB

❍ B. NTDS.DIT

❍ C. RES.LOG

❍ D. RES3.LOG

Answer B is correct. NTDS.DIT is the file that contains the AD data. Answer A is incorrect because this is clearly a misspelling of NTDS.DIT. Answers C and D are incorrect because neither is the correct name for placeholder files used by AD to conserve space on the hard disk. The correct names for these files are RES1.LOG and RES2.LOG.

Question 2

Scott Keating is a system administrator who has been diligently performing backups of his system state data every 90 days. After 85 days, a server fails because of a hard disk failure. Scott installs a new hard disk and then reinstalls Windows Server 2003. When this is complete, he intends to restore from his last backup. Scott calls a friend to refresh him on the correct steps, and he is surprised when his friend advises him that his backups are too old and that he is better off simply running DCPromo.exe. Scott doesn't agree with this advice. Who is correct?

❍ A. Scott is correct. The age of file backups does not matter.

❍ B. The friend is correct. AD has a time limit of 30 days on AD restores. The AD replication process will replace data that is older than this anyway, so Windows 2003 prevents it from being restored.

❍ C. Scott is correct. Although the data is old, he can reply upon AD replication to clear up any problems that might arise.

❍ D. The friend is correct. Because the backed-up files are older than the default expiration period for the garbage-collection process, Scott could introduce inconsistencies into AD.

Answer D is correct. You can adjust the garbage-collection process to fit your backup schedule. However, you should never attempt to restore data from a backup that is older than the garbage-collection process interval (the default is 60 days). Answer A is incorrect because the age of the files does matter. Answer B is incorrect because there is no 30-day limit of restores. Answer C is incorrect because AD replication will not fix the bad data.

Question 3

By default, garbage collection takes place on a system every 60 days. The DCs in Eric's network have plenty of disk space. In addition, he wants to extend the usefulness of his backups. He decides to change the garbage-collection process to occur every 90 days. Which tool will Eric use?

❍ A. Eric will use ADSIEdit to change this.

❍ B. Eric will use NTDSUTIL to change this.

❍ C. Eric must use NTDSUTIL and AD Domains and Trusts.

❍ D. Eric must use AD Domains and Trusts to change this.

Answer A is correct. Eric will use ADSIEdit to do this. Answer B is incorrect because, although NTDSUTIL has many uses, changing the garbage collection interval is not one of them. Answers C and D are incorrect because Active Directory Domains and Trusts is a tool used for domain management and has no role here.

Question 4

Moira Chamberlin is a system administrator for an insurance company. Moira accidentally deleted an OU and wants to get it back. Fortunately, she performed a backup of AD one hour before the deletion. Moira starts the DC and does a restore. When she is done, she restarts the server. The server comes back perfectly; however, within 30 minutes, the OU she has just restored is once again deleted. Why did this happen?

❍ A. Although it is possible to get this object back from a restore, it must be an authoritative restore. Moira must have performed a nonauthoritative restore.

❍ B. The backup worked fine. However, because the object had previously been deleted, it must now be re-created. This process assigns a new SID and allows the object name to be reused.

❍ C. When an object is deleted, it is gone forever. Moira should rename one of her current OUs so that it is the same as the deleted object.

❍ D. Moira must wait. AD replication follows a prescribed methodology. Although it looks like it is deleted, after an hour or so, replication will stop and the object will be restored again.

Answer A is correct. An authoritative restore would allow the object to be restored and would force it to be replicated out to all other DCs. If this is not done, AD replication will detect that the object has come back and simply remove it. Answer B is incorrect because objects can indeed be restored with their original SIDs. Answer C is incorrect because renaming an OU would not restore all the permissions and members that once belonged to the original OU. Answer D is incorrect because replication would not fix this problem without an authoritative restore taking place.

Question 5

Lisa Arase is in the process of putting together a network security plan. Because she will be granting many users access to shared folders and printers, she wants to use groups extensively. Lisa's company also has several kiosks in the foyer of company headquarters that visitors can use to browse the Web and access email. Lisa is not sure how she is going to limit the access of users. What method would be the easiest from an administrative standpoint? (Choose the best answer.)

- ❍ A. Because groups can contain only user accounts, Lisa should create groups for her user community and put a firewall between the kiosk machines and her network.
- ❍ B. Lisa should create groups for the employees of her company. For the kiosk machines, Lisa can create a single logon and apply permissions to this group so that users can access the resources they need. Because this can be a single group, this task would not involve a lot of work.
- ❍ C. Because groups can contain both user accounts and computer accounts, Lisa can go ahead and create a single group that includes both users from her company and the computers that operate as kiosks.
- ❍ D. Lisa should create a single logon for the kiosk machines. She should create a group for her employees and assign them permissions, and she should grant the user who is going to be using the kiosks specific permissions to network resources.

Answer C is correct. Groups can contain both user accounts and computer accounts. Although answers A, B, and D are all feasible, they increase the administrative burden for the administrator. Specifically, answer A is incorrect because a firewall would be more difficult to administer than answer C. Answers B and D are incorrect because adding specific user accounts to permission lists is also administratively intensive.

Question 6

To troubleshoot an installation problem with a particular application, the vendor asks you to manually create an application data partition on your domain controller. What utilities could you use to accomplish this? (Check all correct answers.)

- ❑ A. ADSI
- ❑ B. Active Directory Users and Computers
- ❑ C. NTDSUTIL
- ❑ D. DNS administrative console

Answers A and C are correct. You can use ADSI to programmatically create application data partitions or use the NTDSUTIL.exe command-line utility. Answer B is incorrect because Active Directory Users and Computers does not give you the capability to manage application data partitions. Answer D is incorrect because, although application data partitions are required to be in DNS name formats and resemble DNS domain names, you cannot create them with the DNS console.

Question 7

You are the administrator for a Windows Server 2003 domain tree that goes five levels deep in child domains. Users at the deeper levels have complained about how much typing they have to do to enter their login information. Management has also inquired as to whether anything can be done to strengthen authentication security without incurring any additional cost. What can you use to simplify logons as well as make logon authentication more secure, without incurring any additional expense?

- ❍ A. Change the DNS domain name to something more manageable.
- ❍ B. Implement a smart card solution for authentication.
- ❍ C. Implement an alternate UPN suffix.
- ❍ D. Consolidate the child domains into the parent domain.

Answer C is correct. Alternate UPN suffixes simplify logon names because, with a complex child domain such as `@lewisville.texas.studio.insidecorner.com`, you can create a UPN suffix `@Lewisville` for users to use. In addition to being easier for users, it improves the logon security because users aren't using the default logon domains for their authentication. Answer A is incorrect because renaming a child domain four levels deep would still result in a lengthy name. Removing the domain and reinstalling it as a higher child tree or as a new domain tree would have other repercussions that might not be desirable (and wouldn't improve security). Answer B is incorrect because it doesn't meet the requirement of not incurring any extra expense. Answer D is incorrect because it doesn't improve security and could have other consequences in the management of the network (the child domains probably existed as child domains for a reason).

Question 8

Which of the following are the names given to the partitions of data stored within Active Directory? (Choose all correct answers.)

- ❑ A. Domain
- ❑ B. Configuration
- ❑ C. Schema
- ❑ D. Application

Answers A, B, C, and D are all correct. The application partition is new to Windows Server 2003.

Question 9

Christof Mayer is writing contingency plans for recovery of his domain controllers. One of the things he is most concerned about is having the servers run out of space, thereby preventing Active Directory from being capable of making writes to the database. However, Christof's colleague, Colin Martin, tells Christof that he need not worry about this because Active Directory has a reserve of 20MB on each domain controller to account for this very scenario. In fact, the names of these files are NTDS.RES and NTDS.RE2. Christof doubts whether Colin is correct. Who is right?

- ❍ A. Colin is right. These files are "placeholders" that exist to simply consume disk space. This space is kept as a reserve in case the server hard disk runs out of space.
- ❍ B. Colin is almost right. There are indeed files that act as "placeholders" to consume disk space. However, they are called res1.log and res2.log.
- ❍ C. Christof is right. There are no placeholders. Monitoring is the only way to make sure disk space does not run out.
- ❍ D. Christof is right. Active Directory automatically shuts down the server if it runs out of hard disk space. This ensures that database corruption does not occur.

Answer B is correct. Two files, each 10MB in size, act as placeholders. Their names are res1.log and res2.log. Answer A is incorrect because the placeholder file names are incorrect. Answer C is incorrect because the placeholders do exist. Answer D is incorrect because the placeholders would free up disk space to give administrators time to free up space before a shutdown was necessary.

Question 10

You have issued smart cards to a small number of users as part of a pilot program leading up to a full-scale deployment of smart cards. You configure yourself as an enrollment agent, enroll the users, and configure the smart cards as required. You install smart card readers on the user workstations and have the users stop by and pick up their cards so you can explain how they work. The first user you give a card to, Tina Rowe, calls you shortly after leaving your office to tell you that she can't log on with her smart card, although she is still able to log on with her password. Why isn't the smart card working? (Choose the best answer.)

- ❍ A. You need to reinstall the smart card reader drivers on the workstation.
- ❍ B. You need to configure her user account to use the smart card.
- ❍ C. You need to grant Tina the necessary permissions to use the smart card.
- ❍ D. You need to configure the LAN connection on the workstation for smart card logon rather than password.

Answer B is correct. A required step is to use Active Directory Users and Computers to edit the properties of the user accounts that will use smart cards, and check the box for Smart Card is Required for Interactive Logon. Unless this is done, password logon will still be in effect. Answers A and C are incorrect because password logon is still working, so smart card logon has not been configured. Answer D is incorrect because you do not have to configure a LAN connection to use smart card authentication to log in to a domain.

Need to Know More?

Mulcare, Mike and Stan Reimer. *Active Directory for Microsoft Windows Server 2003 Technical Reference*. Redmond, Washington: Microsoft Press, 2003.

Microsoft Corporation. *Microsoft Windows Server 2003 Resource Kit.* Redmond, Washington: Microsoft Press, 2003.

Microsoft Corporation. *Microsoft Windows Server 2003 Deployment Kit.* Redmond, Washington: Microsoft Press, 2003.

Planning and Implementing Group Policy

Terms you'll need to understand:

- ✓ Assigned applications
- ✓ Delegation of control
- ✓ Domain
- ✓ Filtering
- ✓ Group Policy Object (GPO)
- ✓ Inheritance
- ✓ IntelliMirror
- ✓ Linking
- ✓ No Override
- ✓ Organizational Unit (OU)
- ✓ Package
- ✓ Pilot program
- ✓ Published applications
- ✓ Resultant Set of Policy (RSoP)
- ✓ Site
- ✓ Software Installation
- ✓ Storage domain
- ✓ Windows Installer

Techniques you'll need to master:

- ✓ Creating and modifying a Group Policy Object (GPO)
- ✓ Linking an existing GPO
- ✓ Delegating administrative control of Group Policy
- ✓ Modifying Group Policy inheritance
- ✓ Filtering Group Policy settings by associating security groups to GPOs
- ✓ Using the Resultant Set of Policy MMC snap-in
- ✓ Configuring deployment options
- ✓ Deploying and maintaining software by using Group Policy
- ✓ Troubleshooting common problems that occur during software deployment

Microsoft realizes that consumers today, especially those in the business world, are paying far closer attention to the total cost of ownership (TCO) of their systems. TCO can be reduced if there is a uniform way of managing systems on a network. This is the purpose of Group Policy. Group Policy fits into the "change and configuration" space of Microsoft technologies. As you will soon see, Group Policy sits at the heart of Microsoft's TCO and security infrastructures.

Although Group Policy is often associated with configuring security settings within a Windows Server 2003 environment, it is also commonly used for managing applications within corporate environments.

Application management through Group Policy encompasses the entire life cycle of an application, including installation, maintenance (service packs and updates), and uninstallation. By leveraging the Active Directory (AD) infrastructure, software maintenance through Group Policy brings a uniform approach to the task of managing your user environment.

Change and Configuration Basics

Change and configuration management is a term that encompasses a lot of different things. Microsoft also uses terms within change and configuration to describe groups of technologies—such as IntelliMirror. IntelliMirror is actually a catchall term that can be used when discussing change and configuration management in general terms.

Group Policy is one technology that makes up Microsoft's total change and configuration management strategy. Group Policy is actually one element of IntelliMirror.

Change and configuration management is actually a technology solution to a business problem. It forms the foundation for systems management, which is the old term used to describe the various issues that change and configuration management tries to handle. Change and configuration management includes everything from the installation of the base operating system to applying security settings and configuring Internet Explorer. Some of these items are in the realm of Group Policy, while others require additional technologies (such as operating system installations that require Remote Installation Services [RIS] to be installed).

Microsoft includes several technologies in Windows Server 2003 that are dependent on Active Directory and that make up its change and configuration management initiative. This collection of technologies is commonly referred to as IntelliMirror. A quick summary of the benefits of IntelliMirror technologies is as follows:

- Enables administrators to define environment settings for users, groups, and computers. Windows Server 2003 then enforces the settings.
- Allows the Windows 2000 and above operating system to be installed remotely onto compatible computers.
- Enables users' local folders to be redirected to a shared server location, and enables files to be synchronized automatically between the server and the local hard drive for working offline.
- Enables users' desktop settings and applications to roam with them, no matter what computer they use to log on.
- Enables administrators to centrally manage software installation, updating, and removal. Self-healing applications replace missing or corrupted files automatically, without user intervention.
- Makes the computer a commodity. A system can simply be replaced with a new one, and settings, applications, and policies are quickly regenerated on the new system with minimum downtime.

One of the key features of a Windows Server 2003 change and configuration management strategy involves Group Policy, which is the focus of this chapter. After a quick overview of Group Policy, we show you the skills you will need to be successful on the exam.

Group Policy Overview

Group Policy is at the center of a Microsoft network that utilizes Active Directory. Even without configuration by an administrator, every user and computer has Group Policy applied to them.

In earlier versions of the Microsoft network operating system, Group Policy went by the name of System Policies. Group Policy as it is known today first appeared with Windows 2000 Server. It is dependent upon Active Directory to function. Having said that, a scaled-down version of Group Policy, known as Local Policy, is installed on every copy of Windows 2000 Professional and Windows XP.

Group Policy is an integrated solution that solves configuration problems on a large scale. One of the beauties of Group Policy is that it is entirely invisible to the end user. Group Policy can be used to configure desktop settings (wallpaper and so on), to install applications, and to apply security settings. Its broad range of possibilities gives Group Policy its power and, of course, adds to its complexity.

Group Policy supports Windows 2000 clients and up, so Windows 9*x*, NT 4.0, and earlier systems cannot realize the benefits of a Group Policy implementation. As we've alluded, System Policies are available to use with these legacy clients.

Group Policy Objects

The basic unit of Group Policy is the *Group Policy Object (GPO)*. A GPO is a collection of policies that can be applied at the site, domain, and OU levels. Additionally, GPO settings are passed along from a parent object to all child objects in a process known as inheritance.

Windows Server 2003 processes Group Policy in the following order (easily recalled with the acronym LSDOU):

- Local
- Site
- Domain
- OU

Group Policies are stored both within the Active Directory database and in the system volume (SYSVOL) on each domain controller (DC). Later in this chapter, in the "Filtering Group Policy" section, we look at filtering the effects of Group Policy through security groups, but for now we consider a GPO that has not been filtered:

- A GPO that is linked to a site applies to all objects in the site.
- A GPO that is linked to a domain applies to all objects in the domain.
- A GPO that is linked to an OU applies to all objects in the OU.

Although this sounds fairly obvious, it is essential to understanding Group Policy's scope. As an organizational structure becomes more complex and the number of GPOs grows, it becomes harder to keep track of the effects of individual GPOs and the combined effects that multiple GPOs might have. Fortunately, Microsoft has introduced the Resultant Set of Policy (RSoP) snap-in to help with this situation. This snap-in is discussed later in the "Resultant Set of Policy (RSoP)" section of this chapter.

By default, GPO settings that are applied later override settings that are applied earlier. Therefore, a domain GPO overrides settings made by a site GPO. This gives an administrator highly granular control over the policy behavior on a network. As you will see, this default behavior can be modified, if desired.

Nonlocal GPOs

Nonlocal GPOs are stored within Active Directory. Two locations within the Active Directory database are used to store nonlocal GPOs: a Group Policy container and a Group Policy template. A globally unique identifier is used for naming the GPOs, to keep the two locations synchronized.

A *Group Policy container (GPC)* is an Active Directory storage area for GPO settings for both computer and user Group Policy information. In addition to the GPC, Active Directory stores information in a *Group Policy template (GPT)*, which is contained in a folder structure in the SYSVOL folder of domain controllers, located under \WINDOWS\SYSVOL\sysvol\ *domain_name*\Policies.

When a GPO is created, the GPT is created, and the folder name given to the template is the globally unique identifier (GUID) of the GPO. A GUID is a hexadecimal number supplied by the manufacturer of a product that uniquely identifies the hardware or software. A GUID is in the form of 8 characters (numbers or letters) followed by 4, by 4, by 4, and by 12. For example, `{15DEF489-AE24-10BF-C11A-00BB844CE636}` is a valid format for a GUID (braces included).

The GPC contains definitions of the Group Policy, including the version number of the GPO. The GPT stores the physical aspects of the GPO. For instance, a .REG file is required to store any Registry-based changes that need to be made to clients. Because this is a physical file to which the clients need access, it is created and stored in the GPT for replication to all domain controllers.

Local GPOs

So far, we've mentioned local GPOs, but we have not defined them. A local GPO applies only to the local Windows 2000 Professional or Windows XP computer and is *not* a global object because the GPO is not stored within the Active Directory database. Local GPOs are stored on the local hard drive of the client system, in the \winnt\system32\GroupPolicy directory. Nonlocal GPO settings override any local GPO settings applied from the site, domain, or OU levels and are recommended only for use on standalone Windows 2000 Professional and Windows XP systems that are not part of an Active Directory domain.

Because the local GPO does not utilize Active Directory, some AD features that are normally configurable in the Group Policy Editor, such as Folder Redirection and Software Installation, are unavailable.

A Windows 2000 Professional or Windows XP computer can have only one local GPO, although they will process all nonlocal GPOs presented to them by Active Directory.

Creating a Group Policy Object

Creating a GPO is done primarily through the Active Directory Users and Computers management console, which is accessed through Start, Administrative Tools. From within the console, right-click a domain or OU and select Properties; then click the Group Policy tab. You will notice the options such as Add, New, Edit, and Delete. Those are the major commands, and they perform the following functions:

- *Add*—Adds a Group Policy Object link
- *New*—Creates a new GPO
- *Edit*—Modifies an existing GPO
- *Delete*—Removes a GPO, a GPO link, or both

From Active Directory Users and Computers, right-click on the domain name and click Properties. Then click on the Group Policy tab.

Creating a new GPO is as simple as clicking the New button. Clicking New creates a new GPO with a generic name: New Group Policy Object. You will probably want to rename it to something more descriptive, but for our purposes here, we have just left it with the default name supplied by Windows Server 2003.

Modifying Group Policy Objects

When you create a GPO, the default settings that are created do not really accomplish anything. You need to edit the GPO to define the settings that will affect the behavior of objects linked to the GPO. To edit a Group Policy Object, you use the Group Policy Editor. There is no administrative utility for the Group Policy Editor, although it can be invoked in a couple of different ways:

- Through the standalone console
- By editing a GPO

Group Policy Editor As a Standalone Console

The first method of accessing the Group Policy Editor is through a standalone console. First, click Start, Run and type **MMC /A.**

This opens a new, empty Microsoft Management Console (MMC). First, click on the File menu and then select Add/Remove Snap-in. You will see a dialog box like the one in Figure 9.1.

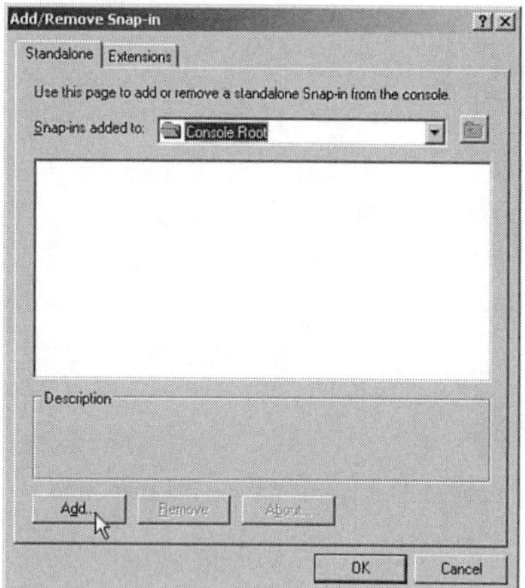

Figure 9.1 The first step in adding a snap-in is to select the Add/Remove Snap-In menu option.

Figure 9.2 shows the next step of the process: selecting Group Policy from the list of available snap-ins. Click the Add button to see this dialog box. Scroll down the list until you find the snap-in shown in Figure 9.2.

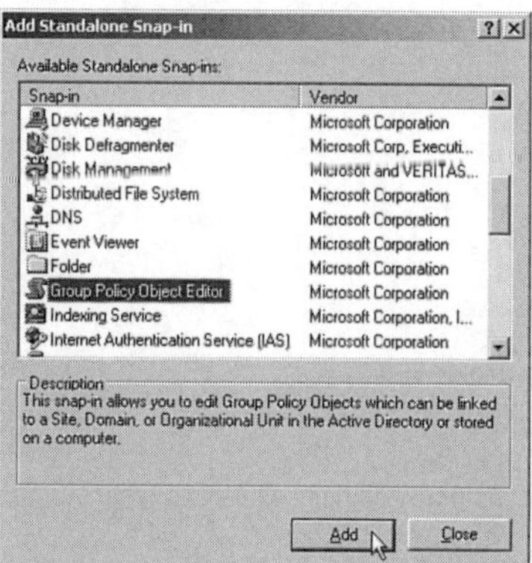

Figure 9.2 The list of snap-ins shows the available standalone snap-ins that can be added to the console.

The next step is the most important and the reason you are stepping through this process. You must define the scope of the Group Policy Editor, which equates to what GPO you will be editing. Figure 9.3 illustrates that the Group Policy Editor defaults to the Local Computer Group Policy Object. Most likely, you will want to edit a nonlocal GPO, so click Browse to look for the desired GPO.

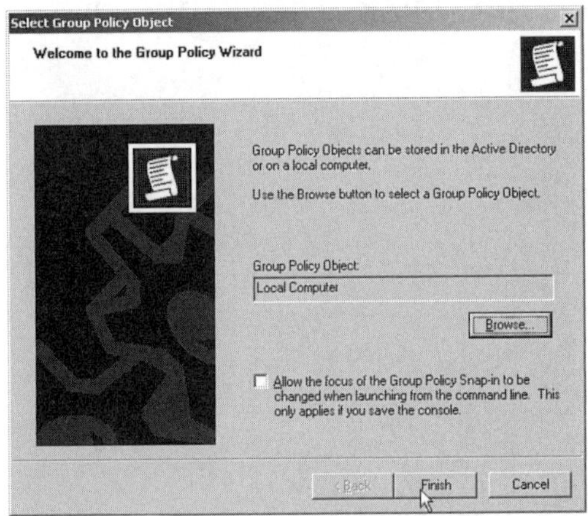

Figure 9.3 You must determine the focus of the Group Policy Editor when you add the snap-in to the console.

As you can see in Figure 9.4, when you browse, you have a number of options. You can browse by domains/OU, sites, computers, or all GPOs. Windows Server 2003 defaults to the current storage domain that you are logged into, but that can be changed by dropping down the list next to Look In.

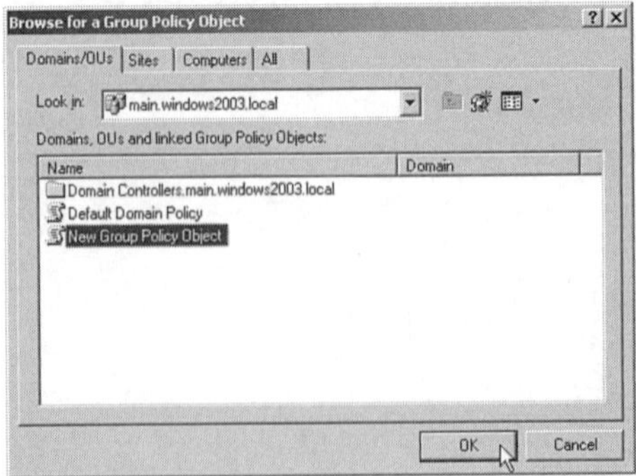

Figure 9.4 You can browse for nonlocal GPOs in the current storage domain, as well as other available domains.

The last option to address is shown back in Figure 9.3, which you see again when you click OK for the choice in Figure 9.4. There is a check box named as follows: Allow the focus of the Group Policy Snap-in to be changed when launched from the command line. This applies only if you save the console. By default, this is not selected, but if you plan to save your console, you might choose to enable this option. It simply enables you to specify a different GPO as the focus of the console if you so choose when entering the command line.

If you plan to edit a particular GPO frequently, you should save the console after you have opened the snap-in and returned to the console screen. Windows Server 2003 prompts you for a filename and saves the file with an .msc extension to your Administrative Tools folder, located in the \Documents and Settings*username*\Start menu\Programs folder. The name that you assign to the console appears as the console name when you browse the Administrative Tools folder in the Start menu, so you should choose something descriptive.

Accessing the Group Policy Editor by Editing a Group Policy Object

The other method of accessing the Group Policy Editor is to simply edit the GPO from the Group Policy tab of a site, domain, or OU's property sheet. This can be accessed from the Active Directory Users and Computers administrative utility.

From Active Directory Users and Computers, right-click an object that has the desired Group Policy Object linked to it. For example, if you want to edit the Default Domain Policy GPO, right-click on the desired domain in Active Directory Users and Computers, click Properties, and then click the Group Policy tab. Click the Edit button, which launches the Group Policy Editor with the GPO that you selected as the focus.

Working Inside the Group Policy Editor

Regardless of whether you open the Group Policy Editor as a standalone console or by editing a GPO in Active Directory Users and Computers, the appearance of the console is the same. Looking at the example console seen in Figure 9.5, you find the following structure:

- *Root container*—This defines the focus of the Group Policy Editor by showing the GPO that is being edited, as well as the fully qualified domain name (FQDN) of the domain controller from which you are editing the GPO. In Figure 9.5, the GPO Default Domain Policy is being edited by win2003svr.main.windows2003.local. If you opened the GPO for editing on a domain controller named ws.main.windows2003.local, the root of the Group Policy Editor would reflect that.

- *Computer Configuration*—This container includes settings specifically covering computer policies. Computer policies are processed when you boot the computer.
- *User Configuration*—This container includes settings that specifically cover user policies. User policies are processed at user logon.
- *Software Settings*—This subcontainer under both the Computer Configuration and User Configuration containers includes Software Installation settings for computers and users.
- *Windows Settings*—This subcontainer under both the Computer Configuration and User Configuration containers includes script and security settings, as well as other policy settings that affect the behavior of the Windows environment.
- *Administrative Templates*—This subcontainer under both the Computer Configuration and User Configuration containers provides the majority of settings for controlling the desktop environment and restricting access to applications, applets, and the appearance of the desktop.

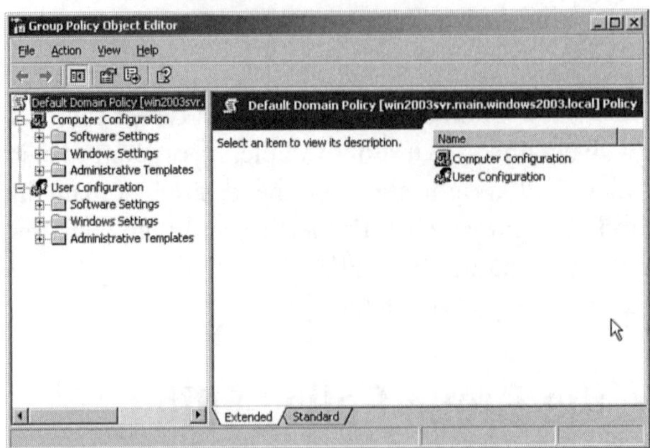

Figure 9.5 Editing a GPO with the Group Policy Editor.

Linking a GPO

As previously mentioned, by default, the effects of GPOs are inherited by all child objects of a parent object, thereby essentially creating a hierarchy of policy objects. That is, a GPO that is linked to a site applies to all computers and users in that site, regardless of their domain membership. A GPO linked to a domain applies to all computers and users within the domain. A GPO applied to an OU applies to all computers and users within the OU. Because of the effects of inheritance and the overriding effects of policies that are applied later in the processing order, it is important to be careful with GPO links. Failure to account for the interaction between different sets of policies can have an adverse impact on your network by introducing undesired behavior of policy recipients.

One important concept to learn is that Group Policy is simply an object created within Active Directory. Creating a new policy does not, within itself, achieve a result. For a Group Policy to be applied, it must first be linked to a container (don't forget the acronym LSDOU). The effects of a GPO are applied to the object(s) to which they are linked.

Before you can link a GPO, you must at least have the permissions necessary to edit a GPO—that is, Read/Write or Full Control permissions. By default, administrators have this capability. As you will see later in this chapter in the section "Delegating Administrative Control of Group Policy," administrators can delegate the authority to perform certain Group Policy functions, such as linking GPOs to nonadministrators.

To link a GPO, open Active Directory Users and Computers (or Active Directory Sites and Services, if you want to link a GPO at the site level) and right-click the domain or OU to which you want to link a GPO. Choose Properties and then the Group Policy tab. Click the Add button, and navigate to select the GPO that you want to link to the particular domain or OU. In Figure 9.6, we have selected an OU called Test OU. As you can see, there are currently no linked GPOs within Test OU. However, if you click on the All tab of the Add a Group Policy Object Link dialog box (after clicking the Add button), as shown in Figure 9.7, you can see all of the GPOs that have been created. Click OK when you are done selecting a GPO to link to. The GPO is now successfully linked to the Test OU.

It is important to note that GPOs *cannot* be linked to the generic Active Directory containers, which include the following:

- Built-In
- Computers
- Users

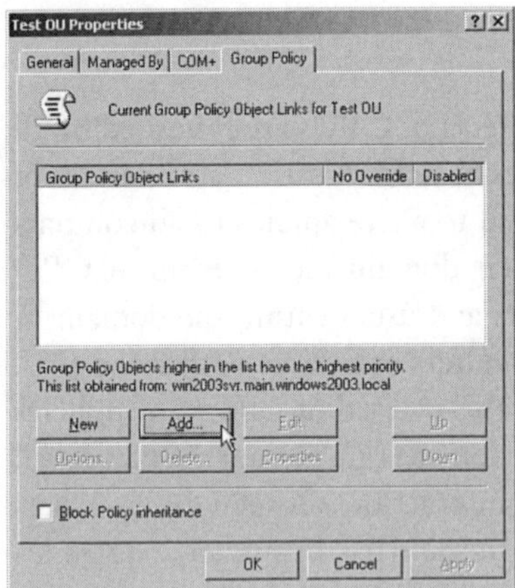

Figure 9.6 You can add or edit an existing GPO.

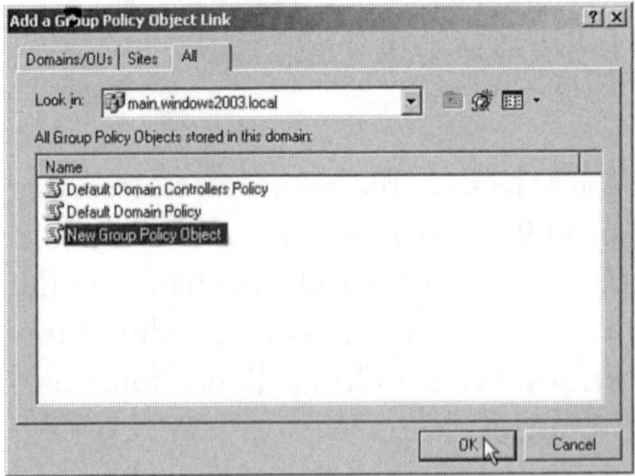

Figure 9.7 Clicking the All tab brings up the entire list of GPOs that are stored in the Active Directory database.

Linking Multiple GPOs

Nonlocal GPOs are stored in the Active Directory database and, in theory, are available to all members of an Active Directory forest. We say *in theory* because, in reality, there are some limitations to GPO linking. First, let's look at how GPOs can and can't be linked.

Multiple GPOs can be linked to a single site, domain, or OU. The converse is also true: Multiple sites, domains, and OUs can all have the same GPO linked to them. Every GPO is stored within Active Directory in the domain in which it was created, which is called its *storage domain*. Although it is usually the case, the storage domain is not necessarily the domain in which the

GPO is linked because there is a significant performance hit when you link GPOs across domains; therefore, Microsoft recommends that you avoid linking a GPO to an object in a different domain.

One last note on linking: It is *not* possible to link to only a subset of a GPO's settings. Group Policy Objects are the most basic unit of Group Policy, so you can link only to an entire GPO.

Cross-Domain GPO Links

It is possible to create GPOs in one domain and have them apply to users and computers in another domain or forest. However, this is not recommended in most cases because computer startup and user logon are slowed, sometimes dramatically, if a domain controller from another domain must process authentication. To apply a GPO, the target of the policy must be capable of reading the GPO and must have the permission to apply Group Policy for the GPO.

Additional authentication mechanisms exist for validating the computer or user account in the remote domain, so processing will not be as fast as when reading a GPO in the same domain. Because of this, normally it is better to create duplicate GPOs in multiple domains rather than attempting to cross-link GPOs to other domains or forests.

Other than the performance issue, there is no real reason not to cross-link domain GPOs above creating multiple duplicate GPOs. In fact, cross-linking a single GPO is actually easier to manage because, if you make a modification to the GPO, the change automatically applies to all users and computers in the target container. Alternatively, you would have to make the change in every GPO that you created to perform the same function.

Delegating Administrative Control of Group Policy

In larger enterprises, network administration is usually distributed among multiple individuals, often at multiple locations in multiple cities. It becomes necessary for more than one person to be able to complete a given task; in some instances, you might need to allow a nonadministrator to have a subset of administrative authority to complete a task. Such would be the case at a small, remote branch office that does not have enough staff to warrant an on-site, full-time systems administrator to manage the servers. To accommodate this, Windows Server 2003 provides the capability for administrators to delegate authority of certain Group Policy tasks.

Keep in mind that the delegation applies only to nonlocal GPOs. Local Group Policy applies to standalone computers only, whereas nonlocal Group Policy requires a Windows domain controller. The rights to administer Group Policy can be found under the <*GPO name*>\User Configuration\Administrative Templates\Windows Components\Microsoft Management Console\Group Policy node, while the GPO is open in the Group Policy Editor.

Managing Group Policy Links

The Delegation of Control Wizard is used to delegate control to users or groups that will manage GPO links. The wizard is accessible by right-clicking on the desired domain or OU in Active Directory Users and Computers and selecting Delegate Control.

When the wizard starts, you must first select the users or groups to which you want to delegate; then click Next. You then should see a window such as that in Figure 9.8, which shows a list of tasks to be delegated. As you can see, the Delegation of Control Wizard can delegate other tasks besides Manage Group Policy Links. For Group Policy, however, only this task is applicable. Simply click Finish after you have made your selection and clicked Next; the wizard requires no other settings.

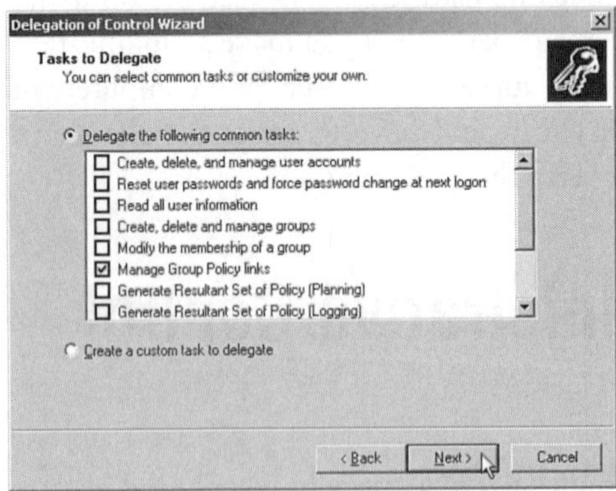

Figure 9.8 The Delegation of Control Wizard is used to delegate control of managing Group Policy links to users and groups.

When you delegate control, you allow the individuals or groups to perform those functions as if they were an administrator. Therefore, it is important not to delegate control indiscriminately.

Creating GPOs

Delegating the capability to create GPOs is accomplished through Active Directory Users and Computers as well. To create a GPO, a user account must belong to the Group Policy Creator Owners administrators group. Double-click the Group Policy Creator Owners group in the Users container, and click the Members tab. Add the users who should be able to create GPOs.

Editing GPOs

You might also want a nonadministrator to have the capability to edit a specific GPO in the domain. The capability for a nonadminister to edit a GPO comes from an administrator delegating administrative control of a specific GPO. Opening the GPO into the Group Policy Editor completes this delegation. Right-click on the GPO name and choose Properties, and then click the Security tab. Add the user(s) you want to have administrative control, and set the appropriate permission levels. At a minimum, a user or group needs Read/Write permissions to edit a GPO, although you could go so far as to grant Full Control, if necessary.

For the exam, you will need to know how Group Policy tasks are delegated, so be sure you know the information in Table 9.1.

Table 9.1 Group Policy Tasks and Their Delegation Methods

Task	Method
Managing Group Policy Links	Delegation of Control Wizard
Creating GPOs	Group Policy Creator Owners membership
Editing GPOs	Security properties of the specific GPO (Group Policy Editor)

Group Policy Inheritance

You know that Group Policy is processed in the order of local, site, domain, and OU (LSDOU). Inheritance, which is enabled by default, is the process by which a policy applied at one level is passed down to lower levels. Objects have parent-child relationships, and parent objects pass down their settings to child objects, thereby forming a hierarchy. The child objects can override parent settings by explicitly defining different policy settings; however, in the absence of a specifically defined setting, the settings from the parent object apply.

Thus, an OU automatically inherits all of the settings from the domain to which it belongs, while at the same time automatically inheriting settings from the site.

In some cases, it is not desirable for inheritance to take effect. Windows Server 2003 therefore allows for two methods of changing the default behavior of setting inheritance:

- Block Policy Inheritance
- No Override

Block Policy Inheritance

Block Policy Inheritance prevents policies higher in the Active Directory structure from being automatically applied at lower levels. You use Block Policy Inheritance to stop settings from higher-level objects from being applied later in the processing order. For example, you can block a domain policy from applying settings to an OU by selecting the check box to Block Policy Inheritance.

To enable Block Policy Inheritance, open the Group Policy tab of an object's properties, as previously discussed. There is a check box in the lower-left corner of the Group Policy property sheet.

You should use the Block Policy Inheritance option with care. When used, it blocks all policies that have been applied at a higher level, and it is not selective.

No Override

As with Block Policy Inheritance, No Override is a method of altering the default behavior of policy inheritance in Windows Server 2003. Unlike Block Policy Inheritance, which is applied at the domain, OU, or local levels, No Override is applied to a GPO *link*. Table 9.2 summarizes these differences.

No Override is used to prevent policies at lower levels in the Active Directory tree from overwriting policies applied from a higher level. This is a way to minimize the effects of multiple GPOs interacting and creating undesirable policy settings. If you want to ensure that a default domain policy is applied regardless of OU polices, use No Override.

If you want to view what objects a GPO is linked to, to determine the effects of setting No Override, open the Group Policy property sheet for an object in Active Directory Users and Computers. Select the desired GPO and click Properties, and then click on the Links tab. Click Find Now to search the default domain, or select a different domain from the drop-down list. Alternatively, you could use the Resultant Set of Policy tool, which is discussed later in the section "Resultant Set of Policy (RSoP)."

Table 9.2 Block Policy Inheritance Versus No Override

Method	Applied To?	Conflict Resolution
Block Policy Inheritance	Domains, OUs, local computers	Defers to No Override
No Override	GPO links	Takes precedence

To configure No Override, open the Group Policy property sheet for an object in Active Directory Users and Computers. Select the GPO in question and click the Options button, at which time you will see the window shown in Figure 9.9.

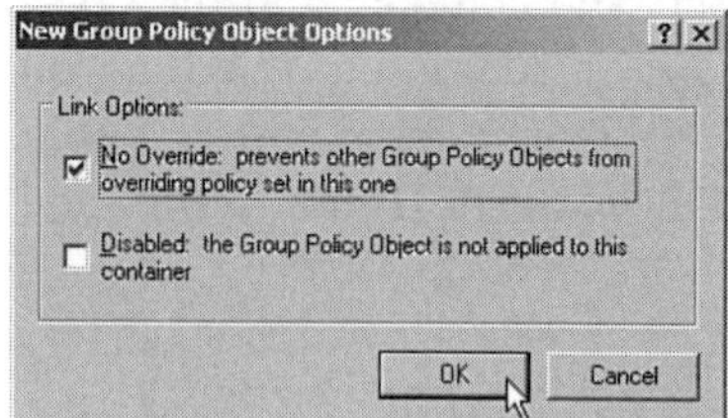

Figure 9.9 Configuring No Override is done through a Group Policy Object's options.

Block Policy Inheritance and No Override can make it extremely complex to troubleshoot policy-related problems on a network, especially as the size of the network and the number of GPOs grows. For that reason, you should avoid using these options whenever possible.

Disabling a GPO

Although it is not exactly the same as the previous methods of preventing policy inheritance, another option prevents the effects of a GPO from being applied to an object (see Figure 9.12). By selecting the Disabled check box, an administrator can prevent the effects of a GPO from being applied to any object within the selected container, such as a domain or an OU.

You might be asking yourself, "Why does this option exist, when I just unlink a GPO to achieve the same result?" The reason you cannot disable a GPO is simple: Suppose that the GPO doesn't do what you expected it to do. In this case, you can simply disable the GPO (rather than unlink it) until you discover the cause of the problem. When the problem is corrected, you can enable the GPO, which is easier than linking the GPO again and having to re-create any custom permissions that you have applied.

Filtering Group Policy

We previously mentioned security groups when delegating control over editing Group Policy Objects. The other time to use security groups in relation to Group Policy is to filter the scope of a GPO. You might have a GPO that applies to an entire OU, for example, yet there are specific objects within the OU that you do not want to be affected by the policies. Through security groups, you can filter out the desired object from the OU and prevent it from having the policy applied to it.

When filtering the effects of a GPO by security group, you are essentially editing the discretionary Access Control List (DACL) on that GPO. Using the DACL, you allow or deny access for users and computers to the GPO based on their memberships in security groups. In addition to DACLs, you have access control entries (ACEs), which are the permission entries within a DACL. ACEs are permissions such as Full Control, Read, Write, and Apply Group Policy.

Two permissions are required for an object to receive policy settings from a GPO, and all authenticated users have these permissions, by default:

- Read
- Apply Group Policy

The easiest way to prevent Group Policy from applying to an object is to remove that object's Apply Policy permission. If Read permission is taken away, an object cannot access the GPO, and, therefore, policy settings will not be applied. Microsoft strongly recommends removing the Apply Group Policy permission as well because it speeds up the time it takes to process Group Policy for an object if unused permissions do not have to be processed.

To reiterate, select the security settings for a GPO by going into the property sheet for a specific GPO and choosing the Security tab.

Filtering affects the entire Group Policy Object. You cannot filter only specific settings within a GPO from applying to a security group. However, you can disable an unused portion of a GPO from applying anywhere if you are not using it.

Lest you think that filtering is the "end all" when it comes to granularly applying GPOs, bear in mind that filtering adds extra processing time to the GPO application because each permission must be checked and verified. Consider applying GPOs selectively to OUs instead of filtering, if possible.

Disabling Unused Portions of a GPO

Windows Server 2003 Group Policy gives you the option of disabling either the Computer Configuration or the User Configuration (or both, but that would be pointless) containers within a GPO. Doing so speeds up Group Policy processing and can be beneficial if you have targeted GPOs that apply only to computers or only to users.

To disable an unused portion, open the Group Policy property sheet for an object, such as a domain (as you have previously done in this chapter). Select the desired GPO and click Properties. As shown in Figure 9.10, the bottom of the page includes the options to disable Computer Configuration and User Configuration settings, to speed up performance.

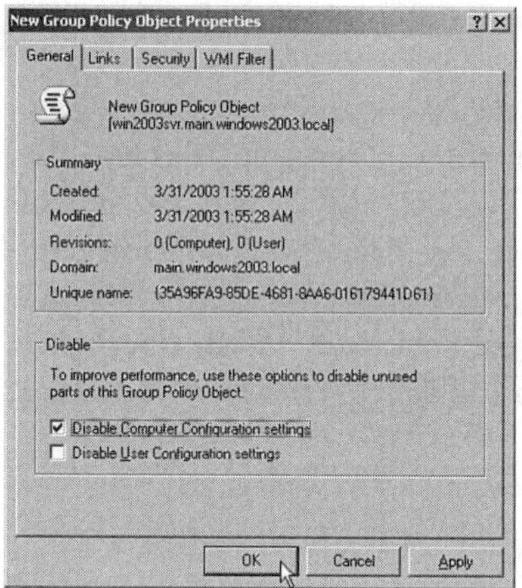

Figure 9.10 Disabling the Computer Configuration or User Configuration settings for a GPO can speed up processing if you have GPOs that apply only to computers or only to users.

Resultant Set of Policy (RSoP)

Group Policy is a powerful tool for configuring users and computers. However, along with its power comes complexity. Previous versions of Microsoft's operating systems sometimes left you to muddle through trying to determine the end result of applying a Group Policy.

As you can imagine, Group Policies can get quite complex as they are layered in sites, domains, and Organizational Units. The result of applying a policy—in other words, the ultimate effect of applying a group of settings to a user or computer—was often quite difficult to determine. Without third-party tools, administrators had to document which Group Policies had been applied to which parts of Active Directory in Microsoft Excel spreadsheets or in databases. Only by working through this information was it possible to troubleshoot or plan a Group Policy implementation.

To assist with these issues in Windows Server 2003, Microsoft introduced a new MMC snap-in called *Resultant Set of Policy (RSoP)*. RSoP is actually a query engine. In effect, it can query about an object (such as a computer or user) and determine what policies have been applied to it. It does this by utilizing Windows Management Instrumentation (WMI).

WMI was first introduced in Windows NT 4.0 and represents Microsoft's strategy to make the Windows platform more manageable. WMI consists of several components. Two of these components are the Common Information Management Object Model (CIMOM) database and agents that are used to both accumulate and store WMI data. The CIMOM database is also known as the WMI repository because WMI uses it to store state data. This is the database that is used by RSoP, so it is mentioned here.

In this context, you can think of WMI as a data store for information regarding Group Policy. It replaces the manual methods of recording this data that were required for documenting previous versions of the operating system. You would be forgiven for assuming that any data about policies being applied to an object would be queried from Active Directory itself; however, in this case, the data is coming from a local data store, WMI. RSoP is an MMC snap-in that both compiles this data and then queries it for you. RSoP works in one of two modes:

- Planning mode
- Logging mode

Note that RSoP can be used to determine details of Group Policies that affect administrative templates, Folder Redirection, and scripts.

Planning Mode

Planning mode gives you the opportunity to apply Group Policies to an object, such as a user or computer, to see the net effect a new policy will have. This enables you to set up "what-if" scenarios.

For instance, let's say that you have a computer that has several Group Policies applied to it through membership to sites, domains, or Organizational Units. As an administrator, you want to configure a new Group Policy. Furthermore, you want to know the net effect if the computer object is moved from one security group to another with Active Directory. This is the purpose of planning mode.

It is possible to run RSoP in planning mode on both local and remote machines. To access remote machines using this utility, you must have one of these three security rights:

- Be a member of the Domain Admins group
- Be a member of the Enterprise Admins group
- Be delegated the Generate Resultant Set of Policy (Planning) rights

In planning mode, you can determine what would happen if a new policy were applied to an object or an object were moved within the directory. When you have determined the net effect, you can make adjustments to your Group Policy planning, if necessary. A good way to think of planning mode is as a "simulator" for new Group Policy settings.

Logging Mode

Logging mode gives you the capability to determine which policies are currently being applied to an object. In this mode, you can generate a report and work out what each of the policies are doing to an object. This is useful for troubleshooting Group Policy problems. A good way to think about logging mode is as a report engine for Group Policy.

Using RSoP Snap-in

We discussed how you could add an MMC snap-in to an empty console. The process for using the RSoP console is the same.

Before you can use the RSoP snap-in, you must generate the RSoP data. This process ensures that all data is written to the WMI database. Clicking on the Action menu and selecting Generate RSoP Data achieves this.

This starts the Resultant Set of Policy Wizard. At this time, you are asked to select whether you will be using logging mode or planning mode.

The screens that follow vary, depending upon which options you choose (logging or planning modes). Logging mode essentially enables you to select the computer against which you want to run the wizard. Planning mode requires that you enter the object that you want to use to simulate the application of a policy. Choosing planning mode displays the dialog box shown in Figure 9.11.

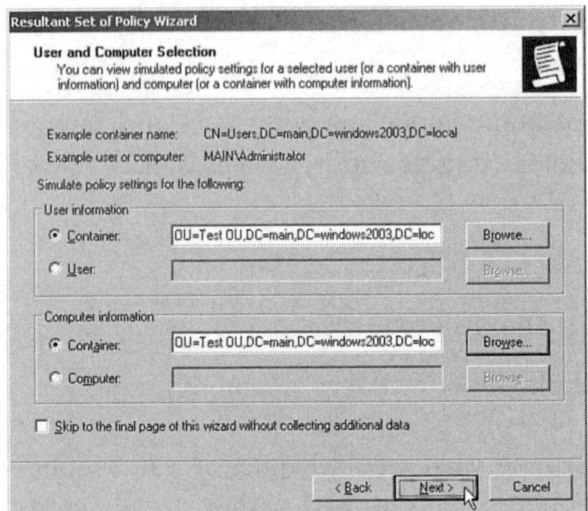

Figure 9.11 The User and Computer Selection option of the Resultant Set of Policy Wizard.

In the lower-left corner of Figure 9.11, you can see the option Skip to the Final Page of This Wizard Without Collecting Additional Data. Doing so skips wizard pages that enable you to configure data about the speed of network connections, loopback settings, and the ability to simulate changes based on user groups.

When the wizard is complete, it is possible to step through each of the options available in Group Policy to see what settings have been applied.

IntelliMirror Concepts

Microsoft has grouped many Group Policy concepts under the name *IntelliMirror*. IntelliMirror is a collection of technologies that work together in Windows Server 2003 to reduce the total cost of ownership (TCO) by simplifying the management of Windows Server 2003 computers.

The features of IntelliMirror are listed here:

- *Data management*—The first feature of IntelliMirror is managing user data. This is implemented in Windows Server 2003 through Folder Redirection. When Folder Redirection and Offline Folders are used, user data can be synchronized between a server copy and a local copy, ensuring that data files are accessible no matter where users are or what computer they log on from.

- *Desktop settings management*—Desktop settings can be stored in profiles that roam with a user so that they are applied whenever a user logs in to a networked computer. Group Policy is used to control what settings should be stored and can control a user's ability to make changes to desktop settings. Group Policy can be used to lock down desktop configurations and define a standard level of security for Windows Server 2003 computers.
- *Software installation and maintenance*—The focus of this chapter, this feature of IntelliMirror allows applications to be published by an administrator for use by defined users and computers. It does this by using the infrastructure provided by Active Directory.

Specifically, the following are the available Windows Server 2003 IntelliMirror technologies and their interdependencies:

- *Active Directory*—This is the cornerstone of IntelliMirror because, without AD, none of the rest would be possible. Active Directory stores the GPOs and other user, group, and computer information, and provides centralized management for Windows Server 2003 networks.
- *Group Policy*—Through Group Policy, you can manage desktop settings and determine what to apply and where to apply it. Group Policy is dependent on Active Directory because it stores global policy information in the Active Directory database. Group Policy is the primary method of managing the IntelliMirror features listed previously.
- *Roaming user profiles*—Roaming user profiles are used to enable user settings such as desktop wallpaper and customized Start menu settings to follow users to whichever computer they log on from. Any changes that are made to the user environment while the user is logged in are saved in the profile, ntuser.dat, and stored in Active Directory.
- *Folder Redirection*—Folder Redirection is one of the primary components of the data management IntelliMirror feature discussed previously. Folder Redirection can be used to seamlessly move the contents of certain local user folders to a network location. Combined with Offline Folders, you can have much greater data protection and availability than by having files stored only on local hard drives.
- *Offline Folders*—Offline Folders is an IntelliMirror capability that allows for the synchronization of files and folders between the local hard drive and a network location. This is particularly useful for users who have laptops because they can use Offline Folders in conjunction with Folder Redirection to ensure that users have full access to their files, regardless of whether they are in the office, on the LAN, or working offline on an airplane.

Software Installation and Maintenance Overview

Through IntelliMirror and, specifically, the Group Policy component, Microsoft has provided the Software Installation and Maintenance feature, which provides a way for administrators to deploy software so that it is always available to users and repairs itself, if necessary. Software Installation and Maintenance is implemented as a Group Policy extension called Software Installation. As shown in Figure 9.12, it is located under both the Computer Configuration and User Configuration containers in a GPO, under the Software Settings nodes.

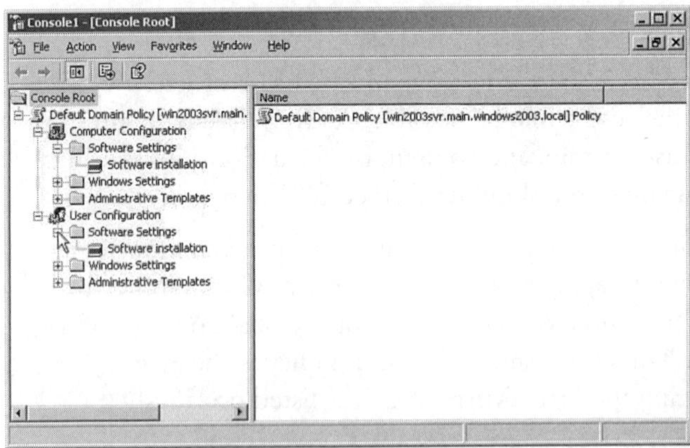

Figure 9.12 The Software Installation extension to Group Policy is located under the Software Settings node in the Computer and User Configuration containers.

Through Software Installation, you can centrally manage each of the following:

- *Deployment of applications*—You can deploy shrink-wrapped applications or custom-built in-house applications. Almost any type of application can be deployed through Software Installation.
- *Upgrades and patches*—Through Software Installation, you can update existing software or even replace it, in the case of a product upgrade. Deploying service packs for operating systems becomes much easier as well.
- *Uninstallation of software*—When a product is no longer in use or is no longer supported by the IT department, you can easily remove it from users' computers without their intervention or having to physically touch each computer that contains the installed software.

The goal of Software Installation is to deploy applications in such a way that whenever users log on to a computer, no matter where they are, they will always have their applications available to them. This technology is often referred to as just-in-time (JIT) because deployment occurs either during user logon or when the user goes to launch a particular application. For example, say that you have assigned Microsoft Word to a particular user. Even though the user has not explicitly installed Microsoft Word himself, he sees the icon on the desktop or in the Start menu. The first time the user attempts to use the program, the system goes out and installs the application automatically—with no user intervention—and launches the program.

Likewise, if the same user attempts to use a feature of the program that is not installed by default, the application will be smart enough to automatically install the missing feature from the network on the fly and allow the user to use it. In the past, installing a missing feature invariably meant manually running the program's setup utility and either reinstalling the entire product to add the missing feature or selecting the missing feature and choosing to update the installation. In either case, this would interrupt the user's workflow and would very likely require a desk-side trip from a desktop support technician.

Requirements for Software Installation

To use the Software Installation extension, the following prerequisites must be met:

- *Active Directory dependency*—Because Group Policy is dependent on Active Directory, it makes sense that you cannot use the Software Installation extension unless you have deployed Active Directory on your network. Software Installation relies on GPOs—which are stored in Active Directory—to determine who can access software that it manages. As with Group Policy, Windows 9*x* and NT 4.0 computers cannot participate in Active Directory.

- *Group Policy dependency*—To use the Software Installation extension, you must be using Group Policy on your network. Because Group Policy is limited to Windows 2000 computers and later, you can manage software only in newer environments. Any legacy Windows 9*x* or NT 4.0 clients cannot receive applications through Group Policy and Software Installation.

The primary function of Software Installation is to deploy software.

Deploying Software with Group Policy and Software Installation

In this section, we explore the Software Installation extension—specifically, the following:

- ➤ Configuring Software Installation properties
- ➤ Deploying a new package
- ➤ Configuring package properties

From setting up the Software Installation extension's global properties to deploying a new package and configuring additional properties for a deployed software package, these topics enable you to deploy software.

On the exam, you will be expected to know how to deploy software using the Software Installation extension and how to configure deployment options.

Software Deployment to Users and Computers

When deploying software, you must decide whether you deploy it to a user or a computer. You should be aware of some differences between the two.

Deploying software to a user means that the deployment follows users as they change computers. This works well for users who share computers. For instance, if a user is part of the accounting group, he might have some software that is specific to the task targeted to him through Group Policy. If this user does an audit of another department, he might use hardware within that department to do his work. Obviously, it is useful if Active Directory detects that the user is on another machine and offers the same software that this user is accustomed to. This is the case if software is targeted at a user—wherever that user logs on, the software remains targeted to him.

Software can also be targeted to computers. In this case, the software is installed on a specific computer (or set of computers) and only those machines. A user logging in to such a machine might have software packages available to him that he will not see anywhere else. This is useful for computers installed in booths or in reception areas or when only certain departments have a license for the software.

This might seem minor, but it is an important distinction between the two. Software targeted at a user "follows" that user; essentially, it knows where the user is and makes sure that the user's environment does not change. Software targeted at a computer essentially belongs to the machine. A user at this machine can use the software package, but only while logged on at that particular piece of hardware.

Other distinctions arise when it comes to assigning and publishing software. These are discussed in the "Assigned Versus Published Applications" section of this chapter.

Configuring Software Installation Properties

To configure the global properties of the Software Installation extension, simply right-click the extension and click Properties. You do this by right-clicking the Software Installation option shown in Figure 9.13. Keep in mind that computer and user settings are independent of each other, so making changes to the computer policy for Software Installation has no effect on the user policy, and vice versa.

The first dialog box that you are presented with when you enter Software Installation Properties is the General tab, shown in Figure 9.13.

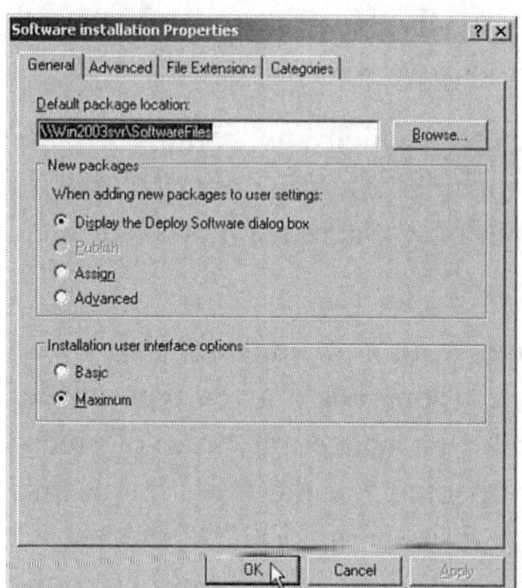

Figure 9.13 The General tab contains information about the default behavior of the Software Installation extension.

The first section on this property sheet enables the administrator to define the default package location for new packages. This should be a network share rather than a local hard-drive path (for example, \\Win2003svr\SoftwareFiles instead of E:\apps), and it is used if you use a centralized distribution location for your software.

The General property sheet also contains settings that define the extension's behavior regarding new package creation. By default, the Deploy Software dialog box is displayed when you choose to create a new package. This dialog box contains the choice to assign or publish a package, thereby enabling you to choose how you want Software Installation to handle a package on a per-instance basis. Unless you strictly publish or assign applications, there is probably no need to change this default setting.

Additionally, the General tab contains the option to define how much information is presented to the user during package installation. By default, only basic information about the software installation is supplied, such as the installation progress meter. Optionally, you can specify that a maximum amount of information and options be shown to the user during installation, which includes all installation messages and dialog boxes being shown during the process.

After the General tab is the Advanced tab. This tab offers advanced options that include the capability to have software uninstall if it falls out of scope. Put another way, because Group Policy is used to deploy software, targeting is performed within its rules. This means that software can be targeted only to users and computers through their membership to a site, domain, or OU. If a user has software installed because of membership to one of these levels, the software can be uninstalled if the user is removed by checking the option Uninstall the Applications When They Fall Out of the Scope of Management.

The Advanced tab also enables you to specify which applications will be advertised to 64-bit clients. An example includes the capability to specify whether applications designed for 32-bit operating systems should be offered to 64-bit systems.

Next is the File Extensions tab. In many cases, your computer will have more than one application installed that is capable of opening a given type of file. This property sheet enables you to pick a file type and set the order of precedence for applications that are capable of opening the file type. If the first application listed isn't available—for example, if it was uninstalled, the second application listed attempts to open the file type. Additionally, if multiple applications are listed and none are installed, the first one on the list is installed.

The last tab is Categories, which is an organizational option. You can create categories to help keep track of where software is deployed. By default, no categories are listed, so you must create them if you want to use this feature. You might choose to create categories for your software based on department, location, or some other naming convention that makes sense for your organization. One popular system is to create categories based on the type of application, such as utilities, office suites, and so on.

Deploying a New Package

To deploy a new package, you must have first copied the installation files to a *distribution point*, which is simply a network share that you designate as a repository for software. Right-click on the Software Installation extension and click New, Package. The dialog box shown in Figure 9.14 appears.

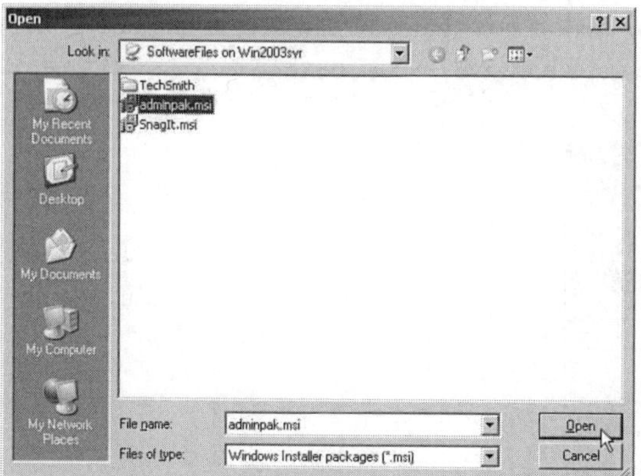

Figure 9.14 The first step in deploying a new package is to select the package that is to be deployed.

In this example, a Windows Installer package for the Admin Pack of Windows Server 2003 is selected, which is located in the SoftwareFiles share on the server Win2003svr. This is the distribution point. When you select the file and click Open, you are presented the dialog box shown in Figure 9.15. You get this dialog box because previously we left the global setting for Software Installation to show these choices when creating a new package rather than defaulting to either Publish or Assign.

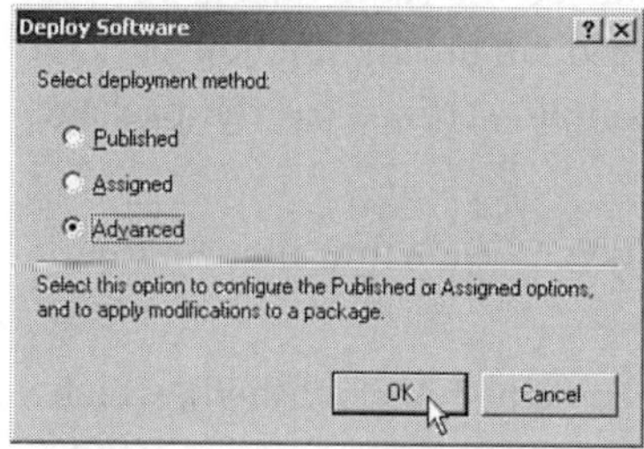

Figure 9.15 After choosing the software package to deploy, you must decide whether to publish or assign it.

It is important to note that the capability to publish applications is available only if the package is being deployed under the User Configuration container. Software deployed to computers does not support publishing, so those packages can be only assigned. When you reach the dialog box shown in Figure 9.15 and you've deployed the package under the Computer Configuration container, the publish option is grayed out.

If you select either Published or Assigned and click OK, the package is deployed without any further prompting. If you select Advanced, the package is deployed, but you are prompted with a dialog box similar to the one in Figure 9.16. This is the same dialog box that you can access later by going into the properties of a package, which we discuss next.

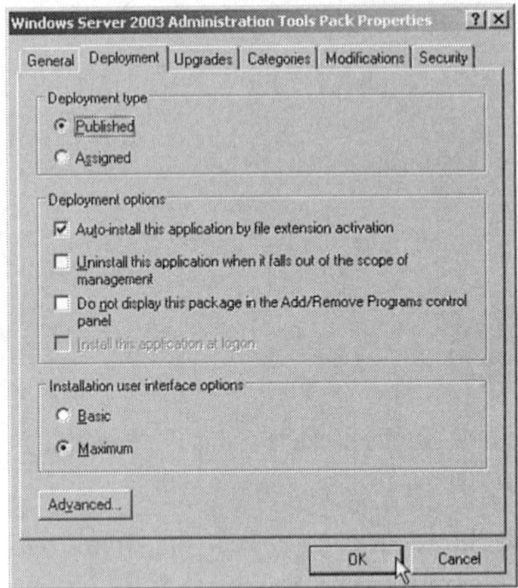

Figure 9.16 You can configure a number of advanced settings for an application after it has been deployed.

Configuring Package Properties

To access a package's properties after you've deployed it, simply right-click on the package and click Properties. You will see the same dialog box that you saw previously if you selected the Advanced tab during the new package deployment. A number of property sheets contain settings for the package. Following is an overview:

- *General*—Contains product information such as the name and version number, as well as contact information.
- *Deployment*—Defines the deployment type (assigned or published), which can also be changed here. In addition, this property sheet contains settings for deployment options, including whether the package should be uninstalled if it falls outside the scope of management and whether it should be displayed in the Add/Remove Programs applet. Advanced deployment options determine whether the language setting should be ignored when installing the software and whether previous installations of the product should be uninstalled if it wasn't installed through Group Policy.

- *Upgrades*—Defines the applications that are to be upgraded by this package and which packages can upgrade this package.
- *Categories*—Determines the categories that the software will be displayed under in the Add/Remove Programs applet.
- *Modifications*—Enables you to apply modifications or transformations to the package, to customize the deployment.
- *Security*—Determines who has what level of access to the package. Through the Security property sheet, you control the deployment of the software to computers, users, and groups.

Assigned Versus Published Applications

A key aspect to consider when deploying software is whether the application will be assigned directly to users or published into Active Directory. When an application is assigned, its icons appear in the Start menu or on the desktop of the user's computer, according to criteria defined by the administrator. The first time a user attempts to launch an assigned application, the software is automatically installed without user or administrator intervention. If a user later uninstalls the application through the Add/Remove Programs applet in the Control Panel, the software still is available to users the next time they log on. If users attempt to launch a program that they thought they had uninstalled, the software simply reinstalls itself and opens. Because the software has been assigned to the user, the user cannot get rid of it. The advantage to this is that users cannot break assigned applications; the software is self-healing, without requiring a traditional desk-side trip from an IT staff member to repair it through a manual reinstall.

On the other hand, administrators can choose to simply publish applications into Active Directory instead of assigning them directly to users. Assigned applications are typically used when users need a particular application to do their job. Published applications are not necessarily required by users to do their jobs, but they are beneficial applications that the administrator wants to make available. A published application shows up in Add/Remove Programs but must be explicitly installed by the user or through file extension invocation (such as double-clicking a .ZIP file and having WinZip installed for you). No icons appear in the Start menu or on the desktop in advance to inform users of the application's availability, and if a user uninstalls the application, it is removed from the computer just as in a traditional uninstall procedure.

Troubleshooting Software Deployment Problems

In a perfect world, you would follow the previous software-deployment phases and roll out an application with no problems whatsoever. Unfortunately, things don't always seem to work out in the real world the way they do in a textbook. Because of this hard reality, let's discuss some of the more common problems you might run into with software deployment and what steps you might take to resolve them.

General Troubleshooting Guidelines

Some general guidelines can be followed in troubleshooting. In many cases, problems can be traced to a lack of necessary permissions. One of the first troubleshooting steps should be to ensure that an appropriate level of permissions exists to access the needed resource. Missing source files or corrupted Windows Installer packages are other potential sources of trouble. You should make sure that the necessary files are available as part of your troubleshooting steps.

Here are some common problems and the things to look for to resolve them.

"Active Directory Will Not Allow the Package to Be Deployed"

This error is usually the result of a corrupt Windows Installer package or the incapability of the Software Installation Group Policy extension to communicate properly with Active Directory.

To resolve this problem, test for connectivity with the DNS server and domain controllers containing the Active Directory database. You can use the `ping` command to establish basic connectivity and browse through My Network Places to the servers to see if you can access the required share directories. To test for a corrupted Windows Installer package, see if you can open the package on another similarly configured computer.

"Cannot Prepare the Package for Deployment"

This error is similar to the previous Active Directory error, in that it can be the result of a corrupt package. Instead of the Software Installation extension not being able to communicate with Active Directory, in this case it cannot communicate with the SYSVOL share.

The troubleshooting steps are the same as with the previous error. Test for connectivity between the workstation and the SYSVOL share on the domain controllers, try from another computer if communication fails, and attempt to install the package on another system if connectivity is fine.

"The Feature You Are Trying to Install Cannot Be Found in the Source Directory"

This type of error is most likely related to permissions or connectivity. Either the user doesn't have the necessary permissions level to access the distribution point, or the distribution point is unavailable over the network. Additionally, you should check to ensure that the source files were not accidentally deleted or moved to another location on the network.

To troubleshoot this error, first make sure that the required source files exist at the distribution point. If they do, make sure that the user attempting to install the feature has connectivity to the server containing the distribution point. If this checks out, check the permissions on the distribution point to see if the user has the required permissions. Most likely, one of these three aspects will be the cause of the error.

Various Installation Error Messages

A number of different error messages can appear when you try to install an application on a workstation. There could be a problem with the Windows Installer packages or a permissions problem in which the user or computer account attempting to install the application doesn't have the necessary level of permissions to complete the installation. The permissions problem could relate to not being able to execute the particular package, not being able to access the distribution point, or not being able to install the application to the target directory on the local hard drive as defined by the package.

To troubleshoot, first determine whether you have the permission to access the distribution point. If you do, copy the package to the local hard drive and attempt to execute it from there. If the package begins installing and fails, ensure that the user account being used has Write permissions to the target directory. If the package gives an error before attempting to install, make sure that the user account has Execute permissions for the package, and test the package on another system to ensure its integrity (that is, to make sure that it is not corrupted).

Shortcuts Still Appear for Removed Applications

This isn't an error message; it is a condition that might exist after uninstalling a managed application. After the user uninstalls an application or the Software Installation extension removes the software when an administrator removes it from the application list, the shortcuts for the application still appear on the Start menu and/or the desktop.

To troubleshoot, determine whether the shortcuts were created by the user or the program. In many cases, users copy shortcuts from the Start menu to the desktop for convenience. The application's installation program would not be aware of this type of user-created shortcut and would not be capable of removing it during the application's uninstallation process.

Another cause might be that the shortcuts point to another installation of the same program. Perhaps the user belongs to multiple GPOs, and the application has been removed from only one of them. Another possibility is that there was a locally installed copy before the installation of the assigned or published application, and those files were not removed.

You should check to see if the shortcuts point to valid programs. If they do, determine why the programs are installed (local install, another GPO, and so on) and if it is appropriate. If the shortcuts do not point to valid applications, simply delete them.

Installed Application Is Suddenly Uninstalled from a User Workstation

This condition almost always occurs when the software deployment option "uninstall this application when it falls outside the scope of management" is selected. However, it could result if a computer or user account was moved outside the influence of the GPO managing the software.

If the computer account was not moved, determine whether a GPO that the user or computer belongs to is still managing the application.

Troubleshooting is often more of an art than a science, but if you remember only to check connectivity, permissions, and the existence of source files, you'll be a long way toward troubleshooting software deployment.

Exam Prep Questions

Question 1

Scott Keating has been asked to design and deploy a new Windows Server 2003–based network. Because the company he has contracted with wants to save money, Scott cannot upgrade each of the clients until the next financial year. This means that his client base will be Windows XP and Windows NT 4.0. Scott has been told that all systems must be managed in a uniform fashion. Group Policy can be used to control user settings and to configure the desktop. Scott decides that he will use Group Policy at the domain level to ensure uniformity. What is the outcome of this choice?

- ❍ A. Scott has chosen a perfect solution. Applying a policy at the domain level means that all clients will be affected by the settings in a uniform fashion.
- ❍ B. Scott has the right idea, but he would be better advised to use Group Policy at the OU level. This would make sure that, although policies are applied uniformly, he would have the flexibility to make exceptions.
- ❍ C. This solution would not work. User-defined Group Policy cannot be applied at the domain level. Domain-level policies are reserved for operating system use only.
- ❍ D. This solution would not work. Group Policy can be used only by Windows 2000 computers and later. In this scenario, Scott would not be able to achieve his objective without upgrading all Windows NT computers to Windows 2000 or greater.

Answer D is correct. Group Policy was first introduced with Windows 2000, and only operating systems of this version or later support it. Answer A is incorrect because all clients are not Windows 2000 or greater, so Group Policy cannot be applied. Answer B is incorrect for the same reason. Answer C is incorrect because, although a default domain-level Group Policy is in place, it is possible for administrators to create their own domain-level policies.

Question 2

Zevi Mehlman, a consultant who is designing a Windows Server 2003 Active Directory network, has been asked to explain why software deployment is important for the client's environment. He says that it is important because it can support the entire life cycle of an application. He is then asked to explain the statement. What will he say?

❍ A. Software deployment can support the entire life cycle of a software application. This means that it can be used to install, maintain (through service packs), and uninstall an application.

❍ B. Software deployment supports the entire life cycle of an application. This includes development, deployment, and removal.

❍ C. *Full life cycle* means that a program can be both installed and maintained. Uninstall is achieved through the Control Panel on the client computers.

❍ D. *Full life cycle* is a term associated with users. It means that software can be provided to a user when the user needs it (just-in-time). However, if a user leaves the company, the software is removed.

Answer A is correct. When we talk about the life cycle of an application, we are talking about deploying it, maintaining it by applying service packs, and uninstalling it automatically if a user goes out of scope. Answer B is incorrect because the software-deployment capabilities of Group Policy have nothing to do with the development of applications. Answer C is incorrect because the life cycle includes the capability to automatically uninstall a program. Answer D is incorrect because the life cycle is not user specific; it is application specific.

Question 3

Bertram Rawe is working as a consultant in Landau. He has been called to a client site to troubleshoot some configuration problems with a Windows Server 2003–based network with Windows XP clients. The client wants to know why configuration settings for Internet Explorer are being applied to some of the computers on his network and not others. The client assures Bertram that he is not using Group Policy within Active Directory for anything. Bertram arrives at the site and quickly fixes the problem. What did Bertram know that the client did not?

❍ A. Bertram knew that Internet Explorer is not configured through Group Policy. Instead, it is configured on a machine-by-machine basis. This was a user education problem; Bertram simply taught the users how to use Internet Explorer.

❍ B. Bertram knew that there are always two Group Policies applied to a Windows Server 2003–based network with Windows XP clients. The first of these is the Local Policy; the second is the default domain policy. Because the configuration was taking place only on certain machines, the options were most likely being configured through Local Policy; this proved to be the case.

❍ C. Bertram knew that the client was mistaken. As a part of the base operating system, Internet Explorer will always be affected by the default domain policy. However, these settings can be overridden by Local Policy.

❍ D. Bertram knew that there are no settings for Internet Explorer in Group Policy. Therefore, the issues had to have been created by users on their own machines.

Answer B is correct. Note the use of the words *most likely*. It is possible through Group Policy filtering for settings to be coming from the domain, but this would be unlikely. It is far more likely that Internet Explorer settings are being configured and applied from the Local Policy on the Windows XP systems. Answer A is incorrect because it is possible for Internet Explorer to be configured via Group Policy. Answer C is incorrect because this statement violates the rules of precedence for Group Policy. Answer D is incorrect because there are indeed settings for Internet Explorer in Group Policy.

Question 4

Software deployment is part of the Windows Server 2003 operating system. What are the requirements for its use? (Choose all that apply.)

❑ A. Active Directory must be present.

❑ B. Group Policy must be both installed and working.

❑ C. Group Policy must be utilized on the network.

❑ D. Security groups must be created to fit the deployment scenario.

Answers A and C are correct. For software deployment to be used, both Active Directory and Group Policy must be installed and functional on the Windows Server 2003 network. Answer B is incorrect because it suggests that Group Policy can be either uninstalled or not installed. Group Policy always exists on a Windows Server 2003 network with Active Directory installed. Answer D is incorrect because user groups cannot be directly targeted for software deployment.

Question 5

Volker Wiora is working on planning for the change and configuration policy of his Windows Server 2003–based network. He wants to apply security settings to all Windows XP–based computers. To allow himself the greatest flexibility, he decides to apply policy to the security group level. A colleague tells him that this should not be done because it is too complex. Volker disagrees, saying that he prefers to use the target groups because it minimizes administrative efforts. Who is correct?

- ❍ A. The colleague is correct. Although this is possible, it is very complex to manage.
- ❍ B. Volker is correct. There are alternative ways of doing this, but this is the least time-consuming administratively.
- ❍ C. The colleague is correct. However, the reason for this does not have to do with complexity; instead, it has to do with Active Directory and the overhead of creating unnecessary replication.
- ❍ D. The colleague is correct. However, the reason is far simpler; it is simply not possible to target Group Policy at security groups.

Answer D is correct. Group Policy cannot be targeted at security groups. Instead, you must target sites, domains, or OU; thus, answer B is incorrect. Groups, however, can be used to perform filtering on the GPO. Answer A is not correct because complexity is simply not an issue (in this case, the option is not possible). Answer C is incorrect because assigning a Group Policy would not create a lot of replication.

Question 6

Younes Dallol works as a system administrator for a law firm. Younes understands Group Policy very well. Younes is asked by one of his colleagues to explain how Group Policy is stored in the network. Younes, of course, answered this correctly. What did Younes reply?

- ❍ A. Younes replied that Group Policy is not actually one thing, but is made up of two things. First, there exists a Group Policy container (GPC) that is stored within Active Directory. Second, there is a Group Policy template. The template is the physical files associated with Group Policy that are stored in the SYSVOL folder on each domain controller.
- ❍ B. Younes replied that Group Policy is a name given to a set of technologies. Rather than being any one thing, it is actually two different things. First, there exists a Group Policy container (GPC) that is stored within SYSVOL. Second, there is a Group Policy template. The template is the physical files associated with Group Policy that are stored in Active Directory on each domain controller.

❍ C. Younes replied that a Group Policy is actually a physical file, usually with a .reg extension. This is stored within Active Directory.

❍ D. Younes replied that a Group Policy is actually a physical file, usually with a .reg extension. This is stored within the SYSVOL volume on each domain controller.

Answer A is correct. Group Policy is actually stored in two places, in a GPC within Active Directory and with the physical files stored in the SYSVOL volume of a domain controller. Answer B is incorrect because it has these two facts reversed. Answer C is incorrect because the physical file associated with Group Policy is never stored within Active Directory. Answer D is incorrect because it gives only half of the story; it does not mention the GPC.

Question 7

You are the network administrator for Jake's Jumpers, Inc., a parachuting tour company. You are implementing several new Group Policy Objects for your network, but they are not all working the way you had planned. What tool or utility can you use to determine what GPO might be responsible for the problems?

❍ A. Use the Resultant Set of Policy snap-in in planning mode.

❍ B. Use filtering on each GPO to prevent it from being applied to the Users group.

❍ C. Use the query feature of Active Directory Users and Computers.

❍ D. Use the Resultant Set of Policy snap-in in logging mode.

Answer D is correct. Resultant Set of Policy in logging mode gives you the capability to determine which policies are currently being applied to an object. In this mode, you can generate a report and work out what each of the policies is doing to an object. Result Set of Policy in planning mode gives you the opportunity to apply Group Policies to an object, such as a user or computer, to see the net effect a new policy will have. This enables you to set up "what-if" scenarios; thus, answer A is incorrect. Filtering is used to selectively allow or deny users or groups the ability to read and apply a Group Policy Object, but it would not typically be used for troubleshooting a GPO application; thus, answer B is incorrect. The query feature of Active Directory Users and Computers is used to perform queries against Active Directory to locate objects such as users, computers, or printers; thus, answer C is incorrect.

Question 8

Bertram Rawe has taken over as system administrator of a Windows Server 2003 network with Active Directory. One of the departments (finance) within the organization has a set of Group Policies applied that limits user access to computers. This has been found to reduce the number of help-desk calls the users generate. Bertram has been asked to apply the same policies to the sales organization. What is the best way to achieve this?

- ❍ A. Bertram should export the properties from the current Group Policy and import them into a new policy. He should then link the new policy to the Organizational Unit that contains the sales team members.
- ❍ B. Bertram should simply link the current policy to the Organizational Unit containing the sales team members.
- ❍ C. Bertram should create a new Group Policy that contains the settings he requires. He should then link this to the Organizational Unit that contains the sales team members.
- ❍ D. Bertram should simply add the sales team members to the same Organizational Unit at the finance group.

Answer B is correct. Because the Group Policy already exists, it is best to simply link it to the container in which the sales team members exist. Answer A is incorrect because it is not possible to simply export Group Policy settings and then import them. Answer C is incorrect because, although this would work, it is administratively time-consuming. Answer D is incorrect because adding the sales team members to the same container as the finance team might have unexpected results (other policies might be in place that would affect the sales team members).

Question 9

Scott Keating has been asked to deploy a software package to users on the network. The users will have the capability to install this software at their discretion. If they do not want the software, they should be able to ignore it. What is the best solution?

- ❍ A. Scott should publish the application to the target objects.
- ❍ B. Scott should assign the software to the target objects.
- ❍ C. Scott should perform a mandatory publication to the target objects.
- ❍ D. Scott should perform a mandatory assignment to the target objects.

Answer A is correct. With a published application, the software shows up in the Add/Remove Programs applet in Control Panel. The user can then choose whether to install the application. Answer B is incorrect because assigning an application causes icons to appear on the users' Start menu. Answers C and D are incorrect because there is no feature to make a mandatory distribution. This terminology is common with Systems Management Server, but not Group Policy.

Question 10

Bertram Rawe has been asked to make a presentation describing software deployment. Part of this presentation involves talking about how users and computers will be targeted. Bertram knows that management would really like to target security groups and that he must address this. What are the only ways software deployment can be targeted?

- ❍ A. Software deployment can be targeted at sites, domains, or OUs only. You cannot target specific security groups.
- ❍ B. Software deployment can be targeted at sites, domains, OUs, and groups. It can target one or all of these at the same time.
- ❍ C. Software deployment targets only security groups.
- ❍ D. Software deployment targets sites, domains, and OUs. The requirement for targeting security groups can also be achieved; however, it involves extensive use of Access Control Lists (ACLs), which can be complex to manage over an enterprise.

Answer D is correct. The requirement for targeting groups can be achieved through ACLs. However, this is complex and should be avoided in an enterprise. Answer A is incorrect because, although it is not possible to target security groups directly, it is possible to achieve the same thing by targeting sites, domains, and OUs, and by changing the ACLs on Group Policy objects. Answer B is incorrect because it is not possible to target groups specifically. Answer C is incorrect because software deployment targets sites, domains, and OUs, not groups.

Need to Know More?

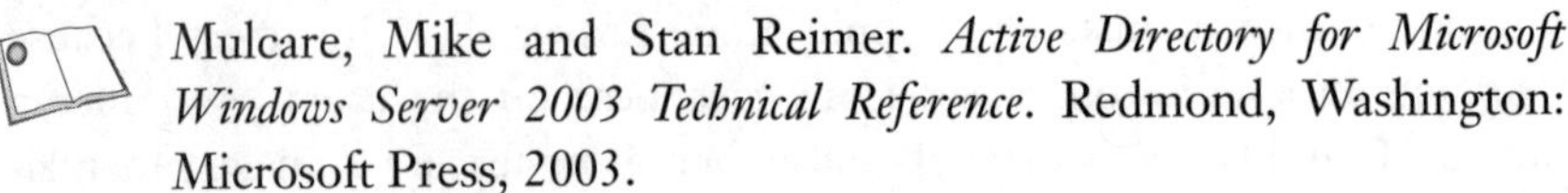

Mulcare, Mike and Stan Reimer. *Active Directory for Microsoft Windows Server 2003 Technical Reference*. Redmond, Washington: Microsoft Press, 2003.

Microsoft Corporation. *Microsoft Windows Server 2003 Resource Kit*. Redmond, Washington: Microsoft Press, 2003.

Microsoft Corporation. *Microsoft Windows Server 2003 Deployment Kit*. Redmond, Washington: Microsoft Press, 2003.

Managing and Maintaining Group Policy

Terms you'll need to understand:

- ✓ Domain name system (DNS)
- ✓ File Replication Service (FRS)
- ✓ **GPUPDATE**
- ✓ Loopback processing
- ✓ Resultant Set of Policies (RSoP)
- ✓ **GPRESULT**

Techniques you'll need to master:

- ✓ Using the **GPUPDATE** tool and its command-line switches
- ✓ Using the **GPRESULT** tool and its command-line switches

Although this chapter is not very long, it is an important one, both for studying for the Microsoft Certified System Engineer (MCSE) exams and for working in the real world. You should be sure that you are familiar with the tools that can be used to troubleshoot problems as they arise. However, it is worth noting that Microsoft tests are based on core operating systems and do not contain questions about resource kit utilities and add-ons. Therefore, this chapter is not intended to be exhaustive coverage regarding the task of troubleshooting Group Policy.

Troubleshooting is always a tricky task—that is why those who are good at it are highly valued. Trying to figure out why Group Policy is not doing everything you thought it would is no exception. Like all good specialists, knowing which tools work in which circumstances is more than half the battle.

Introducing Group Policy Troubleshooting

Later sections spend some time looking at the available tools for troubleshooting Group Policy. First, however, it is a good idea to make the point that Group Policy is actually made up of many different technologies. Thus, there is plenty of room for errors or misunderstandings.

Following are a few of the technologies:

- Active Directory (AD)
- Domain name system (DNS)
- File Replication Service (FRS)
- Windows Server 2003 security groups
- Organizational Units

This list is not exhaustive, but it does offer some insight into where problems could exist. Clearly, this book cannot go into detail about all of these technologies and features. Instead, we concentrate on tools that are specific to Group Policy. However, forewarned is forearmed: As long as you know that issues with Group Policy can come from many different places, you are better prepared for in-depth troubleshooting.

Active Directory and Group Policy

When you get under the hood of Group Policy, you find two components: the Group Policy Container (GPC) and the Group Policy Template (GPT). GPTs are discussed in a moment because they are stored outside AD.

GPCs are objects created within AD. They define what a Group Policy is supposed to do, and they can have permissions assigned to them. Without GPCs, Group Policy would not work. A GPC for a Group Policy exists on every domain controller within a domain and are stored as part of the domain partition in AD. Therefore, GPCs must be replicated—normal AD replication processes take care of this. If AD replication fails, it is highly likely that Group Policy will have problems.

Domain Name System (DNS)

As you already know, the domain name system (DNS) exists to help clients and servers find things on the network, including client computers, shares, printers, or simply services offered by these objects. A Windows Server 2003 network without a fully functional DNS infrastructure is an environment in a world of hurt.

Clients must be capable of reading their Group Policy data. A client reads Group Policy data from domain controllers (DCs). If a client cannot find a DC, Group Policy appears to fail. In fact, the apparent Group Policy error is not caused by Group Policy in this case, but instead by a failure of your DNS infrastructure. When troubleshooting Active Directory problems, you must be able to look not only at Active Directory itself, but also elsewhere, at your core network services such as DNS.

File Replication Service (FRS)

The GPT represents the physical files that make up a Group Policy (for instance, a .reg file that contains Registry settings that must be applied to a target machine). These must be replicated to all DCs in a domain. You might think that this process is taken care of by AD replication, but that is not the case—this task is handled by the File Replication Service instead.

In fact, FRS is a simple file-replication process that runs outside AD replication. By default, it follows the same replication topology, but it does not rely upon the same change processes. Don't forget that, in Windows Server 2003, FRS can be configured to have a unique replication topology. If FRS is broken, Group Policy cannot replicate correctly.

Security Groups

Group Policy can target users and computers through their membership to sites, domains, or Organizational Units. Using OUs as an example, a Group Policy Object (GPO) can be linked to an OU so that all objects within it have the policy applied. However, this does not tell the whole story.

At first you might be tempted to think that the granularity of applying Group Policy seems rather sparse. What if you want to apply a policy to only half the members of an OU? This is possible if you do filtering with security groups. In simple terms, if you do not have permissions to read and apply something (in this case, the GPO), it can't apply to you.

Using this feature can make troubleshooting quite complex. If you use it extensively, you must keep in mind which groups are allowed to access a GPO and which are not. In larger environments, many filtered Group Policy Objects might also result in a performance impact.

As you can see, some things other than specific Group Policies can affect their application. Let's now take a look at some issues you might run into while working with Group Policy.

General Troubleshooting

Considering some of the information just provided, it should be clear that when troubleshooting Group Policy, you should check the simple things first. Participation on a network starts with logging on and being authenticated. This means that TCP/IP connectivity must be present and working.

Simple tasks that you should consider include using the `ping` command to establish that a client has connectivity to a domain controller. Don't forget that, in a Windows Server 2003 environment, it is possible for things to appear to be working when problems actually exist. A good example of this is when users have successfully logged into their workstations using *cached credentials*. To the users, everything appears to be normal and they get the impression that they have authenticated against a domain controller or Global Catalog server—however, this is not the case. In this case, the cached credentials and a cached copy of the policies are applied to the users, masking signs of trouble and making your troubleshooting task more difficult.

Sometimes Group Policy also will not be applied even when a logon to a network works as designed. This is the case with VPN connections: A user might well be working from home with a corporate laptop, but because that user logged on to the machine before establishing the VPN connection, Group Policy will not be applied.

A common tool for troubleshooting is the Event Viewer. The Event Viewer contains log files for many different services. You should always check the Event Viewer logs before digging deeper with other tools. These log files can alert you to unrelated issues such as DNS problems, network connectivity, and corrupt files on the local system.

Always keep in mind that Group Policy is replicated on two different schedules. The GPC is contained with AD; therefore, normal AD replication must take place before a policy will work or be updated. At the same time, FRS must do its job. Not until these two replication topologies reach convergence will a policy function correctly.

Group Policy Application

Group Policy has many uses, and it can sometimes be confusing to think about how exactly they are applied. Note that Group Policies are applied during computer startup and when a user logs on. However, because Group Policy is used to assign scripts to a client, it might also have effects during logoff or when a computer is shut down.

At the same time, Group Policy is also refreshed at intervals. For a workstation, this interval is 90 minutes. However, this is not hard-coded. In fact, a 30-minute random factor is thrown in to stop all clients from refreshing at the same time. This is important when you have changed a Group Policy and are waiting for it to affect a targeted workstation. First, you must wait for AD and FRS replication to take place. Then you must wait for the refresh period to take effect. As always, there is an exception: Domain controllers update their Group Policies every five minutes.

The acronym LSDOU stands for local, site, domain, and Organizational Unit (OU). Users and computers can be targeted to receive Group Policies through their membership to one of these. The order is also important and tells you the precedence. Group Policies set locally on the computer are applied first, followed by those applied at the site level, then Group Policies set at the domain level, and finally those at the OU level.

GPUPDATE

GPUPDATE is a command-line tool that ships with Windows Server 2003. It enables you to manually trigger the refresh of Group Policies from a client machine (a server or a workstation). This is useful when you have changed a Group Policy and want to see the effects immediately.

Table 10.1 details the switches for GPUPDATE.

Table 10.1 GPUPDATE Switches

Switch	Function
/Target:{Computer | User}	Specifies that only User or Computer policy settings are refreshed. By default, both User and Computer policy settings are refreshed.
/Force	Reapplies all policy settings. By default, only policy settings that have changed are applied.
/Wait:{value}	Sets the number of seconds to wait for policy processing to finish. The default is 600 seconds. The value **0** means not to wait. The value **-1** means to wait indefinitely. When the time limit is exceeded, the command prompt returns, but policy processing continues.
/Logoff	Causes a logoff after the Group Policy settings have been refreshed. This is required for Group Policy client-side extensions that do not process policy on a background refresh cycle but do process policy when a user logs on. Examples include user-targeted software installation and folder redirection. This option has no effect if no extensions that require a logoff are called.
/Boot	Causes a reboot after the Group Policy settings are refreshed. This is required for Group Policy client-side extensions that do not process policy on a background refresh cycle but that do process policy at computer startup. Examples include computer-targeted software installation. This option has no effect if no extensions that require a reboot are called.
/Sync	Causes the next foreground policy application to be done synchronously. Foreground policy applications occur at computer bootup and user logon. You can specify this for the user, the computer, or both using the **/Target** parameter. The **/Force** and **/Wait** parameters are ignored if specified.

With the exception of the **/Target:{Computer | User} switch**, don't get wrapped up trying to remember the **GPUPDATE** switches and their functions. It is more important for this exam and for normal operations to understand what **GPUPDATE** does and how it is used.

GPUPDATE is a useful tool, but it doesn't apply settings that occur only during logon. For instance, folder redirection and software installation only take place during logon, and running GPUPDATE will not force these to occur after the fact. Only the logoff and logon process trigger these events.

Group Policy and Precedence

When troubleshooting Group Policies, it is important that you know the order in which they are applied. This is important because settings higher in the hierarchy can be overwritten as other policies are applied.

Earlier we mentioned the LSDOU rule, which should be foremost in your mind. At the same time, some settings can be applied only at the domain level. The most common example of this is password settings for complexity or lifetime. Although settings within Group Policy can be set for these options, they can be applied only to local accounts on a machine, not for anything related to domains (such as a user's own logon).

Group Policy forms a hierarchy, so settings for a child OU are a combination of those linked to the OU itself and those settings inherited from the OU above it (the parent) in the hierarchy. Exceptions occur whenblock inheritance is set at an OU. Block inheritance prevents the usual rules of inheritance from taking place, and settings are not passed down. Of course, this can be defeated by using the Enforce feature (formerly known as No Override.) Make sure you understand that these options apply to an entire Group Policy. You cannot choose a single setting within a Group Policy and force it to be enforced while the rest of the policy follows the usual inheritance rules.

As Group Policies are linked to a container (LSDOU), they are ordered. You can change this link order as often as you like. Policies are applied following the rules of LSDOU; within a container, they are applied in the link order, with the policy that is listed last being applied last.

Loopback Processing

One more wrinkle arises in the processing of Group Policies: *loopback*. Loopback is designed to reverse the usual processing rules. User settings usually override computer settings. In other words, policies that affect a computer are applied when that computer starts up, before a user has even logged on to the machine. When the user logs on, that user's policies are applied, and it is possible for settings for that user to override those already applied to the computer. Furthermore, user configuration settings made in policies targeting the machine are not applied.

What if this is not the way you want things to work? You might have a computer running in a kiosk in your reception area, and you want anyone to be able to log on to use it, but you do not want a user from your community to log on, forget that he has done so, and then give any stranger who wanders up access to your corporate LAN. These types of situations call for *loopback processing*.

Group Policy and Precedence

When troubleshooting Group Policies, it is important that you know the order in which they are applied. This is important because settings higher in the hierarchy can be overwritten as other policies are applied.

Earlier we mentioned the LSDOU rule, which should be foremost in your mind. At the same time, some settings can be applied only at the domain level. The most common example of this is password settings for complexity or lifetime. Although settings within Group Policy can be set for these options, they can be applied only to local accounts on a machine, not for anything related to domains (such as a user's own logon).

Group Policy forms a hierarchy, so settings for a child OU are a combination of those linked to the OU itself and those settings inherited from the OU above it (the parent) in the hierarchy. Exceptions occur whenblock inheritance is set at an OU. Block inheritance prevents the usual rules of inheritance from taking place, and settings are not passed down. Of course, this can be defeated by using the Enforce feature (formerly known as No Override.) Make sure you understand that these options apply to an entire Group Policy. You cannot choose a single setting within a Group Policy and force it to be enforced while the rest of the policy follows the usual inheritance rules.

As Group Policies are linked to a container (LSDOU), they are ordered. You can change this link order as often as you like. Policies are applied following the rules of LSDOU; within a container, they are applied in the link order, with the policy that is listed at the top being applied last.

Loopback Processing

One more wrinkle arises in the processing of Group Policies: *loopback*. Loopback is designed to reverse the usual processing rules. User settings usually override computer settings. In other words, policies that affect a computer are applied when that computer starts up, before a user has even logged on to the machine. When the user logs on, that user's policies are applied, and it is possible for settings for that user to override those already applied to the computer. Furthermore, user configuration settings made in policies targeting the machine are not applied.

What if this is not the way you want things to work? You might have a computer running in a kiosk in your reception area, and you want anyone to be able to log on to use it, but you do not want a user from your community to log on, forget that he has done so, and then give any stranger who wanders up access to your corporate LAN. These types of situations call for *loopback processing*.

- *Logging mode*—This mode of operation enables you to see the net result of the Group Policy settings that have already been applied to your network. Logging mode is used extensively for troubleshooting and analysis of settings that have been applied.

The most common use of RSoP is in logging mode, and that is how we examine it in this troubleshooting-oriented discussion. You will need to add the RSoP snap-in into a blank MMC console before you can start using it. After you have done this, you should have a custom MMC console that looks something like that seen in Figure 10.1.

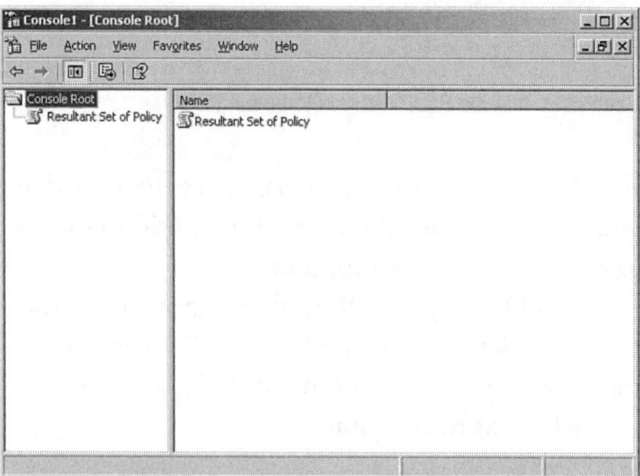

Figure 10.1 The RSoP snap-in must be added to a custom MMC console.

To use RSoP in logging mode after you've created the MMC console for it, perform the following steps.

1. Right-click on Resultant Set of Policy and select Generate RSoP Data from the context menu.

2. The Resultant Set of Policy Wizard starts. Click Next to dismiss the opening page.

3. On the Mode Selection dialog box, select the Logging Mode option and click Next to continue.

4. On the Computer Selection dialog box (see Figure 10.2), select the local or remote computer that the query is to be run for. Additionally, you have the option to display only the results for the user and not the computer by selecting the option Do Not Display Policy Settings for the Selected Computer in the Results (Display User Policy Settings Only). After making your selections, click Next to continue.

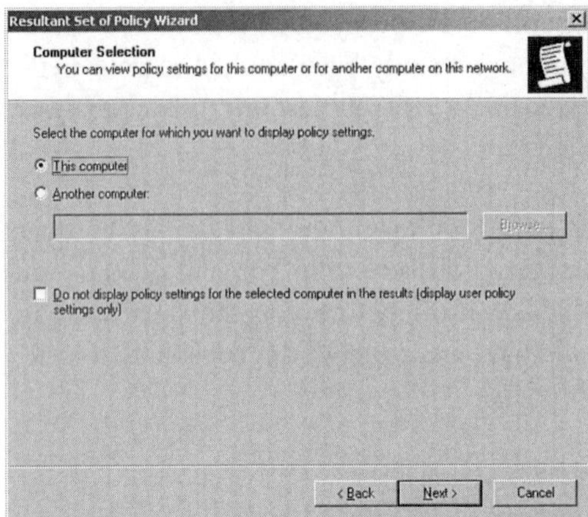

Figure 10.2 Locate and select the computer that the RSoP query is to be run for.

5. On the User Selection dialog box (see Figure 10.3), select the user that the query is to be run for. If you previously selected the option Do Not Display Policy Settings for the Selected Computer in the Results (Display User Policy Settings Only), you will be able to now select the option Do Not Display Policy Settings for the Selected User in the Results (Display Computer Policy Settings Only), if desired. After making your selections, click Next to continue.

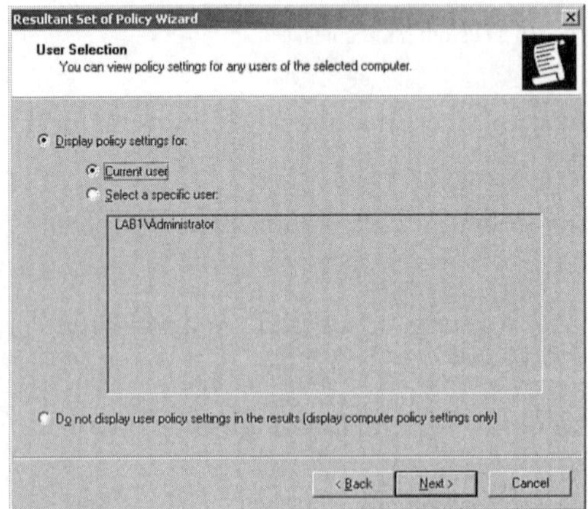

Figure 10.3 Locate and select the user that the RSoP query is to be run for.

6. The Summary of Selections dialog box appears (see Figure 10.4). You have the option here to also gather extended error information by selecting the Gather Extended Error Information option. When you are ready to run the RSoP query, click Finish.

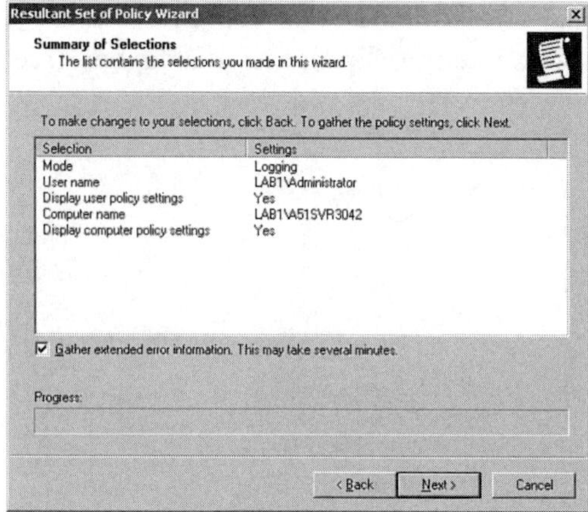

Figure 10.4 The Summary of Selections dialog box enables you to see how the query will be run.

7. The wizard next runs the query as you've configured it. When prompted, click Finish to close the Resultant Set of Policy Wizard.

You can now examine the net result of all applied policies on the user and/or computer. For example, if you were attempting to troubleshoot an issue with the policies that are enforcing the Desktop configuration, you might examine the User Configuration\Administrative Templates\Desktop node, shown in Figure 10.5.

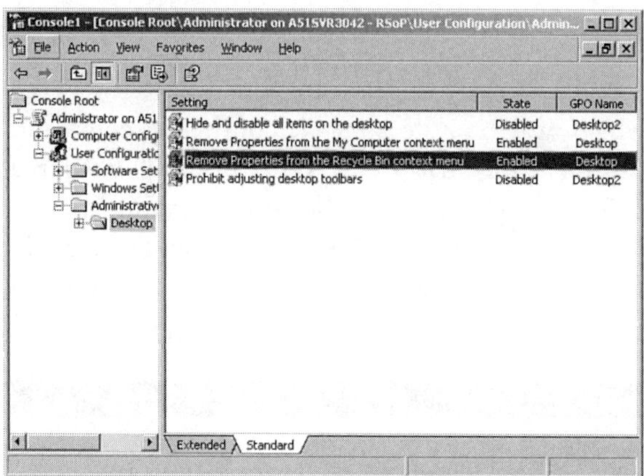

Figure 10.5 You can quickly examine the net effect of the applies policies.

As you can see, you can quickly determine what specific policy items have been configured (items that are not configured do not display in the query results), their status, and the GPO that is enforcing the setting. You can determine what Group Policy Objects are configured for a specific setting by examining the Precedence tab of the setting Properties dialog box (see Figure 10.6).

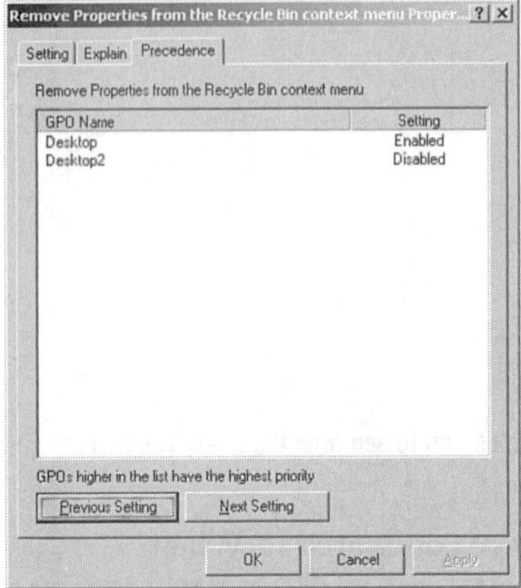

Figure 10.6 The Precedence tab enables you to determine the order in which the Group Policy settings are applied.

In this case, you can see that two GPOs have modified the Remove Properties from the Recycle Bin context menu option. The Desktop GPO has the highest precedence and thus is applying the resultant setting.

GPRESULT

GPRESULT (short for Group Policy Result) is a precursor to RSoP. It has the benefit, depending on which way you look at it, of being command line–driven. Originally, this tool formed part of the Windows 2000 Resource Kit. In Windows Server 2003, it ships as part of the core operating system. GPRESULT gives you data similar to that found in RSoP, but it can more easily be piped to a file for later analysis. The various command-line switches are shown in Table 10.2.

Table 10.2 GPRESULT Switches

Switch	Function
/S system	Specifies the remote system to connect to.
/U [domain\]user	Specifies the user context under which the command should execute.
/P [password]	Specifies the password for the given user context. Prompts for input, if omitted.

(continued)

Table 10.2 GPRESULT Switches *(continued)*	
Switch	**Function**
/SCOPE scope	Specifies whether the user or the computer settings need to be displayed. Valid values are **USER** and **COMPUTER**.
/USER [domain\]user	Specifies the username for which the RSOP data is to be displayed.
/V	Specifies that verbose information should be displayed. Verbose information provides additional detailed settings that have been applied with a precedence of **1**.
/Z	Specifies that the super-verbose information should be displayed. Super-verbose information provides additional detailed settings that have been applied with a precedence of **1** and higher. This enables you to see whether a setting was set in multiple places. See the Group Policy online help topic for more information.

Don't get wrapped up trying to remember the **GPRESULT** switches and their functions. It is more important for this exam and for normal operations to understand what **GPRESULT** does and how it is used.

Running GPRESULT without a command-line parameter gives you an RSoP for the currently logged-on user. The following text is the output from a standard installation of Windows Server 2003 Server:

```
RSOP data for MAIN\Administrator on WIN2003SVR : Logging Mode
--------------------------------------------------------------

OS Type: Microsoft(R) Windows(R) Server 2003, Enterprise Edition
OS Configuration: Primary Domain Controller
OS Version: 5.2.3790
Terminal Server Mode: Remote Administration
Site Name: Default-First-Site-Name
Roaming Profile:
Local Profile: C:\Documents and Settings\Administrator
Connected over a slow link?: No


COMPUTER SETTINGS
------------------
 CN=WIN2003SVR,OU=Domain Controllers,DC=main,DC=windows2003,DC=local
 Last time Group Policy was applied: 6/24/2003 at 7:36:12 AM
 Group Policy was applied from: win2003svr.main.windows2003.local
 Group Policy slow link threshold: 500 kbps
 Domain Name: MAIN
 Domain Type: Windows 2000

 Applied Group Policy Objects
 -----------------------------
```

```
 Default Domain Controllers Policy
 Default Domain Policy
 New Group Policy Object
 Local Group Policy

 The computer is a part of the following security groups
 -------------------------------------------------------
 BUILTIN\Administrators
 Everyone
 BUILTIN\Users
 BUILTIN\Pre-Windows 2000 Compatible Access
 Windows Authorization Access Group
 NT AUTHORITY\NETWORK
 NT AUTHORITY\Authenticated Users
 This Organization
 WIN2003SVR$
 Domain Controllers
 NT AUTHORITY\ENTERPRISE DOMAIN CONTROLLERS

USER SETTINGS
-------------
 CN=Administrator,CN=Users,DC=main,DC=windows2003,DC=local
 Last time Group Policy was applied: 6/24/2003 at 6:43:52 AM
 Group Policy was applied from: win2003svr.main.windows2003.local
 Group Policy slow link threshold: 500 kbps
 Domain Name: MAIN
 Domain Type: Windows 2000

 Applied Group Policy Objects
 -----------------------------
 Default Domain Policy

 The following GPOs were not applied because they were filtered out
 -------------------------------------------------------------------
 New Group Policy Object
 Filtering: Not Applied (Empty)

 Local Group Policy
 Filtering: Not Applied  (Empty)

 The user is a part of the following security groups
 ---------------------------------------------------
 Domain Users
 Everyone
 BUILTIN\Administrators
 BUILTIN\Users
 BUILTIN\Pre-Windows 2000 Compatible Access
 NT AUTHORITY\INTERACTIVE
 NT AUTHORITY\Authenticated Users
 This Organization
 LOCAL
 Enterprise Admins
 Group Policy Creator Owners
 Schema Admins
 Domain Admins
```

As you can see, this offers a lot of data, including which policies are being applied, which security groups the user is a member of, and which policies were filtered.

For Exam 70-296, "Planning, Implementing, and Maintaining a Microsoft Windows Server 2003 Environment for an MCSE Certified on Windows 2000," you should expect to see only questions that relate to the use of the **GPUPDATE** and **GPRESULT** commands. These tools ship with Windows Server 2003 and are not required to be added via the Resource Kit or some other means.

Other Tools

This section exists only for completeness. It lists a few tools that you might want to become more aware of as you work with Group Policies but that will most likely not be on the exam.

Group Policy Management Console (GPMC)

The Group Policy Management Console (GPMC) could revolutionize management of Group Policy. It is a free download, and one wonders why it did not ship with the operating system. You can get it from `www.microsoft.com/windowsserver2003/gpmc/default.mspx`.

GPMC is a tool that offers a plethora of features, such as the capability to administer policies across domains and forests, to perform backups and restores of policy data, and to import or copy them. In addition, it's all scriptable, for ease of use.

The previously mentioned link also offers a good deal of technical documents about this new add-on. We highly recommended that you look into this tool.

GPMONITOR

This utility is part of the Windows Server 2003 Deployment Kit. This kit is available for download at `www.microsoft.com/windowsserver2003/techinfo/reskit/deploykit.mspx`.

`GPMONITOR` actually comes in two parts. The first is a service that runs on the client computers. This service collects policy data from the client and forwards it to a central repository. The second is a viewer tool. A help file with the deployment kit gives more details.

GPOTOOL

This utility is available from the Windows Server 2003 Resource Kit. For details about the contents of the resource kit and a free download of the tools, go to `www.microsoft.com/windowsserver2003/techinfo/reskit/resourcekit.mspx`.

`GPOTOOL` enables you to check consistency, within a domain or across domains, of the Group Policy Container (GPC) and Group Policy Template (GPT) data. This can be used to determine whether you have replication issues.

Exam Prep Questions

Question 1

Ron Porter is a consultant working for a systems-management company. He has been onsite for several months and has run into a Group Policy issue. In this case, he has updated a Group Policy, but it is not being refreshed for some clients. Ron decides to call his partner, Dave, to see if he has any ideas on why this might be. Dave explains how Group Policy replication works, and Ron soon understands the issue and resolves it. What did Dave tell Ron?

❍ A. Dave told Ron that Group Policy is replicated on two different topologies. One is Active Directory replication, and the other is handled by the File Replication Service. These two replication infrastructures must reach convergence if Group policy is to work.

❍ B. Dave told Ron that Group Policy updates can take up to 48 hours to fully replicate (depending on whether they apply to a site, a domain, or an OU.) Ron simply has to wait.

❍ C. Dave told Ron to log off and log back on with a different username. This causes a refresh on the client, thereby making the policy work.

❍ D. Dave told Ron that Group Policy is replicated by Active Directory. This takes time to converge on the network. Patience is a virtue, and Ron simply has to wait 15 minutes.

Answer A is correct. The two replication technologies simply must reach convergence in this case. Answer B is incorrect because although there is no defined window for a policy to replicate, 48 hours is far longer than convergence should take. Answer C is incorrect because logging on and off with a different username is not required. If the policy existed, logging on and off might well resolve it by causing a refresh, but a different username is not required. Answer D is incorrect because policies are replicated by both Active Directory and the File Replication Service.

Question 2

Dwain Kinghorn is a new system administrator. He has been analyzing policies on his Windows Server 2003 network and is confused by a particular policy. The policy is linked to an OU, and a user is a member of that OU. However, the policy is never applied. Everyone else in the OU gets the policy as intended. Dwain called Paul Neilsen, a friend, and asks if he has any ideas on why this might be. Paul offers the solution. What did he say?

- ❍ A. Paul told Dwain that this user must have overridden the settings in this OU with a local policy. Because local policies are applied last, if a setting conflicts, it wins.
- ❍ B. Paul told Dwain that the user has obviously not logged off since the policy was created. Because policies are refreshed only during logon, this policy had been missed.
- ❍ C. Paul told Dwain that security group filtering likely was taking place and that the user does not have permissions to this Group Policy Object.
- ❍ D. Paul told Dwain that the policy replication was probably not complete; Dwain should wait for convergence before worrying about it.

Answer C is correct. Although policies are usually applied at sites, domains, and organizational units, it is possible to filter their application by denying security groups read access to the object. Answer A is incorrect because local policies never override those coming from Active Directory. Answer B is incorrect because it is not true to suggest that policies are refreshed only during logon; some policies are refreshed in the background. Answer D is incorrect because other users were getting this policy.

Question 3

Bertram Rawe wants to know which policies have been applied to him. He is using a Windows XP client. He would rather not install additional tools because he shares the system with someone else. Which tool should he use?

- ❍ A. Group Policy Management Console
- ❍ B. **GPRESULT**
- ❍ C. Resultant Set of Policies
- ❍ D. Active Directory Sites and Services

Answer B is correct. Although either A or C would have provided the answer Bertram requires, the Group Policy Management Console and the Resultant Set of Policies console require the installation of software. Answer D is incorrect because this, too, requires a software installation.

Question 4

Lorena Lardon is trying to find out why a Group Policy targeted at users is not being applied to her computer. She has logged on to her machine, but she cannot figure out what is wrong. When she logs on to another machine, the policy works. Everyone else is also getting the policy. What is a likely reason for this?

- ❍ A. Group Policy refreshes every 90 minutes on a client machine. At logon, the machine uses cached policies that are updated on this interval. Lorena should simply wait 90 minutes.
- ❍ B. FRS has failed on her network; Lorena should address this problem first.
- ❍ C. When Lorena logs on to different machines, her position in the OU infrastructure changes. On the problem machine, it simply is not targeted at her.
- ❍ D. The problem machine has network connectivity issues. Lorena should use PING to make sure she can contact a DC.

Answer D is correct. Lorena is logging on with cached credentials, and the policies are never being read. Answer A is incorrect because policies are always read at logon. Answer B is incorrect because others are getting the policy, and even Lorena does when she logs on to a different machine. Answer C is incorrect because logging on to different machines does not change Lorena's position in the OU structure.

Question 5

Zevi Mehlman is troubleshooting a new Group Policy remotely. He has created a batch file that will be run on the remote clients and will cause them to refresh their policies. The policy that he is testing is a software installation targeting computers. Which command-line tool did Zevi use, and with which switch?

- ❍ A. **GPUPDATE** with the **/Reboot** switch
- ❍ B. **GPRESULT** with the **/Reboot** switch
- ❍ C. **GPUPDATE** with the **/Boot** switch
- ❍ D. **GPRESULT** with the **/Boot** switch

Answer C is correct. GPUPDATE is used to refresh policies. Some policies can be applied on the standard refresh (90 minutes) or simply by running GPUPDATE. However, certain settings, such as software installation with computers, occur only during startup. Therefore, it is necessary to use the `/Boot` switch. Answer A is incorrect because GPUPDATE does not have a reboot switch. Answer

B is incorrect because GPRESULT is used to report on which polices are applied; it cannot refresh policies. Answer D is incorrect because GPRESULT is the wrong tool.

Question 6

You are the network administrator for Tom's Toys, a manufacturer of children's toys and collectibles. You have just finished changing several computer configuration items in the GPO that is linked to your Accounting OU. You want this policy to be enforced immediately upon all clients. What command can you issue from your client computers to cause Group Policy to apply the new changes immediately?

- ❍ A. **gpupdate /target:user**
- ❍ B. **secedit /configure**
- ❍ C. **gpupdate /target:computer**
- ❍ D. **secedit /analyze**

Answer C is correct. You must use the `gpupdate /target:computer` command to immediately cause the computer configuration portion of Group Policy to refresh and update your changes. Computer configuration security policies are not kept in the user configuration portion of Group Policy, so Answer A is incorrect. The `secedit` command is no longer used to refresh Group Policy in Windows Server 2003, so answers B and D are incorrect.

Question 7

You are the network administrator for Tom's Toys, a manufacturer of children's toys and collectibles. You have just finished changing several items in the GPO that is linked to your Accounting OU. One of the items that you have changed was to add a new software installation package to the computer configuration portion of the GPO. What command can you issue to cause Group Policy to be applied immediately and get the software installed as soon as possible?

- ❍ A. **gpupdate /target:user**
- ❍ B. **gpupdate /target:user /sync**
- ❍ C. **gpupdate /target:computer**
- ❍ D. **gpupdate /target:computer /boot**

Answer D is correct. Because the Computer Configuration portion of the GPO was modified, the `/target:computer` switch tells GPUPDATE to update the computer configuration section. The `/boot` switch restarts the computer to complete the application of some policies that occur only at computer startup, such as software installation targeted at a computer. The User Configuration section was not modified, so answers A and B are incorrect. The `/boot` switch is required to complete the software installation, so answer C is incorrect.

Question 8

You are the network administrator for Tom's Toys, a manufacturer of children's toys and collectibles. You have created several GPOs that are linked at various levels within your Active Directory structure. You are preparing to run the Resultant Set of Policies (RSoP) tool to examine the net result of the various GPOs that have been applied on the Accounting OU. In what order are Group Policy Objects applied in Active Directory?

❍ A. Local, site, domain, OU

❍ B. Site, domain, OU, local

❍ C. Domain, OU, local, site

❍ D. OU, local, site, domain

Answer A is correct. The correct Group Policy Object processing order is local, site, domain, OU; thus, answers B, C, and D are incorrect.

Question 9

You are the network administrator for Tom's Toys, a manufacturer of children's toys and collectibles. You have just finished changing several items in the GPO that is linked to your Domain Controllers OU. Assuming that you do not manually refresh the Group Policy settings, how long must you wait before your changes start to be applied?

❍ A. 5 minutes

❍ B. 15 minutes

❍ C. 30 minutes

❍ D. 90 minutes

Answer A is correct. Domain controllers refresh their Group Policy settings every five minutes, by default, so answers B, C, and D are incorrect. Client computers refresh their Group Policy settings every 90 minutes, with a 30-minute random offset so that not all clients will update their Group Policy settings at the same time.

Question 10

Justin Rodino is troubleshooting a Group Policy problem. He has applied the setting targeting computers in an Organizational Unit, but one client has not received it yet. He goes to the workstation and wants to apply the settings immediately. He cannot afford to restart the computer. What is the best way to achieve this?

❍ A. Justin should use the **GPUPDATE** command-line utility.

❍ B. Group Policy can be applied only at startup; therefore, he must restart the computer.

❍ C. Group Policy does not require a restart; the user simply needs to log on and off.

❍ D. Justin should use the **IPCONFIG/FLUSHDNS** command.

Answer A is correct. The GPUPDATE command-line tool can be used to refresh settings at a client computer. Answers B and C are incorrect because different settings are applied at different times. For instance, settings targeting a computer are applied at startup, while settings targeting users are at logon. Either way, to get all new settings, the computer would have to be restarted and the user would have to log on again; doing only one would not achieve the desired result. Answer D is incorrect because the IPCONFIG/FLUSHDNS command would not be used to refresh the Group Policy settings on a computer.

Need to Know More?

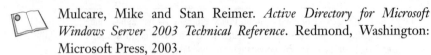

Mulcare, Mike and Stan Reimer. *Active Directory for Microsoft Windows Server 2003 Technical Reference*. Redmond, Washington: Microsoft Press, 2003.

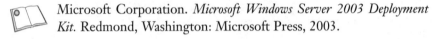

Microsoft Corporation. *Microsoft Windows Server 2003 Resource Kit*. Redmond, Washington: Microsoft Press, 2003.

Microsoft Corporation. *Microsoft Windows Server 2003 Deployment Kit*. Redmond, Washington: Microsoft Press, 2003.

Practice Exam #1

Do not read Chapters 11–14 until you have learned and practiced all the material presented in the chapters of this book. These chapters serve a special purpose; they are designed to test whether you are ready to take Exam 70-296. In these chapters, you will find two practice exams. Each exam is followed by an answer key and brief explanation of correct answers, along with an explanation for why the other answers are incorrect. Reading these chapters before other chapters is like reading the climax of a story and then going back to find out how the story arrived at that ending. Of course, you don't want to spoil the excitement, do you?

How to Take the Practice Exams

Each exam in this book consists of 60 questions and you should complete each test within 120 minutes. The number of questions and the time duration in the actual exam may vary but should be close to this number.

After you have prepared the material presented in the chapters of this book, you should take Practice Exam #1 to check how prepared you are. After the exam is complete, evaluate yourself using the answer key in Chapter 12, "Answer Key to Practice Exam #1". When you evaluate yourself, note the questions that you answered incorrectly, identify the corresponding chapters in the book, and then read and understand that material before taking Practice Exam #2. After you take the second exam, evaluate yourself again and reread the material corresponding to any incorrect answers.

Exam-Taking Tips

Take these exams under your own circumstances, but I strongly suggest that when you take them, you treat them just as you would treat the actual exam at the test center. Use the following tips to get maximum benefit from the exams:

- Before you start, create a quiet, secluded environment where you will not be disturbed for the duration of the exam.
- Provide yourself a few empty sheets of paper before you start. Use some of these sheets to write your answers, and use the others to organize your thoughts. At the end of the exam, use your answer sheet to evaluate your exam with the help of the answer key that follows the sample exam.
- Don't use any reference material during the exam.
- Some of the questions might be vague and require you to make deductions to come up with the best possible answer from the possibilities given. Others might be verbose, requiring you to read and process a lot of information before you reach the actual question.
- As you progress, keep track of the elapsed time and make sure that you'll be able to answer all the questions in the given time limit.

Now it's time to put to the test the knowledge that you've learned from reading this book! Write down your answers to the following questions on a separate sheet of paper. You will be able to take this sample test multiple times this way. After you answer all the questions, compare your answers with the correct answers in Chapter 12. The answer keys for both exams immediately follow each Practice Exam chapter. When you can correctly answer at least 54 of the 60 practice questions (90%) in each Practice Exam, you are ready to start using the PrepLogic Practice Exams CD-ROM at the back of this *Exam Cram 2*. Using the Practice Exams for this *Exam Cram 2*, along with the PrepLogic Practice Exams, you can prepare yourself quite well for the actual 70-296 Microsoft certification exam. Good luck!

Practice Exam #1

Question 1

You are the administrator of a large Windows Server 2003 Active Directory network. Your network consists of 1,500 Windows Server 2003 servers spread out over 150 Organizational Units, with approximately 10 servers each. You have just finished creating a customized security template that specifies the Account Policy and Auditing settings that are required by your organization's corporate policy for specific departments. What is the best way for you to apply this template to only the Sales, Marketing, Production, and Engineering OUs?

- ❍ A. Import the security template at the domain level into a Group Policy Object.
- ❍ B. Import the security template into each required Organizational Unit using a Group Policy Object.
- ❍ C. Script the **secedit.exe** command to apply the security template to the required computers.
- ❍ D. Manually apply the security template to each of the computers.

Question 2

What utilities would you use to raise the domain functional level from Windows 2000 mixed to Windows 2003? (Select two.)

- ❑ A. Group Policy Editor
- ❑ B. Active Directory Users and Computers
- ❑ C. Delegation of Control Wizard
- ❑ D. Active Directory Domains and Trusts

Question 3

Scott Keatinge works in an environment with both Windows Server 2003 and Windows NT clients. He wants to have a fully managed environment. Which technologies will Scott have to use to achieve this? (Select three.)

- ❑ A. Group Policy
- ❑ B. System Policies
- ❑ C. Active Directory
- ❑ D. A legacy Windows NT domain

Question 4

You are a network consultant who has been hired by Carmen's Clown College, Inc. You have been given the task of designing a unique DNS namespace for Carmen's new Windows Server 2003 network. Carmen's already owns the **clowncollege.com** domain, and its ISP is hosting its Web site. Which of the following options represents the best unique DNS namespace?

- ❍ A. **clowncollege.net**
- ❍ B. **corp.clowncollege.com**
- ❍ C. **clowncollege.corp.com**
- ❍ D. **clowncollege.com.corp**

Question 5

Christopher is the network administrator for the Heron Woods Resort Cottages company. Heron Woods rents vacation cottages at several locations along the Eastern Shore of Virginia and Maryland. Christopher needs to implement a solution that will keep the Windows Server 2003 and Windows XP Professional computers at all of his locations up-to-date with the latest security updates, while at the same time installing only those updates that he has specifically approved. Heron Woods has a main office in Chincoteague, Virginia, connected to the Internet by a fractional T1 line. All other locations are considered remote locations and have a dedicated ISDN link connecting them to the main office. What solution can Christopher implement that will allow him to meet his goals of providing available updates and allowing only approved updates to be installed? Christopher has received authorization from the CEO of Heron Woods to add only the absolute minimum number of additional servers as required to provide the best solution meeting the requirements.

❍ A. Christopher should configure all servers and client workstations to connect directly to the Microsoft Windows Update Web servers weekly to download and install any new security updates that are required.

❍ B. Christopher should install an SUS server at each of his locations, including the remote offices, that is configured to automatically synchronize each night with the Windows Update Web servers. Additionally, he should configure Automatic Updates to download and install any new security updates that are required, on a nightly basis, from the local SUS server.

❍ C. Christopher should install an SUS server at each of his locations, including the remote offices. The SUS server at the main office should be configured to automatically synchronize each night with the Windows Update Web servers. The SUS servers at each of the remote offices should be configured to synchronize each night, using the SUS server at the main office as its source. Additionally, he should configure Automatic Updates to download and install any new security updates that are required, on a nightly basis, from the local SUS server.

❍ D. Christopher should install an SUS server at his main office that synchronizes nightly with the Windows Update Web servers. Automatic Updates for all clients, local and remote, should be configured to download and install all approved updates from the main office SUS server on a nightly basis.

Question 6

You have been tasked with creating a report to upper management that details the latest features in Windows. One of the features you need to explain is the process of failback. How do you best explain this concept?

❍ A. Failback is a network communication sent among individual cluster nodes, at intervals of no more than 500 milliseconds, that is used to determine the status of all cluster nodes.

❍ B. Failback is the process of a cluster group moving back to the preferred node after the preferred node has resumed cluster membership.

❍ C. Failback is the process by which NLB clustering hosts determine a new, stable state among themselves and elect a new default host after the failure of one or more cluster nodes.

❍ D. Failback is the process of a cluster group moving from the currently active node to another still functioning node in the cluster group.

Question 7

Greg Smith has been called to troubleshoot a problem on a member server in his domain. A user named Jon Brock says he is logging in to the domain and, although he is being granted access (he can get to the desktop of the server), he cannot access any network resources. Greg checks Jon's account and finds that everything is normal. Jon has been granted access to resources and is a member of several groups that should enable him to access file shares. No one else has reported a problem with the network. Greg visits Jon's office. What is a possible cause for this problem?

❍ A. Jon is typing in the wrong password. He is being granted access to the network, but because he used the wrong password, he is being denied access to network resources.

❍ B. Jon is logging in to the member server using a local user account. This means that he has not yet been validated by the domain and is therefore not allowed access to network resources.

❍ C. Jon's password must be changed. The system is giving him sufficient access to do this, but it will not let him access network resources until the change is confirmed.

❍ D. Jon has to wait for the logon process to complete. AD is complex, and it can take a long time for the security token to be created for a user the first time he logs on.

Question 8

You are the network administrator for Joe's Place, a regional restaurant chain. While at a standards-setting meeting in Redmond, Washington, you are informed that one of your newly installed Windows Server 2003 DHCP servers has stopped leasing addresses. Your assistant administrator has verified that there are plenty of unused leases in the current DHCP scope but cannot determine the cause of the problem. Company policy prohibits the use of any Instant Messaging clients within your internal network. How can your assistant get Remote Assistance from you to help troubleshoot the DHCP server?

❍ A. Use Emergency Management Services to make the request

❍ B. Use the Recovery Console to make the request

❍ C. Use an email-based request

❍ D. Use MSN Messenger to make the request

Question 9

You are the network administrator for Gus Gus Gas Stations, Inc. You need to implement the most secure network environment possible across all servers, both domain controllers and member servers. You do not want to create any new security templates to perform this task. What security templates could you use to provide a higher level of security for your servers? (Choose two.)

- ❑ A. securews.inf
- ❑ B. hisecws.inf
- ❑ C. hisecdc.inf
- ❑ D. securedc.inf

Question 10

You are running an unattended installation of Windows Server 2003 for your enterprise. You want the servers to enable Active Directory. Under which part of the answer file, for an unattended installation of both Windows 2003 and Active Directory, would you specify the command to install Active Directory?

- ❍ A. GuiRunPromo
- ❍ B. GuiRunOnce
- ❍ C. DCInstall
- ❍ D. ADInstall

Question 11

You are the network administrator for Roger's Rockets, a manufacturer of toy rocket kits. You have just completed changing the WLAN security policy that is applied to your Engineering OU. You want this policy to be enforced immediately upon all clients. What command can you issue from your client computers to cause a Group Policy refresh?

- ❍ A. **gpupdate /target:user**
- ❍ B. **secedit /configure**
- ❍ C. **gpupdate /target:computer**
- ❍ D. **secedit /analyze**

Question 12

You are the network administrator of the Gidgets Widgets, LLC, corporate network. You have instructed Andrea, your assistant administrator, to configure file access auditing for all files in the CorpDocs folder on your file server. Where in the Group Policy Editor will Andrea find the options to enable auditing of all types to occur?

❍ A. Account Policies

❍ B. Local Policies

❍ C. Restricted Groups

❍ D. File System

Question 13

Andrea is the network administrator for Purple Pony Wear, Inc., a leading supplier of novelty clothing items. The Purple Pony network consists of 2 Windows Server 2003 computers and 34 Windows XP Professional client computers, 30 of which are laptops that are in use in various remote locations by sales personnel. Andrea wants to create and implement a PKI solution so that her users can use smart cards to log on to their laptop computers, thus increasing the security of the laptop and the Purple Pony network. Priscilla, the president of Purple Pony, is concerned about users removing their smart cards from their laptop computers during their sessions and leaving their laptops logged in without being in front of it. Priscilla would like all laptops to be configured to lock the workstation when the smart card is removed so that open documents will not be lost. What option does Andrea need to configure to ensure that the desired result is achieved?

❍ A. Do Not Allow Smart Card Device Redirection

❍ B. Interactive Logon: Require Smart Card

❍ C. Account Lockout Policy

❍ D. Interactive Logon: Smart Card Removal Behavior

Question 14

Siobhan Chamberlain has been asked to deploy software targeting computers. The software should be available on the client machines but should not necessarily be installed. The concept is that users can simply go to the Add/Remove Programs option in Control Panel and install the applications they need as they want them. At a managers' meeting, Siobhan announces that she intends to publish applications to the computers through Group Policy. Is this a good decision?

- ❍ A. Yes, the difference between assigning and publishing is that an assigned application appears on the Start menu, even if the application is not installed. Published applications do not show up on the Start menu and simply appear in Add/Remove Programs.
- ❍ B. Yes, but Siobhan could have assigned or published the software because the end result when targeting computers is the same.
- ❍ C. No, this will not work. You cannot publish software to a computer. You can only assign software to computers. However, both options are available for users.
- ❍ D. No, this is not the best solution. Siobhan should assign the software to the computers. Published packages appear on the Start Menu.

Question 15

You are preparing to implement a network load-balancing solution for your organization's e-commerce Web site. You will be load-balancing six Windows Server 2003 computers running IIS on the front end, with four Windows Server 2003 computers in a cluster on the back end providing access to an SQL Server 2000 database. You are using the unicast cluster operation mode. In what two ways can you prevent switch port flooding from occurring on the NLB cluster? (Select two.)

- ❑ A. Configure IGMP multicast support for the NLB cluster.
- ❑ B. Place the NLB cluster nodes on a dedicated switch.
- ❑ C. Place the NLB cluster nodes on a dedicate VLAN.
- ❑ D. Configure single affinity for the NLB cluster.

Question 16

You are the network administrator for Tammi's Tours, an island tour company. You are preparing to configure and implement a custom security template across several dozen of your network computers. Your network does not use Active Directory, so you cannot import the custom security template into a Group Policy Object. You know that you will need to use the **secedit** command to most easily implement the custom security template on your computers. What other functions does the **secedit** command have in Windows Server 2003? (Select two.)

- ❑ A. **secedit** can be used to analyze the current security settings.
- ❑ B. **secedit** can be used to refresh the local Group Policy Object on the computers.
- ❑ C. **secedit** can be used to create new custom security templates.
- ❑ D. **secedit** can be used to reset the local Group Policy object on a computer.
- ❑ E. **secedit** can be used to reset a locked-out user account.

Question 17

You are the network administrator for Joe's Place, a regional restaurant chain. While at a standards-setting meeting in Redmond, Washington, you are unsuccessfully attempting to initiate a Remote Desktop for Administration session with one of your Windows Server 2003 servers over the Internet. The server has a publicly accessible IP address, but it is located behind your network's external firewall. You can ping the server from your location and have verified, via a telephone conversation with onsite IT staff, that Remote Desktop is enabled for this server. Your account is a member of the Domain Admins, Enterprise Admins, and Administrators groups for your Active Directory network. What is the most likely reason for the inability to make the Remote Desktop for Administration connection?

- ❍ A. IIS 6.0 is not installed on the server in question.
- ❍ B. TCP port 3389 is being blocked at the external firewall.
- ❍ C. TCP port 8088 is being blocked at the external firewall.
- ❍ D. Your user account does not have the required permissions to use Remote Desktop for Administration.

Question 18

Orin Thomas is a system administrator for a Windows Server 2003 network. He is trying to make a decision about which method users should use to log on to his network. There are four domains in his forest, and he wants to make the logon method as simple for the users as possible. The Smith family owns the company. Three generations of Smiths work in his organization, and he has 25 members of the Smith family working in some context. Family members include David Smith, David Smith II, Darrell Smith, John Smith, John Smith II, and John Smith III. After careful consideration, Orin decides to stick with using the logon method that requires users to know which domains they belong to. Why did Orin make this decision?

- ❍ A. Orin knows that he has some duplicate names on his network. Because a principal name must be unique in a forest, he cannot guarantee that he won't run into problems. To avoid this, he is stuck with forcing the users to enter their domain name.
- ❍ B. Orin has decided that user education is going to be a problem. His user community has been migrated from a Windows NT 4 environment and is used to entering the domain name. Also, the benefits of using principal names are not great.
- ❍ C. Orin eventually wants to collapse two of his domains. By forcing the users to use a domain name, he can more easily identify those who will be affected by such a move and perform a smoother transition.
- ❍ D. It really doesn't make much difference to Orin which method is used. Because, administratively, it does not gain him anything, he decides to make sure that users enter the domain name.

Question 19

Helper Hal is a leading manufacturer of household goods items. You have been hired by the CIO of Helper Hal to design a new DNS namespace for an upcoming Windows Server 2003 deployment. Helper Hal already owns the **helperhal.com** domain name. Helper Hal has its corporate offices in England, with satellite offices in the United States, Canada, India, Germany, and Japan. The corporate office contains five departments: Sales, Production, Support, Facilities, and Finance. Each satellite office has only Sales and Support departments. Child domains exist under **helperhal.com** for each country. Additional child domains exist under these for each department. Which of the following FQDNs for a client named FILESVR042 in the Production department represents the correct DNS namespace? (Select all that apply)

- ❑ A. **filesvr042.production.helperhal.com**
- ❑ B. **filesvr042.uk.helperhal.com**
- ❑ C. **filesvr042.production.uk.helperhal.com**
- ❑ D. **filesvr042.helperhal.com**

Question 20

Siobhan Chamberlain has been tasked with examining the effects of applying a new set of policies to the sales team members of her organization. She knows that it is important that she not create problems for these users; she must be certain of the ultimate effect the new policies are going to have. Which tool should Siobhan use to determine the effect of the new policy settings?

- ❍ A. Group Policy Editor
- ❍ B. The Resultant Set of Policies tool, in Logging mode
- ❍ C. The Resultant Set of Policies tool, in Planning mode
- ❍ D. The Resultant Set of Policies tool, in Test mode

Question 21

You are the network administrator of a Windows Server 2003 Active Directory network. Your company policy states that the network access attempts of all temporary employees are to be tracked, regardless of what workstation they log on to. What auditing options do you need to configure to ensure that you can track the network access of all temporary employees? (Select two.)

- ❑ A. Audit Account Management
- ❑ B. Audit Directory Service Access
- ❑ C. Audit Logon Events
- ❑ D. Audit Privilege Use
- ❑ E. Audit System Events
- ❑ F. Audit Account Logon Events

Question 22

Melissa Wise is a network administrator for a company that uses smart card technology extensively for user logon. The company has recently closed one of its branch offices and, at the same time, is offering a new kiosk service to its clients. Because of the office closing, Melissa decides to utilize those computers for the new kiosk setup, which will include the smart card readers that have been in use for some time at the branch office. To enhance security, Melissa removes the workstations from the domain and puts them in their own workgroup. When she tests the computers after they've been hooked up at the kiosk, she finds that they cannot log on to the network, with her user account or others, even though she is able to hook up her own laptop and log on with her smart card. What might be happening?

- ❍ A. She needs to rejoin the workstations to the domain.
- ❍ B. She needs to configure the user accounts the kiosk computers will use to log in with smart cards.
- ❍ C. She needs to grant "logon locally" permissions to the user accounts.
- ❍ D. She needs to open up the corporate firewall to allow the kiosk computers' traffic to pass.

Question 23

You are the network administrator for Tammi's Tours, an island tour company. You are planning for an upgrade from Windows NT 4.0 on your internal network. The domain **tammistours.com** is already owned by the company and is being hosted by your ISP for mail, FTP, and HTTP services. You have been tasked with creating a new DNS namespace for your Windows Server 2003 network that is easy for users to understand, that provides an easy way to manage separation between the external namespace and the new internal namespace, and that still allows internal users to access both internal and external resources without any special action on their parts. The external namespace will continue to be hosted by your ISP for now. All client computers will be upgraded to Windows XP Professional during this process. Which of the following internal DNS namespaces meets the requirements you have been given?

❍ A. **tammistours.net**

❍ B. **corp.tammistours.com**

❍ C. **tammistours.corp.com**

❍ D. **tammistours.com.corp**

Question 24

You have been tasked with creating a report to upper management that details the latest features in Windows. One of the features you need to explain is the process of failover. How do you best explain this concept?

❍ A. A network communication sent among individual cluster nodes at intervals of no more than 500 milliseconds that is used to determine the status of all cluster nodes

❍ B. The process of a cluster group moving back to the preferred node after the preferred node has resumed cluster membership

❍ C. The process by which NLB clustering hosts determine a new, stable state among themselves and elect a new default host after the failure of one or more cluster nodes

❍ D. The process of a cluster group moving from the currently active node to another still-functioning node in the cluster group

Question 25

You are the network administrator for Good Faith Enterprises, LLC. You want to increase the security of your client workstations, which are all Windows 2000 Professional computers, without causing any adverse effect on network communications between computers. You have already completed this same configuration action on all of your domain controllers and member servers. Which security template should you use to accomplish your goal?

❍ A. securews.inf

❍ B. securedc.inf

❍ C. compatws.inf

❍ D. hisecws.inf

Question 26

Jorg Rosenthal is putting the finishing touches on his Windows 2003 Active Directory design. He has come up with a plan for three domains. He has a naming scheme and a DNS design. He had the plan examined by a consultant who has done a lot of work for the company in the past. The only change that this consultant made was to remind Jorg to add two-way trusts between each of the three domains. Jorg realizes that the consultant probably has never used Windows 2003 Server with Active Directory. How did he come to this realization?

❍ A. The consultant used the wrong terminology. Windows 2003 has "shortcut trusts" but not "two-way trusts."

❍ B. The consultant is correct. Two-way trusts will speed the logon process.

❍ C. Jorg is correct because there is no need to create old style two-way trusts; trusts are created automatically in Windows Server 2003 and are transitive.

❍ D. Jorg realized this because, to install a domain, you must explicitly set up a two-way trust. Therefore, there is no reason to create them after the fact.

Question 27

You are interviewing Chris, a candidate for an assistant administrator position in your company. When you ask her what a standard primary zone is, what answer should she tell you?

- ❍ A. A zone that holds a master copy of the zone data and can transfer or replicate it to all configured servers
- ❍ B. A zone that holds a read-only copy of the zone data
- ❍ C. A zone that has its zone data held within Active Directory
- ❍ D. A zone that contains only resource records necessary to identify the authoritative DNS servers for a zone

Question 28

You are the administrator of a large Windows Server 2003 network. Your company is a leading provider of state-of-the-art satellite communications services for customers all over the world. The CIO of your company is very concerned about user account properties being modified by users who should not have administrative permissions. As part of your efforts to determine who might be modifying user account properties, you have decided to implement auditing. What auditing option should you configure to help you determine who is changing the user account properties on your network?

- ❍ A. Audit Account Management
- ❍ B. Audit Object Access
- ❍ C. Audit Logon Events
- ❍ D. Audit Privilege Use
- ❍ E. Audit System Events
- ❍ F. Audit Account Logon Events

Question 29

You are preparing to implement a network load balancing solution for your organization's e-commerce Web site. You will be load-balancing six Windows Server 2003 computers running IIS on the front end, with four Windows Server 2003 computers in a cluster on the back end providing access to an SQL Server 2000 database. You are trying to decide which clustering mode to use for your back-end servers. What two clustering modes exist? (Select two.)

- ❑ A. Active/Passive
- ❑ B. Passive/Active
- ❑ C. Passive/Passive
- ❑ D. Active/Active

Question 30

You are an assistant network administrator for the Nimbus Flying Broom corporation. You are responsible for 75 Windows XP Professional workstations and 5 Windows Server 2003 member server computers. You have been directed to perform a security analysis on each computer, comparing its settings to those contained in the hisecws.inf template. How you can accomplish your assigned task with the least amount of administrative effort and the fewest number of trips to remote computers?

❍ A. The only way to perform this analysis is to physically visit each computer and use the Security Configuration and Analysis snap-in.

❍ B. You can create a script that runs Security Configuration and Analysis on each computer, collecting the results in a central location for later viewing.

❍ C. You can create a script that runs the **secedit /analyze** command on each computer, collecting the results in a central location for later viewing.

❍ D. You can analyze remote computers from the Security Configuration and Analysis snap-in by targeting it at the desired computer.

Question 31

You are the network administrator for Tammi's Tours, an island tour company. You are planning for an upgrade from Windows NT 4.0 on your internal network. The domain **tammistours.com** is already owned by the company and is being hosted by your ISP for mail, FTP, and HTTP services. Internal DNS services are currently being provided by a BIND version 8.2.1 DNS server. You have been directed to create a new internal DNS solution using Windows Server 2003. The BIND server must be retained for the first six months until the final approval has been given to the Windows Server 2003 DNS server. You have also been directed, as much as possible, to take advantage of the new security and management features that Windows Server 2003 DNS provides. How should you configure the Windows Server 2003 and BIND DNS servers?

❍ A. You should configure the Windows Server 2003 DNS server as a standard secondary server. You should configure the BIND DNS server as a standard primary server.

❍ B. You should configure the Windows Server 2003 DNS server as a standard primary server. You should configure the BIND DNS server as a standard secondary server.

❍ C. You should configure the Windows Server 2003 DNS server to use an Active Directory–integrated zone. You should configure the BIND DNS server as a standard secondary server.

❍ D. You should configure the Windows Server 2003 DNS server to use an Active Directory–integrated zone. You should configure the BIND DNS server as a standard primary server.

Question 32

Bob Muir has been asked to change the password for a user account. Bob is a domain administrator. However, he has tried unsuccessfully to contact the user to get her current password. His boss is worried that an unauthorized person might have the password for this account. What is the best course of action for Bob to take?

❍ A. Bob should delete the user account and re-create it with the new password. The user will call as soon as she is unable to log on.

❍ B. Because Bob is a domain administrator, he does not need the user's current password to make the change.

❍ C. Bob should disable the account. This will force the user to call in with the information Bob needs.

❍ D. Bob should lock out the account. This will force the user to call in with the information Bob needs.

Question 33

You are the network administrator for Roger's Rockets, a manufacturer of toy rocket kits. You are creating a new WLAN security policy for the wireless clients located in the Engineering OU. You have one approved 802.11b WLAN in your organization with an SSID of rogrcktint1. From time to time, the engineering department needs to use a special testing WLAN. The SSID of this testing WLAN changes each time it is implemented. What setting can you configure for the Engineering OU WLAN security policy that will allow these wireless clients to connect to the special testing WLAN when it is available?

❍ A. You will need to update the WLAN security policy every time the special testing WLAN is available.

❍ B. You will need to create a new WLAN security policy in the Engineering OU every time the special testing WLAN is available.

❍ C. You will need to select the Automatically connect to non-preferred networks option.

❍ D. You will need to select the Wireless Network Key (WEP) option.

Question 34

Which of the following constitute the phases of software deployment? (Select all that apply.)

- ❑ A. Preparation
- ❑ B. Distribution
- ❑ C. Targeting
- ❑ D. Pilot
- ❑ E. Installation

Question 35

You are the administrator of a large Windows Server 2003 network. Your company is a leading provider of state-of-the-art satellite communications services for customers all over the world. The CIO of your company is very concerned about who is able to access files and folders located in a sensitive folder named Contacts. What auditing option should you configure to help you determine which users on your network are accessing the files and folders located within the Contacts folder?

- ❍ A. Audit Account Management
- ❍ B. Audit Object Access
- ❍ C. Audit Logon Events
- ❍ D. Audit Privilege Use
- ❍ E. Audit System Events
- ❍ F. Audit Account Logon Events

Question 36

In regard to a network load-balancing cluster, what desirable function do port rules provide?

- ❍ A. They can be used to allow only traffic on specific ports to be load-balanced, dropping all other traffic.
- ❍ B. They assign a unique numerical identifier to each cluster node.
- ❍ C. They specify the IP address that the network load-balancing cluster can be accessed at.
- ❍ D. They specify the IP subnet that the administrative network adapter is to be located on.

Question 37

You are the network administrator for Tammi's Tours, an island tour company. You are implementing a four-node NLB cluster providing Terminal Services to your client computers. All 450 of your client computers are located within a single office building using three different Class C IP subnets. The Terminal Servers will be providing access to a mission-critical application that is used to book and manage tours. Session data is required to be maintained during the connection, but no cookies are used. What type of affinity should you configure to ensure that clients receive the best overall possible service during their connection period?

- ❍ A. None
- ❍ B. Class C
- ❍ C. Multiple
- ❍ D. Single

Question 38

Joanne works for a banking organization. Joanne knows that she should back up her DC regularly, but she has not done so in a while because several urgent projects have required her attention. Also, the server should never be taken offline. She decides to place a call with Microsoft technical support to ask for advice about protecting herself in the case of server failure. What was she told?

- ❍ A. Joanne was told that she should take the server offline so that a backup can be performed. Losing a server for a night, while it is backed up, is far better than losing it for an extended time due to server failure.
- ❍ B. Joanne was told that she should still perform a backup even if the server is being used. Although she won't be able to back up the log files for AD because they are in use, she can still back up the AD database and Registry files. This alone would get the DC functional again.
- ❍ C. Joanne was told not to worry. The database is transactional and can protect itself from failures automatically. Backing up to a file or tape is a precautionary measure that is desirable but not necessary.
- ❍ D. Joanne was told to go ahead and perform a backup of system state data. The DC does not have to be taken offline for this process to take place.

Question 39

Ron Porter wants to make sure that searches for objects across domains are faster. His environment has two buildings, each with its own domains in the same tree. To make searches faster, Ron intends to move a domain controller from his own building into the remote one, and vice versa. Will this make searches across the domain faster?

❍ A. No. To search for an object, the remote domain controller will still have to query servers in its home domain.

❍ B. No. Searches across domains are made at a Global Catalog server; merely being a domain controller would not help.

❍ C. Yes. Because the server would be local to the people doing the search, it would reply faster.

❍ D. Yes. Because it would be in the remote domain, it could query local servers for any data that it needs.

Question 40

You are planning a new DNS namespace for Lou's Log Homes, Inc. Security and redundancy are important factors in your design. Which of the following zone types should you choose to ensure the highest level of security and most redundancy possible?

❍ A. Standard primary

❍ B. Standard secondary

❍ C. Stub

❍ D. Active Directory–integrated

Question 41

You are the network administrator for Jeff's Jeep Tours, an Australian tour company. You are configuring one of your Windows Server 2003 computers so that it will support Remote Desktop for Administration connections. You want two additional nonadministrative personnel to be able to create Remote Desktop connections to the server. What local group do you need to add their user accounts to in order to allow these users to create Remote Desktop for Administration connections?

❍ A. HelpServicesGroup

❍ B. Remote Desktop Users

❍ C. Network Configuration Operators

❍ D. Administrators

Question 42

You are preparing to implement a network load balancing solution for your organization's e-commerce Web site. You will be load-balancing six Windows Server 2003 computers running IIS on the front end, with four Windows Server 2003 computers in a cluster on the back end providing access to an SQL Server 2000 database. Which of the following cluster models is not available in Windows Server 2003?

❍ A. Single-node cluster

❍ B. Multiple-quorum cluster

❍ C. Single-quorum cluster

❍ D. Majority node set cluster

Question 43

You are the network administrator for Nebuchadnezzar Furnaces. Its Windows Server 2003 domain consists of domain controllers, 2 member servers, and 765 Windows XP Professional workstations. Every summer, you hire 30 to 40 temporary employees to assist with additional production and sales needs for the upcoming winter season. Each of these employees is issued a digital certificate for smart card usage, to allow them to securely access the network. The digital certificates have a lifetime of 2 years, by default, due to the configuration of the CA that has issued them. Allison, your CIO, has told you on more than one occasion that she does not like the idea of having unused digital certificates still active. What should you do to increase the level of security of your network?

❍ A. Change the CSP key length

❍ B. Revoke the unused digital certificates

❍ C. Lock the user's accounts

❍ D. Disable the unused digital certificates

Question 44

Volker Wiora is an administrator for a large Windows Server 2003 network. A temporary set of developers will be working for his organization. They will be with the company for only six months. Volker already has a development group defined that exists in an OU called Developers. He had applied Group Policy at this level to control what the developers can do to their systems. The new group of developers is to have an even stricter set of policies applied. Which of the following solutions would work in this situation?

- ❍ A. Volker should create a new set of policies that links these settings to a security group defined for the new developers.
- ❍ B. Volker should create a child OU beneath the current Developers OU. He should then define a new Group Policy and link it to the parent. Through inheritance, this policy will then pass on to the new developers.
- ❍ C. Volker should create a new Group Policy. He should then add the new developers into the current Developers OU. He should link the new Group Policy to the Developers OU. He should create a security group and add the current development team members to it. Finally, he should remove read rights from the new Group Policy object for this security group.
- ❍ D. This cannot be done. Because all the developers are in the same OU, policies applied to it affect either all users or none. You cannot have a situation in which some of the users get the policy and others do not.

Question 45

You are the network administrator for Fast Sloth Enterprises. You need to increase the security of your Windows XP Professional client computers and Windows Server 2003 servers. Which security template should you apply to your workstations to ensure that they have the most secure configuration?

- ❍ A. securews.inf
- ❍ B. hisecdc.inf
- ❍ C. hisecws.inf
- ❍ D. compatws.inf

Question 46

You are the network administrator for Tim's Toys, a specialty top shop. Your internal DNS namespace is **corp.timstoys.com**, and your external DNS namespace is **timstoys.com**. Company policy requires all user logons to consist of the first letter in the first name and the entire last name. For a user named Tim Smith in your internal Windows Server 2003 Active Directory network, which of the following is the correct user principal name (UPN)?

- ❍ A. **tsmith**
- ❍ B. **tsmith@timstoys.com**
- ❍ C. **tsmith@corp**
- ❍ D. **tsmith@corp.timstoys.com**

Question 47

You are the network administrator for Roger's Rockets, a manufacturer of toy rocket kits. You want to require that all wireless clients have the correct WEP key to authenticate to your WLAN. What setting do you need to select in your WLAN security policy?

- ❍ A. Data Encryption (WEP enabled)
- ❍ B. Network authentication (Shared mode)
- ❍ C. The Key is provided to me automatically
- ❍ D. Transmit per IEEE 802.1x

Question 48

You are the network administrator for Stan's Tans, a tanning salon and health spa company. You have been tasked by the CIO to implement and maintain a backup plan for the STANTAN042 file server, on which critical corporate documents are stored. The CIO has specifically tasked you with creating three backups throughout the day at 9 a.m., 12 p.m., and 3 p.m. to back up any changed documents, and one additional backup after working hours at 9 p.m. to back up all data stored on the file server. Documents that are currently being edited are not to be backed up. What option must you select to ensure that this requirement is met?

- ❍ A. Verify data after backup
- ❍ B. Disable volume shadow copy
- ❍ C. Use hardware compression, if available
- ❍ D. Restore security settings

Question 49

In Windows Server 2003, DNS can perform what two types of zone transfers when standard DNS zones are in use? (Select two.)

- ❑ A. Full
- ❑ B. Partial
- ❑ C. Standard
- ❑ D. Incremental

Question 50

You have just composed and sent an email message to a colleague who is located within a different Windows Server 2003 network than your own. The email message has been digitally signed by you using your email certificate. Your root CA uses a third-party certificate from a trusted third-party organization. What will your colleague need to have available to read your email and verify that it originated from you?

- ❍ A. Your private key
- ❍ B. Your public key
- ❍ C. The third-party CA's private key
- ❍ D. The third-party CA's public key

Question 51

How would you determine whether a user had an appropriate level of permissions to execute a managed application?

- ❍ A. Through the Security tab in the package's properties in Software Installation
- ❍ B. Through the Deployment tab in the package's properties in Software Installation
- ❍ C. Through OU membership in Active Directory Users and Computers
- ❍ D. Through GPO membership in Active Directory Users and Computers

Question 52

Active Directory data is stored in a file on all domain controllers. What is the name of this file?

❍ A. NTDS.DIT

❍ B. ADDS.ADT

❍ C. NTDS.ADS

❍ D. ADDS.DIT

Question 53

You are the network administrator for Jeff's Jeep Tours, an Australian tour company. While assisting one of your remote office users with a configuration issue on the user's computer, you have tried unsuccessfully to take control of the user's computer. What possible reasons might explain why you have not been able to take control? (Select two.)

❑ A. Your computer is not configured to allow it to initiate remote control sessions.

❑ B. The remote computer is not configured to allow it to be controlled remotely.

❑ C. A firewall is in place, preventing you from taking control.

❑ D. The Novice is not allowing you to take control of his computer.

Question 54

Hannah is the network administrator for Think Pink Bicycles, Inc. She is attempting to configure the Engineering Organizational Unit in her Windows Server 2003 network with the securews.inf template. There are 30 member file and print servers in this OU, along with approximately 500 Windows XP Professional workstations. Which of the following methods of applying the securews.inf template would be the most administratively efficient?

❍ A. Using the Security Configuration and Analysis snap-in

❍ B. Using the **secedit.exe** command

❍ C. Using Group Policy

❍ D. Using the domain controller Security Policy console

Question 55

You are the network administrator for Stan's Tans, a tanning salon and health spa company. You have been tasked by the CIO to implement and maintain a backup plan for the STANTAN042 file server, on which critical corporate documents are stored. The CIO has specifically tasked you with creating three backups throughout the day at 9 a.m., 12 p.m., and 3 p.m. to back up any changed documents, and one additional backup after working hours at 9 p.m. to back up all data stored on the file server. The backups created throughout the day must be completed as quickly as possible. What backup type should you configure for each of the four daily backup jobs?

- ❍ A. 9 a.m.: differential; 12 p.m.: differential; 3 p.m.: differential; 9 p.m.: incremental
- ❍ B. 9 a.m.: incremental; 12 p.m.: incremental; 3 p.m.: incremental; 9 p.m.: normal
- ❍ C. 9 a.m.: copy; 12 p.m.: copy; 3 p.m.: copy; 9 p.m.: normal
- ❍ D. 9 a.m.: normal; 12 p.m.: normal; 3 p.m.: normal; 9 p.m.: daily

Question 56

Somebody has encrypted a piece of data with your public key. What will you need to decrypt it?

- ❍ A. Your public key
- ❍ B. Your private key
- ❍ C. The other party's public key
- ❍ D. The other party's private key

Question 57

Ester Helwig has been asked to troubleshoot a Group Policy issue. In this case, she has been asked to ensure that a policy is not passed down from a parent OU to a child OU. The current administrator has made sure that the Block Inheritance setting has been turned on, but the policy is still being applied. Why is this? (Choose the best answer.)

- ❍ A. The policy has been set at the parent. The No Override setting has been checked at this level.
- ❍ B. The policy has been misconfigured. The No Override option needs to be set at the child OU.
- ❍ C. Policies applied at parent OUs are always applied to child OUs. This is by design. To prevent this would require a new design for OUs.
- ❍ D. To prevent a policy from being applied, Ester must set No Override in the Local Policies of the client computers.

Question 58

You are the network administrator for Roger's Rockets, a manufacturer of toy rocket kits. You are configuring a new WLAN security policy for the wireless clients that are located in your Accounting OU. You want to provide the maximum level of security for your WLAN by requiring that all computers authenticate to the WLAN upon creating their wireless connection. You want the computer to authenticate using its computer account. You are using a RADIUS server to handle authentication, and the authentication database is Active Directory. What setting do you need to configure in the WLAN security policy?

❍ A. Authenticate as guest when user or computer information is unavailable

❍ B. Transmit per IEEE 802.1x

❍ C. Data Encryption (WEP enabled)

❍ D. Authenticate as computer when computer information is available

Question 59

You are the network administrator for Tim's Toys, a specialty top shop. One of your users has called you to report that she wasn't sure what her password was this morning and tried three times unsuccessfully to log on before remembering the correct password. Now she still cannot log on, even though she is now using the correct password. What do you suspect is the most likely problem?

❍ A. The user's account has been disabled.

❍ B. The user's account has been locked out.

❍ C. The user is over her disk space quota limit.

❍ D. The user's home folder cannot be located.

Question 60

You are the network administrator for Jake's Jumps, a skydiving company. You have just installed a new Windows Server 2003 computer and promoted it to domain controller. You have never used Active Directory on your network. You are creating a new domain named **corp.jakesjumps.com**, which is a delegated DNS namespace off your publicly accessible **jakesjumps.com** domain. After the creation of this first domain, what is the name given to this first domain?

❍ A. Forest roof

❍ B. Forest root

❍ C. Parent domain

❍ D. Child domain

Answer Key to Practice Exam #1

Answer Key

1. B
2. B, D
3. A, B, C
4. A
5. D
6. B
7. B
8. C
9. B, C
10. B
11. C
12. B
13. D
14. C
15. B, C
16. A, C
17. B
18. A
19. B, C
20. C
21. C, F
22. A
23. B
24. D
25. A
26. C
27. A
28. A
29. A, D
30. C
31. C
32. B
33. C
34. A, B, C, D, E
35. B
36. A
37. D
38. D
39. B
40. D
41. B
42. B
43. B
44. C
45. C
46. D
47. B
48. B
49. A, D
50. B
51. A
52. A
53. B, D
54. C
55. B
56. B
57. A
58. D
59. B
60. B

Question 1

Answer B is correct. The best way to apply the settings to only computers that require them is to import the template into a Group Policy Object (GPO) associated with each Organizational Unit (OU) that requires the settings. Importing the security template into the domain-level GPO would apply the settings to all computers in the domain, most likely with unwanted side effects. Therefore, answer A is incorrect. Scripting is not required in this case; therefore, answer C is incorrect. Manually applying the security template would be too time consuming; therefore, answer D is incorrect.

Question 2

Answers B and D are correct. AD Users and Computers and AD Domains and Trusts both allow for raising the domain functional level. Answer A is incorrect because Group Policy Editor allows you to specify the settings for a user or computer that relate to desktop views or software and security policy. Answer C is incorrect because the Delegation of Control Wizard provides a graphical way to assign Active Directory access permissions to individuals with trusted administrative control.

Question 3

Answers A, B, and C are correct. Group Policy cannot work without Active Directory. However, Group Policy does not support Windows NT 4.0 computers; these computers require System Policies for management. Because a Windows Server 2003 environment can deliver System Policies to down-level clients, there is no need to keep a legacy domain on this network; thus, answer D is incorrect.

Question 4

Answer A is correct. The `clowncollege.net` namespace represents a unique Domain Name System (DNS) namespace. `clowncollege.net` would thus become the root of the Active Directory forest and domain structure. Unique DNS namespaces should typically be similar to the original namespace—in this case, `clowncollege.com`. The other options do not represent the best unique

DNS namespace; therefore, answers B, C, and D are incorrect. Answer B presents a delegated namespace, not a unique namespace. Answers C and D are not valid given the current namespace in use.

Question 5

Answer D is correct. Because wide area network (WAN) link usage is not an issue in this scenario and Christopher has received authorization to add only those new servers that are absolutely required, Christopher's best option is to install and configure one Software Update Services (SUS) server at the main office that synchronizes nightly with the Windows Update Web servers. All Automatic Updates clients will then be configured to receive their updates from the home office SUS server.

Question 6

Answer B is correct. Failback is the process of a cluster group moving back to the preferred node after the preferred node has resumed cluster membership. None of the other options adequately define failback; therefore, answers A, C, and D are incorrect.

Question 7

Answer B is correct. Three types of user accounts exist: domain user accounts, local user accounts, and built-in accounts. Domain accounts are designed to allow users to log in to a network and gain access to resources. Local user accounts are used on member servers and Windows Server 2003 Professional systems to allow users to log on to the local computer without network access (as in this instance). Built-in accounts are created by default for administrative purposes. Answer A is incorrect because typing in a bad password would result in the user being unable to see the desktop. Answer C is incorrect because the user would have typed the correct password to access the system. Answer D is incorrect because there should be no lag when the user logs on. When a user logs on, the security token for the user is created. If there is a delay in the creation of the token, the entire logon process is delayed.

Question 8

Answer C is correct. Of the available options, the only valid one is to create and send an email request for Remote Assistance. The email request will contain a special URL that the Expert can use to initiate the Remote Assistance connection via the Microsoft Web site. The Expert will need to download and install an ActiveX applet as part of the connection process. Emergency Management Services and the Recovery Console cannot be used to send Remote Assistance requests; thus, answers A and B are incorrect. MSN Messenger is similar to Windows Messenger but cannot be used to send Remote Assistance requests; thus, answer D is incorrect.

Question 9

Answers B and C are correct. The Highly Secure security templates (hisecws.inf and hisecdc.inf) provide the most secure security environment possible, using only preconfigured default security templates. The Secure templates will increase the baseline security of the servers but still allow for increasing security later, if desired, through the use of the Highly Secure templates; thus, answers A and D are incorrect.

Question 10

Answer B is correct. The `GuiRunOnce` section within the answer file would specify the command `dcpromo` and then specify an additional answer file that is specific to the Active Directory installation. Answer C is incorrect because, although `DCInstall` is a section of the Active Directory answer file, it is not the section that installs the operating system. Answers A and D are invalid answers.

Question 11

Answer C is correct. You must use the `gpupdate /target:computer` command to immediately cause the computer configuration portion of Group Policy to refresh and update your changes. WLAN security policies are not kept in the user configuration portion of Group Policy; thus, answer A is incorrect. The `secedit` command is no longer used to refresh Group Policy in Windows Server 2003; thus, answers B and D are incorrect.

Question 12

Answer B is correct. The Local Policies node of the Group Policy Editor contains three subnodes: Audit Policy, User Rights Assignment, and Security Options. The Audit Policy subnode is where Andrea will find the auditing items she will need to configure. Andrea will not find auditing options in Account Policies, Restricted Groups, or File System; therefore, answers A, C, and D are incorrect.

Question 13

Answer D is correct. By configuring the Smart card removal behavior option (located in the Computer Configuration, Windows Settings, Security Settings, Local Policies, Security Options node of the Group Policy editor) for Lock Workstation, Andrea can achieve the desired results. The other options do not enable this behavior; therefore, answers A, B, and C are incorrect because they do not provide the required solution.

Question 14

Answer C is correct. When making distributions to a computer, the Publish option is grayed out. Software can be assigned only to computers. Answer A is incorrect because it does not state that you cannot publish an application to a computer. Answer B is incorrect because it fails to recognize the difference between assigning and publishing an application. Answer D is incorrect because it mistakenly suggests that published applications show up on the Start menu; they do not.

Question 15

Answers B and C are correct. If the multicast operation mode is configured, you can make use of the new IGMP multicast support function. Because unicast is being used in this case, you have the option of placing the NLB cluster nodes on a dedicated switch or VLAN to eliminate switch port flooding. Answer A assumes the use of multicast mode, which is not the case. The affinity setting is not related to switch port flooding, so answer D is incorrect.

Question 16

Answers A and C are correct. The `secedit` command can be used to analyze a computer, configure a computer, export a computer's security settings to a template, import the settings from a template, validate the context of a template, and create a rollback template; thus, answers B, D, and E are incorrect. You can script `secedit` because it is a command-line tool, allowing you to use it on many computers across your entire network. `gpupdate` is used to refresh Group Policy, so answer B is incorrect. `secedit` cannot be used to reset Group Policy or locked-out accounts, so answers D and E are incorrect.

Question 17

Answer B is correct. The most likely problem is that your external firewall has been configured to block traffic on TCP port 3389 and is thus preventing Remote Desktop Protocol traffic from crossing the firewall. IIS does not need to be installed to use Remote Desktop for Administration; thus, answer A is incorrect. TCP ports 8088 and 8080 are used by the Web Interface for Remote Administration and are not related to Remote Desktop for Administration; thus, answer C is incorrect. Your account does, in fact, have the required permissions because it is a member of the Enterprise Admins, Domain Admins, and Administrators groups in your domain; thus, answer D is incorrect.

Question 18

Answer A is correct. Because this network has a lot of duplicate usernames, it is best at this time to stick with a system that requires users to know their username and domain for logon. Therefore, answers B, C, and D are all incorrect.

Question 19

Answers B and C are correct. Although answer A provided the answer Bertram requires, the Group Policy management Console requires the installation of software. The GPRESULT command line tool and the Resultant Set of Policies snap-in are available by default in Windows XP. Answer D is incorrect because this, too, requires software installation.

Question 20

Answer C is correct. Planning mode enables you to set up "what-if" scenarios for new policy settings. Answer A is not correct because this allows you to create new policies or edit the settings in policies that have already been created, but it does not allow you to determine precisely how they will affect a client. Answer B is incorrect because logging mode does not allow for "what-if" types of scenarios. Answer D is incorrect because the Resultant Set of Policies tool does not have a test mode.

Question 21

Answers C and F are correct. When both the Audit Logon Events and Audit Account Logon Events options are configured, logons and logoffs that use a domain account generate logon or logoff audit events on the local computer as well as the domain controller. A success audit generates an audit entry when a logon attempt succeeds, and a failure audit generates an audit entry when a logon attempt fails. Answers A, B, D, and E do not configure auditing for logon events, so they are all incorrect.

Question 22

Answer A is correct. To use smart card logons, a workstation must belong to a domain. Melissa needs to rejoin them to the domain for the smart card logons to work. Answer B is incorrect because even though user accounts must be configured to log on with smart cards, the scenario states that Melissa's account cannot log on to those computers, although she can log on with her laptop from the kiosk network (making answer D invalid as well). Answer C is incorrect because this right is already given on a workstation, by default.

Question 23

Answer B is correct. The `corp.tammistours.com` namespace is the best option of those presented. This delegated DNS namespace meets all requirements imposed on you by providing complete separation between the internal and external namespaces, as well as allowing internal users to seamlessly access all resources, regardless of their location on the network. The `tammistours.net` namespace represents a unique namespace and could cause confusion among your users; thus, answer A is incorrect. The `tammistours.corp.com` and `tammistours.com.corp` namespaces are invalid; thus, answers C and D are incorrect.

Question 24

Answer D is correct. Failover is the process of a cluster group moving from the currently active node to another still-functioning node in the cluster group. None of the other options adequately define failover; therefore, answers A, B, and C are incorrect.

Question 25

Answer A is correct. By applying the Secure template, securews.inf, you can increase the security of the client workstations without adversely affecting network communications. The other options would cause more delays in network communications; therefore, answers B, C, and D are incorrect.

Question 26

Answer C is correct. Two-way trusts were commonly used in Windows NT 4.0, but they are rarely needed in Windows Server 2003. In this scenario, they serve no purpose. Transitive trusts are created automatically. Answer A is incorrect because this was not merely a terminology issue; two-way trusts still exist in Windows Server 2003 in some instances. Answer B is incorrect because two-way trusts will not aid the logon process here. Answer D is incorrect because this step is not required when installing Windows Server 2003.

Question 27

Answer A is correct. A standard primary zone holds a master copy of a zone and can replicate it to all configured secondary zones in standard text format. Any changes that must be made to the zone are made on the copy stored on the primary. Answer B refers to a standard secondary zone. Answer C refers to an Active Directory–integrated zone. Answer D refers to a stub zone.

Question 28

Answer A is correct. The Audit Account Management option configures auditing to occur for each event of account management on a computer. Typical account-management events include creating a user, creating a group, renaming a user, disabling a user account, and setting or changing a password. A success audit generates an audit entry when any account-management event is successful, and a failure audit generates an entry when any account-management event fails. Answers B, C, D, E, and F do not provide the required auditing result, so all are incorrect.

Question 29

Answers A and D are correct. You can select from either Active/Passive or Active/Active clustering mode. Active/Passive has one node in the cluster online and providing services. All other nodes are online and in a standby state, ready to assume the services if the active node fails. Active/Active has an instance of the clustered service running on all nodes in the cluster. If a node fails, the service instance is transferred to one of the remaining operational nodes. There is no such mode as Passive/Active or Passive/Passive, so answers B and C are incorrect.

Question 30

Answer C is correct. The easiest way to accomplish this task is to create a script that runs the `secedit /analyze` command on the computers and collects the results in a central network location. Answer A is incorrect because you will not have to visit each computer locally. Answer B is incorrect because Security Configuration and Analysis is not scripted. Answer D is incorrect because Security Configuration and Analysis cannot be targeted at a remote computer.

Question 31

Answer C is correct. By configuring the Windows Server 2003 DNS server to use an Active Directory–integrated zone and the BIND DNS server as a standard secondary server, you meet all of the requirements imposed on you. Answers A and B do not meet the requirement to take advantage of the new security and management features that Windows Server 2003 DNS provides, in that they do not use Active Directory–integrated zones. The Windows Server 2003 DNS server will act as a standard primary server to the BIND DNS server, so the BIND DNS server will need to be configured as a standard secondary server; thus, answer D is incorrect.

Question 32

Answer B is correct. Bob does not need the user's password. It is not advisable to change users' passwords without their knowledge, but there might be times when this action is necessary. Using Active Directory Users and Computers, Bob could right-click on the user account and choose Reset Password. Answer A is inadvisable because each user account is associated with a unique SID. Simply deleting and re-creating a user account with the same name will not create an identical account, and all group memberships and permissions would have to be re-created. Answer C would work but is unnecessary to accomplish the task of changing the user password. Answer D is incorrect because an account can be locked only through failed password attempts (if a lockout policy had been configured).

Question 33

Answer C is correct. By creating the WLAN security policy and selecting the Automatically Connect to Nonpreferred Networks option, you can enforce the settings you desire (such as those for authentication and so forth) on preferred networks but still allow wireless clients to connect to nonpreferred networks, if required. Under normal circumstances, you might likely not configure this option because it removes some administrative control that you would otherwise exercise over networks that wireless clients can connect to. There is no need to modify the existing WLAN security policy when the special testing WLAN is available; thus, answer A is incorrect. Likewise, there is no need to create a new WLAN security policy; thus, answer B is incorrect. The Wireless Network Key (WEP) option is not related to this issue; thus, answer D is incorrect.

Question 34

Answers A, B, C, D, and E are correct. The prescribed method of performing a software deployment is to have five phases: preparation, distribution, targeting, pilot, and installation.

Question 35

Answer B is correct. The Audit Object Access option configures auditing to occur upon each user access of an object, such as a file, folder, printer, or Registry key, that has its own system Access Control List (SACL) configured. To configure auditing for object access, you also need to configure auditing specifically on each object that you want to perform auditing on. A success audit generates an audit entry when a user successfully accesses an object, and a failure audit generates an audit entry when a user unsuccessfully attempts to access an object. Answers A, C, D, E, and F do not provide the required audit results of auditing object access and are all incorrect.

Question 36

Answer A is correct. Port rules can be used to allow only traffic on specific ports to be load-balanced. By configuring explicit allow rules for specific ports and an explicit deny rule dropping all other traffic, only the desired traffic will be load-balanced. Answer B is incorrect because port rules have nothing to do with host priority. Answers C and D are incorrect because port rules do not specify an IP address for the cluster.

Question 37

Answer D is correct. By configuring the single affinity setting, you maintain all client requests on the same node for the duration of the session. Single affinity provides the best support for the maintaining of user state data. An affinity setting of None allows inbound client requests to be sent to all cluster nodes and be randomly assigned based on server loading, but it does not maintain session state data; thus, answer A is incorrect. The Class C affinity setting maintains session state data by connecting all users from a single Class C subnet to one specific server. In this case, there is a distinct possibility for server overload because only three IP subnets exist; thus, answer B is incorrect. There is no multiple affinity mode.

Question 38

Answer D is correct. The built-in backup utility can be used to perform an online backup. Answer A is incorrect because it is not necessary to take a server offline before performing a backup. Answer B is incorrect because an online backup can indeed back up the log files. Answer C is incorrect because a system state backup is an important part of the recovery process.

Question 39

Answer B is correct. A Global Catalog server performs searches for objects in other domains. If searches were slow, it would most likely be because there is a problem with the Global Catalog server or there are not enough of them. Answer A is incorrect because, as stated, these queries are done to a Global Catalog server, not between domain controllers. Answer C is incorrect because local searches would not hit the new domain controller. Answer D is incorrect because this process simply does not exist.

Question 40

Answer D is correct. Active Directory–integrated DNS zones store the zone data within the Active Directory database itself, thus allowing for greatly increased security, manageability, and redundancy. When Active Directory–integrated zones are used, all DNS servers operate in a multimaster arrangement, allowing any DNS server to make changes to the zone data. By having multiple DNS servers that are allowed to manage the zone data, dynamic updates are also more redundant because the failure of a single DNS server will not prevent a dynamic update from occurring. Standard zones do not provide security for the zone data as it is transferred in plain text. In addition, standard zones do not have any mechanisms in place to prevent clients from creating or updating records; this makes answers A and B incorrect. Stub zones contain only a small subset of resource records that are required to direct clients to another zone, so answer C is incorrect.

Question 41

Answer B is correct. You must add the user accounts for these two users to the local Remote Desktop Users group on the computer. The HelpServicesGroup is used by Remote Assistance connections; thus, answer A is incorrect. The Network Configuration Operators group is allowed to manage the networking properties of a server; thus, answer C is incorrect. There is no need to add these user accounts to the Administrators group to allow them to create Remote Desktop connections to this server; thus, answer D is incorrect.

Question 42

Answer B is correct. The single mode-cluster, single-quorum cluster, and majority node set cluster models are supported in Windows Server 2003. Thus, answers A and C are incorrect. There is no multiple-quorum cluster model; thus, answer D is incorrect.

Question 43

Answer B is correct. In this scenario, the best option for increasing security is to revoke any unused certificates and immediately publish the Certificate Revocation List (CRL) to all CRL Distribution Points (CDP). Changing the Cryptographic Service Provider (CSP) length will have no effect on certificates that have already been issued, so answer A is incorrect. Locking the user's account is not a good solution because the user accounts should be deleted and the certificates should be revoked; thus, answer C is incorrect. You cannot disable a certificate—you can only revoke it; thus, answer D is incorrect.

Question 44

Answer C is correct. In this case, this is the only solution that would work (although it is rather complex). Answer A is incorrect because Group Polices cannot be applied to a security group. Answer B is incorrect because if the policy is applied to a parent in this manner, it would affect both the members of the parent Organizational Unit and the members of the child Organizational Unit. Answer D is incorrect because it is possible to change who is affected by a policy by altering permissions at the group level.

Question 45

Answer C is correct. Of the given choices, the hisecws.inf template provides the most secure configuration to your Windows XP Professional clients. Answer A is incorrect because the `securews.inf` security template is not the most secure option available. Answer B is incorrect because `hisecdc.inf` is to be applied only to domain controllers. Answer D is incorrect because the `compatws.inf` security template does not provide increased security.

Question 46

Answer D is correct. A UPN consists of two parts: the user principal name prefix (`tsmith`) and the user principal name suffix (`corp.timstoys.com`). Answers A, B, and C are incorrect because they do not represent a full UPN for a user in the `corp.timstoys.com` domain.

Question 47

Answer B is correct. To use WEP to perform WLAN authentication, you must select the Network authentication (Shared mode) option. The Data Encryption (WEP enabled) option specifies that WEP be used to encrypt data placed on the WLAN; thus answer A is incorrect. The Key is provided to me automatically option specifies that the key be dynamically assigned from a key server (such as a RADIUS server); thus answer C is incorrect. The Transmit per IEEE 802.1x option is used to configure how the EAPOL-start message is sent and has nothing to do with WEP; thus answer D is incorrect.

Question 48

Answer B is correct. The Disable volume shadow copy option allows you to turn of the volume shadow copy when running a backup job. When volume shadow copy is disabled, open files will not be backed up. The Verify data after backup option configures the backup job to verify the data in the backup file; thus, answer A is incorrect. The Use hardware compression option configures the backup job to use hardware compression that some backup devices offer; thus, answer C is incorrect. The Restore security settings option applies to how a restoration is performed and specifies the restore security settings for each file and folder, which include permissions, auditing entries, and ownership information; thus, answer D is incorrect.

Question 49

Answers A and D are correct. Windows Server 2003 DNS supports two types of zone transfers: full zone transfers and incremental zone transfers. Full zone transfers are commonly abbreviated as AXFR, and incremental zone transfers are commonly referred to as IXFR. There is no full or partial zone transfer method, so answers B and C are incorrect.

Question 50

Answer B is correct. All that is necessary to read the email and verify that it came from you is your public key, which can be safely transferred to anyone desired. Your private key should never be given out. If your colleague installed the third-party CA's root certificate, your colleague would thus be able to verify the entire certificate chain for your digital certificate.

Question 51

Answer A is correct. The key to this question is the permission to execute a managed application. Permissions for managed applications are set through the Security tab in the package's properties in the Software Installation extension. The Deployment tab is used to configure other package properties, such as whether it is assigned or published; thus, answer B is incorrect. Active Directory Users and Computers is used to control security group membership as a whole rather than setting permissions on a particular resource; thus, answers C and D are incorrect.

Question 52

Answer A is correct. The name of this file is NTDS.DIT. It exists on every domain controller. Answers B, C, and D are incorrect because these files do not exist.

Question 53

Answers B and D are correct. Of the given options, the most likely problems are that the remote computer is not configured to allow you to take remote control or that the Novice is not allowing you to take control. Your local computer is not an issue in the case of not being able to take remote control of an existing Remote Assistance session; thus, answer A is incorrect. Because you already have an existing Remote Assistance connection, the firewall is not the source of your problem; thus, answer C is incorrect.

Question 54

Answer C is correct. Although, in a sense, all of the answers will produce some or all of the results that Hannah needs, only by using Group Policy can Hannah quickly, accurately, and efficiently apply the securews.inf template to all of the computers (member servers and workstations alike) located in the Engineering OU. To apply these settings to the computers located in the Engineering OU, Hannah will need to import the securews.inf template into an existing or new Group Policy Object.

Question 55

Answer B is correct. The only solution that meets the goals of creating three backups as quickly as possible and one backup that backs up all data is answer B; thus, answers A, C, and D are incorrect. Answers C and D have you performing lengthy copy and normal backups during the day, which means that they will not be done as quickly as possible. Answer A uses differential backups during the day, which are still not completed as quickly as incremental backups are.

Question 56

Answer B is correct. In this scenario, because the data has been encrypted with your public key, you would need access to your private key, which should not be a problem. Your private key can be used to decrypt data that has been encrypted using your public key. You cannot decrypt an item using a public key. In addition, because the item was encrypted using your public key, you will not need to have the other party's public or private key.

Question 57

Answer A is correct. Two settings affect inheritance. The first is Block Inheritance. This would prevent policies from being inherited from a parent OU. However, this can be overridden by the No Override setting. Answer B is incorrect because setting No Override at the child level would not prevent inheritance coming from above. Answer C is incorrect because, as described, inheritance can be altered between parent and child OUs. Answer D is incorrect because you cannot set No Override at the local level.

Question 58

Answer D is correct. Selecting the Authenticate As Computer When Computer Information Is Available forces the computer to authenticate itself to the network as soon as the wireless network connection is made. If the computer cannot authenticate, no authentication is performed. The Authenticate As Guest When User or Computer Information Is Unavailable option allows the computer to authenticate using the Guest account if it cannot authenticate using its computer account; thus, answer B is incorrect. The Transmit Per IEEE 802.1x option is used to configure how the EAPOL-start message is sent and has nothing to do with WEP; thus, answer B is incorrect. The Data Encryption (WEP Enabled) option specifies that WEP is to be used to encrypt data placed on the WLAN; thus, answer C is incorrect.

Question 59

Answer B is correct. The most likely problem is that the user's account is now locked out, due to three unsuccessful logon attempts. You will need to unlock the user account from the Account tab of the Properties dialog box for the user account in question. Answer A is incorrect because the user tried unsuccessfully at least three times to log on to her account, which resulted in it becoming locked out. Answers C and D would not prevent a user from logging on to the network and are thus incorrect.

Question 60

Answer B is correct. The first domain that is created in the forest becomes the forest root for that forest. Even though you have created only one domain (the first domain), it is a forest and, thus, the forest root for that forest. Answer A is incorrect because there is no such thing as a forest roof. Answer C is incorrect because a parent domain refers to a domain that has child domains under it, not to the name of the first domain in the forest that is created. Answer D is incorrect because a child domain refers to domains located under a parent domain, not to the name of the first domain in the forest that is created.

Practice Exam #2

Question 1

You are a network administrator preparing for a rollout of Windows Server 2003. In which software-deployment phase would you create and/or modify GPOs?

❍ A. Preparation

❍ B. Distribution

❍ C. Targeting

❍ D. Pilot

❍ E. Installation

Question 2

Rick is the network administrator for Mr. Whippy's Ice Cream. Rick has recently installed and configured an enterprise root CA for his Windows Server 2003 network on a server named CHOCOLATE. He performed no configuration for this new CA other than what was required during the installation process. When he tries to access the Web Enrollment Web pages at **http://CHOCOLATE/certsrv**, he receives a 404 error from Internet Explorer. What is the most likely cause of this problem?

❍ A. Rick forgot to start the Certificate Services service following the completion of the installation process.

❍ B. Rick has not installed Terminal Services on his CA.

❍ C. Rick has not installed IIS on his CA.

❍ D. Rick did not create a new CNAME record for the CA.

Question 3

Austin is the network administrator for the Eternal Light Group, LLC. He is attempting to perform an analysis on a computer using Security Configuration and Analysis. Given the following steps, what is the correct order of performance?

1. Select the security template to be used in the analysis.
2. Right-click on Security Configuration and Analysis, and select Analyze Computer Now.
3. Select the log file to be used in the analysis.
4. Right-click on Security Configuration and Analysis, and select Open database.
5. Right-click on Security Configuration and Analysis, and select Configure Computer Now.
6. Select the database to be used in the analysis.

❍ A. 2, 1, 3, 4, 6, 5

❍ B. 4, 1, 6, 2, 5, 3

❍ C. 4, 6, 1, 3, 2

❍ D. 2, 6, 1, 3, 4

Question 4

You are the network administrator for Jeff's Jeep Tours, an Australian tour company. One of the users in one of your remote locations sent you an email request for Remote Assistance, but it expired before you could assist the user with her problem. You have called the user on the telephone and informed her of the problem with the expired request. You need to have this request answered. What is the easiest way to go about this?

❍ A. Have the user create a new request and send it to you.

❍ B. Have the user extend the lifetime of the initial request.

❍ C. Have the user delete the expired request, causing it to be re-created.

❍ D. Have the user resend the expired request to you.

Question 5

You are the network administrator for Jake's Jumps, a skydiving company. You need to promote a newly installed Windows Server 2003 member server to act as a domain controller. What command-line command will you need to issue to start the promotion process?

❍ A. **dcupgrade**

❍ B. **dcupdate**

❍ C. **dcpromo**

❍ D. **dcpromote**

Question 6

You are preparing to implement a network load balancing solution for your organization's e-commerce Web site. You will be load-balancing six Windows Server 2003 computers running IIS on the front end, with 4 Windows Server 2003 computers in a cluster on the back end providing access to an SQL Server 2000 database. Your e-commerce application makes heavy use of cookies to maintain user session state information during the active connection. What type of filtering mode should you configure to ensure that clients receive the best overall possible service during their connection period?

❍ A. Single Host

❍ B. Disable Port Range

❍ C. Multiple Host

❍ D. Allow Port Range

Question 7

You are the network administrator for Hank's Heroes, a sports card collectibles shop. This morning, one of your users called you to inform you that his user account appears to be locked out and that he cannot log on to the network. Where can you look to see if this user account actually is locked out?

❍ A. The General tab of the user account Properties dialog box

❍ B. The Account tab of the user account Properties dialog box

❍ C. The Saved Queries node of the Active Directory Users and Computer console

❍ D. The Sessions tab of the user account Properties dialog box

Question 8

You are the network administrator for Stan's Tans, a tanning salon and health spa company. One of your users in an office across town has telephoned you, informing you that she needs assistance with the installation of Microsoft Word on her Windows XP Professional computer. You need to correct the problem for the user by taking control of her computer remotely. What methods are available to you to help her with her problem? (Select two.)

❍ A. Remote Desktop for Administration

❍ B. Windows Messenger

❍ C. Emergency Management Services

❍ D. Remote Assistance

❍ E. Web Interface for Remote Administration

Question 9

Hannah is the network administrator for the Wallops Island Rocket Company, Inc. Her network is required to maintain the highest level of security possible without adversely affecting the required operations of its users. For the past 10 weeks, six visiting rocket scientists have been working at her facility on a joint project with another company. Hannah issued each of these users a secure laptop, including a smart card that allows them to securely access and update the rocket systems data stored in SQL databases. These six visiting users have completed their work and have now left the facility, leaving behind their laptop computers and smart cards, as required. Hannah has just completed sanitizing their laptop computers. What should she do next?

❍ A. Delete the data created by the scientists during their stay.

❍ B. Degauss the hard drives installed in the laptop computers the scientists were using.

❍ C. Perform a background check with the FBI, NSA, and NCIS on the scientists.

❍ D. Revoke the smart card certificates that the scientists were issued and immediately publish the CRL to all configured CDPs.

Question 10

Younes is a system administrator for a large company. One of his users, Eric, must have an application targeted at him. Eric is the manager of Finance and belongs to a Finance security group and OU. After he has tested the application, he will want it targeted to his employees. Younes wants to minimize the amount of work he must do now and when the testing is complete. What is the most logical place to target this GPO?

❍ A. Site

❍ B. Domain

❍ C. OU

❍ D. Finance security group

Question 11

You are the network administrator for Herb's Happenings, a public relations firm. You are preparing to create a new IPSec policy that will be used to secure all internal network traffic. What available user authentication methods does IPSec in Windows Server 2003 offer? (Select three.)

❑ A. NTLM v2

❑ B. Kerberos v5

❑ C. Encrypting File System (EFS)

❑ D. Digital certificate

❑ E. Shared secret

❑ F. WEP

Question 12

A DNS resolver performs a recursive query against its local DNS server, asking it to provide the IP address for the host **www.quepublishing.com**. Assuming that the local DNS server is not authoritative for the **quepublishing.com** domain, does not have the answer in its local cache, and is configured for forwarding, what will happen next?

❍ A. The local name server will return an error to the DNS resolver stating that it could not resolve the name as requested.

❍ B. A root name server will make an iterative query to determine the IP address of the **quepublishing.com** domain.

❍ C. A root name server will make an iterative query to determine the IP address of the host **www.quepublishing.com**.

❍ D. The local DNS server will make an iterative query to a root name server to determine the IP address of the host **www.quepublishing.com**.

Question 13

You have just completed an analysis of a computer using the Security Configuration and Analysis snap-in. When you examine the results, you notice several items that have a red X icon next to them. What does this indicate?

❍ A. The items are not defined in the analysis database and were not examined on the computer.

❍ B. The items are defined in the analysis database and on the computer, and match the currently configured setting.

❍ C. The items are defined in the analysis database but not on the computer.

❍ D. The items are defined in the analysis database and on the computer, but do not match the current configured setting.

Question 14

Peter Chamberlain is a system administrator. He has been tasked with fine-tuning Group Policy in his organization. He decides that one of the things he will do is disable certain policies. If he wanted to disable unused portions of a GPO to improve processing times, which portions could he disable? (Select two.)

❑ A. Specific settings within a GPO

❑ B. Windows Settings subcontainer

❑ C. Computer Configuration container

❑ D. User Configuration container

❑ E. Software Settings subcontainer

❑ F. Administrative Templates subcontainer

Question 15

Chris is the network administrator for Island Dreams Tour and Rentals, Inc. She is preparing to implement a smart card solution for her Windows Server 2003 network. All of her client computers are Windows XP Professional desktops and laptops. Some users have both a desktop computer and a laptop computer. Chris wants users to be able to use a single smart card at all times, regardless of what computer they are logging into the network from. Chris does not want any user to be able to log on to the network without using the assigned smart card. What can she configure to enforce this requirement on her users?

❍ A. Do not allow smart card device redirection

❍ B. Interactive logon: Require smart card

❍ C. Account Lockout Policy

❍ D. Interactive logon: Smart card removal behavior

Question 16

You are the network administrator for Jake's Jumps, a skydiving company. You need to demote a newly installed Windows Server 2003 domain controller and reconfigure it to be used as a file server. What command-line command will you need to issue to start the demotion process?

❍ A. **dcremove**

❍ B. **dcuninstall**

❍ C. **dcpromo**

❍ D. **dcdemote**

Question 17

You are the network administrator for Jeff's Jeep Tours, an Australian tour company. You need to connect to the console session of one of your Windows Server 2003 computers to perform some configuration actions. What tools does Windows Server 2003 provide that allows you to do this? (Select two.)

❑ A. The Remote Desktops console

❑ B. The Web Interface for Remote Administration

❑ C. The Remote Desktop Connection Web utility

❑ D. The Remote Desktop Connection utility

Question 18

You are creating a disaster-recovery plan for your organization. You have decided to implement the grandfather, father, son media-rotation method to provide a good mix of backup history and backup media wear. Your plan has been approved by management and implemented for use on the network. After three months, you perform a comprehensive review of the disaster-recovery plan and determine that it does not provide an adequate solution in case the server cannot be started normally. What feature of Windows Server 2003 can you take advantage of to close this gap in your disaster-recovery plan?

❍ A. Volume shadow copy

❍ B. Automated System Recovery

❍ C. Automatic Updates

❍ D. Safe mode

Question 19

You are the network administrator for Hank's Heroes, a sports card collectibles shop. The human resources manager, Jim, has recently retired. Hank's has hired Judy to be Jim's replacement. You need Judy to have all of the same user rights and permissions that Jim had before he left. What is the easiest and most accurate way to accomplish this?

❍ A. Write down all settings configured for Jim's account. Delete Jim's account. Create a new account for Judy with the same settings.

❍ B. Rename Jim's account for Judy, and change the pertinent personal information items, as required.

❍ C. Create a new account for Judy. Add Judy's user account to the Enterprise Admins group until you determine what user rights and permissions she needs.

❍ D. Delete Jim's account. Ask Jim to tell you what user rights and permissions Judy needs. Create a new account for Judy, and assign her the user rights and permissions that Jim said that she needed.

Question 20

Christopher is preparing to use the **secedit.exe** command to analyze the security on one of his member servers. If Christopher is using the secure workstation security template as his comparison point and needs to ensure that the analysis database is clear before importing the security template, which of the following choices represents the correct command that Christopher should enter to perform the analysis?

- ❍ A. **secedit /analyze /overwrite /db c:\sectst\sectst1.sdb /cfg C:\WINDOWS\security\templates\securedc.inf /log c:\sectst\sectst1.log**
- ❍ B. **secedit /configure /db c:\sectst\sectst1.sdb /cfg C:\WINDOWS\security\templates\securedc.inf /log c:\sectst\sectst1.log**
- ❍ C. **secedit /analyze /db c:\sectst\sectst1.sdb /cfg C:\WINDOWS\security\templates\securews.inf /log c:\sectst\sectst1.log**
- ❍ D. **secedit /analyze /overwrite /db c:\sectst\sectst1.sdb /cfg C:\WINDOWS\security\templates\securews.inf /log c:\sectst\sectst1.log**

Question 21

What new feature of Windows Server 2003's DNS service allows you to configure multiple DNS forwarders depending on the destination domain?

- ❍ A. DNS forwarder
- ❍ B. DNS resolver
- ❍ C. Conditional forwarding
- ❍ D. Recursion

Question 22

Jim has recently completed a configuration change to one of his network's firewalls. Now multiple users have called the help desk complaining that they can no longer access external resources. What document did Jim most likely not have in hand that could well have prevented this problem?

- ❍ A. A Security Monitoring policy
- ❍ B. A Firewall Configuration policy
- ❍ C. A Change and Configuration Control policy
- ❍ D. A User Naming Convention policy

Question 23

You are the network administrator for Stan's Tans, a tanning salon and health spa company. One of your users in an office across town has telephoned you, informing you that she needs assistance with the installation of Microsoft Word on her Windows XP Professional computer. You need to correct the problem for the user by taking control of her computer remotely. When you attempt to answer a Remote Assistance request that she has emailed you, you cannot create the connection to her computer. The two offices are connected to each other over a WAN link, with a firewall at each end. What do you suspect is the most likely reason for your inability to create the Remote Assistance connection?

❍ A. Port 3389 is being blocked on one or both of the firewalls.

❍ B. The user's computer is not compatible with Remote Assistance.

❍ C. Your user account does not possess the required permissions to create the connection.

❍ D. Your WAN link is not compatible with the Remote Desktop Protocol.

Question 24

You have recently installed a new Windows Server 2003 computer and promoted it to a domain controller. When you examine the server's disk using Windows Explorer, you notice two 10MB files named RES1.LOG and RES2.LOG. What are these two files used for?

❍ A. They are the transaction logs that are used to temporarily hold transactions before they are written to the directory.

❍ B. They are the directory database files.

❍ C. They are the transaction checkpoint logs.

❍ D. They are reserved files that are used to hold transactions, in case the file system becomes low on disk space.

Question 25

You are the network administrator for Hank's Heroes, a sports card collectibles shop. Judy, the human resources manager, is going on maternity leave and will be away from the office for eight weeks. What should you do with her user account while she is gone?

- ❍ A. Do nothing; Windows Server 2003 automatically archives unused accounts.
- ❍ B. Disable Judy's user account until she gets back.
- ❍ C. Delete Judy's user account and create a new one when she returns to work.
- ❍ D. Change Judy's password and allow her assistant to use it while Judy is gone.

Question 26

You have just completed an analysis of one of your Windows Server 2003 computers using the **secedit.exe** command. How can you view the analysis output produced?

- ❍ A. By running the **secedit.exe /analyze** command with the **–verbose** switch
- ❍ B. By opening the log file in a text editor such as Notepad
- ❍ C. By using the Security Configuration and Analysis snap-in
- ❍ D. By running the **secedit.exe /analyze** command with the **/quiet** switch

Question 27

You are the network administrator for Bob's Boat Tours, a charter tour company. Your network consists of Windows Server 2003 servers and Windows XP Professional SP1 workstations. You use Software Installation to manage several applications for your network users. After removing a graphics application that your company no longer uses, you notice that shortcuts for the application still exist on some of your computers. You check all computers in your network and find that only a handful of computers have this problem. What could be causing this problem? (Select two.)

- ❍ A. The application is not compatible with Windows XP Professional.
- ❍ B. The application has been installed locally by the users.
- ❍ C. The shortcuts were copied or moved from their original location.
- ❍ D. You do not have the required privileges to manage Software Installation for the domain.

Question 28

You are the network administrator for Herb's Happenings, a public relations firm. You are preparing to create a new IPSec policy that will be used to secure all internal network traffic. What available data-encryption methods does IPSec in Windows Server 2003 offer? (Select two.)

- ❑ A. DES
- ❑ B. SHA1
- ❑ C. MD5
- ❑ D. AES
- ❑ E. 3DES

Question 29

You are the network administrator for Jake's Jumps, a skydiving company. You need to demote a newly installed Windows Server 2003 domain controller and reconfigure it for use as a file server. You have issued the command to demote the domain controller from the command line, but the demotion process will not complete. What command can you issue to force the demotion of the domain controller?

- ❍ A. **dcdemote /force**
- ❍ B. **dcpromo /force**
- ❍ C. **dcpromo /forceremoval**
- ❍ D. **dcdemote /forceremoval**

Question 30

You are the network administrator for Stan's Tans, a tanning salon and health spa company. You have several salespeople who travel around the country selling new franchises. Company policy requires users who access the internal corporate network over a remote access connection of any kind to use a smart card for authentication. All of your salespeople have smart cards with smart card certificates and smart card readers. One of your salespeople recently left the company and returned her portable computer and smart card reader, but not her smart card. What should you do to prevent this smart card from being used again?

- ❍ A. Delete the user's account.
- ❍ B. Revoke the user's smart card certificate.
- ❍ C. Format the user's portable computer.
- ❍ D. Disable the user's account.

Question 31

You are concerned about the security of your organization's private internal network. As such, you have configured the firewall to allow traffic on UDP and TCP ports 53 from only one IP address: 192.168.100.133. Your firewall creates dynamic response rules that will allow valid return traffic to the DNS server if it is a response to traffic originating from the DNS server. Your internal network contains four internal DNS servers, and your network users must be able to perform external name resolution, regardless of which DNS server their query is sent to. What should you to do ensure that only the DNS server with IP address 192.168.100.133 makes external DNS queries?

❍ A. Configure the other three DNS servers to forward name-resolution requests for all domains other than the internal namespace to the DNS server with the IP address 192.168.100.133. This server will then perform name resolution by using Internet DNS servers.

❍ B. Disable the other three DNS servers, to prevent them from providing name-resolution services.

❍ C. Configure all four internal DNS servers to be forwarders to an external DNS server.

❍ D. Configure all client computers to use the DNS server with IP address 192.168.100.133 as the primary DNS server.

Question 32

Kim has requested a new smart card certificate from one of her organization's CAs. Her request was not automatically approved and thus has been placed in a queue for administrative approval. You are the network administrator for the organization that Kim is employed by. What must you do to approve her smart card certificate request?

❍ A. You must log in using Kim's user account and supply the approval key for her certificate request.

❍ B. You must use the Active Directory Users and Computers console to locate the Pending Requests folder.

❍ C. You must use the Certificates console to locate the Pending Requests folder.

❍ D. You must use the Certification Authorities console to locate the Pending Requests folder.

Question 33

You are the network administrator for Herb's Happenings, a public relations firm. You are preparing to create a new IPSec policy that will be used to secure all internal network traffic. What available data-hashing methods does IPSec in Windows Server 2003 offer? (Select two.)

- ❑ A. DES
- ❑ B. SHA1
- ❑ C. MD5
- ❑ D. AES
- ❑ E. 3DES

Question 34

You are the network administrator for Bob's Boat Tours, a charter tour company. Your network consists of Windows Server 2003 servers and Windows XP Professional SP1 workstations. You use Software Installation to manage several applications for your network users. You have recently configured a new application to be installed on demand. When users attempt to install the application, they cannot and receive the error message "The feature you are trying to install cannot be found in the source directory." What is the most likely cause of this problem?

- ❍ A. Your DNS server is malfunctioning.
- ❍ B. Your users do not have the correct permissions to access the installation package.
- ❍ C. You do not have the correct permissions to access the installation package.
- ❍ D. The installation packet is corrupt.

Question 35

You are preparing to implement a network load balancing solution for your organization's e-commerce Web site. You will be load-balancing six Windows Server 2003 computers running IIS on the front end, with four Windows Server 2003 computers in a cluster on the back end providing access to an SQL Server 2000 database. Your e-commerce application makes heavy use of cookies to maintain user session state information during the active connection. What type of affinity should you configure to ensure that clients receive the best overall possible service during their connection period?

- ❍ A. None
- ❍ B. Class C
- ❍ C. Multiple
- ❍ D. Single

Question 36

You are the network administrator for Hank's Heroes, a sports card collectibles shop. You are configuring a new backup job to perform backups on your domain controller. You need to ensure that all critical parts of the domain controller are being backed up. What should you back up to accomplish this goal?

- ❍ A. The domain controller's Registry
- ❍ B. The Extensible Storage Engine (ESE)
- ❍ C. The domain controller's System State
- ❍ D. The Knowledge Consistency Checker (KCC)

Question 37

You are the network administrator for Stan's Tans, a tanning salon and health spa company. You need to be able to monitor when client workstations are restarted and shut down. What auditing option should you configure in the GPO that is linked to the Client Computer OU?

- ❍ A. Audit Account Management
- ❍ B. Audit Directory Service Access
- ❍ C. Audit Logon Events
- ❍ D. Audit Privilege Use
- ❍ E. Audit System Events
- ❍ F. Audit Account Logon Events

Question 38

You are the network administrator for Phil's Fillup Stations, Inc. You have been tasked by your CIO to increase the security of all member servers on your network. After examining the security settings configured in the secure and highly secure templates, you have decided that neither completely meets your requirements. You must get the required settings configured as efficiently and safely as possible. Which of the following available options represents the best choice for the required configuration of your servers? (Select two.)

- ❑ A. Create a new (empty) security template and configure the settings you need in it.
- ❑ B. Modify the securews.inf security template, changing and adding options as needed.
- ❑ C. Configure the member server settings from the Local Security Policy console on each member server.
- ❑ D. Configure the security settings you need directly into a Group Policy Object linked to the OU containing the member servers.

Question 39

You are the network administrator for Ken's Karts, a go-cart parts supplier. You have just installed a new Windows Server 2003 computer and promoted it to a domain controller. Your domain has Windows 2000 and Windows Server 2003 domain controllers in it. What is the highest domain functional level that you will be able to operate in?

- ❍ A. Windows 2000 native
- ❍ B. Windows 2000 mixed
- ❍ C. Windows Server 2003
- ❍ D. Windows Server 2003 mixed

Question 40

You are the network administrator for Herb's Happenings, a public relations firm. You have decided to use one of the preconfigured IPSec policies that comes in Windows Server 2003 to secure network traffic on your internal network. Which of the following policies are included with Windows Server 2003? (Select three.)

❑ A. Client (Respond Only)

❑ B. Client (Request Security)

❑ C. Client (Require Security)

❑ D. Server (Respond Only)

❑ E. Server (Request Security)

❑ F. Server (Require Security)

❑ G. Secure Server (Respond Only)

❑ H. Secure Server (Request Security)

❑ I. Secure Server (Require Security)

Question 41

DNS security uses what technology to provide authentication and data integrity?

❍ A. Kerberos v5

❍ B. NTFS

❍ C. EFS

❍ D. PKI

Question 42

When objects are deleted from Active Directory, they are actually tombstoned and marked to be deleted after a specific number of days. Why is this necessary?

❍ A. To reduce replication traffic

❍ B. To give all domain controllers time to become aware of the deletion

❍ C. To allow administrators a chance to undelete the object

❍ D. To allow for error checking of the Active Directory database

Question 43

You are creating a disaster-recovery plan for your organization. You have decided to implement the grandfather, father, son media-rotation method to provide a good mix of backup history and backup media wear. Your plan has been approved by management and implemented for use on the network. After three months, you perform a comprehensive review of the disaster-recovery plan and determine that it does not provide an adequate solution to protect critical operating system files. What additional information should you ensure is backed up when your backup files are created?

❍ A. SYSVOL directory

❍ B. C:\

❍ C. System State

❍ D. All files and folders, on all volumes, on all servers

Question 44

You are the network administrator for Stan's Tans, a tanning salon and health spa company. Your current network environment consists of Windows NT 4.0 BDCs, Windows 2000 domain controllers, Windows 98 clients, and Windows XP Professional clients. You are preparing to install several new Windows Server 2003 domain controllers in your network. What domain functional level will these new domain controllers operate in?

❍ A. Windows 2000 mixed mode

❍ B. Windows 2000 native mode

❍ C. Windows NT mixed mode

❍ D. Windows 2003 native mode

Question 45

You are the network administrator for Bob's Boat Tours, a charter tour company. Your network consists of Windows Server 2003 servers and Windows XP Professional SP1 workstations. You use Software Installation to manage several applications for your network users. This morning, one of your users called you to report that the database application she needs is no longer available on her computer. You have not made any changes to Active Directory in the last week, but your assistant administrator was tasked with ensuring that all user and computer accounts were in their proper OU, by department. No other users report having the same problem. What do you suspect the problem is?

❍ A. The installation package has been deleted from the installation share source.

❍ B. The computer account has been moved to its correct OU.

❍ C. The computer is infected with a virus.

❍ D. The computer needs to have the latest service pack installed.

Question 46

Kim has requested a new smart card certificate from one of her organization's CAs using the Web Enrollment pages. Her request was not automatically approved and thus has been placed in a queue for administrative approval. Kim wants to check on the status of her certificate request to see if the certificate has been approved for issuance. Where can Kim most easily find this information and install the certificate if her request has been approved?

❍ A. She can check the Active Directory Users and Computers console.

❍ B. She can check the Personal Store node in the Certificates console.

❍ C. She can log on to the CA Web Enrollment pages again.

❍ D. She can use the Certificate Request Wizard.

Question 47

Andrea is an administrator for Carmine's Circus Clowns, Inc. She has just recently been hired after the last administrator, oddly enough, ran off to join the circus. Carmine's network includes two domain controllers and three member servers providing file, print, and backup/restoration services. Carime, the president of the company, has instructed Andrea to implement a more secure configuration on all five Windows Server 2003 servers. Andrea has decided to use the secure templates but is not sure what the current configuration is on each server because the last administrator did not keep any records. What is the best way for Andrea to go about getting these servers configured with the secure templates?

❍ A. Andrea should apply the default security template from one of her member servers to all five servers and then apply the securews.inf and securedc.inf templates to them.

❍ B. Andrea should apply the default security template found on each computer to that specific computer. After doing this, she should apply the securews.inf template to her domain controllers and apply the securedc.inf template to her member servers.

❍ C. Andrea should reinstall Windows Server 2003 on all five servers and re-create the domain. After doing this, she should apply the securews.inf and securedc.inf templates to her servers.

❍ D. Andrea should apply the default security template found on each computer to that specific computer. After doing this, she should apply the securedc.inf template to her domain controllers and apply the securews.inf template to her member servers.

Question 48

You are the network administrator for Allison's Alligators, an alligator-wrestling farm in Florida. You have just installed a new Windows Server 2003 computer and promoted it to a domain controller. Your domain has Windows 2000 and Windows Server 2003 domain controllers in it as well as Windows NT 4.0 BDCs. What is the highest domain functional level you will be able to operate in?

❍ A. Windows 2000 native

❍ B. Windows 2000 mixed

❍ C. Windows Server 2003

❍ D. Windows Server 2003 mixed

Question 49

You are the network administrator for Herb's Happenings, a public relations firm. You are preparing to create a new IPSec policy that will be used to secure all internal network traffic. You need to configure this new IPSec policy so that the computers at each end of the connection will communicate with each other and agree on the security parameters that are to be used. What filter action do you need to configure to ensure that this behavior occurs?

❍ A. Permit

❍ B. Block

❍ C. Negotiate

❍ D. Open

Question 50

Chris is the network administrator for Seashell Cruises, Ltd. The Seashell network has recently been upgraded from a mixed environment consisting of Windows 98 clients with Windows NT 4.0 Server and Windows 2000 Server servers. All clients now run Windows XP Professional, and all servers now run Windows Server 2003. Some computers were upgraded in place, while others were clean installations. Chris has recently been hired by Seashell Cruises and wants to establish the security level of her network using the least administrative effort. She has approximately 200 client workstations and 30 servers spread over 2 different locations in the same geographic area, all on the same IP subnet. What method can Chris use to most easily analyze all of her computers and find security problems with them?

❍ A. Use Windows Update locally on each computer to download and install required security updates

❍ B. Use Automatic Updates on each computer to download and install required security updates

❍ C. Install and configure SUS on one of her servers, and configure Automatic Updates on the clients to download and install approved, required security updates

❍ D. Use the MBSA utility to scan her entire subnet to quickly identify security problems and missing security updates on all computers

Question 51

You are the network administrator for Bob's Boat Tours, a charter tour company. Your network consists of Windows Server 2003 servers and Windows XP Professional SP1 workstations. You are creating several new Group Policy Objects to configure various security and desktop settings for your network clients. You need to ensure that you apply the GPOs in the correct order to achieve the desired final result. In what order are Group Policy Objects processed?

❍ A. OU, local, site, domain

❍ B. Domain, OU, local, site

❍ C. Site, domain, OU, local

❍ D. Local, site, domain, OU

Question 52

You are configuring your Windows Server 2003 DNS servers for increased security. You are concerned about the possibility of query responses containing resource records that are not pertinent to the original query. What option can you select that will prevent this from occurring by allowing the DNS server to not cache a resource record if it is not part of the exact DNS domain tree for which the original query was made?

❍ A. BIND Secondaries

❍ B. Enable Round Robin

❍ C. Enable Netmask Ordering

❍ D. Secure Cache Against Pollution

Question 53

You are the network administrator for Hank's Heroes, a sports card collectibles shop. You accidentally deleted a user account belonging to your CEO. You have performed a restoration of the account from last night's backup files. The next day, your CEO reports that he cannot log on to the network. You look for his account in Active Directory Users and Computers and cannot locate it. What is the most likely problem?

❍ A. You performed a nonauthoritative restore operation.

❍ B. You performed an authoritative restore operation.

❍ C. You performed the restore without selecting the Authoritative option in the Windows Backup Utility.

❍ D. You performed the restore without having Backup Operator credentials.

Question 54

You are the network administrator for Stan's Tans, a tanning salon and health spa company. You have just completed changing several user-specific items in the GPO that is linked to your Sales OU. You want this policy to be enforced immediately upon all clients. What command can you issue to cause Group Policy to replicate immediately?

❍ A. **gpupdate /target:user**

❍ B. **secedit /configure**

❍ C. **gpupdate /target:computer**

❍ D. **secedit /analyze**

Question 55

You are the network administrator for Allison's Alligators, an alligator-wrestling farm in Florida. You have just installed a new Windows Server 2003 computer and promoted it to a domain controller. Your domain has Windows 2000 and Windows Server 2003 domain controllers in it as well as Windows NT 4.0 BDCs. You need to enable your Windows NT 4.0 to access resources in your Active Directory domain. What type of trust do you need to create?

❍ A. Realm trust

❍ B. Forest trust

❍ C. Shortcut trust

❍ D. External trust

Question 56

You are preparing to implement a network load balancing solution for your organization's e-commerce Web site. You will be load-balancing six Windows Server 2003 computers running IIS on the front end, with four Windows Server 2003 computers in a cluster on the back end providing access to an SQL Server 2000 database. You are using the unicast cluster operation mode. Which of the following statements are true about the load-balancing adapters installed in your network load-balancing servers? (Select two.)

❑ A. All cluster nodes share an identical unicast MAC address.

❑ B. All cluster nodes retain their original MAC address. In addition, the load-balancing adapters are assigned an additional multicast MAC address.

❑ C. If a network load-balancing server is using the unicast operational mode and has only one network adapter installed, it will be unable to communicate with the other nodes in the network load-balancing cluster.

❍ D. Inbound client requests are sent to all cluster nodes using the multicast MAC address.

Question 57

You are in the process of creating a customized security solution for your network's computers. You want to edit the securedc.inf template in a text editor. Where can you find the preconfigured security templates?

❍ A. %systemroot%\system32\security

❍ B. %systemroot%\security\templates

❍ C. WINNT\security\templates

❍ D. %systemroot%\system32\templates

Question 58

You are the network administrator for Bob's Boat Tours, a charter tour company. Your network consists of Windows Server 2003 servers and Windows XP Professional SP1 workstations. You want to ensure that polices applied at lower levels do not override policies applied at higher levels. What option do you need to select?

❍ A. Block Policy Inheritance

❍ B. No Override

❍ C. Disabled

❍ D. Apply Group Policy

Question 59

Andrea is the network administrator of the Beachside Entertainment Group, Inc., network. Beachside owns and operates several miniature golf centers in resort destinations. Andrea is preparing to implement a smart card solution for use by all employees of Beachside Entertainment because their computers often lack in other forms of security, such as physical security. Beachside has locations in 5 eastern states, with a total of 17 offices, including the corporate offices in Chincoteague, Virginia. Andrea has decided to use self-enrollment for her smart card users. Which of the following items must Andrea take into consideration for her self-enrollment plan to work effectively and securely? (Select two.)

❑ A. Andrea must ensure that all required users get a blank smart card.

❑ B. Andrea should configure her CAs not to automatically issue smart card user certificates when requested.

❑ C. Andrea must ensure that all required users get a ready-to-use smart card.

❑ D. Andrea must ensure that only trusted users are tasked with the job of performing the smart card certificate enrollments.

❑ E. Andrea must ensure that she has selected enough enrollment agents to perform the smart card enrollments for users without getting overburdened.

❑ F. Andrea should configure her CAs to automatically issue smart card user certificates when requested, to ensure that all users get their smart cards operating as quickly as possible.

Question 60

You are preparing to implement a network load balancing solution for your organization's e-commerce Web site. You will be load-balancing six Windows Server 2003 computers running IIS on the front end, with four Windows Server 2003 computers in a cluster on the back end providing access to an SQL Server 2000 database. You are using the unicast cluster operation mode. How many total IP addresses will you need to assign for the network load-balancing portion of the solution?

❍ A. 1

❍ B. 6

❍ C. 7

❍ D. 12

Answer Key to Practice Exam #2

Answer Key

1. C
2. C
3. C
4. D
5. C
6. C
7. B
8. A, D
9. D
10. C
11. B, D, E
12. D
13. D
14. C, D
15. B
16. C
17. A, D
18. B
19. B
20. D
21. C
22. C
23. A
24. D
25. B
26. C
27. B, C
28. A, E
29. C
30. B
31. A
32. D
33. B, C
34. B
35. D
36. C
37. E
38. A, B
39. A
40. A, E, I
41. D
42. B
43. C
44. A
45. B
46. C
47. D
48. B
49. C
50. D
51. D
52. D
53. A
54. A
55. D
56. A, C
57. B
58. B
59. A, B
60. C

Question 1

Answer C is correct. The targeting phase is used to create and/or modify Group Policy Objects (GPOs) that will be the target of the software package. In the preparation phase, you determine who the target will be, but you do not actually create GPOs at that point; thus, answer A is incorrect. The distribution phase involves setting up the source files on distribution points that you have created; thus, answer B is incorrect. The pilot phase involves testing the software on a limited number of users, and the installation phase is the actual deployment; thus, answers D and E are incorrect.

Question 2

Answer C is correct. To use the Certificate Services Web Enrollment pages, Rick must ensure that IIS is installed and configured properly to allow Active Server Pages (ASP) to function properly. For best results, Rick should have installed Internet Information Server (IIS) before installing the Certificate Authority (CA). Answer A is incorrect because Certificate Services starts automatically after the installation. Answer B is incorrect because Terminal Services is not required. Answer D is incorrect because no special modification of DNS is required.

Question 3

Answer C is correct. The correct steps to be used to perform an analysis of a computer with Security Configuration and Analysis are as follows: Select Open Database, select the database, select the security template, select Analyze Computer, and select the log file. Only answer C presents the correct order of operations; answers A, B, and D are all incorrect.

Question 4

Answer D is correct. The easiest way to allow an expired request to be answered is to re-send it. This allows for some of the information that was originally entered to be saved from the expired request. Creating a new request is not the easiest way to solve this problem; thus, answer A is incorrect. After a request has expired, it can be only deleted or re-sent; thus, answer B is incorrect. Deleting the request does not cause it to be automatically re-created; thus, answer C is incorrect.

Question 5

Answer C is correct. The command to promote a member controller to a domain controller is `dcpromo`. Answers A, B, and D are all incorrect because these commands do not exist.

Question 6

Answer C is correct. By using the multiple host filtering mode, you allow all cluster nodes to handle client traffic. When the multiple host filtering mode is configured, you can also configure a client affinity setting. Client affinity determines how cluster nodes will handle repeated client requests during the same session. Single-host filtering does not allow for client affinity, so answer A is incorrect. Port rules are not related to client affinity, so answers B and D are incorrect.

Question 7

Answer B is correct. The Account tab of the user account Properties dialog box alerts you to the account being locked out if the Account Is Locked Out option is selected. You cannot determine the account lockout status from the General or Sessions tabs of the user account Properties dialog box; thus, answers A and D are incorrect. The Saved Queries node of Active Directory Users and Computers also does not provide information about locked-out user accounts; thus, answer C is incorrect.

Question 8

Answers A and D are correct. Windows XP Professional and Windows Server 2003 computers support Remote Desktop for Administration (Remote Desktop) and Remote Assistance. Both Remote Desktop and Remote Assistance allow the Expert to take remote control of the Novice's computer and manage it remotely. Windows Messenger can be used to send Remote Assistance requests, but it cannot be used to actually perform any remote management; thus, answer B is incorrect. Emergency Management Services and the Web Interface for Remote Administration are not designed to be used to remotely administer a client computer; thus, answers C and E are incorrect.

Question 9

Answer D is correct. Hannah should revoke the smart card certificates and immediately publish the Certificate Revocation List (CRL) next. After this, she should also delete any unused user accounts that might have been created for the scientists' use during their visit to Hannah's facility. Answer A is incorrect because deleting the scientists' data will not help her and might actually hurt the company. Answer B is incorrect because degaussing the hard drives is not required. Answer C is incorrect because a background check would typically be done beforehand, not afterward.

Question 10

Answer C is correct. The most logical place to target is an OU. This will allow Younes to target Eric for testing and then target everyone else in the Finance group when the testing is complete. Answer A is incorrect because this would target everyone in the same site as Eric, which likely includes users outside Finance. This would work for testing but would make it difficult to roll out to other Finance members later. Answer B is incorrect for similar reasons, but, in this case, everyone in the domain would be targeted. Answer D is incorrect because you cannot explicitly target security groups.

Question 11

Answers B, D, and E are correct. The Windows Server 2003 IPSec implementation can use Kerberos v5, digital certificates, or shared secrets to perform user authentication. NT LAN Manager (NTLM) v2 is used for network authentication with Windows 2000 and Windows Server 2003; thus, answer A is incorrect. Encrypting File System (EFS) is used to encrypt files and folders to add extra security to them; thus, answer C is incorrect. Wired Equivalent Privacy (WEP) is used as both an encryption and authentication method on wireless LANs (WLANs); thus, answer F is incorrect.

Question 12

Answer D is correct. If the local DNS server is not authoritative for the requested domain and does not have the answer in its local cache, it performs an iterative query to a root name server if it is configured as a forwarder. The root name server will likely not know the IP address of the host but will be capable of providing the local DNS server with the IP address of another DNS server that is authoritative for the quepublishing.com domain. This DNS server will then be capable of providing the requested name-resolution service for the local DNS server. Answer A is incorrect because the DNS server is configured as a forwarder; it will forward the requests it cannot itself resolve. Answer B is incorrect because the DNS server does not know the IP address to make a query to the `quepublishing.com` domain. Answer C is incorrect because the root DNS server will not do anything until it is asked to do so by another DNS server.

Question 13

Answer D is correct. A red circle with an X icon next to an item in the Security Configuration and Analysis results indicates that the item is present in both the database and the computer, but does not match the current configured setting; thus, answers A, B, and C are all incorrect.

Question 14

Answers C and D are correct. Windows Server 2003 Server Group Policy allows an administrator to disable the Computer Configuration and User Configuration containers from being processed. If either container is disabled, the Windows Settings, Software Settings, and Administrative Templates subcontainers for that container are disabled along with it. You cannot filter specific settings within a GPO; thus, answers A, B, E, and F are incorrect.

Question 15

Answer B is correct. By configuring the Interactive Logon: Require Smart Card Group Policy setting, Chris can ensure that all of her users are required to log on to the network using their smart cards. Smart cards are used to provide the highest level of user authentication available in Windows Server 2003 networks. A user provides a password or PIN to access the digital certificate on the smart card, thus protecting the user's identity from rogue applications and attackers. Through the use of on-card digital signatures, smart cards can ensure that a user's private key is never exposed. Perhaps the single best feature of smart cards is that, unlike software-based private keys, they can be moved at will from one computer to another, with ease. Smart cards can be prevented from being used to access the network after a pre-configured number of incorrect login attempts, protecting them further from dictionary attacks, a type of password-guessing attack in which a password is guessed from a list, or dictionary, of common words and phrases.

Question 16

Answer C is correct. The command to demote a domain controller to a member server is `dcpromo`. Answers A, B, and D do not exist and therefore are incorrect.

Question 17

Answers A and D are correct. The Remote Desktops console and the Remote Desktop Connection utility with the `/console` switch can be used to connect to the console session. The Web Interface for Remote Administration and the Remote Desktop Web utility do not provide access to the console session on a remote server; thus, answers B and C are incorrect.

Question 18

Answer B is correct. The Automated System Restore (ASR) feature is new in Windows Server 2003 and provides a means to restore a server in case all other methods fail or are not available for use. You should consider ASR as a last option and use it only after trying Safe mode, Recovery Console, and the Last Known Good Configuration (LKGC). The ASR set consists of a start-up floppy disk and a standard Windows Backup file. In addition to these two items, you will require your original Windows Server 2003 installation CD-ROM and any mass-storage device drivers (on floppy disk) to perform an ASR recovery action.

Question 19

Answer B is correct. The easiest and most accurate way to ensure that a new employee has the exact same user rights and permissions as a former employee is to either rename the existing user account (and change all pertinent information) or copy the existing user account to a new user account. Manually configuring all of the required user rights and permissions on a new account is a much more difficult task and is likely to yield errors; thus, answers A and D are incorrect. Judy's user account should not be a member of the Enterprise Admins group unless Judy will be performing administrative tasks. As the HR manager, it is unlikely that Judy will be administering the network; thus, answer C is incorrect.

Question 20

Answer D is correct. Only option D meets all of the specified requirements that Christopher has for performing this analysis: He must use the secure template for a member server (securews.inf), and he must ensure that the database is cleared before importing the security template. Option C appears to meet these requirements but does not provide for clearing the database before importing the security template. Answers A and B are incorrect because they show the secure domain controller security template in use.

Question 21

Answer C is correct. A new feature in Windows Server 2003, conditional forwarding, enables you to configure a DNS forwarder with multiple forwarding IP addresses. As an example, you could have all name-resolution requests for the `bigcorp.com` domain sent to one IP address and all other name requests sent to a second, completely different IP address. This allows you to provide for both internal and external name resolution from within the internal network. Forwarding (in general), resolvers, and recursion are not new features of Windows DNS, so answers A, B, and D are incorrect.

Question 22

Answer C is correct. If Jim had used a change and configuration control policy, along with an approved change request, he most likely would not have created the problem he did, as a result of his configuration change on the firewall. Only a change and configuration control policy helps you implement changes to the network in a controlled manner with a documented backout plan; thus, answers A, B, and D are incorrect.

Question 23

Answer A is correct. Port 3389 is required for any Remote Desktop Protocol–based service to function properly. Of the available options, this is the most likely cause of your problems. The user's computer is running Windows XP Professional and has issued the Remote Assistance request; therefore, it is compatible with Remote Assistance. This makes answer B incorrect. You do not require special account permissions to answer a Remote Assistance request; thus, answer C is incorrect. The Remote Desktop Protocol runs on top of any standard TCP/IP connection; thus, answer D is incorrect.

Question 24

Answer D is correct. The RES1.LOG and RES2.LOG files are reserved files that are used to hold disk space for Active Directory when there is low disk space. The EDB.LOG file is the transaction log; thus, answer A is incorrect. The NTDS.DIT file is the directory database file; thus, answer B is incorrect. The EDB.CHK file is the transaction check file; thus, answer C is incorrect.

Question 25

Answer B is correct. When employees will be gone for a period of time but plan to return, you should consider disabling their user account. Having unused active user accounts on your network presents a great risk to the security of your network. You can easily disable Judy's user account until she returns, thus preventing it from becoming a security vulnerability. Windows Server 2003 does not automatically archive unused accounts; thus, answer A is incorrect. Deleting Judy's user account is not a good idea and will require you to re-create it later; thus, answer C is incorrect. Allowing Judy's assistant to use her account is not advisable because Judy most likely has certain user rights and permissions that the assistant does not need; thus, answer D is incorrect.

Question 26

Answer C is correct. Although `secedit.exe` allows you to analyze and configure computers throughout the network from the command line, you cannot easily view the analysis reports created from it, except through Security

Configuration and Analysis. Although it is possible to view the log file in a text editor such as Notepad, it is not easy to accurately determine the results of the analysis, so answer B is incorrect. There is no verbose switch for `secedit`, so answer A is incorrect. The `quiet` switch suppresses output, so answer D is incorrect.

Question 27

Answers B and C are correct. The most likely reason for this problem is that the application has been installed locally by the users, thus creating shortcuts from that installation, or that the users have either copied or moved the shortcuts from their original locations. If the application were not compatible with Windows XP Professional, you would most likely not have been able to install it or use it; thus, answer A is incorrect. Your account does have required privileges to maintain Software Installation, or you would have been denied permission to make the changes you have made; thus, answer D is incorrect.

Question 28

Answers A and E are correct. The Windows Server 2003 IPSec implementation uses Data Encryption Standard (DES) and 3DES for data encryption. The Windows Server 2003 IPSec implementation uses SHA1 and MD5 for data hashing; thus, answers B and C are incorrect. Advanced Encryption Standard (AES) is not used in IPSec; thus, answer D is incorrect.

Question 29

Answer C is correct. The `dcpromo /forceremoval` command can be used to force the demotion and removal of a domain controller if the demotion process does not successfully occur using the `dcpromo` command alone. Answers A, B, and D are all incorrect because these commands do not exist.

Question 30

Answer B is correct. Although you will end up deleting the user's account and probably formatting the user's computer, the first and most important thing you must do to prevent use of the smart card again is to revoke the smart card certificate and immediately publish the CRL to all Certificate Authorities on your network; thus, answers A and C are incorrect. Disabling the user's account is not a required action; thus, answer D is incorrect.

Question 31

Answer A is correct. By configuring the other three internal DNS servers to forward name-resolution queries to the DNS server with the IP address 192.168.100.133, only that one specific DNS server will be making external DNS queries.

Question 32

Answer D is correct. Queued certificates are located in the Pending Requests folder of the Certification Authorities console. You can find and issue this certificate for Kim from this location. Answer A is incorrect because you do not need to use a user's account to approve the certificate request. Answer B is incorrect because certificates are not managed through Active Directory Users and Computers. Answer C is incorrect because certificate requests cannot be managed using the Certificates console.

Question 33

Answers B and C are correct. The Windows Server 2003 IPSec implementation uses SHA1 and MD5 for data hashing. The Windows Server 2003 IPSec implementation uses DES and 3DES for data encryption; thus, answers A and E are incorrect. Advanced Encryption Standard (AES) is not used in IPSec; thus, answer D is incorrect.

Question 34

Answer B is correct. The most likely cause of this problem is that you did not configure the correct permissions on the source share where the installation package is located. A malfunctioning DNS server will not yield this error message; thus, answer A is incorrect. Your permissions to access the installation package are not at issue; thus, answer C is incorrect. When the installation package is corrupt, users typically get the following error: "Active Directory will not allow the package to be deployed." Thus, answer D is incorrect.

Question 35

Answer D is correct. By configuring the Single Affinity setting, you maintain all client requests on the same node for the duration of the session. Single affinity provides the best support for maintaining user state data and is often used when applications running on the cluster generate cookies. Answer A is incorrect because the None affinity setting is not appropriate for applications using cookies. Answer B is incorrect because the Class C affinity setting would likely cause one or more nodes in the cluster to become overloaded and would lead to failure. Answer C is incorrect because this is not a valid affinity option.

Question 36

Answer C is correct. By ensuring that the System State is backed up, you back up all critical files, including the Active Directory database files, the Registry, the SYSVOL folder, and other critical files. You cannot select these items individually; thus, answer A is incorrect. The Extensible Storage Engine (ESE) is the database engine that drives Active Directory; thus, answer B is incorrect. The Knowledge Consistency Checker (KCC) is a service of Active Directory that manages and maintains an accurate replication topology; thus, answer D is incorrect.

Question 37

Answer E is correct. The Audit Account Management option configures auditing to occur for each event of account management on a computer; thus, answer A is incorrect. The Audit Object Access option configures auditing to occur upon each user access of an object, such as a file, folder, printer, or Registry key that has its own system Access Control List (SACL) configured. Thus, Answer B is incorrect. When both the Audit Logon Events and Audit Account Logon Events options are configured, logons and logoffs that use a domain account generate logon or logoff audit events on the local computer as well as the domain controller; thus, answers C and F are incorrect. The Audit Privilege Use option configures auditing to occur every time a user exercises a user right; thus, answer E is incorrect.

Question 38

Answers A and B are correct. Although all four of these options can be used to achieve the desired results, the creation of a new security template and the modification of an existing security template represent the best options available. You can opt to configure the settings using the Local Security Policy console, but this requires you to ensure that you make the same changes on all member servers. Thus, answer C is incorrect. You could also make the changes directly in Group Policy, but this does not give you the opportunity to test your configuration in a lab environment, making it more difficult to locate possible problems before they have a chance to occur on the production network. Thus, answer D is incorrect.

Question 39

Answer A is correct. The highest domain functional level that you can use when Windows 2000 domain controllers exist in the network is Windows 2000 native mode. Windows 2000 mixed mode is required to be used when Windows NT 4.0 BDCs are still in use; thus, answer B is incorrect. Windows Server 2003 mode can be used when only Windows Server 2003 domain controllers are in the network; thus, answer C is incorrect. Windows Server 2003 mixed mode does not exist; thus, answer D is incorrect.

Question 40

Answers A, E, and I are correct. The three preconfigured IPSec policies in Windows Server 2003 are Client (Respond Only), Server (Request Security), and Secure Server (Require Security). Answers B, C, D, F, G, and H are incorrect because there are only three preconfigured IPSec policies.

Question 41

Answer D is correct. DNSSEC uses a PKI-based system in which digital signatures are used to authenticate the zone data. These digital signatures are then encrypted with the private key. The public key, made available through the KEY resource record, and the signature allow a DNS resolver to successfully authenticate the SIG resource record.

Question 42

Answer B is correct. In the multimaster model that Active Directory uses, it is impossible for all domain controllers to always know what the others are doing. When deleting objects, the object must first be tombstoned, thus allowing this change to replicate to all other domain controllers. After the specified time (60 days, by default), all domain controllers will permanently delete this object. This process is known as garbage collection. Garbage collection is not intended to reduce replication traffic—only to keep domain controllers consistent. Thus, answer A is incorrect. After an object is deleted from Active Directory, it must be restored. There is no undelete function; thus, answer C is incorrect. Garbage collection does not perform error checking on the Active Directory database; thus, answer D is incorrect.

Question 43

Answer C is correct. You can select to have the System State information backed up to provide recovery protection for all critical operating system files, including those that are required to properly start and support the operating system. Answer A is incorrect because it does provide a complete backup of all critical information. Answer B is incorrect because this will not cause the System State data to be backed up. Answer D is incorrect because, again, this will not cause the System State data to be backed up. The System State consists of the following items:

- Registry
- COM+ class registration database
- Critical boot and system files
- System files that are protected by Windows File Protection
- Certificate Services database, if the server is a Certificate Authority
- Active Directory directory service, if the server is a domain controller
- SYSVOL directory, if the server is a domain controller
- Cluster service information, if the server is a member of a cluster
- IIS metadirectory, if IIS is installed on the server

Question 44

Answer A is correct. Windows 2000 mixed mode is required when Windows NT 4.0 BDCs are still in use; thus, answers B, C and D are incorrect. Windows 2000 native mode allows for only Windows 2000 and Windows Server 2003 domain controllers, although with reduced functionality; thus, answer B is incorrect. Windows Server 2003 mode allows for only Windows Server 2003 domain controllers; thus, answer D is incorrect. There is no Windows NT mixed mode, so answer C is incorrect.

Question 45

Answer B is correct. The most likely source of the problem is that, while your assistant was moving user and computer accounts to their proper OU, the user's computer account was moved. The new OU does not have the database application linked to it, so it was uninstalled when the computer account fell outside of the scope of management. Deletion of the installation package will not cause an application to be removed from a computer; thus, answer A is incorrect. A virus will likely cause numerous problems but is not the most likely cause of this problem; thus, answer C is incorrect. The status of the latest service pack has no bearing on software installation; thus, answer D is incorrect.

Question 46

Answer C is correct. The easiest way for Kim to check on the status of her requested certificate is to go back to the CA she requested it from via its Web Enrollment pages. If the certificate request has been approved, she will also be able to install the certificate from that location. The Active Directory Users and Computers console and Certificates console will not show pending certificate requests, so answers A and B are incorrect. Using the wizard all over again will not show the status of her requests, so answer D is incorrect.

Question 47

Answer D is correct. When you do not know what the current security configuration is, you should apply the default security template to the computer. Each computer has its own default security template that is created at the time of Windows Server 2003 installation for workstations and member servers and at the time of promotion for domain controllers. You should not apply the default security template from one computer to any other computer. After resetting the security configuration back to a known state by using the default template, the secure templates can be successfully applied to create the desired level of security. Recall that security templates are incremental and only build on the security configuration already configured—they do not reset the computer's security configuration back to the default settings before making any changes. The default security template should be applied only to the computer it originated from; thus, answer A is incorrect. Answer B has the security templates being applied to the wrong computers, so it is incorrect. Answer C stipulates more work than is required and thus is incorrect.

Question 48

Answer B is correct. Windows 2000 mixed mode is required when Windows NT 4.0 BDCs are still in use. Windows 2000 native mode can be used when you have only Windows 2000 and Windows Server 2003 domain controllers; thus, answer A is incorrect. Windows Server 2003 mode can be used when only Windows Server 2003 domain controllers are in the network; thus, answer C is incorrect. Windows Server 2003 mixed mode does not exist; thus, answer D is incorrect.

Question 49

Answer C is correct. If the Negotiate Security action is selected, both computers must agree on the security parameters to be used—meaning that they both must support at least one common set of security parameters from those in the list. The list entries are processed in order of preference, from top to bottom. The first security method shared by both computers is used. The Permit option passes the traffic without the requirement for security; thus, answer A is incorrect. This action is appropriate if you never want to secure traffic to which a rule applies. The Block action silently blocks all traffic from computers specified in the IP filter list; thus, answer B is incorrect. There is no Open Filter action; thus, answer C is incorrect.

Question 50

Answer D is correct. Chris wants to simply determine the security status of her network at this time, not install any updates. Using the MBSA utility is the best option because she can configure a single scan of all computers located on her subnet. After MBSA has completed the scan, she will be able to examine each computer's results separately from the others, quickly determining what areas of their security configuration are weak, in addition to determining what security updates are missing on each computer. Using Windows Update or Automatic Updates to download and install updates does not meet the requirements of the question, so answers A and B are incorrect. Using SUS also does not meet the requirements of the question, which were to simply analyze computers; that makes answer C incorrect.

Question 51

Answer D is correct. Group Policy Objects are applied in the following order: local, site, domain, OU. Thus, answers A, B, and C are incorrect. If more than one GPO exists at a specific level, the GPO that is listed first is applied first, and so forth.

Question 52

Answer D is correct. DNS servers typically cache any names in referral answers, thus expediting the speed of resolving subsequent DNS queries. However, when this feature is in use, the server can determine whether the referred name is polluting or insecure and can discard it. The server thus determines whether to cache the name offered in the referral, depending on whether it is part of the exact DNS domain tree for which the original name query was made.

Question 53

Answer A is correct. You have most likely performed a nonauthoritative restore. If a nonauthoritative restore was done, the restored account would be deleted during the next Active Directory replication cycle, so it would not be found when you looked for it. When an authoritative restore is performed, the property version number is incremented by 100,000 per day since the backup was performed. This makes the restored object's PVN much higher than the PVN on the object that is currently held by the domain controller's replication partners. The restored object is thus replicated to all domain controllers because it is assumed to be the most current version (highest PVN); that makes answer B incorrect. There is no option within Windows Backup to perform an authoritative restore; the restore is done from the command line in Directory Service Restore mode using the `NTDSUTIL` command. Thus, answer C is incorrect. You do not need Backup Operator credentials to perform an authoritative restoration; thus, answer D is incorrect.

Question 54

Answer A is correct. The `gpupdate /target:user` command is used to force Group Policy to refresh for user configuration portions of Group Policy. The `secedit` command is no longer used to refresh Group Policy in Windows Server 2003; thus, answers B and D are incorrect. The `gpupdate /target:computer` is used to force Group Policy to refresh to computer configuration portions of Group Policy; thus, answer C is incorrect.

Question 55

Answer D is correct. External trusts are used for connecting Windows 2003 domains to NT 4.0 domains and for connecting Windows 2003 domains from separate forests that are not connected by a forest trust. Realm trusts, in Windows 2003, enable you to create trust relationships between Windows 2003 and any outside realm that supports the Kerberos 5 protocol; thus, answer A is incorrect. Answer B is incorrect because forest trusts can be established only between Windows 2003 forests, which doesn't meet the needs of the question. Answer C is also incorrect because shortcut trusts are for connecting domains in different trees within the same Windows forest.

Question 56

Answers A and C are correct. Unicast mode should be used only when the network load-balancing servers have two network adapters installed. If only one network adapter is installed, the cluster nodes will not be capable of communicating with each other. When unicast mode is used, all cluster nodes are assigned an identical unicast MAC address that overwrites the MAC address of the load-balancing adapter. The network adapters have only one unicast MAC address when unicast is used, so answer B is incorrect. There is no multicast MAC address in unicast mode, so answer D is incorrect.

Question 57

Answer B is correct. You can locate the preconfigured security templates in the %systemroot%\security\templates folder. For a clean installation of Windows Server 2003 on volume C of a computer, this would be c:\windows\security\templates.

Question 58

Answer B is correct. The No Override option is applied to a GPO link and specifies that policies at lower levels are not to overwrite the policies that have been applied at a higher level. The Block Policy Inheritance option is configured on the Group Policy tab of an object, such as an OU or domain. Thus, answer A is incorrect. The Disabled option is also configured on a GPO link, but it disables the GPO without removing it; thus, answer C is incorrect. The Apply Group Policy permission is used to allow Group Policy to be applied to an object and is not related to preventing policy override; thus, answer D is incorrect.

Question 59

Answers A and B are correct. For Andrea to make her smart card self-enrollment solution work efficiently and securely, she must ensure that all required users get a blank smart card. To increase the security of the solution, Andrea should configure her CAs to not issue smart card user certificates automatically, but to instead place them in the Pending Requests folder, awaiting manual administrative approval. Andrea should also take time to properly educate her users in the procedures to be followed to request a smart card certificate and to enroll the approved certificate. In addition, all users will require training on the proper usage, storage and handling of their smart cards, to prevent loss or damage. The most efficient and secure method of implementing the required smart card solution, as discussed in Chapter 6, "Planning, Implementing, and Maintaining Security Infrastructure," is the one presented in answers A and B; thus, answers C, D, E, and F are all incorrect.

Question 60

Answer C is correct. You will need to assign a total of seven IP addresses for the network load-balancing portion of this solution. Each load-balancing network adapter in the front-end IIS servers requires a dedicated IP address, such as 10.0.25.11–10.0.25.16. In addition, the entire network load-balancing cluster is assigned a virtual IP (VIP) address, such as 10.0.25.10.

Additional Resources

Because *Exam Cram 2* books focus entirely on Microsoft Certification exam objectives, you can greatly broaden your knowledge of Windows Server 2003 by taking advantage of the plethora of technical material available. Books, Web sites, and even Windows Server 2003's built-in Help system offer a wealth of technical insight for network and system administrators. In the following pages, we've compiled a list of valuable resources that you can check out at your leisure.

Book Resources

- Bixler, Dave and Schmied, Will. *MCSE Training Guide: 70-291: Implementing, Managing, and Maintaining a Microsoft Windows Server 2003 Network Infrastructure*. Indianapolis, IN: Que Publishing, 2003.
- Boswell, William. *Inside Windows Server 2003*. Boston, MA: Addison-Wesley, 2003.
- Davies, Joseph and Lee, Thomas. *Microsoft Windows Server 2003 TCP/IP Protocols and Services Technical Reference*. Redmond, WA: Microsoft Press, 2003.
- Honeycutt, Jerry. *Introducing Microsoft Windows Server 2003*. Redmond, WA: Microsoft Press, 2003.
- Microsoft Corporation. *Microsoft Windows Server 2003 Resource Kit*. Redmond, WA: Microsoft Press, 2003.
- Microsoft Corporation. *Microsoft Windows Server 2003 Deployment Kit*. Redmond, WA: Microsoft Press, 2003.

- Mulcare, Mike and Reimer, Stan. *Active Directory for Microsoft Windows Server 2003 Technical Reference*. Redmond, WA: Microsoft Press, 2003.
- Russel, Charlie; Crawford, Sharon; and Gerend, Jason. *Microsoft Windows Server 2003 Administrator's Companion*. Redmond, WA: Microsoft Press, 2003.
- Schmied, Will and Shimonski, Robert. *MCSE 70-293 Training Guide: Planning and Maintaining a Windows Server 2003 Network Infrastructure*. Indianapolis, IN: Que Publishing, 2003.
- Stanek, William. *Windows Server 2003 Administrator's Pocket Consultant*. Redmond, WA: Microsoft Press, 2003.
- Stevens, Richard. *TCP/IP Illustrated, Volume 1, The Protocols*. Boston, MA: Addison-Wesley Publishing, 1994.

Certification-Related Web Sites

- MCSE World, a certification portal for those who have and/or are pursuing the MCSE and MCSA certifications: `www.mcseworld.com`.
- Microsoft's Training and Certification home: `www.microsoft.com/traincert/default.asp`.
- CertCities MCSE certification community: `www.certcities.com/certs/microsoft/`.

Magazine Resources

- *Microsoft Certified Professional Magazine* is directly targeted at those certified by Microsoft: `www.mcpmag.com`.
- *Certification Magazine* specializes in information for IT certified individuals: `www.certmag.com`.
- *Windows & .NET Magazine* focuses specifically on Microsoft technologies: `www.winnetmag.com`.
- *Online Learning* is a resource for professional training and development: `www.onlinelearningmag.com`.
- *Computer* magazine is developed by the IEEE (Institute of Electrical and Electronics Engineers): `www.computer.org/computer/`.
- *PC Magazine* is a staple for technology enthusiasts: `www.pcmag.com`.

Technical Reference Web Sites

- Clustering Services Technology Center, `www.microsoft.com/windowsserver2003/technologies/clustering/default.mspx`.
- Deploying Network Services, `www.microsoft.com/technet/prodtechnol/windowsserver2003/evaluate/cpp/reskit/netsvc/default.asp`.
- Internet Protocol Security Overview, `www.microsoft.com/technet/prodtechnol/windowsserver2003/proddocs/standard/sag_IPSECintroduct.asp`.
- Microsoft Windows Server 2003 Deployment Kit, Designing and Deploying Directory and Security Services, `www.microsoft.com/windowsserver2003/techinfo/reskit/deploykit.mspx`.
- Microsoft Windows Server 2003 Deployment Kit, Designing a Managed Environment, `www.microsoft.com/windowsserver2003/techinfo/reskit/deploykit.mspx`.
- Security Configuration Manager overview, `www.microsoft.com/technet/prodtechnol/windowsserver2003/proddocs/server/se_scm_overview.asp`.
- Security Configuration Manager, `www.microsoft.com/technet/prodtechnol/windowsserver2003/proddocs/entserver/SEconcepts_SCM.asp`.
- Storage Services Technology Center, `www.microsoft.com/windowsserver2003/technologies/storage/default.mspx`.
- SUS home page, `www.microsoft.com/windows2000/windowsupdate/sus`.
- Technical overview of Windows Server 2003 networking and communications, `www.microsoft.com/windowsserver2003/techinfo/overview/netcomm.mspx`.
- Technical overview of Windows Server 2003 security services, `www.microsoft.com/windowsserver2003/techinfo/overview/security.mspx`.
- Windows Server 2003 Deployment Kit: Planning Server Deployments, `http://go.microsoft.com/fwlink/?LinkId=15309`.
- Windows Server 2003 online help "Auditing Security Events," `www.microsoft.com/technet/prodtechnol/windowsserver2003/proddocs/entserver/AuditTN.asp`.
- Windows Server 2003 online help "Network Services," `www.microsoft.com/technet/prodtechnol/windowsserver2003/proddocs/entserver/sag_NPStopnode.asp`.

- Windows Server 2003 online help "Security Configuration Manager," www.microsoft.com/technet/prodtechnol/windowsserver2003/proddocs/entserver/SEconcepts_SCM.asp.
- Windows Server 2003 Reviewer's Guide, www.microsoft.com/windowsserver2003/techinfo/overview/reviewersguide.mspx.

What's on the CD-ROM

This appendix is a brief rundown of what you'll find on the CD-ROM that comes with this book. For a more detailed description of the PrepLogic Practice Tests, Preview Edition exam-simulation software, see Appendix C, "Using PrepLogic Practice Tests, Preview Edition Software." In addition to the PrepLogic Practice Tests, Preview Edition, the CD-ROM includes the electronic version of the book in Portable Document Format (PDF) and several utility and application programs.

PrepLogic Practice Tests, Preview Edition

PrepLogic is a leading provider of certification training tools. Trusted by certification students worldwide, PrepLogic is, we believe, the best practice exam software available. In addition to providing a means of evaluating your knowledge of the Exam Cram 2 material, PrepLogic Practice Tests, Preview Edition features several innovations that help you to improve your mastery of the subject matter.

For example, the practice tests allow you to check your score by exam area or domain to determine which topics you need to study more. Another feature allows you to obtain immediate feedback on your responses in the form of explanations for the correct and incorrect answers.

PrepLogic Practice Tests, Preview Edition exhibits most of the full functionality of the Premium Edition but offers only a fraction of the total questions. To get the complete set of practice questions and exam functionality, visit

PrepLogic.com and order the Premium Edition for this and other challenging exam titles.

Again, for a more detailed description of the PrepLogic Practice Tests, Preview Edition features, see Appendix C.

Using PrepLogic Practice Tests, Preview Edition Software

This Exam Cram 2 includes a special version of PrepLogic Practice Tests—a revolutionary test engine designed to give you the best in certification exam preparation. PrepLogic offers sample and practice exams for many of today's most in-demand and challenging technical certifications. This special Preview Edition is included with this book as a tool to use in assessing your knowledge of the Exam Cram 2 material while also providing you with the experience of taking an electronic exam.

This appendix describes in detail what PrepLogic Practice Tests, Preview Edition is, how it works, and what it can do to help you prepare for the exam. Note that although the Preview Edition includes all the test-simulation functions of the complete retail version, it contains only a single practice test. The Premium Edition, available at PrepLogic.com, contains the complete set of challenging practice exams designed to optimize your learning experience.

Exam Simulation

One of the main functions of PrepLogic Practice Tests, Preview Edition is exam simulation. To prepare you to take the actual vendor certification exam, PrepLogic is designed to offer the most effective exam simulation available.

Question Quality

The questions provided in the PrepLogic Practice Tests, Preview Edition are written to the highest standards of technical accuracy. The questions tap the content of the Exam Cram 2 chapters and help you review and assess your knowledge before you take the actual exam.

Interface Design

The PrepLogic Practice Tests, Preview Edition exam-simulation interface provides you with the experience of taking an electronic exam. This enables you to effectively prepare for taking the actual exam by making the test experience a familiar one. Using this test simulation can help eliminate the sense of surprise or anxiety that you might experience in the testing center because you will already be acquainted with computerized testing.

Effective Learning Environment

The PrepLogic Practice Tests, Preview Edition interface provides a learning environment that not only tests you through the computer, but also teaches the material you need to know to pass the certification exam. Each question comes with a detailed explanation of the correct answer and often provides reasons the other options are incorrect. This information helps to reinforce the knowledge you already have and also provides practical information you can use on the job.

Software Requirements

PrepLogic Practice Tests requires a computer with the following:

- Microsoft Windows 98, Windows Me, Windows NT 4.0, Windows 2000, Windows XP, or Windows Server 2003.
- A recommended 166MHz or faster processor.
- A minimum of 32MB of RAM.
- As with any Windows application, the more memory, the better your performance.
- 10MB of available hard drive space.

Installing PrepLogic Practice Tests, Preview Edition

Install PrepLogic Practice Tests, Preview Edition by running the setup program on the PrepLogic Practice Tests, Preview Edition CD. Follow these instructions to install the software on your computer:

1. Insert the CD into your CD-ROM drive. The Autorun feature of Windows should launch the software. If you have Autorun disabled, click Start and select Run. Go to the root directory of the CD and select setup.exe. Click Open and then click OK.

2. The Installation Wizard copies the PrepLogic Practice Tests, Preview Edition files to your hard drive; adds PrepLogic Practice Tests, Preview Edition to your desktop and Program menu; and installs test engine components to the appropriate system folders.

Removing PrepLogic Practice Tests, Preview Edition from Your Computer

If you elect to remove the PrepLogic Practice Tests, Preview Edition product from your computer, an uninstall process has been included to ensure that it is removed from your system safely and completely. Follow these instructions to remove PrepLogic Practice Tests, Preview Edition from your computer:

1. Select Start, Settings, Control Panel.

2. Double-click the Add/Remove Programs icon.

3. You are presented with a list of software installed on your computer. Select the appropriate PrepLogic Practice Tests, Preview Edition title you want to remove. Click the Add/Remove button. The software is then removed from your computer.

Using PrepLogic Practice Tests, Preview Edition

PrepLogic is designed to be user-friendly and intuitive. Because the software has a smooth learning curve, your time is maximized because you start practicing almost immediately. PrepLogic Practice Tests, Preview Edition has two major modes of study: Practice Test and Flash Review.

Using Practice Test mode, you can develop your test-taking abilities as well as your knowledge through the use of the Show Answer option. While you are taking the test, you can expose the answers along with a detailed explanation of why the given answers are right or wrong. This gives you the ability to better understand the material presented.

Flash Review is designed to reinforce exam topics rather than quiz you. In this mode, you are shown a series of questions but no answer choices. Instead, you are given a button that reveals the correct answer to the question and a full explanation for that answer.

Starting a Practice Test Mode Session

Practice Test mode enables you to control the exam experience in ways that actual certification exams do not allow:

- *Enable Show Answer Button*—Activates the Show Answer button, allowing you to view the correct answer(s) and full explanation(s) for each question during the exam. When this option is not enabled, you must wait until after your exam has been graded to view the correct answer(s) and explanation.
- *Enable Item Review Button*—Activates the Item Review button, allowing you to view your answer choices and marked questions, and to facilitate navigation between questions.
- *Randomize Choices*—Randomizes answer choices from one exam session to the next. This makes memorizing question choices more difficult, therefore keeping questions fresh and challenging longer.

To begin studying in Practice Test mode, click the Practice Test radio button from the main exam-customization screen. This enables the options detailed in the preceding list.

To your left, you are presented with the option of selecting the preconfigured Practice Test or creating your own Custom Test. The preconfigured test has a fixed time limit and number of questions. Custom Tests allow you to configure the time limit and the number of questions on your exam.

The Preview Edition included with this book includes a single preconfigured Practice Test. Get the complete set of challenging PrepLogic Practice Tests at PrepLogic.com, and make certain you're ready for the big exam.

Click the Begin Exam button to begin your exam.

Starting a Flash Review Mode Session

Flash Review mode provides you with an easy way to reinforce topics covered in the practice questions. To begin studying in Flash Review mode, click the Flash Review radio button from the main exam-customization screen. Select either the preconfigured Practice Test or create your own Custom Test.

Click the Best Exam button to begin your Flash Review of the exam questions.

Standard PrepLogic Practice Tests, Preview Edition Options

The following list describes the functions of each of the buttons you see. Depending on the options, some of the buttons will be grayed out and inaccessible or missing completely. Buttons that are appropriate are active. The buttons are as follows:

- *Exhibit*—This button is visible if an exhibit is provided to support the question. An exhibit is an image that provides supplemental information necessary to answer the question.
- *Item Review*—This button leaves the question window and opens the Item Review screen. From this screen, you will see all questions, your answers, and your marked items. You will also see correct answers listed here when appropriate.
- *Show Answer*—This option displays the correct answer with an explanation of why it is correct. If you select this option, the current question is not scored.
- *Mark Item*—Check this box to tag a question that you need to review further. You can view and navigate your Marked Items by clicking the Item Review button (if enabled). When grading your exam, you are notified if you have marked items remaining.
- *Previous Item*—View the previous question.
- *Next Item*—View the next question.
- *Grade Exam*—When you have completed your exam, click to end your exam and view your detailed score report. If you have unanswered or marked items remaining, you are asked whether you want to continue taking your exam or view your exam report.

Time Remaining

If the test is timed, the time remaining is displayed on the upper-right corner of the application screen. It counts down minutes and seconds remaining to complete the test. If you run out of time, you are asked whether you want to continue taking the test or end your exam.

Your Examination Score Report

The Examination Score Report screen appears when the Practice Test mode ends—as the result of time expiration, completion of all questions, or your decision to terminate early.

This screen provides you with a graphical display of your test score with a breakdown of scores by topic domain. The graphical display at the top of the screen compares your overall score with the PrepLogic Exam Competency Score.

The PrepLogic Exam Competency Score reflects the level of subject competency required to pass this vendor's exam. Although this score does not directly translate to a passing score, consistently matching or exceeding this score does suggest that you possess the knowledge to pass the actual vendor exam.

Review Your Exam

From the Your Score Report screen, you can review the exam that you just completed by clicking on the View Items button. Navigate through the items, viewing the questions, your answers, the correct answers, and the explanations for those questions. You can return to your score report by clicking the View Items button.

Get More Exams

The PrepLogic Practice Tests, Preview Edition CD that accompanies your book contains a single PrepLogic Practice Test. Certification students worldwide trust PrepLogic Practice Tests to help them pass their IT certification exams the first time. Purchase the Premium Edition of PrepLogic Practice Tests and get the entire set of all new challenging Practice Tests for this exam. PrepLogic Practice Tests—Because You Want to Pass the First Time.

Contacting PrepLogic

If you want to contact PrepLogic for any reason, including to obtain information about our extensive line of certification practice tests, we invite you to do so. Please contact us online at www.preplogic.com.

Customer Service

If you have a damaged product and need a replacement or refund, please call the following phone number:

1-800-858-7674

Product Suggestions and Comments

We value your input! Please email your suggestions and comments to the following address:

feedback@preplogic.com

License Agreement

YOU MUST AGREE TO THE TERMS AND CONDITIONS OUTLINED IN THE END USER LICENSE AGREEMENT ("EULA") PRESENTED TO YOU DURING THE INSTALLATION PROCESS. IF YOU DO NOT AGREE TO THESE TERMS, DO NOT INSTALL THE SOFTWARE.

Glossary

%SystemRoot%
A universal reference to the directory in which the Windows system files are installed. Typically, %SystemRoot% is C:\Winnt or C:\Windows. By default, clean installations of Windows Server 2003 use the Windows directory. If multiple copies of Windows are installed in a multiboot system, each copy has its own %SystemRoot% directory.

802.1*x*
An IEEE standard that provides for port-based access control (and thus authentication) for both wired and wireless networks. 802.1*x* uses the physical characteristics of a switched LAN to authenticate devices (and users) that are attached to each switch port, and to disallow access from that port if the user or device cannot be successfully authenticated.

802.11
A family of IEEE standards that provides for wireless networking. The 802.11 family is to wireless networking what the 802.3 family is to wired networking. 802.11 includes several standards, including 802.11, 802.11a, 802.11b, and 802.11g. Each standard presents the technical specifications for that type of wireless network.

Active Directory
The directory services included with Windows Server 2003. Based on the DNS hierarchy, Active Directory provides a domain-based directory service for organizing all the objects and services in a Windows Server 2003 network.

Active Directory–integrated zone
A DNS zone file that is stored within the Active Directory data. Rather than being stored in a normal DNS text file, it is replicated among other domain controllers that run DNS (as configured).

Active Directory Users and Computers
A preconfigured MMC console provided in Windows 2000 and Windows Server 2003 Active Directory domains that can be used to administer Active Directory objects.

active screen question
A type of exam question that requires you to configure a dialog box by changing one or more of the options on the dialog box.

application data partition
A new directory partition type in Windows Server 2003 that can be used to store application-specific information in a separate partition, which replicates only with the domain controllers that require this information. In Windows Server 2003, these are commonly used for replication of Active Directory–integrated DNS zones.

assigned applications
An Active Directory software-installation method that can be used to target a computer or a user. Applications that are assigned to a computer are installed on the next restart of the computer. Applications that are assigned to users are advertised to the user and will be installed when the user chooses to do so. Assigned applications can also be installed on demand—for example, installing Microsoft Excel the first time a user attempts to open a file with the .XLS file extension.

auditing
The process of logging information about network activities, such as user logins, system shutdowns, and file access.

authentication
The process of verifying a user's identity on a network.

Authentication Header (AH)
A protocol in the IPSec suite that is used to authenticate IP traffic. The AH is inserted into the original IP packet immediately after the IP header.

authoritative restore
A directory services restoration that restores all selected data and increments the update sequence number (USN) of the data by 100,000 so that the restored objects become the authoritative copies in the domain. This guarantees that these restored objects will be replicated to all other domain controllers during the normal replication cycle.

Automatic Updates
The client side of the Software Update Services (SUS) solution. Automatic Updates can be configured to work with the Microsoft Windows Update Web servers or with internal SUS servers.

build-list-and-reorder questions
An exam question type in which you are required to build a list in the correct order that represents the steps that are necessary to achieve the required result.

built-in account
A user account that is created during the installation of Windows Server 2003, the implementation of Active Directory, or the installation of additional services.

certificate
A credential that is used to authenticate the origin, identity, and purpose of the public half of a public/private key pair. A certificate ensures that the sent and received data is kept secure.

Certificate Authority (CA)
A service that issues digital certificates to users and computers. Additionally, CAs maintain a current list of revoked certificates that are no longer considered valid.

Certificate Revocation List (CRL)
A list maintained by Certificate Authorities that includes all certificates that are no longer valid but that have not yet reached their configured expiration date. Clients validating a certificate can check the CRL to determine whether a presented certificate is still valid.

change management
The planning and implementation processes by which changes are proposed, implemented, and tracked within an organization.

child domain
A Windows Active Directory domain that exists directly beneath a parent domain in a tree hierarchy.

Class A network
The largest of the classes of IP networks. There are 126 Class A networks, each of which is capable of addressing up to 16,777,214 hosts. Class A networks have a first octet between 1 to 126, with a default subnet mask of 255.0.0.0.

Class B network
The second-largest class of IP networks. There are 16,384 Class B networks, each of which is capable of addressing up to 65,534 hosts. Class B networks have a first octet between 128 and 191, with a default subnet mask of 255.255.0.0.

Class C network
The smallest class of IP networks. There are 2,097,152 Class C networks, each of which is capable of addressing up to 254 hosts. Class C networks have a first octet between 192 and 223, with a default subnet mask of 255.255.255.0.

cluster
A group of two or more independent servers that operate together and are viewed and accessed as a single resource. Also referred to as clustering.

cluster resource
A network application, service, or hardware device (such as a network adapter or storage system) that is defined and managed by the cluster service.

cluster resource group
A defined set of resources contained within a cluster. Cluster

resource groups are used as failover units within a cluster. When a cluster resource group fails and cannot be automatically restarted by the cluster service, the entire cluster resource group is placed in an offline status and failed over to another node.

cluster virtual server
A cluster resource group to which a network name and IP address are assigned. Cluster virtual servers are accessible by their NetBIOS name, DNS name, or IP address.

compatible template
A security template that allows members of the Users group to run applications that do not conform to the Windows Logo Program by modifying the default file and Registry permissions that are granted to the Users group.

conditional forwarding
A new feature in Windows Server 2003 DNS that allows administrators to direct DNS requests to other DNS servers based on domain. Also known as intelligent forwarding.

convergence
The process by which network load balancing (NLB) nodes determine a new, stable state among themselves and elect a new default host after the failure of one or more cluster nodes. During convergence, the total load on the NLB cluster is redistributed among all cluster nodes that share the handling of traffic on specific ports, as determined by their port rules.

create-a-tree question
An exam question type in which you are required to create a tree structure to achieve the required result or answer the question at hand.

CRL distribution point (CDP)
A location to which certificate distribution lists are published.

Data Encryption Standard (DES)
A symmetric encryption scheme that requires the sender and the receiver to know the secret key. DES uses a 56-bit key that provides approximately 7.2×10^{16} different key combinations.

dcpromo
The command-line command that is issued to begin the process of promoting a member server to a domain controller.

Default DC Security template
A security template that is automatically created when a member server is promoted to a domain controller (DC). It represents the file, Registry, and system service default security settings for that DC and can later be used to reset those areas to their default configurations.

Default Security template
A security template that is created during the installation of Windows on a computer. This template varies from one computer to the next, depending on whether the installation was performed as a clean installation or an upgrade. This template represents the

default security settings that a computer started with and can thus be used to reset portions of security, as required.

delegation of control
The process by which you can grant nonadministrative users some responsibility for some portion of Active Directory, such as delegating the capability to change users' passwords or add computers to the domain.

discretionary Access Control List (DACL)
An internal list that is attached to files and folders on NTFS-formatted volumes and is configured to specify the level of permissions allowed for different users and groups.

DNS forwarder
A DNS server that has been configured to forward name-resolution queries that it cannot answer to another DNS server.

DNS resolver
Any computer that has been configured with one or more DNS server IP addresses and that performs queries against these DNS servers.

DNS Security (DNSSEC)
A public key infrastructure (PKI)–based system in which authentication and data integrity can be provided to DNS resolvers, as discussed in RFC 2535. Digital signatures are used and encrypted with private keys. These digital signatures can then be authenticated by DNSSEC-aware resolvers by using the corresponding public key. The required digital signature and public keys are added to the DNS zone in the form of resource records.

DNS slave server
A DNS forwarder server that does not try to resolve a resolution request if it doesn't receive a valid response to its forwarded DNS request.

domain
A container in the DNS name hierarchy or the network Organizational Unit for Windows Server 2003 networks.

domain controller
A server that holds a writable copy of the Active Directory data and manages information contained within the Active Directory database. Domain controllers also function as NS servers when Active Directory–integrated zones are used. The Kerberos Key Distribution Center (KDC) is also located on every domain controller.

domain name system (DNS)
A service that dynamically provides name- and address-resolution services in a TCP/IP environment.

domain user account
A user account that exists within an Active Directory network that allows the user to log on to any computer in the network for which he has the required user rights.

drag-and-drop question
An exam question type that requires you to drag source objects into their proper place in the work area.

DumpEL
A command-line–based utility that can be used to quickly collect and search through event logs.

Encapsulating Security Payload (ESP)
A protocol that is used in the IPSec suite to handle data encryption. ESP is usually used with AH to provide the maximum level of security and integrity for data transmitted in IPSec transmissions. ESP uses DES encryption, by default, but it can be configured to use 3DES.

encryption
A mechanism for securing data in which data is translated into a secret code that can be read only with the correct key to translate the secret code back to the original data.

Enterprise Certificate Authority
The first Certificate Authority (CA) in a branch of CAs. It is responsible for assigning certificates to intermediary CAs and other subordinate CAs.

EventCombMT
A GUI-based utility that can be used to quickly collect and search event logs.

Extensible Authentication Protocol (EAP)
An extension to the Point-to-Point Protocol (PPP), as specified in RFC 2284, that provides a means for the primary authentication method to be negotiated during the initiation of the PPP session.

failback
The process of moving a cluster group (either manually or automatically) back to the preferred node, after the preferred node has resumed cluster membership. For failback to occur, it must be configured for the cluster group, including the failback threshold and selection of the preferred node.

failover
The process of a cluster group moving from the currently active node to a designated, functioning node in the cluster group. Failover typically occurs when the active node becomes unresponsive (for any reason) and cannot be recovered within the configured failure threshold period.

File Replication Service (FRS)
A service that provides multimaster file replication for designated directory trees between designated servers that run Windows Server 2003.

filtering
The process of configuring the Discretionary Access Control List (DACL) for a Group Policy Object (GPO) so that only specific users or groups can read and apply the GPO settings.

forest
The logical structure that contains all domains in the Active Directory model.

forest and domain functional levels
Levels of functionality for Active Directory forests and Active Directory domains that determines what unique features they can possess, such as the capability to remain forests and domains that are configured for Windows Server 2003 mode.

forest root
The first domain created within an Active Directory forest becomes the forest root.

fully qualified domain name (FQDN)
A host's complete DNS name, including the hostname and all domains that connect the host to the root domain. The FQDN is typically expressed without a trailing period, with the root domain assumed.

garbage collection
The process of a domain controller examining its database for expired tombstones that can be deleted.

Global Catalog (GC)
A partial replica of every object in an Active Directory database that is used to speed searching.

GPRESULT
A command-line utility that can display the Group Policy settings and Resultant Set of Policy (RSOP) for a user or a computer.

GPUPDATE
A command-line utility that is used to refresh local and Active Directory Group Policy settings, including security settings. The `gpupdate` command replaces the `/refreshpolicy` option for the `secedit` command.

Group Policy Editor
A subset of the Active Directory Users and Computers console that allows the editing of Group Policy Objects.

Group Policy Object (GPO)
A collection of security and configuration settings that are applied to a container in an Active Directory domain.

heartbeat
A network communication sent among individual cluster nodes at intervals of no more than 500 milliseconds (ms), used to determine the status of all cluster nodes.

Highly Secure template
A security template that imposes further restrictions on computers to which it is applied. Whereas the Secure templates require at least NTLM authentication, the Highly Secure templates require NTLMv2 authentication.

hot-area question
An exam question type that requires you to select one or more areas on a graphic to indicate the correct answer to a question.

inheritance
The process by which objects have Group Policy applied to them from all levels and where GPOs are configured that apply to them.

IntelliMirror
The various technologies in Windows Server 2003 that depend on Active Directory and provide for change and configuration management.

Internet Control Message Protocol (ICMP)
A protocol in the TCP/IP suite of protocols that is used for testing connectivity.

Internet Group Management Protocol (IGMP)
One of the core protocols in the TCP/IP suite; a routing protocol that is used as part of multicasting.

Internet key exchange (IKE)
An encryption scheme that allows disparate VPN servers to share encryption key information and makes the IPSec protocol practical in today's environment.

Internet Protocol (IP)
The portion of the TCP/IP protocol suite that is used to provide packet routing.

Internet Security Association and Key Management Protocol/Oakley (ISAKMP/Oakley)
A protocol that is used to share a public key between sender and receiver of a secure connection. ISAKMP/Oakley allows the receiving system to retrieve a public key and then authenticate the sender using digital certificates.

IP address
The 32-bit binary address that is used to identify a TCP/IP host's network and host ID. IPv6 IP addresses are 128 bits in length.

IP Security (IPSec)
A Layer 3 TCP/IP protocol that provides end-to-end security for data in transit.

iterative query
A DNS query that is sent from a DNS server to one or more DNS servers in search of the DNS server that is authoritative for the name being sought.

Kerberos v5
An identity-based security protocol that is based on Internet security standards and used by Windows Server 2003 to authenticate users.

Layer 2 Tunneling Protocol (L2TP)
A VPN protocol that is created by combining the PPTP and L2F tunneling protocols. L2TP is used as the transport protocol in the Windows Server 2003 VPN service, in conjunction with IPSec.

leaf
The end object in a hierarchical tree structure.

linking
The process of associating a Group Policy Object with a container, such as an Organizational Unit.

local user account
A user account that exists only within the scope of the local computer and can be used only to authenticate against the local computer Security Accounts Manager (SAM) database.

loopback processing
An advanced Group Policy Object configuration setting that enables you to make sure that policies that are set for a computer take priority over those that are set at other levels of Active Directory.

member server
A server that is part of the Active Directory domain but does not function as a domain controller. Member servers might be SQL servers, Exchange servers, file servers, print servers, or virtually any other type of server.

Microsoft Baseline Security Analyzer (MBSA)
A utility that can be used to scan computers on a network to look for missing security updates and weak security configurations from either the command line or within the GUI.

Microsoft Management Console (MMC)
A Microsoft Windows framework that is used for hosting administrative tools.

multiple-choice, multiple-answer
A standard exam question type that requires you to choose two or more correct answers from a given list of possibilities.

multiple-choice, single-answer
A standard exam question type that requires you to choose one correct answer from a given list of possibilities.

network load balancing (NLB)
A way to provide highly available solutions in which all incoming connection requests are distributed to members of an NLB cluster using a mathematical algorithm. NLB clustering is best used when clients can connect to any server in the cluster, such as Web sites, Terminal Services servers, and VPN servers.

No Override
An advanced Group Policy configuration action that is used to prevent policies at lower levels in the Active Directory tree from overwriting policies applied from a higher level.

node
In regard to clustering, a node is an individual server within a cluster. In regard to networking, a node is a device that communicates on a network and is identified by a unique address. In hierarchies, a node is a container that contains other containers and data.

nonauthoritative restore
A directory services restoration in which the data that is restored is not automatically considered to be authoritative for the domain and is thus subject to being overwritten or updated during the normal replication cycle.

Organizational Unit (OU)
A container that provides for the logical grouping of objects within Active Directory, for ease of administration and configuration.

package
A Windows Installer (.MSI) file that contains a database of information that contains all of the instructions to add an application to or remove an application from a computer.

parent domain
The domain that shares the same DNS namespace with one or more child domains under it.

pilot program
A phase of the software-deployment process in which you deploy your software package to a select group of users, groups, and computers that are representative of the whole that you will target for this package.

Point-to-Point Tunneling Protocol (PPTP)
A protocol that is used by Microsoft and others to create VPNs.

port rules
A configuration that is used to determine what types of traffic are to be load-balanced across the cluster nodes.

primary DNS server
The name server that contains the master copy of a zone file. Also called a primary master.

primary master
See primary DNS server.

primary zone
A DNS zone that contains the master copies of resource records for a domain.

principle of least privilege
An administrative principle that states that users are given only the minimum privileges required to perform the specific set of tasks they have been assigned.

private IP address
An IP address range reserved for private (non–Internet-connected) networks. There are private address ranges in the Class A, Class B, and Class C address blocks.

published applications
A software-installation method that uses Active Directory and advertises the presence of an application to a user, but does not automatically install the application for the user.

quorum disk
The disk drive that contains the definitive cluster-configuration data. Clustering with MSCS requires the use of a quorum disk and requires continuous access to the data contained within the quorum disk. The quorum disk contains vital data about the nodes participating in the cluster, the applications and services defined within the cluster resource group, and the status of each node and cluster resource. The quorum disk is typically located on a shared storage device.

recursive query
A DNS query that is used to request an authoritative answer or an answer indicating that there is no resolution for a DNS lookup.

registered IP address
Any block of addresses registered with the Internet Assigned Names Authority (IANA).

Remote Access Dial-In User Service (RADIUS)
An industry-standard security protocol that is used to authenticate client connections.

Remote Assistance
A Remote Desktop Protocol–based service in Windows XP and Windows Server 2003 that allows a Novice to ask for and receive help from an Expert over a TCP/IP network connection.

Remote Desktop for Administration
A Remote Desktop Protocol–based service that enables administrators to remotely connect to and administer Windows XP and Windows Server 2003 computers. Remote Desktop for Administration replaces Terminal Services Administration mode in Windows 2000.

Remote Desktop Protocol (RDP)
A terminal communications protocol that is based on the industry-standard T.120 multichannel conferencing protocol.

resource record
A data record in a DNS zone. Many types of resource records are available. For example, an address resource record is the data record that describes the address-to-name relationship for a host.

restoration
The process of replacing or re-creating data on a computer using a set of backup media.

Resultant Set of Policy (RSoP)
An MMC snap-in that enables you to determine how various Group Policies are applied to an object.

reverse lookup
In DNS, an IP address-to-name resolution.

revoked certificate
A digital certificate that has been taken out of use before its configured end of lifetime. Certificates can be revoked for any number of reasons, including loss of keys or employee termination.

root
In a hierarchy, the container that holds all other containers.

root Certificate Authority (CA)
A Certificate Authority that forms the top of the CA hierarchy.

schema
A description of object classes and the attributes that the object classes must and can possess.

secedit.exe
The command-line equivalent of the Security Configuration and Analysis snap-in.

secondary DNS server
A server that provides name resolution for a zone but cannot be used to modify the zone. It contains a read-only copy of the zone file. Also known as a secondary master.

secure dynamic update
A secure method used by Active Directory–integrated zones that allows the DHCP service to automatically update DNS when the DHCP server grants and expires DHCP leases.

Secure template
A security template that increases the level of security configured on a computer to which it is applied above the default configuration. Secure templates prevent the use of the LAN Manager (LM) authentication protocol. Windows 9*x* clients need to have Active Directory Client Extensions installed to enable NTLMv2 to allow them to communicate with Windows 2000 and later clients and servers using these templates. These templates also impose additional restrictions on anonymous users, such as preventing them from enumerating account and share information.

Security Configuration and Analysis snap-in
An MMC snap-in that is used to configure, analyze, and implement security templates on a local computer. It can be used to create templates that are imported into GPOs for application to larger groups of computers.

security log
A log that is found in the Event Viewer and that contains auditing entries.

security template
A text file that contains settings that configure the security settings of the computer or computers to which it is applied. Several preconfigured security templates come with Windows Server 2003; you can edit and create your own custom ones, as required.

single sign-on
A feature in Windows Server 2003 that enables users to log in to the network with a single username and password, and receive access to a host of network resources. The user does not have to enter any additional usernames or passwords to gain access to network shares, printers, or other network resources.

site
A group of well-connected TCP/IP subnets.

snap-in
A tool that you can add to the MMC.

software installation
The process by which software can be installed over the network, onto managed computers, using Group Policy Objects in Active Directory. Software can be either assigned or published.

Software Update Services (SUS)
An add-on service for Windows 2000 and Windows Server 2003 networks that provides the functionality of a Windows Update Web server on the internal network.

SUS enables you to select which available updates are authorized for distribution to network clients, thus ensuring that only the updates you have tested and approved are installed.

standalone CA
A Certificate Authority that can be used with or without Active Directory. Certificate requests are set to pending until an administrator approves the request.

standard primary zone
A DNS zone file that holds the master writable copy of a zone and can transfer it to all configured secondary zones.

standard secondary zone
A DNS zone file that holds a read-only copy of the zone file and is used to provide increased reliability and performance.

Start of Authority (SOA) record
In a DNS zone file, a record that is used to provide the zone parameters to all the DNS servers for the zone. The SOA record also provides the name of the primary server and the person who is in charge of the domain.

storage domain
The domain in which a GPO is stored. GPOs are stored in the domain in which they were created.

stub zone
A new DNS zone type in Windows Server 2003 that contains only the required resource records that are needed to identify the authoritative DNS servers for another zone.

subordinate CA
Typically the lowest level in a Certificate Authority hierarchy. Subordinate CAs issue certificates directly to users and network hosts.

suffix
A domain extension that indicates the root domain. For example, `.com` is a domain suffix.

SYSVOL
A shared folder on an NTFS partition on every AD domain controller that contains information (scripts, group policy information, and so on) that is replicated to other domain controllers in the domain. The SYSVOL folder is created during Active Directory installation.

Terminal Services
A Remote Desktop Protocol (RDP)-based service offered by Windows NT, Windows 2000, and Windows Server 2003 that allows thin clients to connect to the server and utilize applications that are stored on the server.

testlet (quizlet) exam format
An examination format that typically consists of 10 or more questions of varying types, as well as a significant amount of background material that must be read and understood to successfully answer the questions. The testlet format is also known as the quizlet or case study format.

top-level domain (TLD)
A domain that exists directly underneath the root domain.

Transmission Control Protocol/Internet Protocol (TCP/IP)
The suite of communications protocols used to connect hosts on the Internet.

transport mode
Used to secure traffic with IPSec, typically between servers or clients and servers. End-to-end security creates a secure channel for trustworthy communication.

tree
A logical group of Windows Server 2003 domains that share a common DNS namespace.

Triple Data Encryption Standard (3DES)
A more secure variant of the DES standard that encrypts data by using three different 56-bit keys in succession. 3DES thus extends the DES key to 168 bits, providing approximately 6.2×10^{57} different keys.

tunnel mode
The use of IPSec in a mode in which two endpoints have been configured to create a tunnel, such as when a VPN tunnel is created.

universal group
A Windows 2003 security group that can be used anywhere within a domain tree or forest; universal groups can be used only when Windows 2003 has been converted to native mode.

universal group caching
A feature that enables users in universal groups to log on without the presence of a GC server. This feature can be used after a domain has been raised to the Windows 2003 functional level.

Universal Naming Convention (UNC)
A naming convention that is used to define a resource on a Windows Server 2003 network. A share named DOCS on the server SERVER1 could be accessed using the UNC path of \\SERVER1\DOCS.

update sequence number
A 64-bit number that keeps track of changes as they are written to copies of the Active Directory. As changes are made, this number increments by one.

UPN suffix
The part of the UPN that comes after the `@` symbol and is typically the domain name for a user account. Alternate UPN suffixes can be created to allow for improved logon security or simply shorter UPNs for users.

user logon name
Commonly referred to as the pre–Windows 2000 logon name, such as will.

user principal name (UPN)
The full DNS domain name of an Active Directory user account, such as `will@corp.mcseworld.com`.

validity period
The length of time for which a digital certificate is valid.

virtual private network (VPN)
A mechanism for providing secure, private communications that uses a public network (such as the Internet) as the transport method. VPNs use a combination of encryption and authentication technologies to ensure data integrity and security.

volume shadow copy
A new feature in Windows Server 2003 that provides distinctly different functions. The first function allows the Windows Backup Utility (or `ntbackup` from the command line) to back up open files, as if they were closed. The second feature provides a means of creating and storing up to 64 historical versions of files that are located within a network share.

Windows 2000 mixed mode
Allows Windows NT 4.0 domain controllers to exist and function within a Windows 2003 domain. This is the default setting when Active Directory is installed, although it can be changed to native mode.

Windows 2000 native mode
The mode in which all domain controllers in a domain have been upgraded to Windows 2003 and there are no longer NT 4.0 domain controllers. An administrator explicitly puts Active Directory into native mode, at which time it cannot be returned to mixed mode without removing and reinstalling Active Directory.

Windows 2003 functional level
The highest functional level of either the domain or the forest in Windows 2003. This functional level implements all the new features of Windows 2003 Active Directory, but at the expense of some backward compatibility.

Windows Installer
The MSIEXEC.EXE service that manages the installation of software on computers.

wireless LAN (WLAN)
A local area network that uses one of the 802.11 standards, such as 802.11b or 802.11a.

workgroup
A grouping of computers and resources that uses a decentralized authentication and management system.

zone
A domain for which a DNS server is authoritative.

zone transfer
The process of copying DNS resource records from a primary zone to a secondary zone.

Index

Symbols

Numbers

A

B

C

D

G

H

I

J-L

M

N

How can we make this index more useful? Email us at indexes@quepublishing.com

O

P

Q

R

S

How can we make this index more useful? Email us at indexes@quepublishing.com

T

U

How can we make this index more useful? Email us at indexes@quepublishing.com

V

W

X-Z